3,000 Quotations from the Writings of George MacDonald

3,000 Quotations from the Writings of George MacDonald

Harry Verploegh
compiler

WIPF & STOCK · Eugene, Oregon

Wipf and Stock Publishers
199 W 8th Ave, Suite 3
Eugene, OR 97401

3,000 Quotations From the Writings of George MacDonald
By MacDonald, George and Verploegh, Harry

ISBN 13: 978-1-5326-8860-7
Publication date 4/12/2019
Previously published by Fleming H. Revell Co., 1996

Preface

Years ago, when I was still a teenager, I discovered a book entitled *Unspoken Sermons* by George MacDonald. I remember one Sunday afternoon when I sat down and read it from cover to cover.

A normal teenage boy does not customarily read sermons on a Sunday afternoon, and I was a normal teenage boy. Maybe I should have spent more time reading sermons, but I didn't.

However, these were not normal sermons, and George MacDonald was not a customary writer. And I could never forget one sermon especially, called "The New Name."

For years I thought I was the only one who knew about George MacDonald and his unusual insights. But then, as I began reading C. S. Lewis, I found that Lewis had "discovered" MacDonald long before I had. In fact, Lewis acknowledged, "I have never concealed the fact that I regarded him as my master; indeed I fancy I have never written a book in which I did not quote from him."

As an atheist at Oxford, Lewis admired the writing of MacDonald. He assumed that MacDonald was a good writer "in spite of being a Christian." "It was a pity," Lewis wrote, "that he had that bee in his bonnet about Christianity." But the nudge that MacDonald's writings gave Lewis started his movement toward Jesus Christ.

After his conversion, Lewis began reviving interest in materials of George MacDonald until today almost all of MacDonald's works have been reprinted.

MacDonald himself was a bit of a maverick. Born in 1824 in the Scottish Highlands, he was raised in a solid, loving Christian home. He married the daughter of a London merchant and entered the ministry when he was twenty-six years old. Two years later, however, he was forced to resign because of some of his unorthodox views.

He left the pastorate but continued preaching and lecturing. Increasingly, he turned to writing. First he attempted poetry and fantasies, but then he felt he could reach a larger audience by writing novels, and soon he became known for his novels, children's stories, and short stories, as well.

With eleven children, MacDonald didn't always find it easy to put bread on the table, but in spite of problems with finances and his health, there was no bitterness. He rejoiced in the goodness of God.

He continued to be a student of Scripture and he continued to speak in churches in England and Scotland. One statement regarding Scripture characterizes MacDonald's biblical outlook: "I am always finding out meaning which I did not see before, and which I now cannot see perfectly—for, of course, till my heart is like Christ's great heart, I cannot fully know what He meant."

Years ago, as I read his *Unspoken Sermons,* I felt that same excitement of discovery coupled with a deep humility that my present understanding is still very imperfect.

As I said, most everything that MacDonald wrote a hundred years ago has now been brought back in print.

But recently in some musty old copies of a British publication, *The Christian World Pulpit,* I discovered a cache of MacDonald sermons. These were not "unspoken sermons"; indeed, they were spoken, preached at various churches in England and Scotland, and taken down verbatim as he preached them.

These "spoken sermons," therefore, though edited from the original publication, are not as smooth as his writings, but perhaps convey a little more of the heartbeat of this great man. In editing, I have tried to retain the flavor of the spoken sermon but have removed some of the repetition and extraneous material that would not be meaningful today.

May these "spoken sermons" affect you as profoundly as MacDonald's book of *Unspoken Sermons* affected me many years ago.

William J. Petersen

Introduction

In an Indiana town on a February afternoon in 1873, a fur-clad and bearded Scot in his mid-fifties, accompanied by his wife and eldest son, glimpsed the advance publicity for his evening lecture. Fluttering on the facade of the courthouse, a blue and silver banner read: "George MacDonald, England, Eminent Scotch Orator, Subject—Robert Burns." The crowd that night was disappointingly small. The eminence of the Victorian man of letters, poet, novelist, preacher, and theologian had perhaps not reached that place, but it did not matter. His American tour had begun auspiciously.

In Boston, three thousand, including several prominent New England literati, Emerson, Longfellow and Beecher Stowe among them, had come to hear the author of the novels *David Elginbrod* (1863), *Alec Forbes of Howglen* (1865), and *Robert Falconer* (1868) lecture on Burns. Then large audiences from New York City to Ann Arbor crowded to hear the LLD from Aberdeen University interpret works of Dante, Milton, and Shakespeare, while churches gladly combined services for a chance to hear him preach.

The Scottish lecturer and cleric was George MacDonald of Aberdeenshire. Born into a highland community of sabbatarian Missionars in 1825, MacDonald was now a popular London preacher-at-large and literary figure. By the end of his tour, his American friends offered him a gift of $1500 as a "copyright testimonial" for the royalties he never received for the sale of his books on their side of the Atlantic. When he died in Italy in 1905 MacDonald had produced fifty-two works. Though it has been 100 years since the publication of his last books, the fifth volume of sermons *The Hope of the Gospel* (1892) and *Lilith* (1895), his masterpiece of myth, MacDonald's remarkable spiritual wisdom and moral insight—woven through poetry, novels, the shorter narratives, and sermons—have stubbornly endured through the efforts of a group of devoted English-speaking readers, the compiler of this anthology, Harry Verploegh, among them. Many of these readers and scholars have been prompted to study MacDonald through the close attention given him by the Christian apologist and Oxford don C. S. Lewis. In the preface to his *George MacDonald An Anthology* (1948), Lewis discussed his admiration for MacDonald's mythmaking gifts and his ability to understand and communicate the mind of Christ and the essentials of the Christian gospel with a compelling combination of severity and tenderness:

> . . . any reader who loves holiness and loves MacDonald . . . can find even in the worst of them [his statements] something that disarms criticism and will come to feel a queer, awkward charm in their very faults. . . . The Divine Sonship is the key-conception which unites all the different elements of his thought. I dare not say that he was never in error; but to speak plainly I know hardly any other writer who seems to be closer, or more continually close, to the Spirit of Christ Himself. Hence his Christ-like union of tenderness and severity. Nowhere else outside the New Testament have I found terror and comfort so intertwined.

MacDonald's earliest hearers among the Congregationalists, however, thought he had missed the essentials of the gospel. It was common enough in the social and theological turmoil of the 1840s and 50s for dissenting churches to refuse appointments to preachers who could not demonstrate their adherence to the Westminster Confession. Because MacDonald was sympathetic to the universalism of the influential evangelical preacher Robert Morison during his university days, he was refused the opportunity to continue teaching in a Sunday school by John Kennedy, a strict Calvinist who led a large Aberdeen congregation. Considering how best to use his talents, MacDonald began to realize that his unorthodox views might deny him advancement as a Congregationalist clergyman should he choose to become one.

Once he obtained his undergraduate degree, he thought of becoming a chemist or a physician, but at that time his father could not support further education for his son. Then came a stint as a private tutor. Finally after considerable hesitation, MacDonald decided to begin theological training at Highbury College, the school for dissenters in London. Once there he found his fellow students unimaginative and the teaching narrowly doctrinal and uninspiring. He thought he might find a vocation as a poet, but he could not yet make a living by his pen, so in 1850, shortly before his marriage at twenty-six to Louisa Powell, he accepted a pastoral appointment to a Congregational chapel in Arundel near Brighton and was ordained the following year. The congregation proved not to be amenable to MacDonald's short sermons, poetical effusions, and remarks on the paltriness of the charities of the wealthy. Members could not understand their new appointee's refusal to declare himself either an Arminian or a Calvinist. Also troubling was his belief in a "future state of probation" for unbelievers (*George MacDonald and His Wife*, pp. 179–80). MacDonald was asked to resign his Arundel appointment after two years, yet he did not see himself as a failure. He and Louisa would live on less and wait for a place where he could "speak God's truth boldly."

MacDonald's boldness is demonstrated in his sermons "The Last Penny" and "Justice" in which he attempts to counteract what he saw as the damaging work of theologians whom he believed did more to "hide the gospel of Christ than many of its adversaries." Hairsplitting arguments about Christ's substitutionary atonement and the imputed righteousness of the believer were for him the "poorest of legal cobwebs spun by spiritual spiders."

> They regard the Father of their spirits as their governor! They yield the idea of the Ancient of Days, "the glad creator," and put in its stead a miserable, puritanical martinet of a God, caring not for righteousness, but for His rights; not for eternal purities, but the goody proprieties. The prophets of such a God take all the glow, all the hope, all the color, all the worth, out of life on earth, and offer you instead what they call eternal bliss—a pale, tearless Hell. Of all things, turn from a mean, poverty-stricken faith. ("Justice")

Except for a one-year preaching appointment that was a happier match, though not extended because of illness, MacDonald was a minister-at-large among those who heard gladly his exalted interpretation of the purifying nature of God's love that strives for their perfection, "even that itself may be perfected—not in itself, but in the object." ("The Consuming Fire")

In this comprehensive collection of his thought, arranged alphabetically by key words, new readers of George MacDonald will discover what one of his editors, Rolland Hein, calls the "strength and captivating moral beauty" of the convictions that for many readers already drawn to his theological ideas, far outweigh his refusal to accept specific tenets of Christian orthodoxy. Throughout his works MacDonald expresses a vision of the divine nature whose heart is our Home, "the one and only goal of the human race." God is both creator and a Trinity of Father, Son, and Holy Spirit and Father, Mother, and Child. God has revealed himself in all created things—nature, animal life, and human beings, but supremely in Jesus Christ who was a child to show us the childlikeness in God's nature. Men and women are deprived of God, not because they are depraved, but because they do not see the Father clearly. They languish in the prisonhouse of the dark and lonely self, a state from which they must "rise and be raised." No one truly lives until he or she chooses to become a child of God. This choice is for most of us, not a sharp about-face, but a process of gradual turning to the light, a response, a submission of the will to God's love and to the words of the Lord. "It was not for our understanding, but for our wills, that Christ came." God does not compel obedience; "he does not make good beasts of us," yet there is no escaping God's desire to

> have His children clean, clear, pure as very snow; . . . that not only shall they with His help make up for whatever wrong they have done, but at length be incapable, by eternal choice of good, under any temptation, of doing the thing that is not divine, the thing that God would not do. ("The Last Penny")

Thus for MacDonald there is no refuge from the love of God, for God refuses to yield us to the selfishness that is killing us. "The love of the Father is a radiant perfection. Love and not self-love is lord of the universe."

The ways in which George MacDonald reshaped the ideas of the mystics, nineteenth-century German thinkers, and English romantic writers for his own uses and registered the influence of Christian Socialism, can now be understood as the literary history of the nineteenth-century is being written. Readers who would like to understand his life and thought in the context of the events and ideas that influenced his mind should begin with William Raeper's 1987 biography *George MacDonald* or Rolland Hein's *George MacDonald: Victorian Myth Maker* (1993), followed by the scholarship on the writer, including Glenn Sadler's edition of MacDonald's letters. Those who wish to read the original works will search out the reprints of MacDonald's five collections of sermons and the novels, as well as the shorter narratives, and essays from which these abstracts have been excerpted. Quotations that appear without pagination are from works where the original editions have not been used.

Virginia Verploegh Steinmetz
January 1996

Abbreviations

This collection has been compiled from the following editions of George MacDonald's works:

- AB *At the Back of the North Wind,* Akron, Ohio: Saalfield Publishing Co., 1927.
- AF *Alec Forbes of Howglen,* London: Hurst and Blackett, Publishers, n.d.
- AN *Annals of a Quiet Neighborhood,* Philadelphia: David McKay, Publisher, n.d.
- DE *David Elginbrod,* Boston: Loring, Publisher, n.d.
- DG *Donal Grant,* Boston: Lothrop Publishing Co., 1883.
- DO *Dish of Orts,* London: Edwin Dalton, 1908.
- DS *Diary of an Old Soul,* Minneapolis: Augsburg Publishing House, 1975.
- E *The Elect Lady,* London: Kegan Paul, Trench, Trubner and Co., Ltd., n.d.
- EA *England's Antiphon,* New York: MacMillan and Co., 1890.
- FS *The Flight of the Shadow,* San Francisco: Harper and Row, Publishers, 1983.
- GC *Guild Court,* Philadelphia: David McKay, Publisher, n.d.
- GK *The Golden Key and Other Stories,* Elgin, Illinois: Scripture Union, 1979.
- GP *Gutta Percha Willie: the Working Genius,* London: Blackie and Son Ltd., n.d.
- GW *God's Word to His Children,* New York: Funk and Wagnalls, 1887.
- HA *Home Again,* London: Kegan Paul, Trench, Trubner and Co., Ltd., 1900.
- HG *Hope of the Gospel,* London: Ward, Lock, Bowden.
- HS *Heather and Snow,* London: Chatto and Windus, 1915.
- L *Lilith,* Grand Rapids, Michigan: Eerdmans, 1981.
- M *Malcolm,* Philadelphia: David McKay, Publisher, n.d.
- ML *The Marquis of Lossie,* London: Kegan Paul, Trench, Trubner and Co., Ltd., n.d.
- MM *Mary Marston,* New York: George Routledge and Sons, Ltd., n.d.

MOL	*The Miracles of Our Lord,* London: Strahan and Co., Publishers, 1870.
P	*The Portent,* San Francisco: Harper and Row, Publishers, 1979.
PI	*Poetical Works,* Volume I, London: Chatto and Windus, 1911.
PII	*Poetical Works,* Volume II, London: Chatto and Windus, 1911.
PC	*The Princess and Curdie,* Elgin, Illinois: Scripture Union, 1979.
PF	*Paul Faber, Surgeon,* Philadelphia: David McKay, Publisher, n.d.
PG	*The Princess and the Goblin,* Elgin, Illinois: Scripture Union, 1979.
PH	*Phantastes,* Grand Rapids, Michigan: Eerdmans, 1981.
RB	*Ranald Bannerman's Boyhood,* Philadelphia: J.B. Lippencott Company, 1890.
RF	*Robert Falconer,* New York: George Routledge and Sons, Ltd., n.d.
RS	*A Rough Shaking,* London: Blackie and Son, Ltd., 1890.
SI	*Unspoken Sermons (Series One),* London: Alexander Strahan, 1867.
SII	*Unspoken Sermons (Series Two),* London: Longmans, Green, and Co., 1895.
SIII	*Unspoken Sermons (Series Three),* London: Longmans, Green, and Co., 1891.
SF	*Salted with Fire,* London: Hurst and Blackett, Ltd., n.d.
SG	*Sir Gibbie,* London: J. M. Dent and Sons, Ltd., 1911.
SGM	*Saint George and Saint Michael,* Philadelphia: David McKay, Publisher, n.d.
SP	*The Seaboard Parish,* Philadelphia: David McKay, Publisher, n.d.
TB	*There and Back,* Boston: D. Lothrop Co., 1891.
TW	*Thomas Wingfold, Curate,* London: Kegan Paul, Trench, Trubner and Co., Ltd., 1906.
V	*The Vicar's Daughter,* London: Sampson Low, Marston, Searle, and Rivington, 1881.
WC	*Wilfred Cumbermede,* Chicago: Belford, Clarke and Co., 1881.
WM	*What's Mine's Mine,* London: Kegan Paul, Trench, Trubner and Co., Ltd., 1900.
WW	*Weighed and Wanting,* Boston: D. Lothrop Co., 1893.

Abandonment

The Old Man of the Earth stooped over the floor of the cave, raised a huge stone, and left it leaning. It disclosed a great hole that went plumb-down. "That is the way," he said. "But there are no stairs." "You must throw yourself in. There is no other way."

GK

No man can ever save his soul. God only can do that. You can glorify him by giving yourself up heart and soul and body and life to his Son. Then you shall *be* saved. That you must leave to *him*, and *do what he tells you.*

M. 53

The things that come out of a man are they that defile him, and to get rid of them a man must go into himself, be a convict, and scrub the floor of his cell.

SG. chap. 40

I sickened at the sight of myself; how should I ever get rid of the demon? The same instant I saw the one escape: I must offer it back to its source—commit it to him who had made it. I must live no more from it but from the source of it; seek to know nothing more of it than he gave me to know by his presence therein. . . . What flashes of self-consciousness might cross me should be God's gift, not of my seeking, and offered again to him in every new self-sacrifice.

WC. chap. 59

I am sometimes almost terrified at the scope of the demands made on me, at the perfection of the self-abandonment required of me; yet outside of such absoluteness can be no salvation. In God we live every commonplace as well as most exalted moment of our being. To trust in *him* when no need is pressing, when things seem going right of themselves, may be harder than when things seem going wrong.

WM. chap. 22

"Lilith," said Mara. "You will not sleep, if you lie there a thousand years, until you have opened your hand and yielded that which is not yours to give or to withhold." "I cannot," she answered. "I would if I could, for I am weary, and the shadows of death are gathering about me"—"They will gather and gather, but they cannot enfold you while yet your hand remains unopened. You may think you are dead, but it will only be a dream; you may think you have come awake, but it will still be only a dream. Open your hand, and you will sleep indeed—then wake indeed"—"I am trying hard, but the fingers have grown together and into the palm"—"I pray you put forth the strength of your will. For the love of life, draw together your forces and break its bonds!"

WM. chap. 40

Let God have his way with you, and not only will all be well, but you shall say, "It is well."

WW. 35

Action

A man must become an actor before he can be a true spectator.

AF. 148

To know about a thing is of no use, except you do it.

AN. 226

To find out what will not do, is a step toward finding out what will do. Moreover, an attempt in itself unsuccessful may set something or other in motion that will help.

AN. 389

Whatever a man does, whether it be the giving up all that he has to go and preach the gospel, or whether it be putting down the smallest rising thought of injustice, of anger and wrong, of selfishness in his soul. The act is where the will of man stands up against liking, against temptation, and leads him simply to do that which God would have him to do, easy or difficult; it may be to mount a throne, it may be to be sawn asunder.

The Christian World Pulpit

Therefore, friends, the practical thing is just this, and it is the one lesson we have to learn, that, whatever our doubts or difficulties may be, we must do the thing we know in order to learn the thing we do not know. But whether we learn it or not, "If you know these things," says the Master, "happy are you if you do them." It is the doing that is everything, and the doing is faith, and there is no division between them.

The Christian World Pulpit

Take him for your master, and he will demand nothing of you which you are not able to perform. This is the open door to bliss.

M

God never gave man a thing to do concerning which it were irreverent to ponder how the Son of God would have done it.

ML. 59

Active faith is the needful response in order that a man may be a child of God, and not the mere instrument upon which his power plays a soulless tune.

MOL. 47

In the act came the cure, without which the act had been confined to the will, and had never taken form in the outstretching. It is the same in all spiritual redemption.

MOL. 53

He sets an open path before us; *we* must walk in it. More, we must be willing to believe that the path is open, that we have strength to walk in it. God's gift glides into man's choice. It is needful that we should follow with our effort in the track of his foregoing power. To refuse is to destroy the gift. His cure is not for such as choose to be invalids.

MOL. 58

Fold the arms of your faith, and wait in quietness until light goes up in your darkness. Fold the arms of your faith I say, but not of your action: think of something that you ought to do, and go and do it, if it be but the sweeping of a room, or the preparing of a meal, or a visit to a friend. Heed not your feelings; do your work.

SI. 177

He who does that which he sees, shall understand; he who is set upon understanding rather than doing, shall go on stumbling and mistaking and speaking foolishness.

SII. 98

Do at once what you must do one day.

SII. 102

Instead of asking yourself whether you believe or not, ask yourself whether you have this day done one thing because he said, *Do it*, or once abstained because he said, *Do not do it*. It is simply absurd to say you believe, or even want to believe, in him, if you do not anything he tells you.

SII. 244

In the things that someone must do, the doer ranks in God's sight, and ought to rank among his fellow men, according to how he does it. The higher the calling the more contemptible the man who therein pursues his own ends. The humblest calling, followed on the principles of the divine caller, is a true and divine calling, be it scavenging, handicraft, shop-keeping, or book-making.

WM. 37

The only way to learn the rules of anything practical is to begin to do the thing. We have enough of knowledge in us—call it insight, call it instinct, call it inspiration, call it natural law, to begin anything required of us.

WW

The one who weighed, is found wanting the most, is the one whose tongue and whose life do not match—who says, "Lord! Lord!" and does not the thing the Lord says.

WW

Everybody knows something that is true to do—that is, something he ought to lose no time in setting about. The true thing is the thing that must not be let alone but done.

WW. 373

Afterlife

I had had very little knowledge of the external shows of death. Strange as it may appear, I had never yet seen a fellow creature pass beyond the call of his fellow mortals—"to think that the one moment the person is here, and the next—who shall say *where*? for we know nothing of the region beyond the grave! Not even our risen Lord thought fit to bring back from Hades any news for the human family standing straining their eyes after their brothers and sisters that have vanished in the dark. Surely it is well, all well, although we know nothing, save that our Lord has been there, knows all about it, and does not choose to tell us. Welcome ignorance, then! the ignorance in which he chooses to leave us. I would rather not know, if he gave me my choice, but preferred that I should not know." And so the oppression passed from me, and I was free.

AN. 497

There is a worse thing than dying never to wake again; there is a worse thing than dying forever, and going soul and brain to the dust; and that is to wake up and find that there is no God! That is the horror of horrors to me—to tell me that I am to live forever, and there is no God! For anything any man knows, who does not believe in a God, it may be so. He cannot tell with certainty that he is going to die forever because he sees no more of those that have gone before. Why should not they go on to some other sphere as they came into this one? Without any warning or any choice, they do not know until they find themselves here. Why should it not be so in another state of existence? But to find yourselves there without a God! There is no use praying to be killed, because there is no God to hear your prayer. You can no more annihilate yourselves than make yourselves. The whole thing would be utter misery.

The Christian World Pulpit

About death you know nothing. God has never told us anything about it but that the dead are alive to him, and that one day, they will be again to us. We do not *know* anything about it, I repeat; but the world beyond the doors of death must be as homelike a place as this world is.

DG. 33

Well may they think of death as the one thing to be right zealously avoided, and forever lamented! Who would forsake even the windowless hut of his sorrow for the poor mean place they imagine the Father's house! Why, many of them do not even expect to know their friends there! do not expect to distinguish one from another of all the holy assembly! They will look in many faces, but never to recognize old friends and lovers! A fine savior of men is their Jesus! Glorious lights they shine in the world of our sorrow, holding forth a word of darkness, of dismalest death! Is the Lord such as they believe him? "Good-bye, then, good Master!" cries the human heart. "I thought you could save me, but, alas, you cannot.

If you save the part of our being which can sin, you let the part that can love sink into hopeless perdition: you are not he that should come; I look for another! You would destroy and not save me! Your Father is not my Father; your God is not my God! Ah, to whom shall we go? He has *not* the words of eternal life, this Jesus, and the universe is dark as chaos! O Father, this your Son is good, but we need a greater Son than he. Never will your children love you under the shadow of this new law, that they are *not* to love one another as you love them!" How does that man love God—of what kind is the love he bears him—who is unable to believe that God loves every throb of every human heart toward another?

Did not the Lord die that we should love one another, and be one with him and the Father, and is not the knowledge of difference essential to the deepest love? Can there be oneness without difference? harmony without distinction? Are all to have the same face? then why faces at all? If the plains of heaven are to be crowded with the same one face over and over forever, but one moment will pass ere by monotony bliss shall have grown ghastly.

HG. 105–106

To annihilate the past of our earthly embodiment would be to crush under the heel of an iron fate the very idea of tenderness, human or divine.

HG. 108

If after death we should be conscious that we yet live, we shall even then, I think, be no more able to prove a further continuance of life, than we can now prove our present being. It may be easier to believe—that will be all.

MOL. 186

We constantly act on grounds which we cannot prove, and if we cannot feel so sure of life beyond the grave as of common everyday things, at least the want of proof ought neither to destroy our hope concerning it, nor prevent the action demanded by its bare possibility.

MOL. 186

It may seem strange that our Lord says so little about the life to come—as we call it, though in truth it is one life with the present as the leaf and the blossom are one life. . . . He seems always to have taken it for granted, ever turning the minds of his scholars toward that which was deeper and lay at its root—the life itself—the oneness with God and his will, upon which the continuance of our conscious being follows of necessity, and without which if the latter were possible, it would be for human beings an utter evil.

MOL. 187

When he speaks of the world beyond, it is as *his Father's house.* He says there are many mansions there. He attempts in no way to explain. Man's own imagination, enlightened of the spirit of truth and working with his experience and affections, was a far safer guide than his intellect with the best schooling which even our Lord could have given it.

MOL. 188

These miracles of our Lord are the nearest we come to news of any kind concerning—I cannot say *from*—the other world. I except of course our Lord's own resurrection. Of that I shall yet speak as a miracle, for miracle it was, as certainly as any of our Lord's, whatever interpretation be put upon the word.

MOL. 189

In God's dealings there are no exceptions. His laws are universal as he is infinite. Jesus wrought no new thing—only the works of the Father. What matters it that the dead come not back to us, if we go to them? *What matters it?* It is tenfold better. Dear as home is, he who loves it best must know that what he calls home is not home, is but a shadow of home, is but the open porch of a home, where all the winds of the world rave by turns, and the glowing fire of the true home casts lovely gleams from within.

MOL. 192

The dead must have their sorrow too, but when they find it is well with them, they can sit and wait by the mouth of the coming stream better than those can wait who see the going stream bear their loves down to the ocean of the unknown. The dead sit by the river-mouths of Time: the living mourn upon its higher banks.

MOL. 192

It is vain to look into that which God has hidden; for surely it is by no chance that we are left . . . in the dark.

MOL. 194

The region beyond is so different from ours, so comprising in one surpassing excellence all the goods of ours, that any attempt of the had-been-dead to describe it would have resulted in the most wretched of misconceptions.

MOL. 195

If one knew for certain that there was no life beyond this, then the noble thing would be to make the best of this, yea even then to try after such things as are written in the Gospel as we call it—for they *are* the noblest. That I am sure of, whatever I may doubt. But not to be sure of annihilation, and yet choose it to be true, and act as if it were true, seems to me to indicate a nature at strife with immortality—bound for the dust by its own choice—of the earth, and returning to the dust.

MOL. 217

Probably we are not capable of being told in words what the other world is. But even the very report through the ages that the dead came back, as their friends had known them, with the old love unlost in the grave, with the same face to smile and bless, is precious indeed. That they remain the same in all that made them lovely, is the one priceless fact—if we may but hope in it as a fact. That we shall behold, and clasp, and love them again follows of simple necessity. We cannot be sure of the report as if it were done before our own eyes, yet what a hope it gives even to him whose honesty and his faith together make him, like Martha, refrain speech, not daring to say *I believe* of all that is reported! I think such a one will one day be able to believe more than he even knows how to desire.

MOL. 219

The future lies dark before us, with an infinite hope in the darkness. To be at peace concerning it on any other ground than the love of God would be an absolute loss. Better fear and hope and prayer, than knowledge and peace without the prayer.

MOL. 221

That men should not limit him, or themselves in him, to the known forms of humanity; and for another, that the best hope might be given them of a life beyond the grave; that their instinctive desires in that direction might thus be infinitely developed and assured.

MOL. 268

It is to me a matter of positively no interest whether or not, in any sense, the matter of our bodies shall be raised from the earth. It is enough that we shall possess forms capable of revealing ourselves and of bringing us in contact with God's other works; forms in which the idea, so blurred and broken in these, shall be carried out—remaining so like, that friends shall doubt not a moment of the identity, becoming so unlike, that the tears of recognition shall be all for the joy of the gain and the gratitude of the loss.

MOL. 269

Wherefore should he not be so far the God of the dead, if during the time allotted to them here, he was the faithful God of the living? What God-like relation can the ever-living, life-giving, changeless God hold to creatures who partake not of his life, who have death at the very core of their being, who are not worth their Maker's keeping alive?

SI. 234

"All live to him." With him death is not. Your life sees our life, O Lord. All of whom *all* can be said, are present to you. You think about us, eternally more than we think about you. The little life that burns within the body of this death glows unquenchable in your true-seeing eyes. If you forget us for a moment then indeed death would be. But to you we live. The beloved pass from our sight, but they pass not from yours.

SI. 234

If God could see us before we were, and make us after his ideal, that we shall have passed from the eyes of our friends can be no argument that he beholds us no longer. "All live to him."

SI. 235

He of whom God thinks, lives. He takes to himself the name of *Their God*. The Living One cannot name himself after the dead when the very Godhead lies in the giving of life. Therefore they must be alive. If he speaks of them, remembers his own loving thoughts of them, would he not have kept them alive if he could; and if he could not, how could he create them? Can it be an easier thing to call into life than to keep alive?

SI. 236

That which made the body what it was in the eyes of those who loved us will be tenfold there.

SI. 240

Every eye shall see the beloved, every heart will cry, "My own again!—more mine because more himself than ever I beheld him!"

SI. 241

What! shall a man love his neighbor as himself, and must he be content not to know him in heaven? Better be content to lose our consciousness, and know ourselves no longer. What! shall God be the God of the families of the earth, and shall the love that he has thus created toward father and mother, brother and sister, wife and child, go moaning and longing to all eternity; or worse, far worse, die out of our bosoms? Shall God be God, and shall this be the end?

SI. 241

God will not take you, has not taken you from me to bury you out of my sight in the abyss of his own unfathomable being, where I cannot follow and find you, myself lost in the same awful gulf. No, our God is an unveiling, a revealing God. He will raise you from the dead, that I may behold you; that that which vanished from the earth may again stand forth, looking out of the same eyes of eternal love and truth, holding the same mighty hand of brotherhood, the same delicate and gentle, yet strong hand of sisterhood, to me, this me that knew you and loved you in the days gone by.

SI. 242

In the changes which, thank God, must take place when the mortal puts on immortality, shall we not feel that the nobler our friends are, the more they are themselves; that the more the idea of each is carried out in the perfection of beauty, the more like they are to what we thought them in our most exalted moods, to that which we saw in them in the rarest moments of profoundest communion, to that which we beheld through the veil of all their imperfections when we loved them the truest?

SI. 244

He gave us to each other to belong to each other for ever. He does not give to take away; with him is no variableness or shadow of turning.

SIII. 195

Our friends will know us then; for their joy, will it be, or their sorrow? Will their hearts sink within them when they look on the real likeness of us? Or will they rejoice to find that we were not so much to be blamed as they thought?

SIII. 246

The notions of Christians, so called, concerning the state into which they suppose their friends to have entered, and which they speak of as a place of blessedness, are yet such as to justify the bitterness of their lamentation over them, and the heathenish doubt whether they shall know them again. Verily it were a wonder if they did! After a year or two of such a fate, they might well be unrecognizable! One is almost ashamed of writing about such follies. The nirvana is grandeur contrasted with their heaven. The early Christians might now and then plague Paul with a foolish question, the answer to which plagues us to this day; but was there ever one of them doubted he was going to find his friends again?

SIII. 259

To understand him better they must be more like him, and to make them more like him he must go away and give them his Spirit—awful mystery which no man but himself can understand.

SP

Even if there be no hereafter, I would live my time believing in a grand thing that ought to be true if it is not. No facts can take the place of truths; and if these be not truths, then is the loftiest part of our nature a waste.

TW

Ambition

The true source of vulgarity, itself the most vulgar thing in the world, is ambition.

DG

The thoroughly simple, those content to be what they are, have the less concern about what they seem. The ambitious, who like to be taken for more than they are, may well be annoyed when they are taken for less.

DG. 2

Fame is the applause of the many, and the judgment of the many is foolish; therefore the greater the fame, the more is the foolishness that swells it, and the worse is the foolishness that longs after it. Aspiration is the sole escape from ambition. He who aspires—that is, endeavors to rise above himself—neither lusts to be higher than his neighbor nor seeks to mount in his opinion. What light there is in him shines the more that he does nothing to be seen of men. He stands in the mist between the gulf and the glory, and looks upward. He loves not his own soul, but longs to be clean.

HG. 201

Ambition is the desire to be above one's neighbor; and here there is no possibility of comparison with one's neighbor: no one knows what the white stone contains except the man who receives it. Here is room for endless aspiration toward the unseen ideal; none for ambition. Ambition would only be higher than others; aspiration would be high. Relative worth is not only unknown—to the children of the kingdom it is unknowable. Each esteems the other better than himself.

SI. 114

We shall be God's children on the little hills and in the fields of that heaven, not one desiring to be before another any more than to cast that other out; for ambition and hatred will then be seen to be one and the same spirit.

SII. 52

Ambition in every shape has to do with *things*, with outward advantages for the satisfaction of self-worship; it is that form of pride, foul shadow of Satan, which usurps the place of aspiration. The sole ambition that is of God is the ambition to rise above oneself; all other is of the devil.

SII. 56

No grasping or seeking, no hungering of the individual, shall give motion to the will: no desire to be conscious of worthiness shall order the life; no ambition whatever shall be a motive of action; no wish to surpass another be allowed a moment's respite from death.

SII. 215

The Lord's is a kingdom in which no man seeks to be above another: ambition is of the dirt of this world's kingdoms.

SIII. 100

Anger

Never will his righteous anger make him unfair to us, make him forget that we are dust.

HG. 33

There is a good anger and a bad anger. There is a wrath of God, and there is a wrath of man that works not the righteousness of God. Anger may be as varied as the color of the rainbow. God's anger can be nothing but Godlike, therefore divinely beautiful, at one with his love, helpful, healing, restoring; yet is it verily and truly what we call anger. How different is the anger of one who loves from that of one who hates! yet is anger anger. There is the degraded human anger, and the grand, noble, eternal anger. Our anger is in general degrading, because it is in general impure.

SIII. 189

It is to me an especially glad thought that the Lord came so near us as to be angry with us.

SIII. 189

The more we think of Jesus being angry with us, the more we feel that we must get nearer and nearer to him—get within the circle of his wrath, out of the sin that makes him angry, and near to him where sin cannot come. There is no quenching of his love in the anger of Jesus. The anger of Jesus is his recognition that we are to blame; if we were not to blame, Jesus could never be angry with us; we should not be of his kind, therefore not subject to his blame.

SIII. 189

Where we do that we ought not, and could have helped it, be moved to anger against us, O Christ! do not treat us as if we were not worth being displeased with; let not our faults pass as if they were of no weight. Be angry with us, Holy Brother, wherein we are to blame; where we do not understand, have patience with us, and open our eyes, and give us strength to obey, until at length we are the children of the Father even as you. For though you are lord and master and savior of them that are growing, you are perfect lord only of the true and the safe and the free, who live in your light and are divinely glad: we keep you back from your perfect lordship. Make us able to be angry and not sin; to be angry nor seek revenge the smallest; to be angry and full of forgiveness. We will not be content until our very anger is love.

SIII. 191

I think sometimes his anger is followed, yea, accompanied by an astounding gift, fresh from his heart of grace.

SIII. 192

He knows what to do, for he is love. He is love when he gives, and love when he withholds; love when he heals, and love when he slays. Lord, if thus you look upon men in your anger, what must a full gaze be from your eyes of love!

SIII. 192

Animals

To believe that God made many of the lower creatures merely for prey, or to be the slaves of a slave, and writhe under the tyrannies of a cruel master who will not serve his own master; that he created and is creating an endless succession of them to reap little or no good of life but its cessation . . . is to believe in a God who, so far as one portion at least of his creation is concerned, is a demon. But a creative demon is an absurdity; and were such a creator possible, he would not be God, but must one day be found and destroyed by the real God.

HG. 208

Do you believe in immortality for yourself? I would ask any reader who is not in sympathy with my hope for the animals. If not, I have no argument with you. But if you do, why not believe in it for them? Verily, were immortality no greater a thing for the animals than it seems for men to some who yet profess to expect it, I should scarce care to insist on their share in it.

HG. 212

The teachers of the nation have unwittingly, it seems to me through unbelief, wronged the animals deeply by their silence anent the thoughtless popular presumption that they have no hereafter; thus leaving them deprived of a great advantage to their position among men. But I suppose they, too, have taken it for granted that the Preserver of man and beast never had a thought of keeping one beast alive beyond a certain time; in which case heartless men might well argue he did not care how they wronged them, for he meant them no redress. Their immortality is no new faith with me, but as old as my childhood.

HG. 212

Are these not worth making immortal? How, then, were they worth calling out of the depth of no-being? It is a greater deed, to make be that which was not, than to seal it with an infinite immortality: did God do that which was not worth doing?

HG. 213

What he thought worth making, you think not worth continuing made! You would have him go on forever creating new things with one hand, and annihilating those he had made with the other—for I presume you would not prefer the earth to be without animals! If it were harder for God to make the former go on living than to send forth new, then his creatures were no better than the toys which a child makes, and destroys as he makes them. For what good, for what divine purpose is the Maker of the sparrow present at its death, if he does not care what becomes of it?

HG. 213

What is he there for . . . if he have no care that it go well with his bird in its dying, that it be neither comfortless nor lost in the abyss? If his presence be no good to the sparrow, are you very sure what good it will be to you when your hour comes? Believe it is not by a little only that the heart of the universe is tenderer, more loving, more just and fair, than yours or mine.

HG. 213

If you did not believe you were yourself to outlive death, I could not blame you for thinking all was over with the sparrow; but to believe in immortality for yourself, and not care to believe in it for the sparrow, would be simply hard-hearted and selfish. If it would make you happy to think there was life beyond death for the sparrow as well as for yourself, I would gladly help you at least to hope that there may be.

HG. 214

I know of no reason why I should not look for the animals to rise again, in the same sense in which I hope myself to rise again—which is, to reappear, clothed with another and better form of life than before.

HG. 214

If the Father will raise his children, why should he not also raise those whom he has taught his little ones to love?

HG. 214

Love is the one bond of the universe, the heart of God, the life of his children: if animals can be loved, they are lovable; if they can love, they are yet more plainly lovable: love is eternal; how then should its object perish?

HG. 214

Is not our love to the animals a precious variety of love? And if God gave the creatures to us, that a new phase of love might be born in us toward another kind of life from the same fountain, why should the new life be more perishing than the new love? Can you imagine that, if, hereafter, one of God's little ones were to ask him to give again one of the earth's old loves—kitten, or pony, or squirrel, or dog, which he had taken from him, the Father would say no? If the thing was so good that God made it for and gave it to the child at first who never asked for it, why should he not give it again to the child who prays for it because the Father had made him love it? What a child may ask for, the Father will keep ready.

HG. 215

That there are difficulties in the way of believing thus, I grant; that there are impossibilities, I deny. Perhaps the first difficulty that occurs is the many forms of life which we cannot desire again to see. But while we would gladly keep the perfected forms of the higher animals, we may hope that those of many other kinds are as transitory as their bodies, belonging but to a stage of development.

HG. 215

All animal forms tend to higher: why should not the individual, as well as the race, pass through stages of ascent? If I have myself gone through each of the typical forms of lower life on my way to the human—a supposition by antenatal history rendered probable—and therefore may have passed through any number of individual forms of life, I do not see why each of the lower animals should not as well pass upward through a succession of bettering embodiments.

HG. 216

I grant that the theory requires another to complement it; namely, that those men and women who do not even approximately fulfill the conditions of their elevated rank, who will not endeavor after the great human-divine idea, striving to ascend, are sent away back down to that stage of development, say of fish or insect or reptile, beyond which their moral nature has refused to advance. Who has not seen or known men who *appeared* not to have passed, or indeed in some things to have approached, the development of the more human of the lower animals!

HG. 216

Let those take care who look contemptuously upon the animals, lest, in misusing one of them, they misuse some ancestor of their own, sent back, as the one mercy for him, to reassume far past forms and conditions—far past in physical, that is, but not in moral development—and so have another opportunity of passing the self-constituted barrier.

HG. 217

If we believe in the progress of creation as hitherto manifested, also in the marvelous changes of form that take place in every individual of certain classes, why should there be any difficulty in hoping that old lives may reappear in new forms? The typal soul reappears in higher formal type; why may not also the individual soul reappear in higher form?

HG. 217

I know no cause of reasonable difficulty in regard to the continued existence of the lower animals, except the present nature of some of them. But what Christian will dare to say that God does not care about them?—and he knows them as we cannot know them. Great or small, they are his. Great are all his results; small are all his beginnings.

HG. 219

That we have to send many of his creatures out of this phase of their life because of their hurtfulness in this phase of ours, is to me no stumbling-block. The very fact that this has always had to be done, the long-protracted combat of the race with such, and the constantly repeated though not invariable victory of the man, has had an essential and incalculable share in the development of humanity, which is the rendering of man capable of knowing God; and when their part to that end is no longer necessary, changed conditions may speedily so operate that the wolf shall dwell with the lamb, and the leopard lie down with the kid. The difficulty may go for nothing in view of the forces of that future with which this loving speculation concerns itself.

HG. 219

"The hope that the creation itself also," as something besides and other than God's men and women, "shall be delivered from the bondage of corruption, into the liberty of the glory of the children of God." The creation then is to share in the deliverance and liberty and glory of the children of God. Deliverance from corruption, liberty from bondage, must include escape from the very home and goal of corruption, namely death—and that in all its kinds and degrees. When you say then that for the children of God there is no more death, remember that the deliverance of the creature is from the bondage of corruption into the glorious liberty of the children of God.

HG. 222

If such then be the words of the apostle, does he, or does he not, I ask, hold the idea of the immortality of the animals? If you say all he means is, that the creatures alive at the coming of the Lord will be set free from the tyranny of corrupt man, I refer you to what I have already said of the poverty of such an interpretation, accepting the failure of justice and love toward those that have passed away, are passing, and must yet, ere that coming, be born to pass away forever. For the man whose heart aches to adore a faithful creator, what comfort lies in such good news! He must perish for lack of a true God! O lame conclusion to the grand prophecy! Is God a mocker, who will not be mocked?

HG. 223

Is there a past to God with which he has done? Is Time too much for him? Is he God enough to care for those that happen to live at one present time, but not God enough to care for those that happen to live at another present time? Or did he care for them, but could not help them? Shall we not rather believe that the vessels of less honor, the misused, the maltreated, shall be filled full with creative wine at last?

HG. 223

Shall not the children have little dogs under the Father's table, to which to let fall plenty of crumbs? If there was such provision for the sparrows of our Lord's time of sojourn, and he will bring yet better with him when he comes again, how should the dead sparrows and their sorrows be passed over of him with whom is no variableness, neither shadow of turning?

HG. 224

Would the deliverance of the creatures into the groaned-for liberty have been much worth mentioning, if within a few years their share in the glory of the sons of God was to die away in death? . . . The gifts of God are without repentance.

HG. 224

The new heaven and the new earth will at least be a heaven and an earth! What would the newest earth be to the old children without its animals? Barer than the heavens emptied of the constellations that are called by their names. Then, if the earth must have its animals, why not the old ones, already dear? The sons of God are not a new race of sons of God, but the old race glorified: Why a new race of animals, and not the old ones glorified?

HG. 225

The apostle says they are to share in the liberty of the sons of God: will it not then be a liberty like ours, a liberty always ready to be offered on the altar of love? What sweet service will not that of the animals be, thus offered! How sweet also to minister to them in their turns of need! For to us doubtless will they then flee for help in any difficulty, as now they flee from us in dread of our tyranny.

HG. 225

What lovelier feature in the newness of the new earth, than the old animals glorified with us, in their home with us—our common home, the house of our Father—each kind an unfailing pleasure to the other! Ah, what horses! Ah, what dogs! Ah, what wild beasts, and what birds in the air!

HG. 225

When the sons, then, are free, when their bodies are redeemed, they will lift up with them the lower creation into their liberty.

HG. 230

Perfection in their kind awaits also the humbler inhabitants of our world, its advent to follow immediately on the manifestation of the sons of God: for our sakes and their own they have been made subject to vanity; for our sakes and their own they shall be restored and glorified, that is, raised higher with us.

HG. 230

Has the question no interest for you? It would have much, had you now what you must one day have—a heart big enough to love any life God has thought fit to create.

HG. 231

Had the Lord cared no more for what of his Father's was lower than himself, than you do for what of your Father's is lower than you, you would not now be looking for any sort of redemption.

HG. 231

The new heavens and the new earth in which dwell the sons of God are to be inhabited by blessed animals also—inferior, but risen—and, I think, yet to rise in continuous development.

HG. 232

If the Lord said very little about animals, could he have done more for them than tell men that his Father cared for them? He has thereby awakened and is wakening in the hearts of men a seed his Father planted.

HG. 234

Our behavior to the animals, our words concerning them, are seed, either good or bad, in the hearts of our children. No one can tell to what the animals might not grow, even here on the old earth under the old heaven, if they were but dealt with according to their true position in regard to us. They are, in sense very real and divine, our kindred.

HG. 234

That the rights of the animals are so much less than ours does not surely argue them the less rights! They have little, and we have much; ought they therefore to have less and we more? Must we not rather be the more honorably anxious that they have their little to the full?

HG. 239

The Lord is mindful of his own, and will save both man and beast.

HG. 242

A beast does not know that he is a beast, and the nearer a man gets to being a beast the less he knows it.

PC. chap. 8

The bliss of the animals lies in this, that, on their lower level, they shadow the bliss of those—few at any moment on the earth—who do not "look before and after, and pine for what is not" but live in the holy carelessness of the eternal *now*.

SG. chap. 2

Anxiety

It has been well said that no man ever sank under the burden of the day. It is when tomorrow's burden is added to the burden of today, that the weight is more than a man can bear. Never load yourselves so, my friends. If you find yourselves so loaded, at least remember this: it is your own doing, not God's. He begs you to leave the future to him, and mind the present. What more or what else could he do to take the burden off you? Nothing else would do it. Money in the bank wouldn't do it. He cannot do tomorrow's business for you beforehand to save you from fear about it. That would derange everything. What else is there but to tell you to trust in him, irrespective of the fact that nothing else but such trust can put our hearts at peace, from the very nature of our relation to him as well as the fact that we need these things. We think that we come nearer to God than the lower animals do by our foresight. But there is another side to it. We are like to him with whom there is no past or future, with whom a day is as a thousand years, and a thousand years as one day, when we live with large bright spiritual eyes, doing our work in the great present, leaving both past and future to him to whom they are ever present, and fearing nothing, because he is in our future, as much as he is in our past, as much as, and far more than, we can feel him to be in our present. Partakers thus of the divine nature, resting in that perfect All-in-all in whom our nature is eternal too, we walk without fear, full of hope and courage and strength to do his will, waiting for the endless good which he is always giving as fast as he can get us able to take it in.

AN. 203

You have a disagreeable duty to do at twelve o'clock. Do not blacken nine and ten and eleven, and all between with the color of twelve. Do the work of each, and reap your reward in peace. So when the dreaded moment in the future becomes the present, you shall meet it walking in the light, and that light will overcome its darkness.

AN. 206

One thing is clear in regard to every trouble—that the natural way with it is straight to the Father's knee. The Father is father *for* his children, else why did he make himself their father?

HG. 115

Tomorrow makes today's whole head sick, its whole heart faint. When we should be still, sleeping or dreaming, we are fretting about an hour that lies a half sun's-journey away!

SII. 49

The care that is filling your mind at this moment, or but waiting until you lay the book aside to leap on you—that need which is no need is a demon sucking at the spring of your life. "No; mine is a reasonable care—an unavoidable care, indeed." Is it something you have to do this very moment? "No." Then you are allowing it to usurp the place of something that is required of you this moment. "There is nothing required of me at this moment." Nay but there is—the greatest thing that can be required of man. "Pray, what is it?" Trust in the living God. . . . "I do trust him in spiritual matters." Everything is an affair of the spirit.

SII. 49

You are ready to be miserable over trifles, and do not believe God good enough to care for your care: I would reason with you to help you rid of your troubles, for they hide from you the thoughts of your God.

SII. 52

With every haunting trouble then, great or small, the loss of thousands or the lack of a shilling, go to God, and appeal to him, the God of your life, to deliver you, his child, from that which is unlike him, therefore does not belong to you, but is antagonistic to your nature. If your trouble is such that you cannot appeal to him, the more need you should appeal to him! Where one cannot go to God, there is something specially wrong.

SII. 55

If you let thought for the morrow, or the next year, or the next month, distress you; if you let the chatter of what is called the public, peering purblind into the sanctuary of motive, annoy you; if you seek or greatly heed the judgment of men, capable or incapable, you set open your windows to the mosquitoes of care, to drown with their buzzing the voice of the Eternal!

SII. 55

If you tell me that but for care, the needful work of the world would be ill done—"What work," I ask, "can that be, which will be better done by the greedy or anxious than by the free, fearless soul? Can care be a better inspirer of labor than the sending of God? If the work is not his work, then, indeed, care may well help it, for its success is loss. But is he worthy the name of man who, for the fear of starvation, will do better work than for the joy that his labor is not in vain in the Lord? I know as well as you that you are not likely to get rich that way; but neither will you block up the gate of the kingdom of heaven against yourself."

SII. 55

The will of God must be to us all in all; to our whole nature the life of the Father must be the joy of the child; we must know our very understanding his—that we live and feed on him every hour in the closest, veriest way: to know these things in the depth of our knowing, is to deny ourselves, and take God instead. To try after them is to begin the denial, to follow him who never sought his own. So must we deny all anxieties and fears. When young we must not mind what the world calls failure; as we grow old, we must not be vexed that we cannot remember, must not regret that we cannot do, must not be miserable because we grow weak or ill: we must not mind anything.

SII. 216

All the morning he was busy . . . with his heart in trying to content himself beforehand with whatever fate the Lord might intend for him. As yet he was more of a Christian philosopher than a philosophical Christian. The thing most disappointing to him he would treat as the will of God for him, and try to make up his mind to it, persuading himself it was the right and best thing—as if he knew it (to be) the will of God. He was thus working in the region of supposition and not of revealed duty: in his own imagination, and not in the will of God. . . . There is something in the very presence and actuality of a thing to make one able to bear it; but a man may weaken himself for bearing what God intends him to bear, by trying to bear what God does not intend him to bear. . . . We have no right to school ourselves to an imaginary duty. When we do not know, then what he lays upon us is *not to know.*

WM. chap. 41

Atonement

He who trusts in the atonement instead of in the Father of Jesus Christ fills his fancy with the chimeras of a vulgar legalism, not his heart with the righteousness of God.

HG. 131

Some of you say we must trust in the finished work of Christ; or again, our faith must be in the merits of Christ—in the atonement he has made, in the blood he has shed: all these statements are a simple repudiation of the living Lord, *in whom* we are told to believe, who, by his presence with and in us, and our obedience to him, lifts us out of darkness into light, leads us from the kingdom of Satan into the glorious liberty of the sons of God.

SII. 240

No manner or amount of belief *about him* is the faith of the New Testament. With such teaching I have had a lifelong acquaintance, and declare it most miserably false. But I do not now mean to dispute against it; except the light of the knowledge of the glory of God in the face of Christ Jesus make a man sick of his opinions, he may hold them to doomsday for me; for no opinion, I repeat, is Christianity, and no preaching of any plan of salvation is the preaching of the glorious gospel of the living God. Even if your plan, your theories, were absolutely true, the holding of them with sincerity, the trusting in this or that about Christ, or in anything he did or could do, the trusting in anything but himself, his own living self, is a delusion. Many will grant this heartily, and yet the moment you come to talk with them, you find they insist that to believe in Christ is to believe in the atonement, meaning by that only and altogether their special theory about the atonement; and when you say we must believe in the atoning Christ, and cannot possibly believe *in* any theory concerning the atonement, they go away and denounce you, saying, "He does not believe in the atonement!" If I explain the atonement otherwise than they explain it, they assert that I deny the atonement; nor count it of any consequence that I say I believe in the atoner with my whole heart, and soul, and strength, and mind. This they call *contending for the truth*! Because I refuse an explanation which is not in the New Testament, though they believe it is, because they can think of no other, one which seems to me as false in logic as detestable in morals, not to say that there is no spirituality in it whatever, therefore I am not a Christian! What wonder men such as I have quoted refuse the Christianity they suppose such "believers" to represent! I do not say that with this sad folly may not mingle a potent faith in the Lord himself; but I do say that the importance they place on theory is even more sadly obstructive to true faith than such theories themselves: while the mind is occupied in inquiring,

"Do I believe or feel this thing right?"—the true question is forgotten: "Have I left all to follow him?" To the man who gives himself to the living Lord, every belief will necessarily come right; the Lord himself will see that his disciple believes aright concerning him. If a man cannot trust him for this, what claim can he make to faith in him? It is because he has little or no faith, that he is left clinging to preposterous and dishonoring ideas, the traditions of men concerning his Father, and neither his teaching nor that of his apostles. The living Christ is to them but a shadow; the all but obliterated Christ of their theories no soul can thoroughly believe in: the disciple of such a Christ rests on his work, or his merits, or his atonement!

What I insist upon is, that a man's faith shall be in the living, loving, ruling, helping Christ, devoted to us as much as ever he was, and with all the powers of the Godhead for the salvation of his brethren. It is not faith that he did this, that his work wrought that—it is faith in the man who did and is doing everything for us that will save him: without this he cannot work to heal spiritually, any more than he would heal physically, when he was present to the eyes of men. Do you ask, "What is faith in him?" I answer, The leaving of your way, your objects, your self, and the taking of his and him; the leaving of your trust in men, in money, in opinion, in character, in atonement itself, *and doing as he tells you.* I can find no words strong enough to serve for the weight of this necessity—this obedience. It is the one terrible heresy of the church, that it has always been presenting something else than obedience as faith in Christ. The work of Christ is not the Working Christ, any more than the clothing of Christ is the body of Christ. If the woman who touched the hem of his garment had trusted in the garment and not in him who wore it, would she have been healed? And the reason that so many who believe *about* Christ rather than in him, get the comfort they do, is that, touching thus the mere hem of his garment, they cannot help believing a little in the live man inside the garment. It is not wonderful that such believers should so often be miserable; they lay themselves down to sleep with nothing but the skirt of his robe in their hand—a robe too, I say, that never was his, only by them is supposed his—when they might sleep in peace with the living Lord in their hearts. Instead of so knowing Christ that they have him in them saving them, they lie wasting themselves in soul-sickening self-examination as to whether they are believers, whether they are really trusting in the atonement, whether they are truly sorry for their sins—the way to madness of the brain, and despair of the heart. Some even ponder the imponderable—whether they are of the elect, whether they have an interest in the blood shed for sin, whether theirs is a saving faith—when all the time the man who died for them is waiting to begin to save them from every evil—and first from this self which is consuming them with trouble about its salvation; he will set them free, and take them home to the bosom of the Father—if only they will mind what he says to them—which is the beginning, middle, and end of faith. If, instead of searching into the mysteries of corruption in their own charnel-houses, they would but awake and arise from the dead, and come out into the light which Christ is waiting to give them, he would begin at once to fill them with the fullness of God.

"But I do not know how to awake and arise!"

I will tell you: Get up, and do something the Master tells you; so make yourself his disciple at once. Instead of asking yourself whether you believe or not, ask yourself whether you have this day done one thing because he said, Do it, or once abstained because he said, Do not do it. It is simply absurd to say you believe, or even want to believe in him, if you do not do anything he tells you. If you can think of nothing he ever said as having had an atom of influence on your doing or not doing, you have too good ground to consider yourself no disciple of his. Do not, I pray you, worse than waste your time in trying to convince yourself that you are his disciple notwithstanding—that for this reason or that you still have cause to think you believe in him. What though you should succeed in persuading yourself to absolute certainty that you are his disciple, if, after all, he say to you, "Why did you not do the things I told you? Depart from me; I do not know you!" Instead of trying to persuade yourself, if the thing be true you can make it truer; if it be not true, you can begin at once to make it true, to *be* a disciple of the Living One—by obeying him in the first thing you can think of in which you are not obeying him. We must learn to obey him in everything, and so must begin somewhere: let it be at once, and in the very next thing that lies at the door of our conscience! Oh fools and slow of heart, if you think of nothing but Christ, and do not set yourselves to do his words! you but build your houses on the sand. What have such teachers not to answer for who have turned your regard away from the direct words of the Lord himself, which are spirit and life, to contemplate plans of salvation tortured out of the words of his apostles, even were those plans as true as they are false! There is but one plan of salvation, and that is to believe in the Lord Jesus Christ; that is, to take him for what he is—our master, and his words as if he meant them, which assuredly he did. To do his words is to enter into vital relation with him, to obey him is the only way to be one with him. The relation between him and us is an absolute one; it can nohow begin to *live* but in obedience: it *is* obedience. There can be no truth, no reality, in any initiation of at-one-ment with him, that is not obedience. What! have I the poorest notion of a God, and dare think of entering into relations with him, the very first of which is not that what he saith, I will do? The thing is eternally absurd, and comes of the father of lies. I know what he whispers to those to whom such teaching as this is distasteful: "It is the doctrine of works!" But one word of the Lord humbly heard and received will suffice to send all the demons of false theology into the abyss. He says the man that does not do the things he tells him, builds his house to fall in utter ruin. He instructs his messengers to go and baptize all nations, "teaching them to observe all things whatsoever I have commanded you." Tell me it is faith he requires: do I now know it? and is not faith the highest act of which the human mind is capable? But faith in what? Faith in what he is, in what he says—a faith which can have no existence except in obedience—a faith which *is* obedience. To do what he wishes is to put forth faith in him. For this the teaching of men has substituted this or that belief *about* him, faith in this or that supposed design of his manifestation in the flesh. It was himself, and God in him that he manifested; but faith in him and his father thus manifested, they make altogether secondary to acceptance of the paltry contrivance of a juggling morality, which they attribute to God and his Christ, imagining it the atonement and "the plan of salvation." "Do you put faith in *him,*" I ask, "or in the doctrines and commandments of men?" If you say "In him"—"Is it then possible," I return, "that you do not see that, above all things and all thoughts, you are bound to obey him?"

SII. 240–247

Tell me something that you have done, are doing, or are trying to do because he told you. If you do nothing that he says, it is no wonder that you cannot trust in him and are therefore driven to seek refuge in the atonement, as if something he had done, and not he himself in his doing were the atonement.

SII. 248

What does it matter how you understand, or what you understand, so long as you are not of one mind with the Truth, so long as you and God are not *at one,* do not atone together?

SII. 248

One thing must surely be plain—that the punishment of the wrongdoer makes no atonement for the wrong done.

SIII. 112

When the man says, "I did wrong; I hate myself and my deed; I cannot endure to think that I did it!" then, I say, is atonement begun. Without that, all that the Lord did would be lost. He would have made no atonement. Repentance, restitution, confession, prayer for forgiveness, righteous dealing thereafter, is the sole possible, the only true make-up for sin. For nothing less than this did Christ die.

SIII. 128

The work of Jesus Christ on earth was the creative atonement, because it works atonement in every heart. He brings and is bringing God and man, and man and man, into perfect unity: "I in them and you in me, that they may be made perfect in one."

SIII. 128

If punishment be no atonement, how does the fact bear on the popular theology accepted by every one of the opposers of what they call Christianity, as representing its doctrines? Most of us have been more or less trained in it, and not a few of us have thereby, thank God, learned what it is—an evil thing, to be cast out of intellect and heart. Many imagine it dead and gone, but in reality it lies at the root (the intellectual root only, thank God) of much the greater part of the teaching of Christianity in the country; and is believed in—so far as the false *can* be believed in—by many who think they have left it behind, when they have merely omitted the truest, most offensive modes of expressing its doctrines.

SIII. 133

God is bound to punish sin, and to punish it to the uttermost. His justice requires that sin be punished. But he loves man, and does not want to punish him if he can help it. Jesus Christ says, "I will take his punishment on me." God accepts his offer, and lets man go unpunished—on a condition. His justice is more than satisfied by the punishment of an infinite being instead of a world of worthless creatures. The suffering of Jesus is of greater value than that of all the generations, through endless ages, because he is infinite, pure, perfect in love and truth, being God's own everlasting Son. God's condition with man is that he believe in Christ's atonement thus explained.

SIII. 143

I believe in Jesus Christ. Nowhere am I requested to believe *in* any thing, or *in* any statement, but everywhere to believe in God and in Jesus Christ. In what you call *the atonement,* in what you mean by the word, what I have already written must make it plain enough I do not believe. God forbid I should, for it would be to believe a lie, and a lie which is to blame for much nonacceptance of the gospel in this and other lands.

SIII. 156

I believe in the atonement, call it the *a-tone-ment,* or the *at-one-ment,* as you please. I believe that Jesus Christ *is* our atonement; that through him we are reconciled to, made one with God. There is not one word in the New Testament about reconciling God to us; it is we that have to be reconciled to God.

SIII. 156

He made atonement! *We* sacrifice to God!—it is God who has sacrificed his own Son to us; there was no way else of getting the gift of himself into our hearts.

SIII. 158

If the joy that alone makes life worth living, the joy that God is such as Christ, be a true thing in my heart, how can I but believe in the atonement of Jesus Christ? I believe it heartily, as God means it.

SIII. 158

Who is the mover, the causer, the persuader, the creator of the repentance, of the passion that restores fourfold?—Jesus, our propitiation, our atonement. He is the head and leader, the prince of the atonement. He could not do it without us, but he leads us up to the Father's knee: he makes us make atonement.

SIII. 158

That I will and can make atonement, thanks be to him who is my atonement, making me at one with God and my fellows! He is my life, my joy, my lord, my owner, the perfecter of my being by the perfection of his own.

SIII. 159

No atonement is necessary to him but that men should leave their sins and come back to his heart.

SIII. 160

We are never told to believe in the atonement; we are told to believe in Christ.

WM

What moment a man feels that he belongs to God utterly, the atonement is there, the Son of God is reaping his harvest.

WM. 14

Belief/Unbelief

It is by the vision in our souls, the feeling and perception in our souls, of what

God is, that we are able to believe in him. Let a man once see God as Christ saw him, and he believes. Any glimmer of the truth in regard to our Lord's nature helps him believe—enables him to go on, and on, and on.

The Christian World Pulpit

If anyone insists on believing nothing but what he has seen something like, I leave him to his misery and the mercy of God.

DG

There are things he cannot do until we believe in Christ.

DG

Poor misbelieving birds of God, we hover about a whole wood of the trees of life, venturing here and there a peck, as if their fruit might be poison, and the design of our creation was our ruin: we shake our wise, owl-feathered heads and declare they cannot be the trees of life, because that is too good to be true. Ten times more consistent are they who deny there is a God at all than they who fancy they believe in a middling kind of a God, in whom they place indeed a fitting faith.

DG. 11

Not only is it impossible for a low man to believe a thousandth part of what a noble man can, but a low man cannot believe anything as a noble man believes it. The men of Nazareth could have believed in Jesus as their savior from the Romans; as their savior from their sins they could not believe in him, for they loved their sins.

HG. 79

If a man can believe that there is a God, he may well believe that, having made creatures capable of hungering and thirsting for him, he must be capable of speaking a word to guide them in their feeling after him. And if he is a grand God, a God worthy of being God, yea (his metaphysics even may show the seeker), if he is a God capable of being God, he will speak the clearest, grandest word of guidance which he can utter intelligible to his creatures.

MOL. 2

The common kind of belief in God is rationally untenable. Half to an insensate nature, half to a living God, is a worship that cannot stand. God is all in all, or no God at all.

MOL. 33

It is heart alone that can satisfy heart. It is the love of God alone that can gather to itself the love of his children. To believe in an almighty being is hardly to believe in a God at all. To believe in a being who, in his weakness and poverty, if such could be, would die for his creatures, would be to believe in a God indeed.

MOL. 38

Jesus did not care to be believed in as the doer of the deed, save the deed itself were recognized as given him of the Father. If they saw him only, and not the Father through him, there was little gained indeed.

MOL. 152

"Help my unbelief." It is the very triumph of faith. The unbelief itself cast like any other care on him who cares for us, is the highest exercise of belief. It is the greatest effort lying in the power of the man. No man can help doubt. The true man alone, that is, the faithful man, can appeal to the Truth to enable him to believe what is true and refuse what is false. How this applies especially to our own time and the need of the living generations is easy to see. Of all prayers it is the one for us.

MOL. 178

Our power of belief depends greatly on our power of imagining a region in which the things might be. I do not see how some people *could* believe what to others may offer small difficulty. Let us beware lest what we call faith be but the mere assent of a mind which has cared and thought so little about the objects of its so-called faith, that it has never seen the difficulties they involve. Some such believers are the worst antagonists of true faith—the children of the Pharisees of old.

MOL. 228

. . . He was getting rather stupid—one of the chief signs of which was that he believed less and less in things he had never seen.

PC. 19

A man will please God better by believing some things that are not told him, than by confining his faith to those things that are expressly said—said to arouse in us the truth-seeing faculty, the spiritual desire, the prayer for the good things which God will give to them that ask him.

SI. 55

If you believed in God you would find it easy to believe the word. You would not even need to inquire whether he had *said* it: you would know that he meant it.

SI. 62

Let us then dare something. Let us not always be unbelieving children. Let us keep in mind that the Lord, not forbidding those who insist on seeing before they will believe, blesses those who have not seen and yet have believed—those who trust in him more than that, who believe without the sight of the eyes, without the hearing of the ears.

SI. 62

To believe in him is to do as he does, to follow him where he goes. We must believe in him *practically*—altogether practically, as he believed in his Father; not as one concerning whom we have to hold something, but as one whom we have to follow out of the body of this death into life eternal.

SII. 2

To hold a thing with the intellect is not to believe it. A man's real belief is that which he lives by; and that which the man I mean lives by, is the love of God, and obedience to his law, so far as he has recognized it. Those hideous doctrines are outside him; he *thinks* they are inside, but no matter; they are not true, and they cannot really be inside any good man. They are sadly against him; for he cannot love to dwell on any of those supposed characteristics of his God; he acts and lives nevertheless in a measure like the true God. What a man believes, is the thing he does.

SII. 239

Some of you say we must trust in the finished work of Christ; or again, our faith must be in the merits of Christ—in the atonement he has made—in the blood he has shed: all these statements are a simple repudiation of the living Lord, *in whom* we are told to believe, who, by his presence with and in us, and our obedience to him, lifts us out of darkness into light, leads us from the kingdom of Satan into the glorious liberty of the sons of God. No manner or amount of belief *about him* is the faith of the New Testament.

SII. 240

Instead of asking yourself whether you believe or not, ask yourself whether you have this day done one thing because he said, Do it, or once abstained because he said, Do not do it. It is simply absurd to say you believe, or even want to believe in him, if you do not anything he tells you.

SII. 244

One chief cause of the amount of unbelief in the world is that those who have seen something of the glory of Christ set themselves to theorize concerning him rather than to obey him. In teaching men, they have not taught them Christ, but taught them about Christ.

SIII. 135

Little knows the world what a power among men is the man who simply and really believes in him who is the Lord of the world to save men from their sins.

SF

The only possibility of believing in a God seems to me to lie in finding an idea of a God large enough, grand enough, pure enough, lovely enough to be fit to believe in.

TW. 43

Complaint against God is far nearer to God than indifference about him.

WM. chap. 39

We are always disbelieving in him because things do not go as we intend and desire them to go. We forget that God has larger ends, even for us, than we can see, so his plans do not fit ours.

WW. 49

He who does not believe in God must be a truster in that which is lower than himself.

WW. 50

Bible

For I thought with myself, if I could get them to like poetry and beautiful things in words, it would not only do them good, but help them see what is in the Bible, and therefore love it more. For I never could believe that a man who did not find God in other places as well as in the Bible ever found him there at all. And I always thought, that to find God in other books enabled us to see clearly that he was *more* in the Bible than in any other book, or all other books put together.

AN. 183

The true heart goes to the blessed Book, not as an idolater, but as a disciple; not to worship the Book, but to learn the will of him who made the Book, and who has made his spirit to understand the Book.

GW. 113

Sad, indeed, would the whole matter be, if the Bible had told us *everything* God meant us to believe. But herein is the Bible itself greatly wronged. It nowhere lays claim to be regarded as *the* Word, *the* Way, *the* Truth. The Bible leads us to Jesus, the inexhaustible, the ever-unfolding Revelation of God. It is Christ "in whom are hid all the treasures of wisdom and knowledge," not the Bible, save as leading to him.

SI. 52

If we were once filled with the mind of Christ, we should know that the Bible had done its work, was fulfilled, and had for us passed away, that thereby the Word of our God might abide for ever.

SI. 54

The one use of the Bible is to make us look at Jesus, that through him we might know his Father and our Father, his God and our God. Until we thus know him, let us hold the Bible dear as the moon of our darkness, by which we travel toward the east; not dear as the sun whence her light comes, and toward which we haste, that, walking in the sun himself, we may no more need the mirror that reflected his absent brightness.

SI. 55

I cannot admit for a moment that there is anything in the Bible too mysterious to be looked into; for the Bible is a *revelation*, an unveiling. True, into many things uttered there I can see only a little way. But that little way is the way of life; for the depth of their mystery is God.

SI. 72

This story may not be just as the Lord told it, and yet may contain in its mirror as much of the truth as we are able to receive, and as will afford us scope for a life's discovery. The modifying influence of the human channels may be essential to God's revealing mode.

SI. 132

No word . . . is fully a Word *of* God until it is a Word *to* man, until the man therein recognizes God. This is that for which the word is spoken. The words of God are as the sands and the stars—they cannot be numbered; but the end of all and each is this—to reveal God.

SI. 142

Satan quotes Scripture as a verbal authority; our Lord meets him with a Scripture by the truth in which he regulates his conduct.

SI. 145

As no Scripture is of private interpretation, so is there no feeling in a human heart which exists in that heart alone—which is not, in some form or degree, in every heart.

SII. 116

How many, failing to trust God, fall back on *a text*, as they call it! It sprang from the pride that will understand what it cannot, before it will obey what it sees. He that will understand *first* will believe a lie—a lie from which obedience alone will at length deliver him.

SIII. 138

Every man must read the Word for himself. One may read it in one shape, another in another: all will be right if it be indeed the Word they read, and they read it by the lamp of obedience. He who is willing to do the will of the Father shall know the truth of the teaching of Jesus. The spirit is "given to them that obey him."

SIII. 167

In the Bible men are constantly recognized as righteous men who are far from perfectly righteous.

SIII. 216

The Bible never deals with impossibilities, never demands of any man at any given moment a righteousness of which at that moment he is incapable; neither does it lay on any man any other law than that of perfect righteousness. It demands of him righteousness; when he yields that righteousness of which he is capable, content for the moment, it goes on to demand more: the common sense of the Bible is lovely.

SIII. 216

Body

The body is a lantern; it must not be a dark lantern; the glowing heart must show in the shining face.

HG. 182

Evil has been constantly at work, turning our house of the body into a prison; rendering it more opaque and heavy and insensible; casting about it bands and cerements, and filling it with aches and pains.

HG. 228

The freest soul, the purest of lovers, the man most incapable of anything mean, would not, for all his mighty liberty, yet feel absolutely at large while chained to a dying body—nor the less hampered, but the more, that that dying body was his own. The redemption of the body, therefore, the making of it for the man a genuine, perfected, responsive house-alive, is essential to the apostle's notion of a man's deliverance. The new man must have a new body with a new heaven and earth.

HG. 228

A body like the Lord's is, I imagine, necessary to bring us into true and perfect contact with the creation, of which there must be multitudinous phases whereof we cannot now be even aware.

HG. 229

The way in which both good and indifferent people alike lay the blame on their bodies, and look to death rather than God-aided struggle to set them at liberty, appears to me low and cowardly: it is the master fleeing from the slave, despising at once and fearing him.

HG. 229

We must hold the supremacy over our bodies, but we must not despise body; it is a divine thing. Body and soul are in the image of God; and the Lord of life was last seen in the glorified body of his death. I believe that he still wears that body.

HG. 229

We shall do better without these bodies that suffer and grow old—which may indeed, as some think, be but the outer cases, the husks of our real bodies. Endlessly helpful as they have been to us, and that, in a measure, incalculable, through their very subjection to vanity, we are yet surely not in altogether and only helpful company, so long as the houses wherein we live have so many spots and stains in them which friendly death, it may be, can alone wash out—so many weather-eaten and self-engendered sores which the builder's hand, pulling down and rebuilding of fresh and nobler material, alone can banish.

HG. 230

I hold that he took again the same body in which he had walked about on the earth, suffered, and yielded unto death. In the same body—not merely the same form, in which he had taught them, he appeared again to his disciples, to give them the final consolations of a visible presence, before departing for the sake of a yet higher presence in the spirit of truth, a presence no longer limited by even the highest forms of the truth.

MOL. 260

The body with all its limitations, with all its partition-walls of separation, is God's, and there must be some way in which even *it* can come into a willed relation with him to whom it is nearer even than to ourselves, for it is the offspring of his will, or as the prophets of old would say—the work of his hands.

MOL. 264

After he had once ascended to the Father, he not only appeared to his disciples again and again, but their hands handled the word of life, and he ate in their presence. He had been to his Father, and had returned that they might know him lifted above the grave and all that region in which death has power; that as the elder brother, free of the oppressions of humanity, but fulfilled of its tenderness, he might show himself captain of their salvation.

MOL. 265

Upon the body he inhabited, death could no longer lay his hands, and from the vantage-ground he thus held, he could stretch down the arm of salvation to each and all.

MOL. 266

In regard of this glorified body of Jesus, we must note that it appeared and disappeared at the will of its owner; and it would seem also that other matter yielded and gave it way; yes, even that space itself was in some degree subjected to it. Upon the first of these, the record is clear. If any man say he cannot believe it, my only answer is that I can. If he ask how it *could* be, the nearest I can approach to an answer is to indicate the region in which it may be possible: the borderland where thought and matter meet is the region where all marvels and miracles are generated.

MOL. 266

The wisdom of this world can believe that matter generates mind: what seems to me the wisdom from above can believe that mind generates matter—that matter is but the manifest mind. On this supposition matter may well be subject to mind; much more, if Jesus be the Son of God, his own body must be subject to his will.

MOL. 266

It may be objected that although this might be credible of the glorified body of even the human resurrection, it is hard to believe that the body which suffered and died on the cross could become thus plastic to the will of the indwelling spirit. But I do not see why that which was born of the spirit of the Father, should not be so interpenetrated and possessed by the spirit of the Son, that, without the loss of one of its former faculties, it should be endowed with many added gifts of obedience.

MOL. 267

There is no massing of men with God. When he speaks of gathered men, it is as a spiritual *body*, not as a *mass*.

SI. 112

Who could wish his material body which has indeed died over and over again since he was born, never remaining for one hour composed of the same matter, its endless activity depending upon its endless change, to be fixed as his changeless possession, such as it may then be, at the moment of death, and secured to him in worthless identity for the ages to come? A man's material body will be to his consciousness at death no more than the old garment he throws aside at night, intending to put on a new and better in the morning.

SI. 237

What is the use of this body of ours? It is the means of revelation to us, the *camera* in which God's eternal shows are set forth.

SI. 238

It is by the body that we come in contact with nature, with our fellow men, with all their revelations of God to us. It is through the body that we receive all the lessons of passion, of suffering, of love, of beauty, of science. It is through the body that we are both trained outwards from ourselves, and driven inwards into our deepest selves to find God. There is glory and might in this vital evanescence, this slow, glacier-like flow of clothing and revealing matter, this ever uptossed rainbow of tangible humanity. It is no less of God's making than the spirit that is clothed therein.

SI. 238

The meek who have found that their Lord spoke true, and have indeed inherited the earth, who have seen that all matter is radiant of spiritual meaning, who would not cast a sigh after the loss of mere animal pleasure, would, I think, be the least willing to be without a body, to be unclothed without being again clothed upon.

SI. 239

We need not only a body to convey revelation to us, but a body to reveal us to others. The thoughts, feelings, imaginations which arise in us, must have their garments of revelation whereby shall be made manifest the unseen world within us to our brothers and sisters around us; else is each left in human loneliness. Now, if this be one of the uses my body served on earth before, the new body must be like the old. Nay, it must be the same body, glorified as we are glorified, with all that was distinctive of each from his fellows more visible than ever before.

SI. 240

We shall always need bodies to manifest and reveal us to each other—bodies, then, that fit the soul with absolute truth of presentment and revelation.

SII. 133

It is the soul that makes the body. When we are the sons of God in heart and soul, then shall we be the sons of God in body too: "we shall be like him, for we shall see him as he is."

SII. 133

The body of man does not exist for the sake of its hidden secrets; its hidden secrets exist for the sake of its outside—for the face and the form in which dwells revelation: its outside is the deepest of it. So Nature as well exists primarily for her face, her look, her appeals to the heart and the imagination, her simple service to human need, and not for the secrets to be discovered in her and turned to man's farther use.

SII. 196

Death can only kill my body; he cannot make me his captive.

SIII. 17

Let no man who wants to do something for the soul of a man lose a chance of doing something for his body.

SP. 238

Books

Which is the real possessor of a book—the man who has its original and every following edition, and shows, to many an admiring and envying visitor, now this, now that, in binding characteristic, with possessor-pride; yea, from secret shrine is able to draw forth and display the author's manuscript, with the very shapes in which his thoughts came forth to the light of day—or the man who cherishes one little, hollow-backed, coverless, untitled, bethumbed copy, which he takes with him in his solitary walks and broods over in his silent chamber, always finding in it some beauty or excellence or aid he had not found before—which is to him in truth as a live companion?

HG. 96

For what makes the thing a book? Is it not that it has a soul—the mind in it of him who wrote the book? Therefore only can the book be possessed, for life alone can be the possession of life. The dead possess their dead only to bury them.

HG. 96

Does not he, then, who loves and understands his book, possess it with such possession as is impossible to the other? Just so may the world itself be possessed—either as a volume unread, or as the wine of a soul, "the precious life-blood of a master-spirit, embalmed and treasured up on purpose to a life beyond life." It may be possessed as a book filled with words from the mouth of God, or but as the golden-clasped covers of that book; as an embodiment or incarnation of God himself; or but as a house built to sell.

HG. 96

Childlikeness

Those parents act foolishly who wish to explain everything to their children—most foolishly. No; teach your child to obey, and you give him the most precious lesson that can be given to a child.

DO. 307

The child sees things as the Father means him to see them, as he thought of them when he uttered them. For God is not only the Father of the child, but of the childhood that constitutes him a child, therefore the childness is of the divine nature.

HG. 57

To cease to wonder is to fall plumb-down from the childlike to the commonplace—the most undivine of all moods intellectual. Our nature can never be at home among things that are not wonderful to us.

HG. 58

The Father . . . revealed his things to babes, because the babes were his own little ones, uncorrupted by the wisdom or the care of this world, and therefore able to receive them. The others, though his children, had not begun to be like him, therefore could not receive them. The Father's things could not have got anyhow into their minds without leaving all their value, all their spirit, outside the unchildlike place. The babes are near enough whence they come to understand a little how things go in the presence of their Father in heaven, and thereby to interpret the words of the Son.

HG. 159

The child who has not yet "walked above a mile or two from" his "first love" is not out of touch with the mind of his Father. Quickly will he seal the old bond when the Son himself, the first of the babes, the one perfect babe of God, comes to lead the children out of the lovely "shadows of eternity" into the land of the "white celestial thought."

HG. 160

As God is the one only real Father, so is it only to God that any one can be a perfect child. In his garden only can childhood blossom.

HG. 160

Jesus represented God; the spirit of Jesus reveals God. The represented God a man may refuse; many refused the Lord; the revealed God no one can refuse; to see God and to love him are one. He can be revealed only to the child; perfectly, to the pure child only. All the discipline of the world is to make men children, that God may be revealed to them.

HG. 163

No wisdom of the wise can find out God; no words of the God-loving can reveal him. The simplicity of the whole natural relation is too deep for the philosopher. The Son alone can reveal God; the child alone understand him.

HG. 163

No man, when first he comes to himself, can have any true knowledge of God; he can only have a desire after such knowledge. But while he does not know him at all, he cannot become in his heart God's child; so the Father must draw nearer to him. He sends therefore his Firstborn, who does know him, is exactly like him, and can represent him perfectly. Drawn to him, the children receive him, and then he is able to reveal the Father to them.

HG. 163

The Elder Brother companies with the younger, and makes him yet more a child like himself. He interpenetrates his willing companion with his obedient glory. He lets him see how he delights in his Father, and lets him know that God is his Father too. He rouses in his little brother the sense of their Father's will; and the younger, as he hears and obeys, begins to see that his Elder Brother must be the very image of their Father. He becomes more and more of a child, and more and more the Son reveals to him the Father. For he knows that to know the Father is the one thing needful to every child of the Father, the one thing to fill the divine gulf of his necessity.

HG. 164

Verily we must be born from above, and be good children, or become even to our self-loving selves, a scorn, a hissing, and an endless reproach.

MM

No amount of evil, not to say in the face, but in the habits, or even in the heart of the child, can make it cease to be a child, can annihilate the divine idea of childhood which moved in the heart of God when he made that child after his own image. It is the essential of which God speaks, the real by which he judges, the undying of which he is the God.

SI. 5

The blessedness is the perceiving of the truth—the blessing is the truth itself—the God-known truth, that the Lord has the heart of a child.

SI. 12

"He that sees the essential in this child, the pure childhood, sees that which is the essence of me," grace and truth—in a word, childlikeness. It follows not that the former is perfect as the latter, but it is the same in kind, and therefore, manifest in the child, reveals that which is in Jesus.

SI. 13

To receive a child in the name of Jesus is to receive Jesus; to receive Jesus is to receive God; therefore to receive the child is to receive God himself.

SI. 14

To receive the child because God receives it, or for its humanity, is one thing; to receive it because it is like God, or for its childhood, is another.

SI. 15

The subject kneels in homage to the kings of the earth: the Heavenly King takes his subject in his arms.

SI. 15

When we receive the child in the name of Christ, the very childhood that we receive to our arms is humanity. We love its humanity in its childhood, for childhood is the deepest heart of humanity—its divine heart; and so in the name of the child we receive all humanity.

SI. 16

God is represented in Jesus, for that God is like Jesus: Jesus is represented in the child, for that Jesus is like the child. Therefore God is represented in the child, for that he is like the child. God is childlike. In the true vision of this fact lies the receiving of God in the child.

SI. 17

"He that receives me receives him that sent me." To receive a child in the name of God is to receive God himself. How to receive him? As alone he can be received—by knowing him as he is. To know him is to have him in us. And that we may know him, let us now receive this revelation of him, in the words of our Lord himself.

SI. 17

Let me then ask, do you believe in the incarnation? And if you do, let me ask further, Was Jesus ever less divine than God? I answer for you, Never. He was lower, but never less divine. Was he not a child then? You answer, "Yes, but not like other children." I ask, "Did he not look like other children?" If he looked like them and was not like them, the whole was a deception, a masquerade at best. I say he was a child, whatever more he might be. Childhood belongs to the divine nature.

SI. 19

In this, then, is God like the child: that he is simply and altogether our friend, our father—our more than friend, father, and mother—our infinite, love-perfect God. Grand and strong beyond all that human imagination can conceive of poet-thinking and kingly action, he is delicate beyond all that human tenderness can conceive of husband or wife, homely beyond all that human heart can conceive of father or mother.

SI. 21

How terribly . . . have the theologians misrepresented God in the measures of the low and showy, not the lofty and simple humanities! Nearly all of them represent him as a great King on a grand throne, thinking how grand he is, and making it the business of his being and the end of his universe to keep up his glory, wielding the bolts of a Jupiter against them that take his name in vain. They would not allow this, but follow out what they say, and it comes much to this. Brothers, have you found our king? There he is, kissing little children and saying they are like God.

SI. 22

It is his childlikeness that makes him our God and Father. The perfection of his relation to us swallows up all our imperfections, all our defects, all our evils; for our childhood is born of his fatherhood.

SI. 24

We must become as little children, and Christ must be born in us; we must learn of him, and the one lesson he has to give is himself: he does first all he wants us to do; he is first all he wants us to be. We must not merely do as he did; we must see things as he saw them, regard them as he regarded them; we must take the will of God as the very life of our being; we must neither try to get our own way, nor trouble ourselves as to what may be thought or said of us. The world must be to us as nothing.

SII. 210

God is; Jesus is not dead; nothing can be going wrong, however it may look so to hearts unfinished in childness.

SIII. 23

The wise and prudent must make a system and arrange things to his mind before he can say, *I believe.* The child sees, believes, obeys—and knows he must be perfect as his Father in heaven is perfect.

SIII. 224

A parent must respect the spiritual person of his child, and approach it with reverence, for that too looks the Father in the face and has an audience with him into which no earthly parent can enter even if he dared to desire it.

SP. chap. 23

And the mother's heart more than any other God has made is like him in power of loving. Alas that she is so seldom like him in wisdom—so often thwarting the work of God, and rendering more severe his measures with her child by her attempts to shield him from his law, and save him from saving sorrow.

WW. 55

Choice

My Father has taken the trouble to get me just far enough from him in order to let me know and choose him. Then am I of his kind when I know him, and choose him, and go back to him. This thing is what he wants us to know.

GW

If we, choosing, against our liking, do the right, go on so until we are enabled by doing it to see into the very loveliness and essence of the right, and know it to be altogether beautiful, and then at last never think of doing evil, but delight with our whole souls in doing the will of God, why then, do you not see, we combine the two, and we are free indeed, because we are acting like God out of the essence of our nature, knowing good and evil, and choosing the good with our whole hearts and delighting in it?

GW. 32

There is a door wide to the jewelled wall not far from any one of us, even when he least can find it.

RF

The door must be opened by the willing hand, ere the foot of Love will cross the threshold. He watches to see the door move from within.

SII. 56

He will carry us in his arms until we are able to walk; he will carry us in his arms when we are weary with walking; he will not carry us if we will not walk.

SII. 83

Christ Jesus

Let me glorify God that Jesus took not on him the nature of nobles, but the seed of Adam.

AN. 22

When Christ has had his way with you, you would as soon ask for anything that he did not like as you would beg of God to destroy the universe he had created. There would be nothing to you desirable that is not desirable in his eyes.

The Christian World Pulpit

The love of Christ is an awful thing. There is nothing in that which goes half way, or which makes exception. The Son of God loves so utterly that he will have his children clean, and if hurt and sorrow, pain and torture, will do to deliver any one of them from the horrible thing, from the death that he cherishes at the very root of his soul, the loving Christ, though it hurts him all the time, and though he feels every sting himself, will do it.

The Christian World Pulpit

Do not take from the glory of the words of Christ; do not be afraid to claim from him what he gives you, and would have you take. Claim him, man, woman, boy, girl, claim him as your own; for without him you are as nothing. Claim him, by taking the will of God for your one care, your one object, your one desire; and Christ will be yours altogether. "Behold I stand at the door, and knock: if any man hear my voice, and open the door, I will come in to him, and will sup with him, and he with me." Partaking of the same food together—that food being the very will of God: "it is my meat and drink to do thy will." That is the very food concerning which our Lord says: "man shall not live by bread alone, but by every word that proceeds out of the mouth of God." That is the will of God; it is the very food and drink of the true heart; and when Jesus and the man who has opened to him the door sit down together, it is to share together in the understanding of the will of the Father of both—that Father to whom he went when he said: "Go to my brethren, and say to them, I ascend unto my Father, and your Father; and to my God and your God."

The Christian World Pulpit

"Don't you know that, besides being himself, and just because he is himself, Jesus is the living picture of God?"

DG

"Nothing but Christ himself, your lord and friend and brother, not all the doctrines about him, even if every one of them were true, can save you."

DG

Jesus Christ is the very God I want. I want a father like him, like the Father of him who came as our Big Brother to take us home. No other than the God exactly like Christ can be the true God.

DG. 15

The reality of Christ's nature is not to be proved by argument. He must be beheld.

DO. 206

The sum of the whole matter is this: the Son has come from the Father to set the children free from their sins; the children must hear and obey him, that he may send forth judgment unto victory.

HG. 21

This was the task to which he was baptized; this is yet his enduring labor. "This is my blood of the new covenant which is shed for many unto the sending away of sins." What was the new covenant? "I will make a new covenant with the house of Israel and with the house of Judah; not according to the covenant which they brake, but this: I will put my law in their inward parts, and write it in their hearts, and will be their God, and they shall be my people."

HG. 35

He is the refuge of the oppressed. By its very woes, as by bitterest medicine, he is setting the world free from sin and woe.

HG. 65

The Lord loved the world and the things of the world, not as the men of the world love them, but finding his Father in everything that came from his Father's heart.

HG. 97

Jesus represented God; the spirit of Jesus reveals God.

HG. 163

The only merit that could live before God is the merit of Jesus—who of himself, at once, untaught, unimplored, laid himself aside, and turned to the Father, refusing his life save in the Father. Like God, of himself he chose righteousness, and so merited to sit on the throne of God. In the same spirit he gave himself afterward to his Father's children, and merited the power to transfuse the life-redeeming energy of his spirit into theirs: made perfect, he became the author of eternal salvation unto all them that obey him.

HG. 199

It is a word of little daring, that Jesus had no thought of merit in what he did—that he saw only what he had to be, what he must do—I speak after the poor fashion of a man lost in what is too great for him, yet is his very life.

HG. 199

What matters today, or tomorrow, or ten thousand years to Life himself, to Love himself! He is coming, is coming, and the necks of all humanity are stretched out to see him come!

L. 245

He is our Lord and Master, Elder Brother, King, Savior, the divine Man, the human God: to believe in him is to give ourselves up to him in obedience, to search out his will and do it.

M. 69

Jesus did the works of him who sent him: as Jesus did so God does.

MOL. 105

The Savior had no tinge of that jealousy of rival teaching—as if truth could be two, and could avoid being one—which makes so many of his followers grasp at any waif of false argument. He knew that all good is of God, and not of the devil. All were *with* him who destroyed the power of the devil.

MOL. 165

Jesus is the express image of God's substance, and in him we know the heart of God. To nourish faith in himself was the best thing he could do for the man.

MOL. 197

In Christ we have an ever-growing revelation. He is the resurrection and the life. As we know him we know our future.

MOL. 222

They would have made him a king: he would make them poor in spirit, mighty in aspiration, all kings and priests unto God.

MOL. 240

There is more hid in Christ than we shall ever learn, here or there either; but they that begin first to inquire will soonest be gladdened with revelation; and with them he will be best pleased, for the slowness of his disciples troubled him of old. To say that we must wait for the other world, to know the mind of him who came to this world to give himself to us, seems to me the foolishness of a worldly and lazy spirit.

SI. 54

The Son of God *is* the Teacher of men, giving to them of his Spirit—that Spirit which manifests the deep things of God, being to a man the mind of Christ.

SI. 54

To mistake the meaning of the Son of man may well fill a man with sadness.

SI. 70

Think what an abyss of truth was our Lord, out of whose divine darkness, through that revealing countenance, that uplifting voice, those hands whose tenderness has made us great, broke all holy radiations of human significance. Think of his understanding, imagination, heart, in which lay the treasures of wisdom and knowledge. Must he not have known, felt, imagined, rejoiced in things that would not be told in human words, could not be understood by human hearts? Was he not always bringing forth out of the light inaccessible? Was not his very human form a veil hung over the face of the truth that, even in part by dimming the effulgence of the glory, it might reveal? What could be conveyed must be thus conveyed: an infinite More must lie behind.

SI. 127

Our Lord never thought of being original.

SI. 189

It was not for himself he came to the world—not to establish his own power over the doings, his own influence over the hearts of men: he came that they might know the Father who was his joy, his life. The sons of men were his Father's children like himself: that the Father should have them all in his bosom was the one thought of his heart: that should be his doing for his Father, cost him what it might! He came to do his will, and on the earth was the same he had been from the beginning, the eternal first. He was not interested in himself, but in his Father and his Father's children.

SII. 4

Demands, unknown before, are continually being made on the Christian: it is the ever fresh rousing and calling, asking and sending of the Spirit that works in the children of obedience. When he thinks he has attained, then he is in danger; when he finds the mountain he has so long been climbing show suddenly a distant peak, radiant in eternal whiteness, and all but lost in heavenly places, a peak whose glory-crowned apex it seems as if no human foot could ever reach—then is there hope for him; proof there is then that he has been climbing, for he beholds the yet unclimbed; he sees what he could not see before; if he knows little of what he is, he knows something of what he is not. He learns ever afresh that he is not in the world as Jesus was in the world; but the very wind that breathes courage as he climbs is the hope that one day he shall be like him, seeing him as he is.

SII. 34

The mission undertaken by the Son was not to show himself as having all power in heaven and earth, but to reveal his Father, to show him to men such as he is, that men may know him, and knowing, trust him.

SII. 44

The Lord never pretended anything, whether to his enemy or his mother; he is The True.

SII. 82

Christ is our righteousness, not that we should escape punishment, still less escape being righteous, but as the live, potent creator of righteousness in us, so that we, with our wills receiving his spirit, shall like him resist unto blood, striving against sin; shall know in ourselves, as he knows, what a lovely thing is righteousness, what a mean, ugly, unnatural thing is unrighteousness. He *is* our righteousness, and that righteousness is no fiction, no pretense, no imputation.

SII. 104

Everything must at length be subject to man, as it was to The Man. When God can do what he will with a man, the man may do what he will with the world; he may walk on the sea like his Lord; the deadliest thing will not be able to hurt him: "He that believes on me, the works that I do shall he do also; and greater than these shall he do."

SII. 126

He brothers us. He takes us to the knees of the Father, beholding whose face we grow sons indeed. Never could we have known the heart of the Father, never felt it possible to love him as sons, but for him who cast himself into the gulf that yawned between us. In and through him we were foreordained to the sonship: sonship, even had we never sinned, never could we reach without him. We should have been little children loving the Father indeed, but children far from the sonhood that understands and adores.

SII. 129

He is the express image of the Father, by which we, his imperfect images, are to read and understand him: imperfect, we have yet perfection enough to spell toward the perfect.

SII. 136

He is God our Savior: it is because God is our Savior that Jesus is our Savior. The God and Father of Jesus Christ could never possibly be satisfied with less than giving himself to his own! The unbeliever may easily imagine a better God than the common theology of the country offers him; but not the lovingest heart that ever beat can even reflect the length and breadth and depth and height of that love of God which shows itself in his Son—one, and of one mind, with himself.

SII. 143

All the growth of the Christian is the more and more life he is receiving. At first his religion may hardly be distinguishable from the mere prudent desire to save his soul; but at last he loses that very soul in the glory of love, and so saves it.

SII. 144

I will call no one Master but Christ—and from him I learn that his quarrel with us is that we will not do what we know, will not come to him that we may have life.

SII. 175

He that has looked on the face of God in Jesus Christ, whose heart overflows, if ever so little, with answering love, sees God standing with full hands to give the abundance for which he created his children, and those children hanging back, refusing to take, doubting the God-heart which knows itself absolute in truth and love.

SII. 195

To know a primrose is a higher thing than to know all the botany of it—just as to know Christ is an infinitely higher thing than to know all theology, all that is said about his person, or babbled about his work.

SII. 196

Jesus *must* have hated anything like display. God's greatest work has never been done in crowds, but in closets; and when it works out from thence, it is not upon crowds, but upon individuals. A crowd is not a divine thing. It is not a body.

SII. 198

Christ is the way out, and the way in; the way from slavery, conscious or unconscious, into liberty; the way from the unhomeliness of things to the home we desire but do not know; the way from the stormy skirts of the Father's garments to the peace of his bosom. To picture him, we need not only endless figures, but sometimes quite opposing figures: he is not only the door of the sheepfold, but the shepherd of the sheep; he is not only the way, but the leader in the way, the rock that followed, and the captain of our salvation.

SII. 210

We must become as little children, and Christ must be born in us; we must learn of him, and the one lesson he has to give is himself: he does first all he wants us to do; he is first all he wants us to be. We must not merely do as he did; we must see things as he saw them, regard them as he regarded them; we must take the will of God as the very life of our being; we must neither try to get our own way, nor trouble ourselves as to what may be thought or said of us. The world must be to us as nothing.

SII. 210

We must not fail to see, or seeing ever forget, that, when Jesus tells us we must follow him, we must come to him, we must believe in him, he speaks first and always as *the Son* of the Father—and that in the active sense, as the obedient God, not merely as one who claims the sonship for the ground of being and so of further claim.

SII. 218

To believe in him is to do as he does, to follow him where he goes. We must believe in him *practically*—altogether practically, as he believed in his Father; not as one concerning whom we have to hold something, but as one whom we have to follow out of the body of this death into life eternal. It is not to follow him to take him in any way theoretically, to hold this or that theory about why he died, or wherein lay his atonement: such things can be revealed only to those who follow him in his active being and the principle of his life—who do as he did, live as he lived. There is no other following.

SII. 218

Christ sought not his own, sought not anything but the will of his Father: we have to grow diamond-clear, true as the white light of the morning. Hopeless task!—were it not that he offers to come himself, and dwell in us.

SII. 221

He who will not part with all for Christ is not worthy of him and cannot know him.

SII. 254

I say none but he who does right, can think right; you cannot *know* Christ to be right until you do as he does, as he tells you to do; neither can you set him forth, until you know him as he means himself to be known, that is, as he is.

SII. 259

The truth in Jesus is his relation to his Father; the righteousness of Jesus is his fulfillment of that relation. Meeting this relation, loving his Father with his whole being, he is not merely alive as born of God; but, giving himself with perfect will to God, choosing to die to himself and live to God, he therein creates in himself a new and higher life; and, standing upon himself, has gained the power to awake life, the divine shadow of his own, in the hearts of us his brothers and sisters, who have come from the same birth-home as himself, namely, the heart of his God and our God, his Father and our Father, but who, without our Elder Brother to do it first, would never have chosen that self-abjuration which is life, never have become alive like him.

SIII. 10

This choice of his own being, in the full knowledge of what he did; this active willing to be the Son of the Father, perfect in obedience—is that in Jesus which responds and corresponds to the self-existence of God. Jesus rose at once to the height of his being, set himself down on the throne of his nature, in the act of subjecting himself to the will of the Father as his only good, the only *reason* of his existence.

SIII. 11

The whole being and doing of Jesus on earth is the same as his being and doing from all eternity, that whereby he is the blessed Son-God of the Father-God; it is the shining out of that life that men might see it. It is a being like God, a doing of the will of God, a working of the works of God, therefore an unveiling of the Father in the Son, that men may know him.

SIII. 16

I know your Father, for he is my Father; I know him because I have been with him from eternity. You do not know him; I have come to you to tell you that as I am, such is he; that he is just like me, only greater and better. He only is the true, original good; I am true because I seek nothing but his will. He only is all in all; I am not all in all, but he is my Father, and I am the Son in whom his heart of love is satisfied.

SIII. 16

The life of Jesus is the light of men, revealing to them the Father.

SIII. 20

The Christ in us is our own true nature made blossom in us by the Lord, whose life is the light of men that it may become the life of men.

SIII. 22

Everyone who desires to follow the Master has the spirit of the Master, and will receive more, that he may follow closer, nearer, in his very footsteps. He is not called on to prove to this or that or any man that he has the light of Jesus; he has to let his light shine.

SIII. 28

If the Lord were to appear this day in England as once in Palestine, he would not come in the halo of the painters or with that wintry shine of effeminate beauty, of sweet weakness, in which it is their helpless custom to represent him.

SIII. 37

Jesus Christ is the *only* likeness of the living Father.

SIII. 44

Our mediator is the Lord himself, the spirit of light, a mediator not sent by us to God to bring back his will, but come from God to bring us himself.

SIII. 47

When we take into our understanding, our heart, our conscience, our being, the glory of God, namely Jesus Christ as he shows himself to our eyes, our hearts, our consciences, he works on us, and will keep working, until we are changed to the very likeness we have thus mirrored in us; for with his likeness he comes himself, and dwells in us.

SIII. 51

When we receive his image into our spiritual mirror, he enters with it. Our thought is not cut off from his. Our open, receiving thought is his door to come in. When our hearts turn to him, that is, opening the door to him, that is, holding up our mirror to him; then he comes in, not by our thought only, not in our idea only, but he comes himself and of his own will—comes in as we could not take him, but as he can come.

SIII. 52

The life of Jesus has, through light, become life in us; the glory of God in the face of Jesus, mirrored in our hearts, has made us alive; we are one with God for ever and ever.

SIII. 54

What it cost the Son to get so near to us that we could say *Come in*, is the story of his life. He stands at the door and knocks, and when we open to him he comes in, and dwells with us, and we are transformed to the same image of truth and purity and heavenly childhood.

SIII. 54

The Lord Jesus, by free, potent communion with their inmost being, will change his obedient brethren until in every thought and impulse they are good like him, unselfish, neighborly, brotherly like him, loving the Father perfectly like him, ready to die for the truth like him, caring like him for nothing in the universe but the will of God, which is love, harmony, liberty, beauty, and joy.

SIII. 55

When a man is, with his whole nature, loving and willing the truth, he is then a live truth. But this he has not originated in himself. He has seen it and striven for it, but not originated it. The one originating, living, visible truth, embracing all truths in all relations, is Jesus Christ. He is true; he is the live Truth. His truth, chosen and willed by him, the ripeness of his being, the flower of his sonship which is his nature, the crown of his one topmost perfect relation acknowledged and gloried in, is his absolute obedience to his Father. The obedient Jesus is Jesus the Truth. He is true and the root of all truth and development of truth in men.

SIII. 79

His likeness to Christ is the truth of a man, even as the perfect meaning of a flower is the truth of a flower. . . . As Christ is the blossom of humanity, so the blossom of every man is the Christ perfected in him.

SIII. 80

Christ . . . is the Lord of life; his life is the light of men; the light mirrored in them changes them into the image of him, the Truth; and thus *the Truth, who is the Son, makes them free.*

SIII. 82

Christ died to save us, not from suffering, but from ourselves; not from injustice, far less from justice, but from being unjust. He died that we might live—but live as he lives, by dying as he died who died to himself.

SIII. 96

I ought to know what I say, for I have been from all eternity the Son of him from whom you issue, and whom you call your Father, but whom you will not have your Father: I know all he thinks and is; and I say this, that my perfect freedom, my pure individuality, rests on the fact that I have not another will than his. My will is all for his will, for his will is right. He is righteousness itself.

SIII. 103

I believe in Jesus Christ, the eternal Son of God, my Elder Brother, my Lord and Master; I believe that he has a right to my absolute obedience whereinsoever I know or shall come to know his will; that to obey him is to ascend the pinnacle of my being; that not to obey him would be to deny him.

SIII. 153

I believe that he died that I might die like him—die to any ruling power in me but the will of God—live ready to be nailed to the cross as he was, if God will it.

SIII. 153

I believe and pray that he will give me what punishment I need to set me right, or keep me from going wrong. I believe that he died to deliver me from all meanness, all pretense, all falseness, all unfairness, all poverty of spirit, all cowardice, all fear, all anxiety, all forms of self-love, all trust or hope in possession; to make me merry as a child, the child of our Father in heaven, loving nothing but what is lovely, desiring nothing I should be ashamed to let the universe of God see me desire.

SIII. 153

I believe that he is my Savior from myself, and from all that has come of loving myself, from all that God does not love, and would not have me love—all that is not worth loving; that he died that the justice, the mercy of God, might have its way with me, making me just as God is just, merciful as he is merciful, perfect as my Father in heaven is perfect.

SIII. 153

It is only in him that the soul has room. In knowing him is life and its gladness. The secret of your own heart you can never know; but you can know him who knows its secret.

SP. chap. 13

Impressed as I am with the truth of his nature, the absolute devotion of his life, and the essential might of his being, I yet obey not [Christ], I shall not only deserve to perish, but in that very refusal draw ruin on my head.

TW

We are not real human beings until we are of the same mind with Christ.

WW

There are many who would save the pathetic and interesting and let the ugly and provoking take care of themselves! Not so with Christ, nor those who have learned of him!

WW

Humility, the worship of the Ideal—that is, of the man Christ Jesus—is the only lifter-up of the head.

WW. 60

Christ in You

The indwelling of Jesus in the soul of man, who shall declare!

SIII. 52

The dwelling of Jesus in us is the power of the spirit of God upon us; for "the Lord is that spirit," and that Lord dwelling in us, we are changed "even as from the Lord the spirit." When we think Christ, Christ comes; when we receive his image into our spiritual mirror, he enters with it. Our thought is not cut off from his. Our open receiving thought is his door to come in. When our hearts turn to him, that is, opening the door to him, that is, holding up our mirror to him: then he comes in, not by our thought only, not in our idea only, but he comes himself, and of his own will—comes in as we could not take him, but as he can come and we receive him—enabled to receive by his very coming the one welcome guest of the whole universe.

SIII. 52

What it cost the Son to get so near to us that we could say *Come in,* is the story of his life. He stands at the door and knocks, and when we open to him he comes in, and dwells with us, and we are transformed to the same image of truth and purity and heavenly childhood. Where power dwells, there is no force; where the spirit-Lord is, there is liberty. The Lord Jesus, by free, potent communion with their inmost being, will change his obedient brethren until in every thought and impulse they are good like him, unselfish, neighborly, brotherly like him, loving the Father perfectly like him, ready to die for the truth like him, caring like him for nothing in the universe but the will of God, which is love, harmony, liberty, beauty, and joy.

SIII. 54

Christians

It now ought not to be possible to mistake a Christian for a man of the world. His very dealings with every man that comes near him have something to show, something that Christ would have done that a man of the world would not do.

GW. 122

They were salt which must remember that it is salt; which must live salt, and choose salt, and be salt. For the whole worth of salt lies in its being salt; and all the saltness of the moral salt lies in the will to be salt. To lose its saltness, then, is to cease to exist, save as a vile thing whose very being is unjustifiable. What is to be done with saltless salt!—with such as would teach religion and know not God!

HG. 174

The man who goes to church every Sunday, and yet trembles before chance, is a Christian only because Christ has claimed him; is not a Christian as having believed in him. I would not be hard. There are so many degrees in faith! A man may be on the right track, may be learning of Christ, and be very poor and weak. But I say there is no *standing* room, no reality of reason, between absolute faith and absolute unbelief.

MOL. 34

It is better to be an atheist who does the will of God, than a so-called Christian who does not.

PF

We are and remain such creeping Christians, because we look at ourselves and not at Christ; because we gaze at the marks of our own soiled feet, and the trail of our own defiled garments. . . . Each, putting his foot in the footprint of the Master, and so defacing it, turns to examine how far his neighbor's footprint corresponds with that which he still calls the Master's, although it is but his own. Or, having committed a petty fault, I mean a fault such as only a petty creature could commit, we mourn over the defilement to ourselves, and the shame of it before our friends, children, or servants, instead of hastening to make the due confession and amends to our fellow, and then, forgetting our own paltry self with its well-earned disgrace, lift up our eyes to the glory which alone will quicken the true man in us, and kill the peddling creature we so wrongly call our *self.*

SI. 170

All the growth of the Christian is the more and more life he is receiving. At first his religion may hardly be distinguishable from the mere prudent desire to save his soul; but at last he loses that very soul in the glory of love, and so saves it; self becomes but the cloud on which the white light of God divides into harmonies unspeakable.

SII. 144

Is there not many a Christian who, having *begun* to deny himself, yet spends much strength in the vain and evil endeavor to accommodate matters between Christ and the dear self—seeking to save that which so he must certainly lose—in how different a way from that in which the Master would have him lose it!

SII. 222

To a man who loves righteousness and his fellow men, it must always be painful to be misunderstood; and misunderstanding is specially inevitable where he acts on principles beyond the recognition of those around him, who, being but half-hearted Christians, count themselves the lawgivers of righteousness, and charge him with the very things it is the aim of his life to destroy. The Lord himself was accused of being a drunkard and a keeper of bad company—and perhaps would in the present day be so regarded by not a few calling themselves by his name, and teaching temperance and virtue. He lived on a higher spiritual platform than they understand, acted from a height of the virtues they would inculcate, loftier than their eyes can scale.

SIII. 232

While men count themselves Christians on any other ground than that they are slaves of Jesus Christ, the children of God, and free from themselves, so long will they use the servants of the Master despitefully. "Do not hesitate," says the Lord, "to speak the truth that is in you; never mind what they call you; proclaim from the housetop; fear nobody."

SIII. 233

A man may sink by such slow degrees that, long after he is a devil, he may go on being a good churchman or a good dissenter, and thinking himself a good Christian. Continuously repeated sin against the poorest consciousness of evil must have a dread rousing. There are men who never wake to know how wicked they are, until, lo, the gaze of the multitude is upon them!—the multitude staring with self-righteous eyes, doing like things themselves, but not yet found out; sinning after another pattern, therefore the hardest judges, thinking by condemnation to escape judgment. But there is nothing covered that shall not be revealed.

SIII. 242

We have no right to school ourselves to an imaginary duty. When we do not know, then what he lays upon us is *not to know*, and to be content not to know. The philosopher is he who lives in the thought of things, the Christian is he who lives in the things themselves. The philosopher occupies himself with God's decree, the Christian with God's will; the philosopher with what God may intend, the Christian with what God wants *him to do.*

WM. 40

Christianity

To object to Christianity as selfish is utter foolishness; Christianity alone gives any hope of deliverance from selfishness. Is it selfish to desire love? Is it selfish to hope for purity and the sight of God? What better can we do for our neighbor than to become altogether righteous toward him?

HG. 198

No worst thing ever done in the name of Christianity, no vilest corruption of the church, can destroy the eternal fact that the core of it is in the heart of Jesus.

M

Christianity must not, could not interfere with the discipline needful for its own fulfillment, could not depose the schoolmaster that leads unto Christ.

MOL. 214

It is the punishment of the true Love, and is continually illustrated and fulfilled: if I know anything of the truth of God, then the objectors to Christianity, so far as I am acquainted with them, do not; their arguments, not in themselves false, have nothing to do with the matter; they see the thing they are talking against, but they do not see the thing they think they are talking against.

SII. 100

The Christian religion, throughout its history, has been open to more corrupt misrepresentation than ever the Jewish could be, for as it is higher and wider, so must it yield larger scope to corruption: Have we learned Christ in false statements and corrupted lessons about him, or have we learned *himself*? Nay, true or false, is only our brain full of things concerning him, or does he dwell himself in our hearts, a learnt, and ever being learnt lesson, the power of our life?

SII. 233

How many are there not who seem capable of anything for the sake of the church or Christianity, except the one thing its Lord cares about—that they should do what he tells them.

SIII. 188

"What is Christianity, then?"
"God in Christ, and Christ in man."

TW. 78

Respect and graciousness from each to each is of the very essence of Christianity, independently of rank, or possession, or relation.

WM

Either God is altogether such as Christ, or the Christian religion is a lie.

WW. 43

Church

The Church is part of God's world.

AN. 5

What idea could a man have of religion who knew nothing of it except from what goes on in churches?

DG. 11

Individual life is the life of the church.

MOL. 42

Every man had a cure of his own; every woman had a cure of her own—all one and the same in principle, each individual in the application of the principle. This was the foundation of the true church. And yet the members of that church will try to separate upon individual and unavoidable differences!

MOL. 99

It is the half-Christian clergy of every denomination that are the main cause of the so-called failure of the church of Christ.

PF

The great heresy of the church of the present day is unbelief in this Spirit. The mass of the church does not believe that the Spirit has a revelation for every man individually—a revelation as different from the revelation of the Bible as the food in the moment of passing into living brain and nerve differs from the bread and meat.

SI. 54

It is the one terrible heresy of the church, that it has always been presenting something else than obedience as faith in Christ.

SII. 243

How many are there not who seem capable of anything for the sake of the church or Christianity, except the one thing its Lord cares about—that they should do what he tells them! He would deliver them from themselves into the liberty of the sons of God, make them his brothers; they leave him to vaunt their church. His commandments are not grievous; they invent commandments for him, and lay them, burdens grievous to be borne, upon the necks of their brethren. God would have us sharers in his bliss—in the very truth of existence; they worship from afar, and will not draw nigh.

SIII. 188

Church or chapel is *not* the place for divine service. It is a place of prayer, a place of praise, a place to feed on good things, a place to learn of God, as what place is not? It is a place to look in the eyes of your neighbor, and love God along with him. But the world in which you move, the place of your living and loving and labor, not the church you go to on your holiday, is the place of divine service. Serve your neighbor, and you serve him.

SIII. 228

"See how, even in the services of the church, as they call them, they will accumulate gorgeousness and cost. Had I my way . . . I would never have any vessel used in the Eucharist but wooden platters and wooden cups."

"But are we not to serve him with our best?" said my wife.

"Yes, with our very hearts and souls, with our absolute being. But all external things should be in harmony with the spirit of his revelation. And if God chose that his Son should visit the earth in homely fashion, in homely fashion likewise should be everything that enforces and commemorates that revelation. All church-form should be on the other side from show and expense. Let the money go to build decent houses for God's poor, not to give them his holy bread and wine out of silver and gold and precious stones—stealing from the significance of the content by the meretricious grandeur of the [container]. I would send all the church-plate to fight the devil with his own weapons in our overcrowded cities, and in our villages where the husbandmen are housed like swine, by giving them room to be clean, and decent air from heaven to breathe. When the people find the clergy thus in earnest, they will follow them fast enough, and the money will come in like salt and oil on the sacrifice."

SP. 51–52

Clergy

A clergyman, of all men, should be slow to take offense, for if he does, he will never be free or strong to reprove sin. And it must sometimes be his duty to speak severely to those, especially the good, who are turning their faces the wrong way. It is of little use to reprove the sinner, but it is worthwhile sometimes to reprove those who have a regard for righteousness, however imperfect they may be. "Reprove not a scorner, lest he hate you; rebuke a wise man, and he will love you."

AN. 234

It is the half-Christian clergy of every denomination that are the main cause of the so-called failure of the church of Christ.

PF

Many a thief is a better man than many a clergyman, and miles nearer to the gate of the kingdom.

TW

Coercion

The truth is this: he wants to make us in his own image, *choosing* the good, *refusing* the evil. How should he effect this if he were *always* moving us from within, as he does at divine intervals, toward the beauty of holiness?

SI. 173

God gives us room *to be*; does not oppress us with his will; "stands away from us," that we may act from ourselves, that we may exercise the pure will for good.

SI. 174

Nor will God force any door to enter in. He may send a tempest about the house; the wind of his admonishment may burst doors and windows, yea, shake the house to its foundations; but not then, not so, will he enter. The door must be opened by the willing hand, ere the foot of Love will cross the threshold. He watches to see the door move from within.

SII. 56

Comfort

God's comfort must ever be larger than man's grief, else were there gaps in his Godhood.

HG. 105

Such, surely, is the heart of the comfort the Lord will give those whose love is now making them mourn; and their present blessedness must be the expectation of the time when the true lover shall find the restored the same as the lost—with precious differences: the things that were not like the true self, gone or going; the things that were loveliest, lovelier still; the restored not merely more than the lost, but more the person lost than he or she that was lost. For the things which made him or her what he or she was, the things that rendered lovable, the things essential to the person, will be more present, because more developed.

HG. 110

The Lord has come to wipe away our tears. He is doing it; he will have it done as soon as he can; and until he can, he would have them flow without bitterness; to which end he tells us it is a blessed thing to mourn, because of the comfort on its way. Accept his comfort now, and so prepare for the comfort at hand. He is getting you ready for it, but you must be a fellow worker with him, or he will never have done. He *must* have you pure in heart, eager after righteousness, a very child of his Father in heaven.

HG. 116

Comfort yourselves, then, brothers and sisters; he to whom the Son will reveal him shall know the Father; and the Son came to us that he might reveal him. "Eternal Brother," we cry, "show us the Father. Be yourself to us, that in you we may know him. We, too, are his children: let the other children share with you in the things of the Father."

HG. 164

God is the God of comfort, known of man as the refuge, the life-giver, or not known at all.

SII. 181

Let us comfort ourselves in the thought of the Father and the Son. So long as there dwells harmony, so long as the Son loves the Father with all the love the Father can welcome, all is well with the little ones.

SIII. 22

Commandments

The Lord cared little for the letter of his own commands; he cared all for the spirit, for that was life.

MOL. 95

It is a beautiful thing to obey the rightful source of a command: it is a more beautiful thing to worship the radiant source of our light, and it is for the sake of obedient vision that our Lord commands us. For then our heart meets his: we see God.

SI. 200

Then the road to eternal life is the keeping of the commandments? Had the Lord not said so, what man of common moral sense would ever dare say otherwise? What else can be the way into life but the doing of what the Lord of life tells the creatures he has made, and whom he would have live forever, that they must do? It is the beginning of the way. If a man had kept all those commandments, yet would he not therefore have in him life eternal; nevertheless, without keeping of the commandments, there is no entering into life; the keeping of them is the path to the gate of life; it is not life, but it is the way—so much of the way to it. Nay, the keeping of the commandments, consciously or unconsciously, has closest and essential relation to eternal life.

SII. 9

Is there no meaning in the word *keep*, or *observe*, except it be qualified by *perfectly*? Is there no keeping but a perfect keeping?

"None that God cares for."

There I think you utterly wrong. That no keeping but a perfect one will *satisfy* God, I hold with all my heart and strength; but that there is none else he cares for, is one of the lies of the enemy. What father is not pleased with the first tottering attempt of his little one to walk? What father would be satisfied with anything but the manly step of the full-grown son?

SII. 10

There must be a keeping of the commandments, which, although anything but perfect, is yet acceptable to the heart of him from whom nothing is hid.

SII. 11

The immediate end of the commandments never was that men should succeed in obeying them, but that, finding they could not do that which yet must be done, finding the more they tried the more was required of them, they should be driven to the source of life and law—of their life and his law—to seek from him such reinforcement of life as should make the fulfillment of the law as possible, yea, as natural, as necessary.

SII. 11

The commandments can never be kept while there is a strife to keep them; the man is overwhelmed in the weight of their broken pieces. It needs a clean heart to have pure hands, all the power of a live soul to keep the law—a power of life, not of struggle; the strength of love, not the effort of duty.

SII. 17

Have you . . . kept the commandments? Have you, unsatisfied with the result of what keeping you have given them, and filled with desire to be perfect, gone kneeling to the Master to learn more of the way to eternal life? or are you so well satisfied with what you are, that you have never sought eternal life, never hungered and thirsted after the righteousness of God, the perfection of your being? If this latter be your condition, then be comforted; the Master does not require of you to sell what you have and give to the poor. *You* follow him! *You* go with him to preach good tidings!—you who care not for righteousness! You are not one whose company is desirable to the Master. Be comforted, I say; he does not want you; he will not ask you to open your purse for him; you may give or withhold, it is nothing to him. What! is he to be obliged to come to one outside his kingdom—to the untrue, the ignoble—for money? Bring him a true heart, an obedient hand: he has given his lifeblood for that; but your money—he neither needs it nor cares for it.

SII. 26

When in keeping the commandments you have found the great reward of loving righteousness—the further reward of discovering that, with all the energy you can put forth, you are but an unprofitable servant; when you have come to know that the law can be kept only by such as need no law; when you have come to feel that you would rather pass out of being than live on such a poor, miserable, selfish life as alone you can call yours; when you are aware of a something beyond all that your mind can think, yet not beyond what your heart can desire—a something that is not yours, seems as if it never could be yours, which yet your life is worthless without; when you have come, therefore, to the Master with the cry, "What shall I do that I may inherit eternal life?"—it may be then that he will say to you, "Sell all that you have, and give to the poor, and come, follow me." If he do, then will you be of men most honorable, if you obey; of men most pitiable, if you refuse. Until then, you would be of no comfort to him, no pleasure to his friends.

SII. 28

Condemnation

Not for any or all of his sins that are past shall a man be condemned; not for the worst of them need he dread remaining unforgiven.

HG. 9

It is true the memory of the wrongs we have done is, or will become, very bitter; but not for those is condemnation; and if that in our character which made them possible were abolished, remorse would lose its worst bitterness in the hope of future amends. "This is the condemnation, that light is come into the world, and men loved darkness rather than light, because their deeds were evil."

HG. 10

We may be sure of this, that no man will be condemned for any sin that is past; that, if he be condemned, it will be because he would not come to the light when the light came to him; because he would not cease to do evil and learn to do well; because he hid his unbelief in the garment of a false faith, and would not obey; because he imputed to himself a righteousness that was not his; because he preferred imagining himself a worthy person, to confessing himself everywhere in the wrong, and repenting. We may be sure also of this, that, if a man becomes the disciple of Christ, he will not leave him in ignorance as to what he has to believe; he shall know the truth of everything it is needful for him to understand. If we do what he tells us, his light will go up in our hearts.

SII. 251

No man is condemned for anything he has done; he is condemned for continuing to do wrong. He is condemned for not coming out of the darkness, for not coming to the light.

SIII. 175

God gives every man time. There is a light that lightens sage and savage, but the glory of God in the face of Jesus may not have shined on this sage or that savage. The condemnation is of those who, having seen Jesus, refuse to come to him, or pretend to come to him but do not the things he says.

SIII. 177

Conscience

We were not meant to be creatures of feeling; we were meant to be creatures of conscience, first of all, and then of consciousness toward God—a sense of his presence; and if we go on, the feeling will come all right. Our feelings will blossom as a rose just from the very necessity of things.

GW. 11

This is what God put in your hands. He says: "I tell you I am: act you upon that; for I know your conscience moves you to it; act you upon that, and you will find whether I am or not, and what I am."

GW. 117

She was sorely troubled with what is, by huge discourtesy, called a bad conscience—being in reality a conscience doing its duty so well that it makes the whole house uncomfortable.

SG. chap. 37

"Can a conscience ever get too fastidious, Ian?"—"The only way to find out is always to obey it."

WM. chap. 9

Contentment

I do not think that the road to contentment lies in despising what we have not got. Let us acknowledge all good, all delight that the world holds, and be content without it. But this we can never be except by possessing the one thing, without which I do not merely say no man ought to be content, but no man *can* be content—the Spirit of the Father.

AN. 213

No man can have the consciousness of God with him and not be content; I mean that no man who has not the Father so as to be eternally content in him alone, can possess a sunset or a field of grass or a mine of gold or the love of a fellow creature according to its nature—as God would have him possess it.

SII. 36

If you are not content, it is because God is not with you as you need him, not with you as he would be with you, as you *must* have him, for you need him as your body never needed food or air, need him as your soul never hungered after joy, or peace, or pleasure.

SII. 36

As for any influence from the public offices of religion, a contented soul may glide through them all for a long life, unstruck to the last, buoyant and evasive as a bee among hailstones.

TW. chap. 7

Creation

The whole creation is groaning after an unforeseen yet essential birth—groaning with the necessity of being freed from a state that is but a transitional and not a true one, from a condition that nowise answers to the intent in which existence began. In both the lower creation and the higher, this same groaning of the fettered idea after a freer life seems the first enforced decree of a holy fate, and itself the first movement of the hampered thing toward the liberty of another birth.

HG. 208

A creative demon is an absurdity; and were such a creator possible, he would not be God, but must one day be found and destroyed by the real God.

HG. 208

God has subjected the creation to vanity, in the hope that the creation itself shall be delivered from the bondage of corruption into the glorious liberty of the children of God. For this double deliverance—from corruption and the consequent subjection to vanity—the creation is eagerly watching.

HG. 220

The creation groans and travails—"but ourselves also, which have the first-fruits of the spirit, even we ourselves groan within ourselves, waiting for . . . the redemption of our body." We are not free . . . until our body is redeemed; then all the creation will be free with us. He regards the creation as part of our embodiment. The whole creation is waiting for the manifestation of the sons of God—that is, the redemption of their body, the idea of which extends to their whole material envelopment, with all the life that belongs to it.

HG. 227

A body like the Lord's is, I imagine, necessary to bring us into true and perfect contact with the creation, of which there must be multitudinous phases whereof we cannot now be even aware.

HG. 229

The kingdom comes not with observation, and the working of the leaven of its approach must be chiefly unseen. Like the creative energy itself, it works "in secret shadow, far from all men's sight."

MOL. 49

In the grand process of existence, destruction is one of the phases of creation; for the inferior must ever be giving way for the growth of the superior: the husk must crumble and decay, that the seed may germinate and appear.

MOL. 251

As the whole creation passes on toward the sonship, death must ever be doing its sacred work about the lower regions, that life may ever arise triumphant, in its ascent toward the will of the Father.

MOL. 251

Daring to interpret the work of the Father from the work of the Son, I would humbly believe that all destruction is for creation—that, even for this, death alone is absolutely destroyed—that, namely, which stands in the way of the outgoing of the Father's will, then only completing its creation when men are made holy.

MOL. 258

When the sons of God show as they are, taking, with the character, the appearance and the place, that belong to their sonship; when the sons of God sit with *the* Son of God on the throne of their Father; then shall they be in potency of fact the lords of the lower creation, the bestowers of liberty and peace upon it: then shall the creation, subjected to vanity for their sakes, find its freedom in their freedom, its gladness in their sonship. The animals will glory to serve them, will joy to come to them for help. Let the heartless scoff, the unjust despise! the heart that cries *Abba, Father*, cries to the God of the sparrow and the oxen; nor can hope go too far in hoping what God will do for the creation that now groans and travails in pain because our higher birth is delayed.

SII. 134

"All things were made" not *by*, but "*through* him."

SIII. 5

The Father, in bringing out of the unseen the things that are seen, made essential use of the Son, so that all that exists was created *through* him.

SIII. 5

The word *creation* applied to the loftiest success of human genius, seems to me a mockery of humanity, itself in process of creation.

SIII. 5

The power by which he created the worlds was given him by his Father; he had in himself a greater power than that by which he made the worlds. There was something made, not *through* but *in* him; something brought into being by himself. Here he creates in his grand way, in himself, as did the Father. "That which was made *in* him was *life*."

SIII. 6

He could not have been employed by the Father in creating, save in virtue of the life that was *in* him.

SIII. 6

The one interminable mystery . . . a mystery that must be a mystery to us for ever—not because God will not explain it, but because God himself could not make us understand it—is first, how he can be self-existent, and next, how he can make other beings exist: self-existence and creation no man will ever understand.

SIII. 7

Regarding the matter from the side of the creature—the cause of his being is antecedent to that being; he can therefore have no knowledge of his own creation; neither could he understand that which he can do nothing like.

SIII. 7

If we could make ourselves, we should understand our creation, but to do that we must be God. And of all ideas this—that, with the self-dissatisfied, painfully circumscribed consciousness I possess, I could in any way have caused myself, is the most dismal and hopeless. Nevertheless, if I be a child of God, I must be *like* him, like him even in the matter of this creative energy. There must be something in me that corresponds in its childish way to the eternal might in him. . . . The question now is: What was that life, the thing made *in* the Son—made by him inside himself, not outside him—made not *through* but *in* him—the life that was his own, as God's is his own?

SIII. 7

God is Love. Love is the deepest depth, the essence of his nature, at the root of all his being. It is not merely that he could not be God, if he had made no creatures to whom to be God; but love is the heart and hand of his creation; it is his right to create, and his power to create as well. The love that foresees creation is itself the power to create.

SIII. 8

No thought, human or divine, can be conveyed from man to man save through the symbolism of the creation. The heavens and the earth are around us that it may be possible for us to speak of the unseen by the seen; for the outermost husk of creation has correspondence with the deepest things of the Creator.

SIII. 31

The precious things of the earth, the coal and the diamonds, the iron and clay and gold, may be said to have come from his hands; but the live things come from his heart—from near the same region whence ourselves we came.

SIII. 254

Crime

No crime can be committed against a creature without being committed also against the creator of that creature; therefore surely the first step for any one who has committed such a crime must be to humble himself before God, confess the sin, and ask forgiveness and cleansing.

TW

Except a man has God dwelling in him, he may be, or may become, capable of any crime within the compass of human nature.

TW. 58

Nor must I fail to remind the man who has committed no grievous crime, that except he has repented of his evil self and abjured all wrong, he is not safe from any even the worst offense.

TW. 67

"Our crimes are friends that will hunt us either to the bosom of God, or the pit of hell."

TW. 88

Cross

To tell the truth, I feel a good deal younger. For then I only knew that a man had to take up his cross; whereas now I know that a man has to follow him.

AN. chap. 1

Friends, our cross may be heavy, and the *via dolorosa* rough; but we have claims on God, yea the right to cry to him for help. He has spent, and is spending himself to give us our birthright, which is righteousness. Though we shall not be condemned for our sins, we cannot be saved but by leaving them; though we shall not be condemned for the sins that are past, we shall be condemned if we love the darkness rather than the light, and refuse to come to him that we may have life. God is offering us the one thing we cannot live without—his own self: we must make room for him; we must cleanse our hearts that he may come in; we must do as the Master tells us, who knew all about the Father and the way to him—*we must deny ourselves, and take up our cross daily, and follow him.*

SII. 208

God's eternal denial of himself, revealed in him who for our sakes in the flesh took up his cross daily, will have been developed in the man; his eternal rejoicing will be in God—and in his fellows, before whom he will cast his glad self to be a carpet for their walk, a footstool for their rest, a stair for their climbing.

SII. 215

There is no magnifying of himself. *He first* denies himself, and takes up his cross—then tells us to do the same. The Father magnifies the Son, not the Son himself; the Son magnifies the Father.

SII. 220

Every day until then we have to take up our cross; every hour to see that we are carrying it. A birthright may be lost for a mess of pottage, and what Satan calls a trifle must be a thing of eternal significance.

SII. 222

When he died on the cross, he did that, in the wild weather of his outlying provinces, in the torture of the body of his revelation, which he had done at home in glory and gladness.

SIII. 9

Christ died to save us, not from suffering, but from ourselves; not from injustice, far less from justice, but from being unjust. He died that we might live—but live as he lives, by dying as he died who died to himself that he might live unto God. If we do not die to ourselves, we cannot live to God, and he that does not live to God, is dead.

SIII. 96

Paul glories in the cross of Christ, but he does not trust in the cross: he trusts in the living Christ and his living Father.

SIII. 129

Death

Death is not a breaker but a renewer of ties.

AF

We so often choose death, the thing that separates and kills, for everything that parts us from our fellow, and everything that parts us from God, is a killing of us.

The Christian World Pulpit

There is a worse thing than dying never to wake again; there is a worse thing than dying forever, and going soul and brain to the dust; and that is to wake up and find that there is no God! That is the horror of horrors to me—to tell me that I am to live forever, and there is no God! For anything any man knows, who does not believe in a God, it may be so. He cannot tell with certainty that he is going to die forever because he sees no more of those that have gone before. Why should not they go on to some other sphere as they came into this one? Without any warning or any choice, they do not know until they find themselves here. Why should it not be so in another state of existence? But to find yourselves there without a God! There is no use praying to be killed, because there is no God to hear your prayer. You can no more annihilate yourselves than make yourselves. The whole thing would be utter misery.

The Christian World Pulpit

As to death, the fact is we know next to nothing about it.

DG

About death you know nothing. God has never told us anything about it but that the dead are alive to him, and that one day, they will be again to us. We do not *know* anything about it, I repeat; but the world beyond the doors of death must be as homelike a place as this world is.

DG. 33

A Christian who looks gloomy at the mention of death, still more, one who talks of his friends as if he had lost them, turns the bushel of his little-faith over the lamp of the Lord's light.

HG. 180

Death is but our visible horizon, and our look ought always to be focused beyond it. We should never talk as if death were the end of anything.

HG. 180

When you say then that for the children of God there is no more death, remember that the deliverance of the creature is from the bondage of corruption into the glorious liberty of the children of God.

HG. 223

Death is the divine cure of many ills.

MOL. 182

What did our Lord mean by those words—"The damsel is not dead, but sleeps"? Not certainly that, as we regard the difference between death and sleep, his words were to be taken literally; not that she was only in a state of coma or lethargy; not even that it was a case of suspended animation as in catalepsy; for the whole narrative evidently intends us to believe that she was dead after the fashion we call death. That this was not to be dead after the fashion our Lord called death, is a blessed and lovely fact.

Neither can it mean, that she was not dead as others, in that he was going to wake her so soon; for they did not know that, and therefore it could give no ground for the expostulation, "Why make ye this ado, and weep?"

Nor yet could it come *only* from the fact that to his eyes death and sleep were so alike, the one needing the power of God for awaking just as much as the other.

MOL. 199–200

The Lord brings his assurance, his knowledge of what we do not know, to feed our feeble faith. It is as if he told us that our notion of death is all wrong, that there is no such thing as we think it; that we should be nearer the truth if we denied it altogether, and gave to what we now call death the name of sleep, for it is but a passing appearance, and no right cause of such misery as we manifest in its presence.

MOL. 202

When he raised the dead, the Son did neither more nor less nor other than the work of the Father—what he is always doing; he only made it manifest a little sooner to the eyes and hearts of men.

MOL. 203

If the Father ceased the Son must cease. It was the darkness between God and his creatures that gave room for and was filled with their weeping and wailing over their dead. To them death must appear an unmitigated and irremediable evil. How frightful to feel as they felt! to see death as they saw it! Nothing could help their misery but that faith in the infinite love which he had come to bring them; but how hard it was to persuade them to receive it! And how many weeping generations of loving hearts must follow! His Father was indeed with them all, but how slowly and painfully would each learn the one precious fact!

MOL. 209

Joy of all joys! The dead come back!

MOL. 213

One main doubt and terror which drives men toward the revelation in Jesus, is this strange thing Death. How shall any man imagine he is complete in himself, and can do without a Father in heaven, when he knows that he knows neither the mystery when he sprung by birth, nor the mystery to which he goes by death? God has given us room away from himself as Robert Browning says:—

> God, whose pleasure brought
> Man into being, stands away,
> As it were, an hand-breadth off, to
> give
> Room for the newly-made to live,
> And look at Him from a place apart,
> And use His gifts of brain and heart.

MOL. 214

Whence I came and whither I go are dark: how can I live in peace without the God who ordered it thus? Faith is my only refuge—an absolute belief in a being so much beyond myself, that he can do all for this *me* with utter satisfaction to this *me*, protecting all its rights, jealously as his own from which they spring, that he may make me at last one with himself who is my deeper self, inasmuch as his thought of me is my life. And not to know him, even if I could go on living and happy without him, is death.

MOL. 215

It is our low faithlessness that makes us misjudge it, and nothing but faith could make us judge it aright. And that, while in faithlessness, we should thus misjudge it, is well. In what it appears to us, it is a type of what we are without God. But there is no falsehood in it. The dust must go back to the dust. He who believes in the body more than in the soul, cleaves to this aspect of death: he who believes in thought, in mind, in love, in truth, can see the other side—can rejoice over the bursting shell which allows the young oak to creep from its kernel-prison. The lower is true, but the higher overcomes and absorbs it.

MOL. 220

"When that which is perfect is come, then that which is in part shall be done away." When the spirit of death is seen, the body of death vanishes from us. Death is God's angel of birth. We fear him. The dying stretches out loving hands of hope toward him.

MOL. 221

I do not believe that death is to the dying the dreadful thing it looks to the beholders. I think it is more like what the spirit may then be able to remember of its own birth as a child into this lower world, this porch of the heavenly.

MOL. 221

At length, O God, will you not cast Death and Hell into the lake of Fire—even into your own consuming self? Death shall then die everlastingly.

Then indeed will you be all in all. For then our poor brothers and sisters, every one—O God, we trust in you, the Consuming Fire—shall have been burnt clean and brought home. For if their moans, myriads of ages away, would turn heaven for us into hell—shall a man be more merciful than God? Shall, of all his glories, his mercy alone not be infinite?

SI. 48

Am I going to die? You know, if only from the cry of your Son, how terrible that is; and if it comes not to me in so terrible a shape as that in which it came to him, think how poor to bear I am beside him. I do not know what the struggle means; for, of the thousands who pass through it every day, not one enlightens his neighbor left behind; but shall I not long with agony for one breath of your air, and not receive it? shall I not be torn asunder with dying?—I will question no more: Father, into your hands I commend my spirit. For it is your business, not mine. You will know every shade of my suffering; you will care for me with your perfect fatherhood; for that makes my sonship, and enwraps and enfolds it.

SI. 185

It is imperative on us to get rid of the tyranny of things. See how imperative: let the young man cling with every fiber to his wealth, what God can do he will do; his child shall not be left in the hell of possession. Comes the angel of death—and where are the things that haunted the poor soul with such manifold hindrance and obstruction?

SII. 37

The man wakes from the final struggle of death, in absolute loneliness—such a loneliness as in the most miserable moment of deserted childhood he never knew. Not a hint, not a shadow of anything outside his consciousness reaches him. . . . Soon misery will beget on imagination a thousand shapes of woe, which he will not be able to rule, direct, or even distinguish from real presences.

SII. 108

All that is not God is death.

SII. 163

I bear witness that my Father is such as I. In the face of death I assert it, and dare death to disprove it. Kill me; do what you will and can against me; my Father is true, and I am true in saying that he is true. Danger or hurt cannot turn me aside from this my witness. Death can only kill my body; he cannot make me his captive.

SIII. 17

The whole strife and labor and agony of the Son with every man, is to get him to die as he died. All preaching that aims not at this, is a building with wood and hay and stubble.

SIII. 20

If we cannot fully . . . give ourselves to the Father, then we have not yet laid hold on that for which Christ has laid hold on us. The faith that a man may, nay, must put in God, reaches above earth and sky, stretches beyond the farthest outlying star of the creatable universe. The question is not at present, however, of removing mountains, a thing that will one day be simple to us, but of waking and rising from the dead *now*.

SIII. 21

Death and grief bring out the great family likenesses in the living as well as in the dead.

SP

It is for the sake of the resurrection that death exists.

SP

The Lord of Life is with you, and that is real company, even in dying, when no one else can be with you.

TW. 87

There are a thousand individual events in the course of every man's life, by which God takes a hold of him—a thousand breaches by which he would and does enter, little as the man may know it. But there is one universal and unchanging grasp he keeps on the race, yet not as the race, for the grasp is on every solitary single individual that has a part in it. That grasp is—death in its mystery. To whom can the man who is about to die in absolute loneliness and go he cannot tell whither, flee for refuge from the doubts and fears that assail him, but to the Father of his being?

TW. 94

You will be dead so long as you refuse to die.

WM. chap. 31

Death is the door to the temple-house, whose God is not seated aloft in motionless state, but walks about among his children, receiving his pilgrim sons in his arms, and washing the sore feet of the weary ones.

WW. 43

We have yet learned but little of the blessed power of death. We call it an evil! It is a holy, friendly thing.

WW. 43

Deeds

It is the deed that stirs the man; it is the thing you do, and not what you feel.

GW. 11

The man whose deeds are evil, fears the burning. But the burning will not come the less that he fears it or denies it. Escape is hopeless. For Love is inexorable. Our God is a consuming fire. He shall not come out until he has paid the uttermost penny.

SI. 46

Am I going to do a good deed? Then, of all times—Father, into your hands; lest the enemy should have me now.

SI. 184

The Lord cared neither for isolated truth nor for orphaned deed. It was truth in the inward parts, it was the good heart, the mother of good deeds, he cherished.

SII. 6

God seems to take pleasure in working by degrees; the progress of the truth is as the permeation of leaven, or the growth of a seed: a multitude of successive small sacrifices may work more good in the world than many a large one. . . . It is the *Being* that is the precious thing. Being is the mother to all little Doings as well as the grown-up Deeds and the mighty heroic Sacrifice; and these little Doings, like the good children of the house, make the bliss of it.

WW. 4

Desire

Our longing desires can no more exhaust the fullness of the treasures of the Godhead, than our imagination can touch their measure.

SI. 24

Such as ask amiss may sometimes have their prayers answered. The Father will never give the child a stone that asks for bread; but I am not sure that he will never give the child a stone that asks for a stone. If the Father says, "My child, that is a stone; it is no bread"; and the child answers, "I am sure it is bread; I want it"; may it not be well he should try his bread?

SII. 92

Man finds it hard to get what he wants, because he does not want the best; God finds it hard to give, because he would give the best, and man will not take it.

SII. 142

Many a man will gnaw at a lie all his life, and perish of want.

WM. 19

When we wish what he does not wish, we are not more against him than against our real selves. We are traitors to the human when we think anything but the will of God desirable, when we fear our very life.

WM. 32

Who in any measure seeing what Christ sees and feeling as Christ feels, would rest in the enjoyment of beauty while so many are unable to desire it?

WW

Discipleship

He who heard to obey was his disciple.

HG. 82

If a disciple be blessed because of any one thing, every other blessing is either his, or on the way to become his; for he is on the way to receive the very righteousness of God. Each good thing opens the door to the one next it, so to all the rest.

HG. 151

The Lord does not hesitate to call his few humble disciples the salt of the earth; and every century since has borne witness that such indeed they were—that he spoke of them but the simple fact. Where would the world be now but for their salt and their light!

HG. 173

Their Master set them to be salt against corruption, and light against darkness; and our souls answer and say, Lord, they have been the salt, they have been the light of the world!

HG. 174

Salt only preserves from growing bad; it does not cause anything to grow better. His disciples are the salt of the world, but they are more. Therefore, having warned the human salt to look to itself that it be indeed salt, he proceeds: "You are the light of the world, a city, a candle," and so resumes his former path of persuasion and enforcement: "It is so, therefore make it so."—"You are the salt of the earth; therefore be salt."—"You are the light of the world; therefore shine."—"You are a city; be seen upon your hill."—"You are the Lord's candles; let no bushels cover you. Let your light shine." Every disciple of the Lord must be a preacher of righteousness.

HG. 175

In business, the custom of the trade must be understood by both contracting parties, else it can have no place, either as law or excuse, with the disciple of Jesus.

HG. 181

Some seem to take this to mean that the disciple must go against his likings because they are his likings; must be unresponsive to the tendencies and directions and inclinations that are his, because they are such, and his; they seem to think something is gained by abstinence from what is pleasant, or by the doing of what is disagreeable—that to thwart the lower nature is in itself a good. Now I will not dare say what a man may not get good from, if the thing be done in simplicity and honesty. I believe that when a man, for the sake of doing the thing that is right, does in mistake that which is not right, God will take care that he be shown the better way—will perhaps use the very thing which is his mistake to reveal to him the mistake it is. I will allow that the mere effort of will, arbitrary and uninformed of duty, partaking of the character of tyranny and even schism, may add to the man's power over his lower nature; but in that very nature it is God who must rule and not the man, however well he may mean.

SII. 211

He is all for the Father; we must be all for the Father too, else are we not following him. To follow him is to be learning of him, to think his thoughts, to use his judgments, to see things as he saw them, to feel things as he felt them, to be hearted, souled, minded, as he was—that so also we may be of the same mind with his Father. This is to deny self and go after him; nothing less, even if it be working miracles and casting out devils, is to be his disciple.

SII. 219

"But I do not know how to awake and arise!"

I will tell you: Get up, and do something the Master tells you; so make yourself his disciple at once. Instead of asking yourself whether you believe or not, ask yourself whether you have this day done one thing because he said, Do it, or once abstained because he said, Do not do it. It is simply absurd to say you believe, or even want to believe in him, if you do not anything he tells you. If you can think of nothing he ever said as having had an atom of influence on your doing or not doing, you have too good ground to consider yourself no disciple of his.

SII. 244

There is no life for any man other than the same kind that Jesus has; his disciple must live by the same absolute devotion of his will to the Father's; then is his life one with the life of the Father.

SIII. 12

I believe that to be the disciple of Christ is the end of being; that to persuade men to be his disciples is the end of teaching.

SIII. 156

Doubt

The more ignorant a man is, the more capable is he of being absolutely certain of many things—with such certainty, that is, as consists in the absence of doubt.

M. 53

The very first step toward action is the death-warrant of doubt.

ML. 24

No man can help doubt. The true man alone, that is, the faithful man, can appeal to the Truth to enable him to believe what is true, and refuse what is false. How this applies especially to our own time and the need of the living generations, is easy to see. Of all prayers it is the one for us.

MOL. 178

To deny the existence of God may, paradoxical as the statement will at first seem to some, involve less unbelief than the smallest yielding to doubt of his goodness. I say *yielding*; for a man may be haunted with doubts, and only grow thereby in faith.

SII. 201

Doubts are the messengers of the Living One to rouse the honest. They are the first knock at our door of things that are not yet, but have to be, understood.

SII. 201

Doubt must precede every deeper assurance; for uncertainties are what we first see when we look into a region hitherto unknown, unexplored, unannexed.

SII. 201

To know that our faith is weak is the first step toward its strengthening; to be capable of distrusting is death; to know that we are, and cry out, is to begin to live—to begin to be made such that we cannot distrust—such that God may do anything with us and we shall never doubt him. Until doubt is impossible, we are lacking in the true, the childlike knowledge of God; for either God is such that one *may* distrust him, or he is such that to distrust him is the greatest injustice of which a man can be guilty. If then we are able to distrust him, either we know God imperfect, or we do not know him.

SII. 202

If you cannot trust him to let you know what is right, but think you must hold this or that before you can come to him, then I justify your doubts in what you call your worst times, but which I suspect are your best times in which you come nearest to the truth—those, namely, in which you fear you have no faith.

SII. 252

A doubter is not without faith. The very fact that he doubts shows that he has some faith.

SP

Duty

The best preparation is the present well seen to, the last duty done.

AN. 206

You have a disagreeable duty to do at twelve o'clock. Do not blacken nine and ten and eleven, and all between, with the color of twelve. Do the work of each, and reap your reward in peace. So when the dreaded moment in the future becomes the present, you shall meet it walking in the light, and that light will overcome its darkness.

AN. 206

Our business is not to speculate what we would do in other circumstances, but to perform the duty of the moment, the one true preparation for the duty to come.

EA. 227

Depart from evil, and do good. The duty that lies at your door, do it, be it great or small.

HG. 30

Even if our supposed merit were of the positive order, and we did every duty perfectly, the moment we began to pride ourselves upon the fact we should drop into a hell of worthlessness. What are we for but to do our duty?

HG. 191

Not anxious to know our duty, or knowing it and not doing it, how shall we understand that which only a true heart and a clean soul can ever understand?

MOL. 19

We shall one day forget all about duty, and do everything from the love of the loveliness of it, the satisfaction of the rightness of it.

PF. 206

If a man lay himself out to do the immediate duty of the moment, wonderfully little forethought, I suspect, will be found needful. That forethought only is right which has to determine duty, and pass into action. To the foundation of yesterday's work well done, the work of the morrow will be sure to fit.

SII. 47

The things readiest to be done, those which lie, not at the door but on the very table, of a man's mind, are not merely in general the most neglected, but even by the thoughtful man, the oftenest let alone, the oftenest postponed.

SII. 52

Do at once what you must do one day. As there is no escape from payment, escape at least the prison that will enforce it. Do not drive Justice to extremities. Duty is imperative; it must be done. It is useless to think to escape the eternal law of things; yield of yourself, nor compel God to compel you.

SII. 102

"When you shall have done all the things that are commanded you, say, We are unprofitable servants; we have done that which it was our duty to do." Duty is a thing prepaid: it can never have desert. There is no claim on God that springs from us: all is from him.

SII. 193

The man is a true man who chooses duty; he is a perfect man who at length never thinks of duty, who forgets the name of it. The duty of Jesus was the doing in lower forms than the perfect that which he loved perfectly, and did perfectly in the highest forms also. Thus he fulfilled all righteousness.

SIII. 73

One who went to the truth by mere impulse, would be a holy animal, not a true man. Relations, truths, duties, are shown to the man away beyond him, that he may choose them, and be a child of God, choosing righteousness like him.

SIII. 73

The moral philosopher who regards duties only as facts of his system; nay, even the man who regards them as truths, essential realities of his humanity, but goes no farther, is essentially a liar, a man of untruth. He is a man indeed, but not a true man. He is a man in possibility, but not a real man yet.

SIII. 73

No man can order his life, for it comes flowing over him from behind. . . . The one secret of life and development is not to devise and plan but to fall in with the forces at work—to do every moment's duty aright—that being the part in the process allotted to us: and let come—not what will, for there is no such thing—but what the eternal thought wills for each of us, has intended in each of us from the first.

SG. chap. 44

Those who gain no experience are those who shirk the King's highway for fear of encountering the Duty seated by the roadside.

TW. chap. 17

We have no right to school ourselves to an imaginary duty. When we do not know, then what he lays upon us is *not to know*, and to be content not to know.

WM

Enemy

Will a man ever love his enemies? He may come to do good to them that hate him; but when will he pray for them that despitefully use him and persecute him? When? When he is the child of his Father in heaven. Then shall he love his neighbor as himself, even if that neighbor be his enemy.

SI. 217

Is it then reasonable to love our enemies? God does; therefore it must be the highest reason. But is it reasonable to expect that man should become capable of doing so? Yes; on one ground: that the divine energy is at work in man, to render at length man's doing divine as his nature is.

SI. 218

Why should we love our enemies? The deepest reason for this we cannot put in words, for it lies in the absolute reality of their being, where our enemies are of one nature with us, even of the divine nature. Into this we cannot see, save as into a dark abyss. But we can adumbrate something of the form of this deepest reason if we let the thoughts of our heart move upon the face of the dim profound.

SI. 219

If, owing you love, he gives you hate, you, owing him love, have yet to pay it.

SII. 106

Evil

However absurd the statement may appear to one who has not yet discovered the fact for himself, the cause of every man's discomfort is evil, moral evil—first of all, evil in himself, his own sin, his own wrongness, his own unrightness.

HG. 3

Foolish is the man, and there are many such men, who would rid himself or his fellows of discomfort by setting the world right, by waging war on the evils around him, while he neglects that integral part of the world where lies his business, his first business—namely, his own character and conduct.

HG. 4

The bad that lives in us, our evil judgments, our unjust desires, our hate and pride and envy and greed and self-satisfaction—these are the souls of our sins, our live sins, more terrible than the bodies of our sins, namely, the deeds we do, inasmuch as they not only produce these loathsome things, but make us loathsome as they.

HG. 11

Evil is not human; it is the defect and opposite of the human; but the suffering that follows it is human, belonging of necessity to the human that has sinned: while it is by cause of sin, suffering is *for* the sinner, that he may be delivered from his sin. For that they were indeed created.

HG. 14

The man may recognize the evil in him only as pain; he may know little and care nothing about his sins; yet is the Lord sorry for his pain. He cries aloud, "Come unto me, all you that labor and are heavy laden, and I will give you rest." He does not say, "Come unto me, all you that feel the burden of your sins"; he opens his arms to all weary enough to come to him in the poorest hope of rest. Right gladly would he free them from their misery—but he knows only one way: he will teach them to be like himself, meek and lowly, bearing with gladness the yoke of his Father's will. This is the one, the only right, the only possible way of freeing them from their sins, the cause of their unrest. With them the weariness comes first; with him the sins: there is but one cure for both—the will of the Father. That which is his joy will be their deliverance!

HG. 16

Equally is it common sense that, if a man would be delivered from the evil in him, he must himself begin to cast it out, himself begin to disobey it, and work righteousness.

HG. 20

Every one will, I presume, confess to more or less misery. Its apparent source may be this or that; its real source is, to use a poor figure, a dislocation of the juncture between the created and the creating life. This primal evil is the parent of evils unnumbered, hence of miseries multitudinous, under the weight of which the arrogant man cries out against life, and goes on to misuse it, while the child looks around for help—and who shall help him but his Father! The Father is with him all the time, but it may be long ere the child knows himself in his arms.

HG. 66

Evil, that is, physical evil, is a moral good—a mighty means to a lofty end. Pain is an evil; but a good as well, which it would be a great injury to take from the man before it had wrought its end. Then it becomes all evil, and must pass.

MOL. 42

The man whose deeds are evil, fears the burning. But the burning will not come the less that he fears it or denies it. Escape is hopeless. For Love is inexorable. Our God is a consuming fire. He shall not come out until he has paid the uttermost farthing.

SI. 46

It was not this and that fault he had come to set right, but the primary evil of life without God, the root of all evils, from hatred to discourtesy.

SII. 46

There is no half-way house of rest, where ungodliness may be dallied with, nor prove quite fatal.

SII. 114

What makes me evil and miserable is that the thing spoiled in me is the image of the Perfect.

SII. 115

However bad I may be, I am the child of God, and therein lies my blame. Ah, I would not lose my blame! In my blame lies my hope.

SII. 120

If a man ceased to be *capable* of evil, he must cease to be a man.

SF

Ignorant creatures who do not yet understand anything go about asking why God permits evil. *We* know why!

SF. 36

Evil that is not seen to be evil by one willing and trying to do right, is not counted evil to him. It is evil only to the person who either knows it to be evil, or does not care whether it be or not.

WM

The darkness knows neither the light nor itself; only the light knows itself and the darkness also. None but God hates evil and understands it.

WM. chap. 39

Evil is a hard thing for God himself to overcome. Yet thoroughly and altogether and triumphantly will he overcome it; and that not by crushing it underfoot—any god of man's idea could do that!—but by conquest of heart over heart, of life in life, of life over death.

WW. 33

Evil cannot be destroyed without repentance.

WW. 49

Faith

This thing of faith means the whole recognized relation of man to God and his fellows; it is the right position of the human soul which is made to understand the truth—the right position of that soul toward the truth. Taking it in its simplest original development, it is the highest effort of the whole human intellect, imagination, and will, in the highest direction. Never does our nature put forth itself in such power, with such effort, with such energy, as when it has faith in God.

The Christian World Pulpit

Faith is simply the greatest work that man can do.

The Christian World Pulpit

Faith is the trying of the things unseen—the putting of them to the test; and whatever your doubts and fears are, try God by obedience, and then you will get help to carry you on. Less than that will not do.

The Christian World Pulpit

Faith is the trying of the things that you do not see, and that you cannot be sure about. A thing that you do not see, and which not seeing you have doubts about, you can yet try—that is faith. And if you are honest, that will be a great opportunity and a great help to you. It will start a fresh faith which you have not thought of before, and give your life a new impulse. Faith is intended to put to the test the unseen world of truth, law, hope, redemption. God grant us all faith enough to carry us on from point to point until the faith shall vanish into light, and we have never to think about faith more, nor to think about church more, nor the Bible more, nor prayer more, but our whole being shall be a delighted consciousness of the presence of God and his Christ.

The Christian World Pulpit

How few are those whose faith is simple and mighty in the Father of Jesus Christ, waiting to believe all that he will reveal to them!

DE

Faith, in its simplest, truest, mightiest form, is to do his will in the one thing revealing itself at the moment as duty. The faith that works miracles is an inferior faith to this.

DG

Therefore, friends, the practical thing is just this, and it is the one lesson we have to learn, that, whatever our doubts or difficulties may be, we must do the thing we know in order to learn the thing we do not know. But whether we learn it or not, "If you know these things," says the Master, "happy are you if you do them." It is the doing that is everything, and the doing is faith, and there is no division between them.

GW. 117

Faith in its true sense does not belong to the intellect alone, nor to the intellect first, but to the conscience, to the will; and that man is a faithful man who says, "I cannot prove that there is a God, but, O God, if you hear me anywhere, help me to do your will." There is faith. "Do this," and he does it. It is obedience, friends, that is faith; it is doing that thing which you, let me say, even only suppose to be the will of God; for if you are wrong, and do it because you think it is his will, he will set you right. It is the turning of the eye to the light; it is the sending of the feet into the path that is required, putting the hands to do the things which the conscience says ought to be done.

GW. 117

Need and the upward look, the mood ready to believe when and where it can, the embryonic faith, is dear to him whose love would have us trust him.

HG. 78

"Our Lord speaks of many coming up to his door confident of admission, whom yet he sends from him. Faith is obedience, not confidence."

ML

Active faith is the needful response in order that a man may be a child of God, and not the mere instrument on which his power plays a soulless tune.

MOL. 47

We have neither humility enough to be faithful, nor faith enough to be humble.

MOL. 107

The power to work is a diviner gift than a great legacy. But these are individual affairs to be settled individually between God and his child. They cannot be pronounced upon generally because of individual differences. But here as there, now as then, the lack is *faith.*

MOL. 112

A man may say, "How can I have faith?" I answer, "How can you indeed, who do the thing you know you ought not to do, and have not begun to do the thing you know you ought to do? How should you have faith?"

MOL. 113

Faith in God will do more for the intellect at length than all the training of the schools.

MOL. 136 (note)

If any one ask how Jesus could marvel, I answer, Jesus could do more things than we can well understand. The fact that he marveled at the great faith, shows that he is not surprised at the little, and therefore is able to make all needful and just, yea, and tender allowance.

MOL. 143

The man who can go to sleep without faith in God has yet to learn what being is. He who knows not God cannot, however, have much to lose in losing being.

MOL. 216

That man is perfect in faith who can come to God in the utter death of his feelings and his desires, without a glow or an aspiration, with the weight of low thoughts, failures, neglects, and wandering forgetfulness, and say to him, "You are my refuge, because you are my home."

SI. 25

The faith that limits itself to the promises of God seems to me to partake of the paltry character of such a faith in my child—good enough for a Pagan, but for a Christian a miserable and wretched faith. Those who rest in such faith would feel yet more comfortable if they had God's bond instead of his word, which they regard not as the outcome of his character, but as a pledge of his honor. They try to believe in the truth of his word, but the truth of his Being, they understand not. In his oath they persuade themselves that they put confidence: in *himself* they do not believe, for they know him not.

SI. 59

To believe what he has not said is faith indeed, and blessed. For that comes of believing in him.

SI. 62

"If you have faith and doubt not, if you shall say to this mountain, 'Be removed and cast into the sea,' it shall be done." Good people . . . have been tempted to tempt the Lord their God upon the strength of this saying. . . . Happily for such, the assurance to which they would give the name of faith generally fails them in time.

SI. 147

Faith is that which, knowing the Lord's will, goes and does it; or, not knowing it, stands and waits, content in ignorance as in knowledge, because God wills; neither pressing into the hidden future, nor careless of the knowledge which opens the path of action.

SI. 147

The faith which will remove mountains is that confidence in God which comes from seeking nothing but his will.

SI. 149

Thus the will of Jesus, in the very moment when his faith seems about to yield, is finally triumphant. It has no *feeling* now to support it, no beatific vision to absorb it. It stands naked in his soul and tortured, as he stood naked and scourged before Pilate. Pure and simple and surrounded by fire, it declares for God. The sacrifice ascends in the cry, *My God.* The cry comes not out of happiness, out of peace, out of hope. Not even out of suffering comes that cry. It was a cry *in* desolation, but it came out of Faith. It is the last voice of Truth, speaking when it can but cry. The divine horror of that moment is unfathomable by human soul. It was blackness of darkness. And yet he would believe. Yet he would hold fast. God was his God yet. *My God*—and in the cry came forth the Victory, and all was over soon. Of the peace that followed that cry, the peace of a perfect soul, large as the universe, pure as light, ardent as life, victorious for God and his brethren, he himself alone can ever know the breadth and length, and depth and height.

SI. 166

Then fold the arms of your faith, and wait in quietness until light goes up in your darkness. Fold the arms of your faith I say, but not of your action: think of something that you ought to do, and go and do it, if it be but the sweeping of a room, or the preparing of a meal, or a visit to a friend. Heed not your feelings: Do your work.

SI. 177

Our vision is so circumscribed, our theories are so small—the garment of them not large enough to wrap us in; our faith so continually fashions itself to the fit of our dwarf intellect, that there is endless room for rebellion against ourselves: we must not let our poor knowledge limit our not so poor intellect, our intellect limit our faith, our faith limit our divine hope; reason must humbly watch over all—reason, the candle of the Lord.

SII. 90

A man's faith shall be in the living, loving, ruling, helping Christ, devoted to us as much as ever he was, and with all the powers of the Godhead for the salvation of his brethren. It is not faith that he did this, that his work wrought that—it is faith in the man who did and is doing everything for us that will save him: without this he cannot work to heal spiritually, any more than he would heal physically, when he was present to the eyes of men.

SII. 242

Do you ask, "What is faith in him?" I answer, The leaving of your way, your objects, your self, and the taking of his and him; the leaving of your trust in men, in money, in opinion, in character, in atonement itself, *and doing as he tells you.* I can find no words strong enough to serve for the weight of this necessity—this obedience. It is the one terrible heresy of the church, that it has always been presenting something else than obedience as faith in Christ.

SII. 243

Faith in what? Faith in what he is, in what he says—a faith which can have no existence except in obedience—a faith which *is* obedience. To do what he wishes is to put forth faith in him.

SII. 246

It is faith that saves us—but not faith in any work of God—it is faith in God himself.

SII. 250

The poorest faith in the living God, the God revealed in Christ Jesus, if it be vital, true, that is obedient, is the beginning of the way to know him, and to know him is eternal life. If you mean by faith anything of a different kind, that faith will not save you.

SII. 250

A faith . . . that God does not forgive me because he loves me, but because he loves Jesus Christ, cannot save me, because it is a falsehood against God: if the thing were true, such a gospel would be the preaching of a God that was not love, therefore in whom was no salvation, a God to know whom could not be eternal life. Such a faith would damn, not save a man; for it would bind him to a God who was anything but perfect.

SII. 251

Your faith! . . . Your theory is not your faith, nor anything like it. Your faith is your obedience; your theory I know not what. Yes, I will gladly leave you without any of what you call faith. Trust in God. Obey the word—every word of the Master. That is faith; and so believing, your opinion will grow out of your true life, and be worthy of it.

SIII. 151

[Abraham's faith] . . . was no mere intellectual recognition of the existence of a God. . . . It was that faith which is one with action: "He went out, not knowing whither he went." The very act of believing in God after such a fashion that, when the time of action comes, the man will obey God, is the highest act, the deepest, loftiest righteousness, and the spirit of it will work until the man is perfect.

SIII. 214

What springs from myself and not from God is evil: it is a perversion of something of God's. Whatever is not of faith is sin; it is a stream cut off—a stream that cuts itself off from its source and thinks to run on without it.

SIII. 262

A doubter is not without faith. The very fact that he doubts shows that he has some faith.

SP

It is not a belief in immortality that will deliver a man from the woes of humanity, but faith in the God of life, the Father of lights, the God of all consolation and comfort. Believing in him, a man can leave his friends, and their and his own immortality, with everything else—even his and their love and perfection, with utter confidence in his hands. Until we have the life in us, we shall never be at peace. The living God dwelling in the heart he has made, and glorifying it by inmost speech with himself—that is life, assurance, and safety. Nothing less is or can be such.

TW. 94

The thing that is not true cannot find its way to the home of faith; if it could, it would be at once rejected with a loathing beyond utterance.

WM

Faith . . . must be of the purest, and may be of the strongest. In few other circumstances can it have such an opportunity—can it rise to equal height. It may be its final lesson, and deepest. God is in it just in his seeming to be not in it—that we may choose him in the darkness of the feeling, stretch out the hand to him when we cannot see him, verify him in the vagueness of the dream, call to him in the absence of impulse, obey him in the weakness of the will.

WW. 43

Family

The true idea of the universe is the whole family in heaven and earth. All the children in this part of it, the earth, at least, are not good children; but however far, therefore, the earth is from being a true portion of a real family, the life-germ at the root of the world, that by and for which it exists, is its relation to God the Father of men.

HG. 132

The whole divine family is made up of numberless human families, that in these, men may learn and begin to love one another. God, then, would make of the world a true, divine family.

HG. 133

The primary necessity to the very existence of a family is peace.

HG. 133

Many a human family is no family, and the world is no family yet, for the lack of peace.

HG. 133

Wherever peace is growing, there, of course, is the live peace, counteracting disruption and disintegration, and helping the development of the true essential family.

HG. 133

The one question, therefore, as to any family is, whether peace or strife be on the increase in it; for peace alone makes it possible for the binding grass-roots of life—love, namely, and justice—to spread throughout what were else but a wind-blown heap of still drifting sand.

HG. 133

We must not fear what man can do to us, but commit our way to the Father of the Family.

HG. 139

Those whom our Lord felicitates are all the children of one family; and everything that can be called blessed or blessing comes of the same righteousness.

HG. 151

Father and Son

All that the children want is their Father.

HG. 38

The relation of the Father and the Son contains the idea of the universe. Jesus tells his disciples that his Father had no secrets from him; that he knew the Father as the Father knew him. The Son must know the Father; he only could know him—and knowing, he could reveal him; the Son could make the other, the imperfect children, know the Father, and so become such as he. All things were given unto him by the Father, because he was the Son of the Father: for the same reason he could reveal the things of the Father to the child of the Father. The child-relation is the one eternal, ever-enduring, never-changing relation.

HG. 162

The Father knows the Son, and sends him to us that we may know him; the Son knows the Father, and dies to reveal him.

HG. 162

Omniscience is a consequence, not an essential of the divine nature. God knows because he creates. The Father knows because he orders. The Son knows because he obeys. The knowledge of the Father must be perfect; such knowledge the Son neither needs nor desires. His sole care is to do the will of the Father. Herein lies his essential divinity.

MOL. 79

Not only does he not claim perfect knowledge, but he disclaims it. Hc speaks once, at least, to his Father with an *if it be possible*. Those who believe omniscience essential to divinity, will therefore be driven to say that Christ was not divine. This will be their punishment for placing knowledge on a level with love.

MOL. 79

The Fatherhood and the Sonship are one, save that the Fatherhood looks down lovingly, and the Sonship looks up lovingly.

SI. 20

The Father said, That is a stone. The Son would not say, That is a loaf. No one creative *fiat* shall contradict another. The Father and the Son are of one mind. The Lord could hunger, could starve, but would not change into another thing what his Father had made one thing.

SI. 138

The Father shall order what comes next. The Son will obey.

SI. 146

The Holy Child, the Son of the Father, has nothing to conceal, but all the Godhead to reveal.

SI. 164

This is the faith of the Son of God. God withdrew, as it were, that the perfect will of the Son might arise and go forth to find the will of the Father. It is possible that even then he thought of the lost sheep who could not believe that God was their Father; and for them, too, in all their loss and blindness and unlove, cried, saying the word they might say, knowing for them that *God* means *Father* and more.

SI. 169

Think, brothers, think, sisters, we walk in the air of an eternal fatherhood. Every uplifting of the heart is a looking up to the Father. Graciousness and truth are around, above, beneath us, yes, *in* us. When we are least worthy, then, most tempted, hardest, unkindest, let us yet commend our spirits into his hands.

SI. 186

The joy of the Lord's life, that which made it life to him, was the Father; of him he was always thinking, to him he was always turning. I suppose most men have some thought of pleasure or satisfaction or strength to which they turn when action pauses, life becomes for a moment still, and the wheel sleeps on its own swiftness: with Jesus it needed no pause of action, no rush of renewed consciousness, to send him home; his thought was ever and always his Father. To its home in the heart of the Father his heart ever turned. That was his treasure-house, the jewel of his mind, the mystery of his gladness, claiming all degrees and shades of delight, from peace and calmest content to ecstasy. His life was hid in God. No vain show could enter at his eyes; every truth and grandeur of life passed before him as it was; neither ambition nor disappointment could distort them to his eternal childlike gaze; he beheld and loved them from the bosom of the Father.

SII. 3

It was not for himself he came to the world—not to establish his own power over the doings, his own influence over the hearts of men: he came that they might know the Father who was his joy, his life. The sons of men were his Father's children like himself: that the Father should have them all in his bosom was the one thought of his heart: that should be his doing for his Father, cost him what it might! He came to do his will, and on the earth was the same he had been from the beginning, the eternal first. He was not interested in himself, but in his Father, and in his Father's children. He did not care to be himself called *good*. It was not of consequence to him. He was there to let men see the goodness of the Father in whom he gloried. For that he entered the weary dream of the world, in which the glory was so dulled and clouded. You call me good! you should know my Father!

SII. 4

The Lord's greatness consisted in his Father's being greater than he: he who calls into being is greater than the one who is called. The Father was always the Father, the Son was always the Son; yet the Son is not of himself, but by the Father; he does not live by his own power, like the Father. If there were no Father, there would be no Son. All that is the Lord's is the Father's, and all that is the Father's he has given to the Son. The Father was all in all to the Son, and the Son no more thought of his own goodness than an honest man thinks of his honesty. When the good man sees goodness, he thinks of his own evil: Jesus had no evil to think of, but neither does he think of his goodness; he delights in his Father's. "Why do you call me good?"

SII. 5

The mission undertaken by the Son was not to show himself as having all power in heaven and earth, but to reveal his Father, to show him to men such as he is, that men may know him, and knowing, trust him.

SII. 44

He saw it was not good for man to be alone, so has he never been alone himself; from all eternity the Father has had the Son, and the never-begun existence of that Son I imagine an easy outgoing of the Father's nature; while to make other beings—beings like us, I imagine the labor of a God, an eternal labor.

SII. 141

God has never been contented to be alone even with the Son of his love, the prime and perfect idea of humanity, but that he has from the first willed and labored to give existence to other creatures who should be blessed with his blessedness—creatures whom he is now and always has been developing into likeness with that Son—a likeness for long to be distant and small, but a likeness to be for ever growing: perhaps never one of them yet, though unspeakably blessed, has had even an approximate idea of the blessedness in store for him.

SII. 141

The worst heresy, next to that of dividing religion and righteousness, is to divide the Father from the Son—in thought or feeling or action or intent; to represent the Son as doing that which the Father does not himself do. Jesus did nothing but what the Father did and does.

SII. 143

He is the Son of the Father as the Son who obeys the Father, as the Son who came expressly and only to do the will of the Father, as the messenger whose delight it is to do the will of him that sent him. At the moment he says *Follow me*, he is following the Father; his face is set homeward.

SII. 218

Jesus Christ is the eternal Son of the eternal Father; that from the first of firstness Jesus is the Son, because God is the Father—a statement imperfect and unfit because an attempt of human thought to represent that which it cannot grasp, yet which it so believes that it must try to utter it even in speech that cannot be right. I believe therefore that the Father is the greater, that if the Father had not been, the Son could not have been.

SIII. 3

I worship the Son as the human God, the divine, the only Man, deriving his being and power from the Father, equal with him as a son is the equal at once and the subject of his father—but *making himself the equal of his Father in what is most precious in Godhead, namely, Love.*

SIII. 4

Because of that eternal love which has no beginning, the Father must have the Son. God could not love, could not be love, without making things to love: Jesus has God to love; the love of the Son is responsive to the love of the Father.

SIII. 9

The life of Christ is this—negatively, that he does nothing, cares for nothing for his own sake; positively, that he cares with his whole soul for the will, the pleasure of his Father. Because his Father is his Father, therefore he will be his child.

SIII. 10

He made himself what he is by *deathing* himself into the will of the eternal Father, through which will he was the eternal Son—thus plunging into the fountain of his own life, the everlasting Fatherhood, and taking the Godhead of the Son. This is the life that was made *in* Jesus: "That which was made in him was life."

SIII. 12

Because we are come out of the divine nature, which chooses to be divine, we must *choose* to be divine, to be of God, to be one with God, loving and living as he loves and lives, and so be partakers of the divine nature, or we perish. Man cannot originate this life; it must be shown him, and he must choose it. God is the Father of Jesus and of us—of every possibility of our being; but while God is the Father of his children, Jesus is the father of their sonship; for in him is made the life which is sonship to the Father.

SIII. 13

Let us not forget that the devotion of the Son could never have been but for the devotion of the Father, who never seeks his own glory one atom more than does the Son; who is devoted to the Son, and to all his sons and daughters, with a devotion perfect and eternal, with fathomless unselfishness.

SIII. 16

It is not the fact that God created all things, that makes the universe a whole; but that he through whom he created them loves him perfectly, is eternally content in his Father, is satisfied to be because his Father is with him. It is not the fact that God is all in all, that unites the universe; it is the love of the Son to the Father.

SIII. 18

He has shown us the Father not only by doing what the Father does, not only by loving his Father's children even as the Father loves them, but by his perfect satisfaction with him, his joy in him, his utter obedience to him. He has shown us the Father by the absolute devotion of a perfect son. He is the Son of God because the Father and he are one, have one thought, one mind, one heart. Upon this truth—I do not mean the dogma, but the truth itself of Jesus to his Father—hangs the universe; and upon the recognition of this truth—that is, upon their becoming thus true—hangs the freedom of the children, the redemption of their whole world.

SIII. 96

"I and the Father are one" is the center-truth of the universe; and the circumfering truth is "that they also may be one in us."

SIII. 97

The Father magnifies the Son, not the Son himself; the Son magnifies the Father.

SIII. 220

Jesus alone knows the Father and can reveal him.

SG. 153

Fear

"Let us have grace, whereby we may serve God acceptably with reverence and godly fear, for our God is a consuming fire." We have received a kingdom that cannot be moved—whose nature is immovable: let us have grace to serve the Consuming Fire, our God, with divine fear; not with the fear that cringes and craves, but with the bowing down of all thoughts, all delights, all loves before him who is the life of them all, and will have them all pure.

SI. 30

The fear of God will cause a man to flee, not from him, but from himself; not from him, but to him, the Father of himself, in terror lest he should do him wrong or his neighbor wrong.

SI. 32

Fear is nobler than sensuality. Fear is better than no God, better than a god made with hands.

SI. 36

The worship of fear is true, although very low: and though not acceptable to God in itself, for only the worship of spirit and of truth is acceptable to him, yet even in his sight it is precious.

SI. 36

Because we easily imagine ourselves in want, we imagine God ready to forsake us.

SII. 44

It is not alone the first beginnings of religion that are full of fear. So long as love is imperfect, there is room for torment. That love only which fills the heart—and nothing but love can fill any heart—is able to cast out fear, leaving no room for its presence. What we find in the beginnings of religion, will hold in varying degree, until the religion, that is, the love, be perfected.

SII. 157

The thing that is unknown, yet known to be, will always be more or less formidable. When it is known as immeasurably greater than we, and as having claims and making demands on us, the more vaguely these are apprehended, the more room is there for anxiety; and when the conscience is not clear, this anxiety may well mount to terror.

SII. 157

Naturally the first emotion of man toward the being he calls God, but of whom he knows little, is fear.

SII. 158

Where it is possible that fear should exist, it is well it should exist, cause continual uneasiness, and be cast out by nothing less than love.

SII. 158

In him who does not know God, and must be anything but satisfied with himself, fear toward God is as reasonable as it is natural, and serves powerfully toward the development of his true humanity.

SII. 158

Fear is natural, and has a part to perform nothing but itself could perform in the birth of the true humanity. Until love, which is the truth toward God, is able to cast out fear, it is well that fear should hold; it is a bond, however poor, between that which is and that which creates—a bond that must be broken, but a bond that can be broken only by the tightening of an infinitely closer bond. Verily, God must be terrible to those that are far from him; for they fear he will do, yea, he is doing with them what they do not, cannot desire, and can ill endure.

SII. 158

A God who will die for his creatures, and insists on giving himself to them, insists on their being unselfish and blessed like himself. That which is the power and worth of life they must be, or die; and the vague consciousness of this makes them afraid. They love their poor existence as it is; God loves it as it must be—and they fear him.

SII. 159

Although he loves them utterly, he does not tell them there is nothing in him to make them afraid. That would be to drive them from him for ever. While they are such as they are, there is much in him that cannot but affright them; they ought, they do well to fear him. . . . To remove that fear from their hearts, save by letting them know his love with its purifying fire, a love which for ages, it may be, they cannot know, would be to give them up utterly to the power of evil. Persuade men that fear is a vile thing, that it is an insult to God, that he will none of it—while they are yet in love with their own will, and slaves to every movement of passionate impulse, and what will the consequence be? That they will insult God as a discarded idol, a superstition, a falsehood, as a thing under whose evil influence they have too long groaned, a thing to be cast out and spit upon. After that how much will they learn of him?

SII. 160

If then any child of the Father finds that he is afraid before him, that the thought of God is a discomfort to him, or even a terror, let him make haste—let him not linger to put on any garment, but rush at once in his nakedness, a true child, for shelter from his own evil and God's terror, into the salvation of the Father's arms, the home whence he was sent that he might learn that it was home.

SII. 163

No glory even of God *should* breed terror; when a child of God is afraid, it is a sign that the word *Father* is not yet freely fashioned by the child's spiritual mouth. The glory can breed terror only in him who is capable of being terrified by it; while he is such it is well the terror should be bred and maintained, until the man seek refuge from it in the only place where it is not—in the bosom of the glory.

SII. 164

Endless must be our terror, until we come heart to heart with the fire-core of the universe, the first and the last and the living One.

SII. 166

Oh, the joy to be told, by Power himself, the first and the last, the living one—told what we can indeed then see *must* be true, but which we are so slow to believe—that the cure for trembling is the presence of Power; that fear cannot stand before Strength; that the visible God is the destruction of death; that the one and only safety in the universe is the perfect nearness of the Living One! God is being; death is nowhere! What a thing to be taught by the very mouth of him who knows!

SII. 166

The glory of the mildest show of the Living One is such that even the dearest of his apostles, the best of the children of men, is cowed at the sight. He has not yet learned that glory itself is a part of his inheritance, yea is of the natural condition of his being; that there is nothing in the man made in the image of God alien from the most glorious of heavenly shows: he has not learned this yet, and falls as dead before it—when lo, the voice of him that was and is and is for evermore, telling him not to be afraid—for the very reason, the one only reason, that he is the first and the last, the living one!

SII. 167

The reason then for not fearing before God is, that he is all-glorious, all-perfect. Our being needs the all-glorious, all-perfect God. The children can do with nothing less than the Father; they need the Infinite One.

SII. 170

Fear is a wholesome element in the human economy; they are merely silly who would banish it from all association with religion.

WM

There is no religion in fear; religion is love, and love casts out fear; but until a man has love, it is well he should have fear.

WM

Until a man has love, it is well he should have fear. So long as there are wild beasts about, it is better to be afraid than secure.

WM. chap. II

The disgrace of fearing anything except doing wrong, few human beings are capable of conceiving, fewer still of actually believing.

WW. 38

Feelings

It is not always those who utter best who feel most.

DE

We were not meant to be creatures of feeling; we were meant to be creatures of conscience, first of all, and then of consciousness toward God—a sense of his presence; and if we go on, the feeling will come all right. Our feelings will blossom as a rose just from the very necessity of things.

GW. 11

It is the deed that stirs the man; it is the thing you do, and not what you feel.

GW. 11

There is no such thing in the world as liberty, except under the law of liberty; that is, the acting according to the essential laws of our own being—not our feelings which come and go.

GW. 28

Our feelings, especially where a wretched self is concerned, are notably illogical.

PF. 136

A man does not live by his feelings any more than by bread, but by the Truth, that is, the Word, the will, the uttered Being of God.

SI. 141

He could not see, could not feel him near; and yet it is "*My* God" that he cries. Thus the will of Jesus, in the very moment when his faith seems about to yield, is finally triumphant. It has no *feeling* now to support it, no beatific vision to absorb it. It stands naked in his soul and tortured, as he stood naked and scourged before Pilate. Pure and simple and surrounded by fire, it declares for God.

SI. 166

So long as we have nothing to say to God, nothing to do with him, save in the sunshine of the mind when we feel him near us, we are poor creatures, willed upon, not willing. . . . And how in such a condition do we generally act? Do we sit mourning over the loss of our feelings? or worse, make frantic efforts to rouse them?

SI. 172

God does not, by the instant gift of his Spirit, make us always feel right, desire good, love purity, aspire after him and his will. Therefore either he will not, or he cannot. If he will not, it must be because it would not be well to do so. If he cannot, then he would not if he could; else a better condition than God's is conceivable to the mind of God—a condition in which he could save the creatures whom he has made, better than he can save them.

SI. 173

Troubled soul, you are not bound to feel, but you are bound to arise. God loves you whether you feel or not. You cannot love when you will, but you are bound to fight the hatred in you to the last. Try not to feel good when you are not good, but cry to him who is good. He changes not because you change. No, he has an especial tenderness of love toward you for that you are in the dark and have no light, and his heart is glad when you do arise and say, "I will go to my Father." For he sees you through all the gloom through which you cannot see him. Will his will. Say to him: "My God, I am very dull and low and hard; but you are wise and high and tender, and you are my God. I am your child. Forsake me not."

SI. 177

They had a feeling, or a feeling had them, until another feeling came and took its place. When a feeling was there, they felt as if it would never go; when it was gone they felt as if it had never been; when it was returned, they felt as if it had never gone.

WM. chap. 16

Forgiveness

If he pleases to forget anything, then he can forget it. And I think that is what he does with our sins—that is, after he has got them away from us, once we are clean from them altogether. It would be a dreadful thing if he forgot them before that.

AN. chap. 28

If he were not . . . constantly pardoning our sins, what would become of us! We should soon be overwhelmed with our wrongdoings, not to say our mistakes and blunders.

DG. 20

God's forgiveness is as the burst of a spring morning into the heart of winter; and he will make us pay the uttermost farthing: to let us go without that, would be the forgiveness of a demon, not of the eternally loving God.

DG. 42

Unable to believe in the forgiveness of their Father in heaven, imagining him not at liberty to forgive or incapable of forgiving forthright; not really believing him God our Savior, but a God bound, either in his own nature or by a law above him and compulsory upon him, to exact some recompense or satisfaction for sin, a multitude of teaching men have taught their fellows that Jesus came to bear our punishment and save us from hell. They have represented a result as the object of his mission—the said result nowise to be desired by true man save as consequent on the gain of his object.

HG. 8

You are such a Father, that you take our sins from us and throw them behind your back.

M

Christ is God's Forgiveness.

SI. 76

Forgiveness can never be indifference. Forgiveness is love toward the unlovely.

SI. 78

God is forgiving us every day—sending from between him and us our sins and their fogs and darkness. Witness the shining of his sun and the falling of his rain, the filling of their hearts with food and gladness, that he loves them that love him not. When some sin that we have committed has clouded all our horizon, and hidden him from our eyes, he, forgiving us, ere we are, and that we may be, forgiven, sweeps away a path for this his forgiveness to reach our hearts, that it may be causing our repentance destroy the wrong, and make us able even to forgive ourselves. For some are too proud to forgive themselves, until the forgiveness of God has had its way with them.

SI. 79

God's love is ever in front of his forgiveness.

SI. 80

God's love is the prime mover, ever seeking to perfect his forgiveness, which latter needs the human condition for its consummation. The love is perfect, working out the forgiveness. God loves where he cannot yet forgive—where forgiveness in the full sense is as yet simply impossible, because no contact of hearts is possible, because that which lies between has not yet begun to yield to his holy destruction.

SI. 80

When the man has, with his whole nature, cast away his sin, there is no room for forgiveness anymore, for God dwells in him, and he in God.

SI. 81

It may be an infinitely less evil to murder a man than to refuse to forgive him. The former may be the act of a moment of passion: the latter is the heart's choice. It is spiritual murder, the worst, to hate, to brood over the feeling that excludes, that, in our microcosm, kills the image, the idea of the hatred.

SI. 83

God holds the unforgiving man with his hand, but turns his face away from him. If, in his desire to see the face of his Father, he turns his own toward his brother, then the face of God turns round and seeks his, for then the man may look on God and not die. With our forgiveness to our neighbor, in flows the consciousness of God's forgiveness to us; or even with the effort, we become capable of believing that God can forgive us.

SI. 84

No man who will not forgive his neighbor, can believe that God is willing, yea wanting, to forgive *him*. . . . If God said "I forgive you" to a man who hated his brother, and if (as is impossible) that voice of forgiveness should reach the man, what would it mean to him? How would the man interpret it? Would it not mean to him, "You may go on hating. I do not mind it. You have had great provocation and are justified in your hate"? No doubt God takes what wrong there is, and what provocation there is, into the account: but the more provocation, the more excuse that can be urged for the hate, the more reason, if possible, that the hater should be delivered from the hell of his hate.

SI. 84

Man would think, not that God loved the sinner, but that he forgave the sin, which God never does. *Every* sin meets with its due fate—inexorable expulsion from the paradise of God's Humanity.

SI. 85

He loves the sinner so much that he cannot forgive him in any other way than by banishing from his bosom the demon that possesses him.

SI. 85

Forgiveness . . . is not love merely, but love *conveyed as love* to the erring, so establishing peace toward God, and forgiveness toward our neighbor.

SI. 86

All sin is unpardonable. There is no compromise to be made with it. We shall not come out except clean, except having paid the uttermost farthing.

SI. 88

Without the Spirit no forgiveness can enter the man to cast out the satan. Without the Spirit to witness with his spirit, no man could know himself forgiven, even if God appeared to him and said so. The full forgiveness is . . . when a man feels that God is forgiving him; and this cannot be while he opposes himself to the very essence of God's will.

SI. 89

For him that speaks against the Spirit of Truth, against the Son of God revealed *within* him, he is beyond the teaching of that Spirit now. For how shall he be forgiven? The forgiveness would touch him no more than a wall of stone. Let him know what it is to be without the God he has denied. Away with him to the Outer Darkness! Perhaps *that* will make him repent.

SI. 97

It is the divine glory to forgive.

SI. 229

It were a small boon indeed that God should forgive men, and not give himself. It would be but to give them back themselves, and less than God just as he is will not comfort men for the essential sorrow of their existence. Only God the gift can turn that sorrow into essential joy: Jesus came to give them God, who is eternal life.

SII. 44

You require us to forgive: surely you forgive freely! Bound you may be to destroy evil, but are you bound to keep the sinner alive that you may punish him, even if it make him no better?

SII. 191

They tell me I must say *for Christ's sake*, or you will not pardon: it takes the very heart out of my poor love to hear that you will not pardon me except because Christ has loved me; but I give you thanks that nowhere in the record of your Gospel does one of your servants say any such word.

SII. 191

"All manner of sin and blasphemy," the Lord said, "shall be forgiven men; but the blasphemy against the spirit shall not be forgiven." God speaks, as it were, in this manner: "I forgive you everything. Not a word more shall be said about your sins—only come out of them; come out of the darkness of your exile; come into the light of your home, of your birthright, and do evil no more. Lie no more; cheat no more; oppress no more; slander no more; envy no more; be neither greedy nor vain; love your neighbor as I love you; be my good child; trust in your Father. I am light; come to me, and you shall see things as

I see them, and hate the evil thing. I will make you love the thing which now you call good and love not. I forgive all the past."

SIII. 177

"I thank thee, Lord, for forgiving me, but I prefer staying in the darkness: forgive me that too"—"No; that cannot be. The one thing that cannot be forgiven is the sin of choosing to be evil, of refusing deliverance. It is impossible to forgive that. It would be to take part in it."

SIII. 178

To side with wrong against right, with murder against life, cannot be forgiven. The thing that is past I pass, but he who goes on doing the same, annihilates this my forgiveness, makes it of no effect. Let a man have committed any sin whatever, I forgive him; but to choose to go on sinning—how can I forgive that?

SIII. 178

God may forgive and punish; and he may punish and not forgive, that he may rescue.

SIII. 181

He cannot forgive the man who will not come to the light because his deeds are evil. Against that man his fatherly heart is *moved with indignation.*

SIII. 181

Ask him to forgive you and make you clean and set things right for you. If he will not do it, then he is not the savior of men, and was wrongly named Jesus.

TW. 58

Some things seem the harder to forgive the greater the love. It is but a false seeming, thank God, and comes only of selfishness, which makes both the love and the hurt seem greater than they are.

WW. 531

Freedom

To serve God, the source of our being, our own glorious Father, is freedom; in fact, is the only way to get rid of all bondage.

AN

While God's will is our law, we are but a kind of noble slaves; when his will is our will, we are free children.

DE, bk. III. 12

When a man heartily confesses, leaving excuse to God, the truth makes him free; he knows that the evil has gone from him, as a man knows that he is cured of his plague.

DG

If we, choosing, against our liking, do the right, go on so until we are enabled by doing it to see into the very loveliness and essence of the right, and know it to be altogether beautiful, and then at last never think of doing evil, but delight with our whole souls in doing the will of God, why then, do you not see, we combine the two, and we are free indeed, because we are acting like God out of the essence of our nature, knowing good and evil, and choosing the good with our whole hearts and delighting in it?

GW. 32

He is the refuge of the oppressed. By its very woes, as by bitterest medicine, he is setting the world free from sin and woe.

HG. 65

Those who cannot see how the human will should be free in dependence upon the will of God, have not realized that the will of God made the will of man; that, when most it pants for freedom, the will of man is the child of the will of God, and therefore that there can be no natural opposition or strife between them.

MOL. 55

A free will is not the liberty to do whatever one likes, but the power of doing whatever one sees ought to be done, even in the very face of otherwise overwhelming impulse. There lies freedom indeed.

MOL. 56

A great deal of what is called freedom of thought is merely the self-assertion which would persuade itself of a freedom it would possess but cannot without an effort too painful for ignorance and self-indulgence. The man would *feel* free without being free.

MOL. 122

To assert one's individuality is not necessarily to be free: it *may* indeed be but the outcome of absolute slavery.

MOL. 122

God made our individuality as well as, and a greater marvel than, our dependence; made our *apartness* from himself, that freedom should bind us divinely dearer to himself.

SI. 175

It may seem to a man the first of his slavery when it is in truth the beginning of his freedom. Never soul was set free without being made to feel its slavery.

SII. 38

Our Lord teaches us that the truth, known by obedience to him, will make us free: our freedom lies in living the truth of our relations to God and man.

SII. 189

One who went to the truth by mere impulse would be a holy animal, not a true man. Relations, truths, duties, are shown to the man away beyond him, that he may *choose* them and be a child of God, choosing righteousness like him. Hence the whole sad victorious human tale and the glory to be revealed.

SIII. 73

Obeying the will that is the cause of his being, the cause of that which demands of itself to be true, and that will being righteousness and love and truth, he begins to stand on the apex of his being, to know himself divine. He begins to feel himself free.

SIII. 78

The truth—not as known to his intellect, but as revealed in his own sense of being true, known by his essential consciousness of his divine condition, without which his nature is neither his own nor God's—trueness has made him free.

SIII. 78

Not any abstract truth, not all abstract truth, not truth its very metaphysical self, held by purest insight into entity, can make any man free; but the truth done, the truth loved, the truth lived by the man; the truth *of* and not merely *in* the man himself; the honesty that makes the man himself a child of the honest God.

SIII. 79

When my being is consciously and willedly in the hands of him who called it to live and think and suffer and be glad—given back to him by a perfect obedience—I thenceforward breathe the breath, share the life of God himself. Then I am free, in that I am true—which means one with the Father. And freedom knows itself to be freedom.

SIII. 81

The liberty of the God who would have his creature free, is in contest with the slavery of the creature who would cut his own stem from his root that he might call it his own and love it; who rejoices in his own consciousness, instead of the life of that consciousness; who poises himself on the tottering wall of his own being, instead of the rock on which that being is built. Such a one regards his own dominion over himself—the rule of the greater by the less, inasmuch as the conscious self is less than the self—as a freedom infinitely larger than the range of the universe of God's being. If he says, "At least I have it my own way!" I answer, you do not know what is your way and what is not. You know nothing of whence your impulses, your desires, your tendencies, your likings come. They may spring now from some chance, as of nerves diseased; now from some roar of a wandering bodiless devil; now from some infant hate in your heart; now from the greed or lawlessness of some ancestor you would be ashamed of if you knew him; or, it may be, now from some far-piercing chord of a heavenly orchestra; the moment it comes up into your consciousness, you call it your own way, and glory in it.

SIII. 91

"You shall know the truth, and the truth shall make you free. I am the truth, and you shall be free as I am free. To be free, you must be sons like me. To be free you must *be* that which you have to be, that which you are created. To be free you must give the answer of sons to the Father who calls you. To be free you must fear nothing but evil, care for nothing but the will of the Father, hold to him in absolute confidence and infinite expectation. He alone is to be trusted."

SIII. 96

The only free man, then, is he who is a child of the Father. He is a servant of all, but can be made the slave of none: he is a son of the lord of the universe. He is in himself, in virtue of his truth, free. He is in himself a king. For the Son rests his claim to royalty on this, that *he was born and came into the world to bear witness to the truth.*

SIII. 97

Free Will

He has set before us a way that we may turn, and, of our own free will, run back to him, embrace the Father's knees, and be lifted to the Father's heart.

GW. 28

God has . . . put us just so far away from him that we can exercise the divine thing in us, our own will, in returning toward our source. Then we shall learn the fact that we are infinitely more great and blessed in being the outcome of a perfect self-constituting will, than we could be by the conversion of any imagined independence of origin into fact for us—a truth no man *can* understand, feel, or truly acknowledge, save in proportion as he has become one with his perfect origin, the will of God.

MOL. 54

Those who cannot see how the human will should be free in dependence on the will of God, have not realized that the will of God made the will of man; that, when most it pants for freedom, the will of man is the child of the will of God, and therefore that there can be no natural opposition or strife between them. Nay, more, the whole labor of God is that the will of man should be free as his will is free—in the same way that his will is free—by the perfect love of the man for that which is true, harmonious, lawful, creative.

MOL. 55

If a man say, "But might not the will of God make my will with the intent of overriding and enslaving it?" I answer, such a will could not create, could not be God, for it involves the false and contrarious. That would be to make a will in order that it might be no will. To create in order to uncreate is something else than divine.

MOL. 55

A free will is not the liberty to do whatever one likes, but the power of doing whatever one sees ought to be done, even in the very face of otherwise overwhelming impulse. There lies freedom indeed.

MOL. 56

God gives us room *to be*; does not oppress us with his will; "stands away from us," that we may act from ourselves, that we may exercise the pure will for good. Do not, therefore, imagine me to mean that we can do anything of ourselves without God. If we choose the right at last, it is all God's doing, and only the more his that it is ours, only in a far more marvelous way his than if he had kept us filled with all holy impulses precluding the need of choice. For up to this very point, for this very point, he has been educating us, leading us, pushing us, driving us, enticing us, that we may choose him and his will, and so be tenfold more his children, of his own best making, in the freedom of the will found our own first in its loving sacrifice to him, for which in his grand fatherhood he has been thus working from the foundations of the earth, than we could be in the most ecstatic worship flowing from the divinest impulse, without this *willing* sacrifice.

SI. 174

The stronger the pure will of the man to be true; the freer and more active his choice; the more definite his individuality, ever the more is the man and all that is his, Christ's. Without him he could not have been; being, he could not have become capable of truth; capable of truth, he could never have loved it; loving and desiring it, he could not have attained to it.

SIII. 80

He gives us the will wherewith to will, and the power to use it, and the help needed to supplement the power, whatever in any case the need may be; but we ourselves must will the truth, and for that the Lord is waiting, for the victory of God his Father in the heart of his child. In this alone can he see of the travail of his soul, in this alone be satisfied. The work is his, but we must take our willing share.

SIII. 80

Gifts/Giver/Giving

The gift which makes all other gifts a thousandfold in value, is the gift of the Holy Spirit, the spirit of the child Jesus, who will take of the things of Jesus, and show them to you—make you understand them, that is—so that you shall see them to be true, and love him with all your heart and soul, and your neighbor as yourselves.

AN. 208

The glory of that Father is not in knowing himself God, but in giving himself away—in creating and redeeming and glorifying his children.

HG. 89

To create for the knowledge of himself, and then not give himself, would be injustice even to cruelty; and if God give himself, what other reward—there can be no *further*—is not included, seeing he is Life and all her children—the All in all?

HG. 197

In giving, a man receives more than he gives, and the *more* is in proportion to the worth of the thing given.

MM

His gifts are to the overflowing of the cup; but when the cup would overflow, he deepens its hollow and widens its brim. Our Lord is profuse like his Father, yea, will, at his own sternest cost, be lavish to his brethren.

MOL. 24

What a mighty gift of God is this very common thing—these eyes to see with—that light which enlightens the world, this sight which is the result of both.

MOL. 67

God is exhaustless in giving where the human receiving holds out.

MOL. 138

A man might throw a lordly gift to his fellow, like a bone to a dog, and damn himself in the deed. You may insult a dog by the way you give him his bone.

PF. 207

He gives himself to us—shall not we give ourselves to him? Shall we not give ourselves to each other whom he loves?

SI. 21

For God to give a man because he asked for it that which was not in harmony with his laws of truth and right, would be to damn him—to cast him into outer darkness.

SI. 25

Our God, we will trust you. Shall we not find you equal to our faith? One day, we shall laugh ourselves to scorn that we looked for so little from you; for your giving will not be limited by our hoping.

SI. 60

Every highest human act is just a giving back to God of that which he first gave to us. "You, God, have given me: here again is your gift. I send my spirit home." Every act of worship is a holding up to God of what God has made us. "Here, Lord, look what I have received: feel with me in what you have made me, in this your own bounty, my being. I am your child, and know not how to thank you save by uplifting the heave-offering of the overflowing of your life, and calling aloud, 'It is yours: it is mine. I am yours, and therefore I am mine.'"

SI. 182

I give myself back to you. Take me, soothe me, refresh me, "make me over again." Am I going out into the business and turmoil of the day, where so many temptations may come to do less honorably, less faithfully, less kindly, less diligently than the Ideal Man would have me do?—Father, into your hands.

SI. 184

Are you so well satisfied with what you are, that you have never sought eternal life, never hungered and thirsted after the righteousness of God, the perfection of your being? If this latter be your condition, then be comforted; the Master does not require of you to sell what you have and give to the poor. *You* follow him! *You* go with him to preach good tidings!—you who care not for righteousness! You are not one whose company is desirable to the Master. Be comforted, I say: he does not want you; he will not ask you to open your purse for him; you may give or withhold; it is nothing to him. What! is he to be obliged to one outside his kingdom—to the untrue, the ignoble, for money?

SII. 26

It were a small boon indeed that God should forgive men, and not give himself. It would be but to give them back themselves; and less than God just as he is will not comfort men for the essential sorrow of their existence. Only God the gift can turn that sorrow into essential joy: Jesus came to give them God, who is eternal life.

SII. 44

It is hard on God, when his children will not let him give; when they carry themselves so that he must withhold his hand, lest he harm them. To take no care that they acknowledge whence their help comes, would be to leave them worshipers of idols, trusters in that which is not.

SII. 48

The real good of every gift it is essential, first, that the giver be in the gift—as God always is, for he is love—and next, that the receiver know and receive the giver in the gift.

SII. 74

No gift unrecognized as coming from God is at its own best; therefore many things that God would gladly give us, things even that we need because we are, must wait until we ask for them, that we may know whence they come: when in all gifts we find him, then in him we shall find all things.

SII. 74

Every gift of God is but a harbinger of his greatest and only sufficing gift—that of himself.

SII. 74

God is ever seeking to lift us up into the sharing of his divine nature; God's kings, such men, namely, as with Jesus have borne witness to the truth, share his glory even on the throne of the Father. See the grandeur of the creative love of the Holy! Nothing less will serve it than to have his children, through his and their suffering, share the throne of his glory! If such be the perfection of the Infinite, should that perfection bring him under bonds and difficulties, and not rather set him freer to do the thing he would in the midst of opposing forces? If his glory be in giving himself, and we must share therein, giving ourselves, why should we not begin here and now?

SII. 87

Man finds it hard to get what he wants, because he does not want the best; God finds it hard to give, because he would give the best, and man will not take it.

SII. 142

The God and Father of Jesus Christ could never possibly be satisfied with less than giving himself to his own!

SII. 143

The careless soul receives the Father's gifts as if it were a way things had of dropping into his hand . . . yet is he ever complaining, as if someone were accountable for the checks which meet him at every turn. For the good that comes to him, he gives no thanks—who is there to thank? At the disappointments that befall him he grumbles—there must be someone to blame!

SII. 225

The true share, in the heavenly kingdom throughout, is not what you have to keep, but what you have to give away. The thing that is mine is the thing I have with the power to give it. The thing I have *no* power to give a share in, is nowise mine; the thing I cannot share with everyone, cannot be essentially my own.

SIII. 252

The heart of man cannot hoard. His brain or his hand may gather into its box and hoard, but the moment the thing has passed into the box, the heart has lost it and is hungry again. If a man would *have*, it is the Giver he must have. . . . Therefore all that he makes must be free to come and go through the heart of his child; he can enjoy it only as it passes, can enjoy only its life, its soul, its vision, its meaning, not itself.

SP. chap. 32

It is not what God can give us, but God that we want.

WC. chap. 59

His end in giving us being is that his humblest creature should at length possess himself, and be possessed by him.

WM. 29

God

Because our God is so free from stain, so loving, so unselfish, so good, so altogether what he wants us to be, so holy, therefore all his works declare him in beauty; his fingers can touch nothing but to mold it into loveliness; and even the play of his elements is in grace and tenderness of form.

AN. 211

The only name that will do for our God is, "I am that I am." There is no describing it: "I am." And for us, friends, when we are nearest God, it is just when we are in the knowledge that he *is*.

The Christian World Pulpit

No other than the God exactly like Christ can be the true God.

DG. 15

It is better to trust in work than in money; God never buys anything, and is forever at work.

DG. 22

It is God we want, not heaven! God, not an imputed righteousness! remission, not mere letting off! love, not endurance for the sake of another, even if that other be the one loveliest of all.

DG. 27

Easy to please is he—hard indeed to satisfy.

DG. 42

Omnipotence that could do and not do the same thing at the same moment, were an idea too absurd for mockery; an omnipotence that could at once make a man a free man, and leave him a self-degraded slave—make him the very likeness of God, and good only because he could not help being good, would be an idea of the same character—equally absurd, equally self-contradictory.

HG. 20

God's education makes use of terrible extremes. There are last that shall be first, and first that shall be last.

HG. 150

The glory of God's mysteries is, that they are for his children to look into.

HG. 162

If a man can believe that there is a God, he may well believe that, having made creatures capable of hungering and thirsting for him, he must be capable of speaking a word to guide them in their feeling after him.

MOL. 2

If he is a grand God, a God worthy of being God, yea (his metaphysics even may show the seeker), if he is a God capable of being God, he will speak the clearest grandest word of guidance which he can utter intelligible to his creatures.

MOL. 2

God ministers to us so gently, so stolenly, as it were, with such a quiet, tender, loving absence of display, that men often drink of his wine, as these wedding guests drank, without knowing whence it comes—without thinking that the giver is beside them, yea, in their very hearts.

MOL. 21

The God of the light is a faithful, loving, upright, honest, and self-denying being, yea utterly devoted to the uttermost good of those whom he has made.

MOL. 67

To God alone we live or die. Let us fall, as, thank him, we must, into his hands. Let him judge us. Posterity may be wiser than we; but posterity is not our judge.

MOL. 166

In God's dealings there are no exceptions. His laws are universal as he is infinite.

MOL. 192

Destruction itself is holy. It is as if the Eternal said, "I will show myself; but think not to hold me in any form in which I come. The form is not I." The still small voice is ever reminding us that the Lord is neither in the earthquake nor the wind nor the fire; but in the lowly heart that finds him everywhere. The material can cope with the eternal only in virtue of everlasting evanescence.

MOL. 259

God is all in all. He is ever seeking to get down to us—to be the divine man to us. And we are ever saying, "That be far from you, Lord!" We are careful, in our unbelief, over the divine dignity, of which he is too grand to think.

SI. 20

The devotion of God to his creatures is perfect? that he does not think about himself but about them? that he wants nothing for himself, but finds his blessedness in the outgoing of blessedness?

SI. 21

He has not two thoughts about us. With him all is simplicity of purpose and meaning and effort and end—namely, that we should be as he is, think the same thoughts, mean the same things, possess the same blessedness.

SI. 22

He is utterly true and good to us, nor shall anything withstand his will.

SI. 22

The God who is ever uttering himself in the changeful profusions of nature; who takes millions of years to form a soul that shall understand him and be blessed; who never needs to be, and never is, in haste; who welcomes the simplest thought of truth or beauty as the return for seed he has sown on the old fallows of eternity; who rejoices in the response of a faltering moment to the age-long cry of his wisdom in the streets; the God of music, of painting, of building, the Lord of Hosts, the God of mountains and oceans; whose laws go forth from one unseen point of wisdom, and thither return without an atom of loss; the God of history working in time unto Christianity; this God is the God of little children, and he alone can be perfectly, abandonedly simple and devoted. The deepest, purest love of a woman has its well-spring in him. Our longing desires can no more exhaust the fullness of the treasures of the Godhead, than our imagination can touch their measure. Of him not a thought, not a joy, not a hope of one of his creatures can pass unseen; and while one of them remains unsatisfied, he is not Lord over all.

SI. 23

God is not mocked; that he is not a man that he should repent; that tears and entreaties will not work on him to the breach of one of his laws; that for God to give a man because he asked for it that which was not in harmony with his laws of truth and right, would be to damn him—to cast him into the outer darkness. And he knows that out of that prison the childlike, imperturbable God will let no man come until he has "paid the last cent."

SI. 25

That man is perfect in faith who can come to God in the utter dearth of his feelings and desires, without a glow or an aspiration, with the weight of low thoughts, failures, neglects, and wandering forgetfulness, and say to him, "You are my refuge."

SI. 25

Our God is a consuming fire.

SI. 28

He is a consuming fire, that only that which cannot be consumed may stand forth eternal. It is the nature of God, so terribly pure that it destroys all that is not pure as fire, which demands like purity in our worship. He will have purity. It is not that the fire will burn us if we do not worship thus; but that the fire will burn us until we worship thus; yea, will go on burning within us after all that is foreign to it has yielded to its force, no longer with pain and consuming, but as the highest consciousness of life, the presence of God.

SI. 31

At all events, if God showed them these things, God showed them what was true. It was a revelation of himself. He will not put on a mask. He puts on a face. He will not speak out of flaming fire if that flaming fire is alien to him, if there is nothing in him for that flaming fire to reveal. Be his children ever so brutish, he will not terrify them with a lie.

SI. 34

If a man resists the burning of God, the consuming fire of Love, a terrible doom awaits him, and its day will come. He shall be cast into the outer darkness who hates the fire of God. What sick dismay shall then seize upon him! For let a man think and care ever so little about God, he does not therefore exist without God. God is here with him, upholding, warming, delighting, teaching him—making life a good thing to him. God gives him himself, though he knows it not. But when God withdraws from a man as far as that can be without the man's ceasing to be; when the man feels himself abandoned, hanging in a ceaseless vertigo of existence upon the verge of the gulf of his being, without support, without refuge, without aim, without end—for the soul has no weapons wherewith to destroy herself—with no inbreathing of joy, with nothing to make life good; then will he listen in agony for the faintest sound of life from the closed door; then, if the moan of suffering humanity ever reaches the ear of the outcast of darkness, he will be ready to rush into the very heart of the Consuming Fire to know life once more, to change this terror of sick negation, of unspeakable death, for that region of painful hope.

SI. 46

He is not afraid of your presumptuous approach to him. It is you who are afraid to come near him. He is not watching over his dignity. It is you who fear to be sent away as the disciples would have sent away the little children. It is you who think so much about your souls and are so afraid of losing your life, that you dare not draw near to the Life of life, lest it should consume you.

SI. 60

There is a chamber also (O God, humble and accept my speech)—a chamber in God himself, into which none can enter but the one, the individual, the peculiar man—out of which chamber that man has to bring revelation and strength for his brethren. This is that for which he was made—to reveal the secret things of the Father.

SI. 112

The Father said, That is a stone. The Son would not say, That is a loaf. No one creative *fiat* shall contradict another. The Father and the Son are of one mind.

SI. 138

To say *you are God*, without knowing what the *you* means—of what use is it?

God is a name only, except we know *God.* Our Lord did not care to be so acknowledged.

SI. 151

The Lord himself *will* be bound by the changeless laws which are the harmony of the Father's being and utterance. He will *be,* not seem. He will be, and thereby, not therefore, seem.

SI. 153

God does not, by the instant gift of his Spirit, make us always feel right, desire good, love purity, aspire after him and his will. Therefore either he will not, or he cannot. If he will not, it must be because it would not be well to do so. If he cannot, then he would not if he could; else a better condition than God is conceivable to the mind of God—a condition in which he could save the creatures whom he has made, better than he can save them.

SI. 173

He wants to make us in his own image, *choosing* the good, *refusing* the evil. How should he effect this if he were *always* moving us from within, as he does at divine intervals, toward the beauty of holiness? God gives us room *to be*; does not oppress us with his will; "stands away from us," that we may act from ourselves, that we may exercise the pure will for good.

SI. 174

God is, and shall be, All in all.

SI. 214

God changes not. Once God he is always God.

SI. 234

He who has God, has all things, after the fashion in which he who made them has them. To man, woman, and child, I say—if you are not content, it is because God is not with you as you need him, not with you as he would be with you, as you *must* have him: for you need him as your body never needed food or air, need him as your soul never hungered after joy, or peace, or pleasure.

SII. 36

No man can have the consciousness of God with him and not be content; I mean that no man who has not the Father so as to be eternally content in him alone, can possess a sunset or a field of grass or a mine of gold or the love of a fellow creature according to its nature—as God would have him possess it—in the eternal way of inheriting, having, and holding.

SII. 36

Help is always within God's reach when his children want it—their design, to show what God is—not that Jesus was God, but that his Father was God—that is, was what he was, for no other kind of God could be, or be worth believing in, no other notion of God be worth having.

SII. 44

Nor will God force any door to enter in. He may send a tempest about the house; the wind of his admonishment may burst doors and windows, yea, shake the house to its foundations; but not then, not so, will he enter.

SII. 56

We know that the wind blows: why should we not know that God answers prayer?

SII. 66

The glory of God is to give himself.

SII. 73

That God cannot interfere to modify his plans, interfere without the change of a single law of his world, is to me absurd. If we can change, God can change, else is he less free than we—his plans, I say, not principles, not ends: God himself forbid!—change them after divine fashion, above our fashions as the heavens are higher than the earth.

SII. 81

All things are possible with God, but all things are not easy. It is easy for him *to be*, for there he has to do with his own perfect will: it is not easy for him to create—that is, after the grand fashion which alone will satisfy his glorious heart and will, the fashion in which he is now creating us. In the very nature of being—that is, God—it must be hard—and divine history shows how hard—to create that which shall be not himself, yet like himself.

SII. 139

I believe that there is nothing good for me or for any man but God, and more and more of God, and that alone through knowing Christ can we come nigh to him.

SII. 154

Verily God must be terrible to those that are far from him: for they fear he will do, yea, he is doing with them what they do not, cannot desire, and can ill endure.

SII. 158

God being what he is, a God who loves righteousness; a God who, rather than do an unfair thing, would lay down his Godhead, and assert himself in ceasing to be; a God who, that his creature might not die of ignorance, died as much as a God could die, and that is divinely more than man can die, to give him himself; such a God, I say, may well look fearful from afar to the creature who recognizes in himself no imperative good; who fears only suffering, and has no aspiration—only wretched ambition! But in proportion as such a creature comes nearer, grows toward him in and for whose likeness he was begun; in proportion, that is, as the eternal right begins to disclose itself to him; in proportion as he becomes capable of the idea that his kind belongs to him as he could never belong to himself; approaches the capacity of seeing and understanding that his individuality can be perfected only in the love of his neighbor, and that his being can find its end only in oneness with the source from which it came; in proportion, I do not say as he sees these things, but as he nears the possibility of seeing them, will his terror at the God of his life abate; though far indeed from surmising the bliss that awaits him, he is drawing more nigh to the goal of his nature, the central secret joy of sonship to a God who loves righteousness and hates iniquity, does nothing he would not permit in his creature, demands nothing of his creature he would not do himself.

SII. 161

The fire of God, which is his essential being, his love, his creative power, is a fire unlike its earthly symbol in this, that it is only at a distance it burns—that the farther from him, it burns the worse, and that when we turn and begin to approach him, the burning begins to change to comfort, which comfort will grow to such bliss that the heart at length cries out with a gladness no other gladness can reach, "Whom have I in heaven but you? and there is none upon earth that I desire besides you!"

SII. 162

If then any child of the Father finds that he is afraid before him, that the thought of God is a discomfort to him, or even a terror, let him make haste—let him not linger to put on any garment, but rush at once in his nakedness, a true child, for shelter from his own evil and God's terror, into the salvation of the Father's arms.

SII. 163

Endless must be our terror, until we come heart to heart with the fire-core of the universe, the first and the last and the living One.

SII. 166

Men would rather receive salvation from God than God their salvation.

SII. 178

God *owes* something to his creature. This is the beginning of the greatest discovery of all—that God owes *himself* to the creature he has made in his image, for so he has made him incapable of living without him. This, his creatures' highest claim on him, is his divinest gift to them. For the fulfilling of this their claim he has sent his Son, that he may himself, the Father of him and of us, follow into our hearts. Perhaps the worst thing in a theology constructed out of man's dull *possible*, and not out of the being and deeds and words of Jesus Christ, is the impression it conveys throughout that God acknowledges no such obligation.

SII. 182

It is God to whom every hunger, every aspiration, every desire, every longing of our nature is to be referred; he made all our needs—made us the creatures of a thousand necessities—and have we no claim on him? Nay, we have claims innumerable, infinite; and his one great claim on us is that we should claim our claims of him.

SII. 183

The root of every heresy popular in the church draws its nourishment merely and only from the soil of unbelief. The idea that God would be God all the same, as glorious as he needed to be, had he not taken on himself the divine toil of bringing home his wandered children, had he done nothing to seek and save the lost, is false as hell. Lying for God could go no farther. As if the idea of God admitted of his being less than he is, less than perfect, less than all-in-all, less than Jesus Christ! less than Love absolute, less than entire unselfishness! As if the God revealed to us in the New Testament were not his own perfect necessity of lovingkindness, but one who has made himself better than, by his own nature, by his own love, by the laws which he willed the laws of his existence, he needed to be! They would have it that, being unbound, he deserves the greater homage! So it might be, if he were not our Father.

SII. 187

To think of the living God not as our Father, but as one who has condescended greatly, being nowise, in his own willed grandeur of righteous nature, bound to do as he has done, is killing to all but a slavish devotion. It is to think of him as nothing like the God we see in Jesus Christ.

SII. 188

God could not be satisfied with himself without doing all that a God and Father could do for the creatures he had made—that is, without doing just what he has done, what he is doing, what he will do, to deliver his sons and daughters, and bring them home with rejoicing.

SII. 189

Then truly our hearts shall be jubilant, because you are what you are—infinitely beyond all we could imagine. You will humble and raise us up. You have given yourself to us that, having you, we may be eternally alive with your life. We run within the circle of what men call your wrath, and find ourselves clasped in the zone of your love!

SII. 192

Lest it should be possible that any unchildlike soul might, in arrogance and ignorance, think to stand on his rights *against* God, and demand of him this or that after the will of the flesh, I will lay before such a possible one some of the things to which he has a right. . . . He has a claim to be compelled to repent; to be hedged in on every side; to have one after another of the strong, sharp-toothed sheep-dogs of the Great Shepherd sent after him, to thwart him in any desire, foil him in any plan, frustrate him of any hope, until he come to see at length that nothing will ease his pain, nothing make life a thing worth having, but the presence of the living God within him.

SII. 193

God's eternal denial of himself, revealed in him who for our sakes in the flesh took up his cross daily, will have been developed in the man; his eternal rejoicing will be in God—and in his fellows, before whom he will cast his glad self to be a carpet for their walk, a footstool for their rest, a stair for their climbing.

SII. 215

We must draw our life, by the uplooking, acknowledging will, every moment fresh from the living one, the causing life, not glory in the mere consciousness of health and being. It is God feeds us, warms us, quenches our thirst.

SII. 216

God is the heritage of the soul in the ownness of origin; man is the offspring of his making will, of his life; God himself is his birthplace; God is the self that makes the soul able to say *I too, I myself.*

SII. 263

As to what the life of God is to himself, we can only know that we cannot know it—even that not being absolute ignorance, for no one can see that, from its very nature, he cannot understand a thing without therein approaching that thing in a most genuine manner.

SIII. 6

What is the deepest in God? His power? No, for power could not make him what we mean when we say *God.* Evil could, of course, never create one atom; but let us understand very plainly, that a being whose essence was only power would be such a negation of the divine that no righteous worship could be offered him: his service must be fear, and fear only. Such a being, even were he righteous in judgment, yet could not be God. The God himself whom we love could not be righteous were he not something deeper and better still than we generally mean by the word—but, alas, how little can language say without seeming to say something wrong!

SIII. 8

"God is; Jesus is not dead; nothing can be going wrong, however it may look so to hearts unfinished in childness."

SIII. 23

He is not a God who hides himself, but a God who made that he might reveal; he is consistent and one throughout.

SIII. 31

His very being is love and equity and self-devotion, and he will have his children such as himself—creatures of love, of fairness, of self-devotion to him and their fellows. I was born to bear witness to the truth—in my own person to be the truth visible—the very likeness and manifestation of the God who is true. My very being is his witness. Every fact of me witnesses him. He is the truth, and I am the truth.

SIII. 103

He is God beyond all that heart hungriest for love and righteousness could to eternity desire.

SIII. 148

I believe that God is just like Jesus, only greater yet, for Jesus said so. I believe that God is absolutely, grandly beautiful, even as the highest soul of man counts beauty, but infinitely beyond that soul's highest idea—with the beauty that creates beauty, not merely shows it, or itself exists beautiful.

SIII. 154

There is no way of thought or action which we count admirable in man, in which God is not altogether adorable. There is no loveliness, nothing that makes man dear to his brother man, that is not in God, only it is infinitely better in God. He is God our Savior. Jesus is our Savior because God is our Savior. He is the God of comfort and consolation. He will soothe and satisfy his children better than any mother her infant. The only thing he will not give them is—leave to stay in the dark.

SIII. 171

The light of our life, our sole, eternal, and infinite joy, is simply God—God—God—nothing but God, and all his creatures in him. He is all and in all, and the children of the kingdom know it. He includes all things; not to be true to anything he has made is to be untrue to him. God is truth, is life; to be in God is to know him and need no law. Existence will be eternal Godness.

SIII. 221

It cannot be that any creature should know him as he is and not desire him. In proportion as we know him we must desire him, until at length we live in and for him with all our conscious heart.

SIII. 222

God is not a God that hides, but a God that reveals. His whole work in relation to the creatures he has made—and where else can lie his work?—is revelation—the giving them truth, the showing of himself to them, that they may know him, and come nearer and nearer to him, and so he have his children more and more of companions to him. That we are in the dark about anything is never because he hides it, but because we are not yet such that he is able to reveal that thing to us.

That God could not do the thing at once which he takes time to do, we may surely say without irreverence. His will cannot finally be thwarted; where it is thwarted for a time, the very thwarting subserves the working out of a higher part of his will. He gave man the power to thwart his will, that, by means of that same power, he might come at last to do his will in a higher kind and way than would otherwise have been possible to him. God sacrifices his will to man that man may become such as himself, and give all to the truth; he makes man able to do wrong, that he may choose and love righteousness.

SIII. 229

God will be fair to you—so fair!—fair with the fairness of a father loving his own—who will have you clean, who will neither spare you any needful shame, nor leave you exposed to any that is not needful. The thing we have risen above, is dead and forgotten, or if remembered, there is God to comfort us. "If any man sin, we have a comforter with the Father." We may trust God with our past as heartily as with our future. It will not hurt us so long as we do not try to hide things, so long as we are ready to bow our heads in hearty shame where it is fit we should be ashamed. For to be ashamed is a holy and blessed thing.

SIII. 238

All things are God's, not as being in his power—that of course—but as coming from him. The darkness itself becomes light around him when we think that verily he hath created the darkness, for there could have been no darkness but for the light.

SIII. 251

Without God there would not even have been nothing; there would not have existed the idea of nothing, any more than any reality of nothing, but that he exists and called *something* into being.

SIII. 252

Nothingness owes its very name and nature to the being and reality of God. There is no word to represent that which is not God, no word for the *where* without God in it; for it is not, could not be. So I think we may say that the inheritance of the saints is the share each has in the Light.

SIII. 252

All the light is ours. God is all ours. Even that in God which we cannot understand is ours. If there were anything in God that was not ours, then God would not be one God. I do not say we must, or can ever know all in God; not throughout eternity shall we ever comprehend God, but he is our Father, and must think of us with every part of him—so to speak in our poor speech; he must know us, and that in himself which we cannot know, with the same thought, for he is one. We and that which we do not or cannot know, come together in his thought.

SIII. 253

The infinitude of God can only begin and only go on to be revealed, through his infinitely differing creatures—all capable of wondering at, admiring, and loving each other, and so bound all in one in him, each to the others revealing him.

SIII. 253

The ways of God go down into microscopic depths, as well as up into telescopic heights—and with more marvel, for there lie the beginnings of life: the immensities of stars and worlds all exist for the sake of less things than they. So with mind; the ways of God go into the depths yet unrevealed to us; he knows his horses and dogs as we cannot know them, because we are not yet pure sons of God.

SIII. 254

God is, and all is well. All that is needed to set the world right enough for me—and no empyrean heaven could be right for me without it—is, that I care for God as he cares for me; that my will and desires keep time and harmony with his music; that I have no thought that springs from myself apart from him; that my individuality have the freedom that belongs to it as born of his individuality, and be in no slavery to my body, or my ancestry, or my prejudices, or any impulse whatever from region unknown; that I be free by obedience to the law of my being, the live and live-making will by which life is life, and my life is myself. What springs from myself and not from God, is evil; it is a perversion of something of God's. Whatever is not of faith is sin; it is a stream cut off—a stream that cuts itself off from its source, and thinks to run on without it. But light is my inheritance through him whose life is the light of men, to wake in them the life of their father in heaven. Loved be the Lord who in himself generated that life which is the light of men!

SIII. 261

"And the thing that makes me gladdest of all, is just that God is what he is. To know that such a One is God over us, and in us, makes of very being a most precious delight."

SF

God is Love, and God is all and in all! He is no abstraction, but the one eternal Individual! In him Love evermore breaks forth anew into fresh personality in every new consciousness, in every new child of the one creating Father. In every burning heart, in every thing that hopes and fears and is, Love is the creative presence, the center, the sources of life, yea, Life itself; yea, God himself!

SF. 17

He would not be God if he could not or would not do for his creature what that creature can not do for himself, and must have done for him or lose his life.

TW. 62

Nothing is so deadening to the divine as an habitual dealing with the outsides of holy things.

TW. chap. 74

The only perfect idea of life is a unit, self-existent and creative. That is, God, the only One. But to this idea, in its kind, must every life, to be complete as life, correspond; and the human correspondence to self-existence is that the man should round and complete himself by taking in to himself his Origin; by going back and in his own will adopting that Origin. . . . Then has he completed the cycle by turning back upon his history, laying hold of his Cause, and willing his own being in the will of the only I AM.

TW. chap. 76

The only perfect idea of life is—a unit, self-existent and creative. That is, God, the only one. But to this idea, in its kind, must every life, to be complete as life, correspond.

TW. 76

All about us, in earth and air, wherever eye or ear can reach there is a power ever breathing itself forth in signs, now in a daisy, now in a windwaft, a cloud, a sunset; a power that holds constant and sweetest relation with the dark and silent world within us. . . . The same God who is in us, and upon whose tree we are the buds, if not yet the flowers, also is all about us—inside, the Spirit; outside, the Word. And the two are ever trying to meet in us; and when they meet, then the sign without, and the longing within, become one in light, and the man no more walketh in darkness, but knoweth whither he goeth.

TW. 82

In God we live every commonplace as well as most exalted moment of our lives.

WM

Any salvation short of God is no salvation at all.

WM

What God remembers, he thinks of, and what he thinks of, *is*.

WM. 11

Great in goodness, yea absolutely good, God must be, to have a right to make us—to compel our existence, and decree its laws!

WM. 35

Complaint against God is far nearer to God than indifference about him.

WM. chap. 39

Awfully omnipotent is God. For he wills, effects, and perfects the thing which, because of the bad in us, he has to carry out in suffering and sorrow, his own and his Son's.

WW. 23

God and Man

Until a man knows that he is one of God's family, living in God's house, with God upstairs, as it were, while he is at his work or his play in a nursery below-stairs, he can't feel comfortable.

AN. 100

When one has learned to seek the honor that comes from God only, he will take the withholding of the honor that comes from men very quietly indeed.

AN. 173

"I say, you are gods." The children of God must be gods in some sense. Little gods, indeed, but what is their completion and salvation? "You shall sit down with me in my throne, even as I am set down with my Father in his throne."

The Christian World Pulpit

I think God has sometimes great trouble in separating us far enough from himself that he can look round and know us.

The Christian World Pulpit

It is a profound, absolute fact that our relation to God is infinitely nearer than any relation by nature. Our mother does not make us; we come forth of her, but forth also of the very soul of God. We are nearer, unspeakably nearer, infinitely and unintelligibly (to our very poor intellects) nearer to God than to the best, loveliest, dearest mother on the face of the earth.

The Christian World Pulpit

It is God and man, and that is real religion. It is not this observation and that observation; it is my soul and his soul, and then my hands to do his will. That is real religion.

The Christian World Pulpit

"And isn't God a man—and ever so much more than a man?"

DG

God and his sorrows and his joys are the man's inheritance!

DG

The finite that dwells in the infinite, and in which the infinite dwells, is finite no longer. Those who are thus children indeed, are little gods, the divine brood of the infinite Father.

HG. 68

Diversity is in and from God; peculiarity, in and from man. The real man is the divine idea of him; the man God had in view when he began to send him forth out of thought into thinking; the man he is now working to perfect by casting out what is not he, and developing what is he. But in God's real men, that is, his ideal men, the diversity is infinite; he does not repeat his creations; every one of his children differs from every other, and in every one the diversity is lovable.

HG. 110

He only who knows God a little can at all understand man.

HG. 118

When a man gets up and goes out and discharges an obligation, he is an individual; to him God has spoken, and he has opened his ears to hear: God and that man are henceforth in communion.

M. 48

If there be a God at all, it is absurd to suppose that his ways of working should be such as to destroy his side of the highest relation that can exist between him and those whom he has cared to make—to destroy, I mean, the relation of the will of the Creator to the individual will of his creature.

MOL. 105

To arouse the higher, the hopeful, the trusting nature of a man; to cause him to look up into the unknown region of mysterious possibilities—the God so poorly known—is to do infinitely more for a man than to remove the pressure of the direst evil without it. I will go further: To arouse the hope that there may be a God with a heart like our own is more for the humanity in us than to produce the absolute conviction that there is a being who made the heaven and the earth and the sea and the fountains of waters. Jesus is the express image of God's substance, and in him we know the heart of God. To nourish faith in himself was the best thing he could do for the man.

MOL. 197

Whence I came and whither I go are dark: how can I live in peace without the God who ordered it thus? Faith is my only refuge—an absolute belief in a being so much beyond myself, that he can do all for this *me* with utter satisfaction to this *me*, protecting all its rights, jealously as his own from which they spring, that he may make me at last one with himself who is my deeper self, inasmuch as his thought of me is my life. And not to know him, even if I could go on living and happy without him, is death.

MOL. 215

No God to help one to be good now! no God who cares whether one is good or not! if a God, then one who will not give his creature time enough to grow good, even if he is growing better, but will blot him out like a raindrop! Great God, forbid—if you are. If you are not, then this, like all other prayers, goes echoing through the soulless vaults of a waste universe, from the thought of which its peoples recoil in horror. Death, then, is genial, soul-begetting, and love-creating; and Life is nowhere, save in the imaginations of the children of the grave. Whence, then, oh! whence came those their imaginations? Death, you are not my father! Grave, you are not my mother! I come of another kind, nor shall you usurp dominion over me.

MOL. 218

Man is not master in his own house because he is not master in himself, because he is not a law unto himself—is not himself obedient to the law by which he exists. Harmony, that is law, alone is power. Discord is weakness. God alone is perfect, living, self-existent law.

MOL. 225

The essential truth of God it must be that creates its own visual image in the sun that enlightens the world: when man who is the image of God is filled with the presence of the eternal, he too, in virtue of his divine nature thus for the moment ripened to glory, radiates light from his very person.

MOL. 278

The true man can be satisfied only with a God of magnificence.

PF

God is man, and infinitely more. Our Lord became flesh, but did not *become* man. He took on him the form of man: he was man already. And he was, is, and ever shall be divinely childlike. He could never have been a child if he would ever have ceased to be a child, for in him the transient found nothing. Childhood belongs to the divine nature.

SI. 19

The devotion of God to his creatures is perfect? that he does not think about himself but about them? that he wants nothing for himself, but finds his blessedness in the outgoing of blessedness?

SI. 21

The God who is ever uttering himself in the changeful profusions of nature; who takes millions of years to form a soul that shall understand him and be blessed; who never needs to be, and never is, in haste; who welcomes the simplest thought of truth or beauty as the return for seed he has sown upon the old fallows of eternity; who rejoices in the response of a faltering moment to the age-long cry of his wisdom in the streets; the God of music, of painting, of building, the Lord of Hosts, the God of mountains and oceans; whose laws go forth from one unseen point of wisdom, and thither return without an atom of loss; the God of history working in time unto Christianity; this God is the God of little children, and he alone can be perfectly, abandonedly simple and devoted. The deepest, purest love of a woman has its wellspring in him. Our longing desires can no more exhaust the fullness of the treasures of the Godhead, than our imagination can touch their measure. Of him not a thought, not a joy, not a hope of one of his creatures can pass unseen; and while one of them remains unsatisfied, he is not Lord over all.

SI. 23

There is a great difference between a mystery of God that no man understands, and a mystery of God laid hold of, let it be but by one single man.

SI. 42

The Divine creates the Human, has the creative power in excess of the Human. It is the Divine forgiveness that, originating itself, creates our forgiveness, and therefore can do so much more. It can take up all our wrongs, small and great, with their righteous attendance of griefs and sorrows, and carry them away from between our God and us.

SI. 76

The true name is one which expresses the character, the nature, the being, the *meaning* of the person who bears it. It is the man's own symbol—his soul's picture, in a word—the sign which belongs to him and to no one else. Who can give a man this, his own name? God alone. For no one but God sees what the man is, or even, seeing what he is, could express in a name-word the sum and harmony of what he sees. To whom is this name given? To him that overcomes. When is it given? When he has overcome. Does God then not know what a man is going to become? As surely as he sees the oak which is put there lying in the heart of the acorn. Why then does he wait until the man has become by overcoming ere he settles what his name shall be? He does not wait; he knows his name from the first. But as—although repentance comes because God pardons—yet the man becomes aware of the pardon only in the repentance; so it is only when the man has become his name that God gives him the stone with the name upon it, for then first can he understand what his name signifies. It is the blossom, the perfection, the completion, that determines the name; and God foresees that from the first, because he made it so; but the tree of the soul, before its blossom comes, cannot understand what blossom it is to bear, and could not know what the word meant, which, in representing its own unarrived completeness, named itself. Such a name cannot be given until the man *is* the name.

SI. 106

Not only . . . has each man his individual relation to God, but each man has his peculiar relation to God. He is to God a peculiar being, made after his own fashion, and that of no one else; for when he is perfected he shall receive the new name which no one else can understand. Hence he can worship God as no man else can worship him—can understand God as no man else can understand him. This or that man may understand God more, may understand God better than he, but no other man can understand God *as* he understands him.

SI. 110

The name is one "which no man knows except he that receives it."

SI. 110

For each, God has a different response. With every man he has a secret—the secret of a new name. In every man there is a loneliness, an inner chamber of peculiar life into which God only can enter. I say not it is *the innermost chamber.*

SI. 111

There is a chamber also—(O God, humble and accept my speech)—a chamber in God himself, into which none can enter but the one, the individual, the peculiar man—out of which chamber that man has to bring revelation and strength for his brethren. This is that for which he was made—to reveal the secret things of the Father.

SI. 112

By his creation . . . each man is isolated with God; each, in respect of his peculiar making, can say, "*my* God"; each can come to him alone, and speak with him face to face, as a man speaks with his friend. There is no *massing* of men with God. When he speaks of gathered men, it is a spiritual *body,* not a *mass.* For in a body every smallest portion is individual, and therefore capable of forming a part of the body.

SI. 112

Each of us is a distinct flower or tree in the spiritual garden of God—precious, each for his own sake, in the eyes of him who is even now making us—each of us watered and shone upon and filled with life, for the sake of his flower, his completed being, which will blossom out of him at last to the glory and pleasure of the great gardener. For each has within him a secret of the Divinity; each is growing toward the revelation of that secret to himself, and so to the full reception, according to his measure, of the divine.

SI. 112

Each man . . . is in God's sight worth.

SI. 113

God must be God *in* man before man can know that he is God, or that he has received aright, and for that for which it was spoken, any one of his words.

SI. 143

To put God to the question in any other way than by saying, "What will you have me do?" is an attempt to compel God to declare himself, or to hasten his work. . . . The man is therein dissociating himself from God so far that, instead of acting by the divine will from within, he acts in God's face, as it were, to see what he will do. Man's first business is, "What does God want me to do?" not "What will God do if I do so and so?"

SI. 148

So long as we have nothing to say to God, nothing to do with him, save in the sunshine of the mind when we feel him near us, we are poor creatures, willed upon, not willing; reeds, flowering reeds, it may be, and pleasant to behold, but only reeds blown about of the wind; not bad, but poor creatures.

SI. 172

If we choose the right at last, it is all God's doing, and only the more his that it is ours, only in a far more marvelous way his than if he had kept us filled with all holy impulses precluding the need of choice. For up to this very point, for this very point, he has been educating us, leading us, pushing us, driving us, enticing us, that we may choose him and his will, and so be tenfold more his children, of his own best making, in the freedom of the will found our own first in its loving sacrifice to him, for which in his grand fatherhood he has been thus working from the foundations of the earth, than we could be in the most ecstatic worship flowing from the divinest impulse, without this *willing* sacrifice.

SI. 174

In God alone can man meet man. In him alone the converging lines of existence touch and cross not.

SI. 196

The whole constitution of human society exists for the express end, I say, of teaching the two truths by which man lives, Love to God and Love to Man.

SI. 206

He is made for the All, for God, who is the All, is his life. And the essential joy of his life lies abroad in the liberty of the All.

SI. 215

God withholds that man may ask.

SII. 73

God has so far withdrawn from the man, that he is conscious only of that from which he has withdrawn. In the midst of the live world he cared for nothing but himself; now in the dead world he is in God's prison, his own separated self. He would not believe in God because he never saw God; now he doubts if there be such a thing as the face of a man—doubts if he ever really saw one, ever anything more than dreamed of such a thing: he never came near enough to human being, to know what human being really was—so may well doubt if human beings ever were, if ever he was one of them.

SII. 109

After doubt comes reasoning on the doubt: "The only one must be God! I know no one but myself: I must myself be God—none else!" Poor helpless dumb devil!—his own glorious lord god! Yes, he will imagine himself that same resistless force which, without his will, without his knowledge, is the law by which the sun burns, and the stars keep their courses, the strength that drives all the engines of the world. His fancy will give birth to a thousand fancies, which will run riot like the mice in a house but just deserted: he will call it creation, and *his*. Having no reality to set them beside, nothing to correct them by; the measured order, harmonious relations, and sweet graces of God's world nowhere for him; what he thinks, will be, for lack of what God thinks, the man's realities: what others can he have! Soon, misery will beget on imagination a thousand shapes of woe, which he will not be able to rule, direct, or even distinguish from real presences—a whole world of miserable contradictions and cold-fever-dreams.

SII. 109

The most frightful idea of what could, to his own consciousness, befall a man, is that he should have to lead an existence with which God had nothing to do. The thing could not be; for being that is caused, the causation ceasing, must of necessity cease. It is always in, and never out of God, that we can live and do.

SII. 110

Everything must at length be subject to man, as it was to The Man. When God can do what he will with a man, the man may do what he will with the world: he may walk on the sea like his Lord; the deadliest thing will not be able to hurt him: "He who believes in me, the works that I do shall he do also; and greater than these shall he do."

SII. 126

Man finds it hard to get what he wants, because he does not want the best; God finds it hard to give, because he would give the best, and man will not take it.

SII. 142

The man to whom God is all in all, who feels his life-roots hid with Christ in God, who knows himself the inheritor of all wealth and worlds and ages, yea, of power essential and in itself, that man has begun to be alive indeed.

SII. 146

When the man bows down before a power that can account for him, a power to whom he is no mystery as he is to himself; a power that knows whence he came and whither he is going; who knows why he loves this and hates that, why and where he began to go wrong; who can set him right, longs indeed to set him right, making of him a creature to look up to himself without shadow of doubt, anxiety, or fear, confident as a child whom his father is leading by the hand to the heights of happy-making truth, knowing that where he is wrong, the father is right and will set him right; when the man feels his whole being in the embrace of self-responsible paternity—then the man is bursting into his flower; then the truth of his being, the eternal fact at the root of his new name, his real nature, his idea—born in God at first, and responsive to the truth, the being of God, his origin—begins to show itself; then his nature is almost in harmony with itself.

SIII. 77

Nothing but the heart-presence, the humanest sympathy, and whatever deeper thing else may be betwixt, the creating Truth and the responding soul, could make a man go on hoping, until at last he forget himself, and keep open house for God to come and go.

SIII. 80

The man who really knows God, is, and always will be, content with what God, who is the very self of his self, shall choose for him; he is entirely God's, and not at all his own. His consciousness of himself is the reflex from those about him, not the result of his own turning in of his regard upon himself. It is not the contemplation of what God has made him, it is the being what God had made him, and the contemplation of what God himself is, and what he has made his fellows, that gives him his joy. He wants nothing, and feels that he has all things, for he is in the bosom of his Father, and the thoughts of his Father come to him. He knows that if he needs anything, it is his before he asks it; for his Father has willed him, in the might and truth of his fatherhood; to be one with himself.

SIII. 223

Those who think their affairs too insignificant for God's regard, will justify themselves in lying crushed under their seeming ruin. Either we live in the heart of an eternal thought, or we are the product and sport of that which is lower than we.

WM. 4

God only can be ours perfectly; nothing called property can be ours at all.

WM. 32

There is something in the very presence and actuality of a thing to make one able to bear it; but a man may weaken himself for bearing what God intends him to bear, by trying to bear what God does not intend for him to bear.

WM. 40

God cares nothing about keeping a man respectable; he will give his very self to make of him a true man.

WW

God is the one only person, and it is our personality alone, so far as we have any, that can work with God's perfect personality.

WW

The Lord is mindful of his own. He does not forget because we forget. Horror and pain may come, but not because he forgets—nay, just because he does not forget. That is a thing God never does.

WW. 33

God, Care of

Let God let us know that he is there; it is just to let all the rest go away, all the troubles and anxieties of life, and let God say to our hearts, "Here I am, and here you are: you are in my charge, and nothing can hurt you; every thing is well; I am here in peace, and I am leading you through these dreams of the daytime with all those troubles and pains; I am leading you up to my eternal peace, no dull existence, but with a sense of joy such as I have in my own heart, such joy that compelled me to create in you such joy as you have in the sense that you are my child."

The Christian World Pulpit

If God himself sought to raise his little ones without their consenting effort, they would drop from his foiled endeavor. He will carry us in his arms until we are able to walk; he will carry us in his arms when we are weary with walking; he will not carry us if we will not walk.

HG. 83

The poor, the hungry, the weeping, the hated, may lament their lot as if God had forgotten them; but God is all the time caring for them. Blessed in his sight now, they shall soon know themselves blessed. "Blessed are you that weep now, for you shall laugh." Welcome words from the glad heart of the Savior!

HG. 149

Either not a sparrow falls to the ground without him, or there is no God, and we are fatherless children.

MOL. 34

Is not God ready to do unto them even as they fear, though with another feeling and a different end from any which they are capable of supposing? He is against sin: in so far as, and while, they and sin are one, he is against them—against their desires, their aims, their fears, and their hopes; and thus he is altogether and always *for them.*

SI. 36

God has cared to make me for himself.

SI. 115

To be something to God—is not that praise enough? To be a thing that God cares for and would have complete for himself, because it is worth caring for—is not that life enough?

SI. 115

Because we easily imagine ourselves in want, we imagine God ready to forsake us.

SII. 44

The care of the disciples was care for the day, not for the morrow; the word *morrow* must stand for any and every point of the future. The next hour, the next moment, is as much beyond our grasp and as much in God's care, as that a hundred years away. Care for the next minute is just as foolish as care for the morrow, or for a day in the next thousand years—in neither can we do anything, in both God is doing everything. Those claims only of the morrow which have to be prepared today are of the duty of today; the moment which coincides with work to be done, is the moment to be minded; the next is nowhere until God has made it.

SII. 46

We have to do with God who can, not with ourselves where we cannot; we have to do with the Will, with the Eternal Life of the Father of our spirits, and not with the being which we could not make, and which is his care. He is our care; we are his; our care is to will his will; his care, to give us all things. This is to deny ourselves.

SII. 217

God is in every creature that he has made, and in their needs he is needy, and in all their afflictions he is afflicted.

TW

One thing is sure—that God is doing his best for *every* man.

WW. 39

God as Creator

I would rather be what God chose to make me, than the most glorious creature that I could think of. For to have been thought about—born in God's thoughts—and then made by God, is the dearest, grandest, most precious thing in all thinking.

DE. bk. 19

He himself both takes and gives time for the things he most desires, else would he never have made the world.

DG. 11

The Perfect Heart could never have created us except to make us wise, loving, obedient, honorable children of our Father in heaven.

DG. 27

Diversity is in and from God; peculiarity, in and from man. The real man is the divine idea of him; the man God had in view when he began to send him forth out of thought into thinking; the man he is now working to perfect by casting out what is not he, and developing what is he. But in God's real men, that is, his ideal men, the diversity is infinite; he does not repeat his creations; every one of his children differs from every other, and in every one the diversity is lovable. God gives in his children an analysis of himself, an analysis that will never be exhausted. It is the original God-idea of the individual man that will at length be given, without spot or blemish, into the arms of love.

HG. 110

A man who has not created himself, can never secure himself against the inroad of the glorious terror of that Goodness which was able to utter him into being, with all its possible wrongs and repentances. The fact that a man has never, up to any point yet, been aware of aught beyond himself, cannot shut him out who is beyond him, when at last he means to enter.

ML. 65

God made man for lordly skies, great sunshine, gay colors, free winds, and delicate odors; and however the fogs may be needful for the soul, right gladly does he send them away, and cause the dayspring from on high to revisit his children. While they suffer he is brooding over them an eternal day, suffering with them, but rejoicing in their future. He is the God of the individual man, or he could be no God of the race.

MOL. 28

If there be a God at all, it is absurd to suppose that his ways of working should be such as to destroy his side of the highest relation that can exist between him and those whom he had cared to make—to destroy, I mean, the relation of the will of the Creator to the individual will of his creature.

MOL. 105

To arouse the hope that there may be a God with a heart like our own is more for the humanity in us than to produce the absolute conviction that there is a being who made the heaven and the earth and the sea and the fountains of waters.

MOL. 197

How God creates, no man can tell. But as man is made in God's image, he may think about God's work, and dim analogies may arise out of the depth of his nature which have some resemblance to the way in which God works. I say then, that, as we are the offspring of God—the children of his will, like as the thoughts move in a man's mind, we live in God's mind. When God thinks anything, then that thing *is*. His thought of it is its life. Everything is because God thinks it into being.

MOL. 226

It is in virtue of the absolute harmony in him, his perfect righteousness, that God can create at all. If man were in harmony with this, if he too were righteous, he would inherit of his Father a something in his degree correspondent to the creative power in him; and the world he inhabits, which is but an extension of his body, would, I think, be subject to him in a way surpassing his wildest dreams of dominion, for it would be the perfect dominion of holy law—a virtue flowing to and from him through the channel of a perfect obedience.

MOL. 229

All destruction is for creation—that, even for this, death alone is absolutely destroyed—that, namely, which stands in the way of the outgoing of the Father's will, then only completing its creation when men are made holy.

MOL. 258

The wrath will consume what they *call* themselves; so that the selves God made shall appear.

SI. 44

God who has made us can never be far from any man who draws the breath of life—nay, must be in him: not necessarily in his heart, as we say, but still in him.

SI. 92

By his creation, then, each man is isolated with God; each, in respect of his peculiar making, can say, "*my* God"; each can come to him alone, and speak with him face to face, as a man speaks with his friend. There is no *massing* of men with God. When he speaks of gathered men, it is as a spiritual *body*, not a *mass*. For in a body every smallest portion is individual, and, therefore, capable of forming a part of the body.

SI. 112

Shall I not tell him my troubles—how he, even he, has troubled me by making me?—how unfit I am to be that which I am?—that my being is not to me a good thing yet?

SII. 65

All things are possible with God, but all things are not easy. . . . In the very nature of being—that is, God—it must be hard—and divine history shows how hard—to create that which shall be not himself, yet like himself. The problem is, so far to separate from himself that which must yet on him be ever and always and utterly dependent, that it shall have the existence of an individual, and be able to turn and regard him, choose him, and say, "I will arise and go to my Father." . . . I imagine the difficulty of doing this thing, of effecting this creation, this separation from himself such that will in the creature shall be possible—I imagine, I say, that for it God must begin inconceivably far back in the infinitesimal regions of beginnings.

SII. 139

God is life, and the will-source of life. In the outflowing of that life, I know him; and when I am told that he is love, I see that if he were not love he would not, could not create. I know nothing deeper in him than love, nor believe there is in him anything deeper than love—nay, that there can be anything deeper than love. The being of God is love, therefore creation. I imagine that from all eternity he has been creating. As he saw it was not good for man to be alone, so has he never been alone himself—from all eternity the Father has had the Son.

SII. 141

Let no soul think that to say God undertook a hard labor in willing that many sons and daughters should be sharers of the divine nature, is to abate his glory! The greater the difficulty, the greater is the glory of him who does the thing he has undertaken—without shadow of compromise, with no half-success, but with a triumph of absolute satisfaction to innumerable radiant souls!

SII. 142

This is the beginning of the greatest discovery of all—that God owes *himself* to the creature he has made in his image, for so he has made him incapable of living without him. This, his creatures' highest claim upon him, is his divinest gift to them. For the fulfilling of this their claim he has sent his

Son, that he may himself, the Father of him and of us, follow into our hearts.

SII. 182

To speak as a man—the more of vital obligation he lays on himself, the more children he creates, with the more claims on him, the freer is he as Creator and giver of life, which is the essence of his Godhead: to make scope for his essence is to be free.

SII. 188

Could a creator make a creature whose well-being should not depend on himself?

SIII. 89

Nothing can come so close as that which creates; the nearest, strongest, dearest relation possible is between Creator and created. Where this is denied, the schism is the widest; where it is acknowledged and fulfilled, the closeness is unspeakable.

SIII. 91

To live without the eternal creative life is an impossibility; freedom from God can only mean an incapacity for seeing the facts of existence, an incapability of understanding the glory of the creature who makes common cause with his Creator in his creation of him, who wills that the lovely will calling him into life and giving him choice, should finish making him, should draw him into the circle of the creative heart, to joy that he lives by no poor power of his own will, but is one with the causing life of his life, in closest breathing and willing, vital and claimant oneness with the life of all life. Such a creature knows the life of the infinite Father as the very flame of his life, and joys that nothing is done or will be done in the universe in which the Father will not make him all of a sharer that it is possible for perfect generosity to make him. If you say this is irreverent, I doubt if you have seen the God manifest in Jesus.

SIII. 92

I have seen his face and heard his voice in the face and the voice of Jesus Christ; and I say this is our God, the very one whose being the Creator makes it an infinite gladness to be the created.

SIII. 147

I repent me of the ignorance wherein I ever said that God made man out of nothing: there is no nothing out of which to make anything; God is all in all, and he made us out of himself.

WW. 35

God, Existence of

You won't believe this, and therefore naturally you can't quite believe that there is a God at all; for, indeed, a being that was not all light would be no God at all. If you would but let him teach you, you would find your perplexities melt away like the snow in spring, until you could hardly believe you had ever felt them. No arguing will convince you of a God; but let him once come in, and all argument will be tenfold useless to convince you that there is no God. Give God justice. Try him as I have said.

AN. 286

But do not think that God is angry with you because you find it hard to believe. It is not so; that is not like God. He knows perfectly well that what the scientific man calls truth is simply an impossibility with regard to God. When you read a proposition of Euclid, there is a kind of proof which commends itself to your mind and understanding; you say, "So it is, and it cannot be otherwise." But there is no such proof with regard to the mighty God: and God knows it. And therefore I say, if you doubt his existence, he is not angry with you for that.

The Christian World Pulpit

Not all the intellect or metaphysics of the world could prove that there is no God, and not all the intellect in the world could prove that there is a God. If you could prove that there is a God, that implies that you could go all around him, and buttress up his being with your human argument that he should exist.

The Christian World Pulpit

For God alone *is*, and without him we are not. This is not the mere clang of a tinkling metaphysical cymbal; he that endeavors to live apart from God must at length find—not merely that he has been walking in a vain show, but that he has been himself but the phantom of a dream.

DG

Many think it a horrible thing to say there is no God, who never think how much worse a thing it is not to heed him.

HA

Every kind-hearted person who thinks a great deal of being comfortable, and takes prosperity to consist in being well-off, must be tempted to doubt the existence of a God.

ML

If . . . we could prove there is a God, it would be of small avail indeed: we must see him and know him, to know that he was not a demon. But I know no other way of knowing that there is a God but that which reveals *what* he is—the only idea that could be God—shows him in his own self-proving existence—and that way is Jesus Christ as he revealed himself on earth, and as he is revealed afresh to every heart that seeks to know the truth concerning him.

TW. 18

If there be a God . . . then is he God everywhere, and not a maggot can die any more than a Shakespeare be born without him. He is either enough, that is, all in all, or he is not at all.

TW. 40

"My business is not to prove to any other man that there is a God, but to find him for myself. If I should find him, then will be time enough to think of showing him."

TW. 43

If there is no God, annihilation is the one thing to be longed for, with all that might of longing which is the mainspring of human action. In a word, it is not immortality the human heart cries out after, but that immortal, eternal thought whose life is its life, whose wisdom is its wisdom. . . . Dissociate immortality from the living Immortality, and it is not a thing to be desired.

WC. chap. 58

God's beginnings do not *look* like his endings, but they *are* like; the oak *is* in the acorn, though we cannot see it.

WW

God's beginnings are imperceptible, whether in the region of soul or of matter.

WW. 48

Reading my New Testament, I came to see that, if the story of Christ was true, the God that made me was just inconceivably lovely, and that the perfection, the very flower of existence, must be to live the heir of all things, at home with the Father.

WW. 48

God, Face of

The goal of all life is the face of God.

AF

The glory of God is the beauty of Christ's face.

WW. 4

God, Fatherhood of

When people want to walk their own way without God, God lets them try it. And then the devil gets a hold of them. But God won't let him keep them. As soon as they are "wearied in the greatness of their way," they begin to look about for a Savior. And then they find God ready to pardon, ready to help, not breaking the bruised reed—leading them to his own self manifest—with whom no man can fear any longer, Jesus Christ, the righteous lover of men—their Elder Brother—what we call *Big Brother*, you know—one to help them and take their part against the devil, the world, and the flesh, and all the rest of the wicked powers. So you see God is tender—just like the prodigal son's father—only with this difference, that God has millions of prodigals, and never gets tired of going out to meet them and welcome them back, every one as if he were the only prodigal son he had ever had. There's a father indeed!

AN. 263

The Father—the Father—the Father was all in all in the heart of the Son, and because the Father, therefore the children of the Father, all the men and women, savage and refined, throughout the universe.

The Christian World Pulpit

That no keeping but a perfect one will satisfy God, I hold with all my heart and strength; but that there is none else he cares for, is one of the lies of the enemy. What father is not pleased with the first tottering attempt of his little one to walk? What father would be satisfied with anything but the manly step of the full-grown son?

SI. 10

To whom shall a man, whom the blessed God has made, look for what he likes best, but to that blessed God? If we have been indeed enabled to see that God is our Father, as the Lord taught us, let us advance from that truth to understand that he is far more than father—that his nearness to us is beyond the embodiment of the highest idea of father; that the fatherhood of God is but a step toward the Godhood for them that can receive it.

SI. 57

Think, brothers, think, sisters, we walk in the air of an eternal fatherhood. Every uplifting of the heart is a looking up to

The Father. Graciousness and truth are around, above, beneath us, yea, *in* us. When we are least worthy, then, most tempted, hardest, unkindest, let us yet commend our spirits into his hands.

SI. 186

We shall never be able, I say, to rest in the bosom of the Father, until the fatherhood is fully revealed to us in the love of the brothers. For he cannot be our Father, save as he is their Father; and if we do not see him and feel him as their Father, we cannot know him as ours.

SI. 188

The hardest, gladdest thing in the world is, to cry *Father*! from a full heart. I would help whom I may to call thus on the Father.

SII. 115

The refusal to look up to God as our Father is the one central wrong in the whole human affair; the inability, the one central misery: whatever serves to clear any difficulty from the way of the recognition of the Father, will more or less undermine every difficulty in life.

SII. 116

God can no more than an earthly parent be content to have only children: he must have sons and daughters—children of his soul, of his spirit, of his love—not merely in the sense that he loves them, or even that they love him, but in the sense that they love like him, love as he loves. For this he does not adopt them; he dies to give them himself, thereby to raise his own to his heart; he gives them a birth from above; they are born again out of himself and into himself—for he is the one and the all. His children are not his real, true sons and daughters until they think like him, feel with him, judge as he judges, are at home with him, and without fear before him because he and they mean the same thing, love the same things, seek the same ends. For this are we created; it is the one end of our being, and includes all other ends whatever.

SII. 123

He is our Father all the time, for he is true; but until we respond with the truth of children, he cannot let all the father out to us; there is no place for the dove of his tenderness to alight. He is our Father, but we are not his children. Because we are his children, we must become his sons and daughters. Nothing will satisfy him or do for us, but that we be one with our Father! What else could serve! How else should life ever be a good! Because we are the sons of God, we must become the sons of God.

SII. 123

All things were made *through* the Word, but that which was made *in* the Word was life, and that life is the light of men: they who live by this light, that is, live as Jesus lived—by obedience, namely, to the Father, have a share in their own making; the light becomes life in them; they are, in their lower way, alive with the life that was first born in Jesus, and through him has been born in them—by obedience they become one with the Godhead: "As many as received him, to them gave he power to become the sons of God." He does not *make* them the sons of God, but he gives them power to become the sons of God: in choosing and obeying the truth, man becomes the true son of the Father of lights.

SII. 126

While we but obey the law God has laid upon us, without knowing the heart of the Father whence comes the law, we are but slaves—not necessarily ignoble slaves, yet slaves; but when we come to think *with* him, when the mind of the son is as the mind of the Father, the action of the son the same as that of the Father, then is the son *of* the Father, then are we the sons of God.

SII. 127

Children we were; true sons we could never be, save through The Son. He brothers us. He takes us to the knees of the Father, beholding whose face we grow sons indeed. Never could we have known the heart of the Father, never felt it possible to love him as sons, but for him who cast himself into the gulf that yawned between us. In and through him we were foreordained to the sonship: sonship, even had we never sinned, never could we reach without him. We should have been little children loving the Father indeed, but children far from the sonhood that understands and adores.

SII. 129

So are we sons when we begin to cry Father, but we are far from perfected sons. So long as there is in us the least taint of distrust, the least lingering of hate or fear, we have not received the sonship; we have not such life in us as raised the body of Jesus; we have not attained to the resurrection of the dead.

SII. 132

Every child will look in the eyes of the Father, and the eyes of the Father will receive the child with an infinite embrace.

SII. 143

In spite of all our fears and groveling, our weakness, and our wrongs, you will be to us what you are—such a perfect Father as no most loving child-heart on earth could invent the thought of! You will take our sins on yourself, giving us your life to live withal. You bear our griefs and carry our sorrows; and surely you will one day enable us to pay every debt we owe to each other! You will be to us a right generous, abundant Father!

SII. 191

That you do not know me now, as I stand here speaking to you, is that you do not know your own Father, even my Father; that throughout your lives you have refused to do his will, and so have not heard his voice; that you have shut your eyes from seeing him, and have thought of him only as a partisan of your ambitions.

SIII. 37

I believe that God has always done, is always doing his best for every man; that no man is miserable because God is forgetting him; that he is not a God to crouch before, but our Father, to whom the child-heart cries exultant, "Do with me as you will."

SIII. 154

God, Goodness of

If I had not the hope of one day being good like God himself, if I thought there was no escape out of the wrong and badness I feel within me and know I am not able to rid myself of without supreme help, not all the wealth and honors of the world could reconcile me to life.

ML. 42

He is utterly true and good to us, nor shall anything withstand his will.

SI. 22

God chooses to be good, else he would not be God. Man must choose to be good, else he cannot be the son of God. Herein we see the grand love of the Father of men—that he gives them a part, and that a part necessary as his own, in the making of themselves.

SF

God, Image of

It is the business of our human being to know Christ, and nothing else is our business. If it is true that we are made in the image of God, the sole, paramount, all-including and absorbing business of existence is to know that image of God in which we are made, to know it in the living Son of God—the one only ideal man.

The Christian World Pulpit

The things that are really dangerous to us are those that affect the life of the image of the living God; we are so ignorant about that as yet, though it is our deepest nature that there the Father must every moment take care of his child. If he were not, for instance, constantly pardoning our sins, what would become of us! We should soon be overwhelmed with our wrongdoings, not to say our mistakes and blunders.

DG. 20

Surely then inasmuch as man is made in the image of God, nothing less than a love in the image of God's love, all-embracing, quietly excusing, heartily commending, can constitute the blessedness of man; a love not insensible to that which is foreign to it, but overcoming it with good.

DO. 213

Made in the image of God, we see things in the image of his sight.

M. 49

Whatever's no like Christ is no like God.

RF

The truth is this: he wants to make us in his own image, *choosing* the good, *refusing* the evil. How should he effect this if he *were* always moving us from within, as he does at divine intervals, toward the beauty of holiness?

SI. 174

He that is made in the image of God must know him or be desolate.

SII. 61

"But creation is not fatherhood."

Creation in the image of God, is. And if I am not in the image of God, how can the word of God be of any meaning to me? "He called them gods to whom the word of God came," says the Master himself. To be fit to receive his word implies being of his kind. No matter how his image may have been defaced in me: the thing defaced is his image, remains his defaced image—an image yet that can hear his word. What makes me evil and miserable is, that the thing spoiled in me is the image of the Perfect.

SII. 118

Every man is the image of God to every man, and in proportion as we love him, we shall know the sacred fact. The precious thing to human soul is, and one day shall be known to be, every human soul. And if it be so between man and man, how will it not be betwixt the man and his maker, between the child and his eternal Father, between the created and the creating Life?

SII. 155

It is true that nothing but a far closer divinc presence can ever make life a thing fit for a son of man—and that for the simplest of all reasons, that he is made in the image of God, and it is for him absolutely imperative that he should have in him the reality of which his being is the image: while he has it not in him, his being, his conscious self, is but a mask, a spiritual emptiness.

SII. 202

Jesus Christ as he shows himself to our eyes, our hearts, our consciences, he works upon us, and will keep working, until we are changed to the very likeness we have thus mirrored in us; for with his likeness he comes himself, and dwells in us. He will work until the same likeness is wrought out and perfected in us, the image, namely, of the humanity of God, in which image we were made at first, but which could never be developed in us except by the indwelling of the perfect likeness. By the power of Christ thus received and at home in us, we are changed—the glory in him becoming glory in us, his glory changing us to glory.

SIII. 51

I do not know if we may call this having life in ourselves; but it is the waking up, the perfecting in us of the divine life inherited from our Father in heaven, who made us in his own image, whose nature remains in us, and makes it the deepest reproach to a man that he has neither heard his voice at any time, nor seen his shape. He who would thus live must, as a mirror draws into its bosom an outward glory, receive into his "heart of heart" the inward glory of Jesus Christ, *the Truth*.

SIII. 55

God, Knowledge of

To know God as the beginning and end, the root and cause, the giver, the enabler, the love and joy and perfect good, the present one existence in all things and degrees and conditions, is life. And faith, in its simplest, truest, mightiest form, is—to do his will in the one thing revealing itself at the moment as duty. The faith that works miracles is an inferior faith to this—and not what the old theologians call a saving faith.

DG. 1

All knowledge helps to the knowing of God by one who already knows him, inasmuch as there is nothing to be known but has its being in him.

DG. 29

All misery is God *unknown*.

HA. 192

We know what God is in recognizing him as our God.

MOL. 68

The man who can go to sleep without faith in God has yet to learn what being is. He who knows not God cannot, however, have much to lose in losing being.

MOL. 216

I remembered that God was near me. But I did not know what God is then as I know now, and when I thought about him then, which was neither much nor often, my idea of him was not like him; it was merely a confused mixture of other people's fancies about him and my own. I had been told that he was angry with those that did wrong; I had not understood that he loved them all the time, although he was displeased with them and must punish them to make them good.

RB. 35–36

To say *you are God*, without knowing what the *you* means—of what use is it? God is a name only, except we know *God*. Our Lord did not care to be so acknowledged.

SI. 151

The knowledge of the living God *is* eternal life.

SII. 29

To know God present, to have the consciousness of God where he is the essential life, must be absolutely necessary to that life! He that is made in the image of God must know him or be desolate: the child must have the Father! Witness the dissatisfaction, yea desolation of my soul—wretched, alone, unfinished, without him!

SII. 64

That God knows is enough for me; I shall know, if I can know. It would be death to think God did not know; it would be as much as to conclude there was no God to know.

SII. 200

To acknowledge is not to be sure of God.

SII. 201

He who knows God, will find that knowledge open the door of his understanding to all things else. He will become able to behold them from within, instead of having to search wearily into them from without.

SII. 229

Good souls many will one day be horrified at the things they now believe of God. If they have not thought about them, but given themselves to obedience, they may not have done them much harm as yet; but they can make little progress in the knowledge of God, while, if but passively, holding evil things true of him. If, on the other hand, they do think about them, and find in them no obstruction, they must indeed be far from anything to be called a true knowledge of God. But there are those who find them a terrible obstruction, and yet imagine, or at least fear them true: such must take courage to forsake the false in *any* shape, to deny their old selves in the most seemingly sacred of prejudices, and follow Jesus, not as he is presented in the tradition of the elders, but as he is presented by himself, his apostles, and the spirit of truth. There are "traditions of men" after Christ as well as before him, and far worse, as "making of none effect" higher and better things; and we have to look to it, *how we have learned Christ.*

SII. 232

Those who know God, or have but begun to catch a far-off glimmer of his gloriousness, of what he is, regard life as insupportable save God be the All in all, the first and the last.

SII. 254

The man who really knows God, is, and always will be, content with what God, who is the very self of his self, shall choose for him; he is entirely God's, and not at all his own.

SIII. 223

It is only in him that the soul has room. In knowing him is life and its gladness. The secret of your own heart you can never know; but you can know him who knows its secret.

SP. chap. 13

God is God to us not that we may say *he is, but that we may know him*; and when we know him, then we are with him, at home, at the heart of the universe, the heir of all things.

TB. 364

"I cannot see what harm would come of letting us know a little—as much at least as might serve to assure us that there was more of *something* on the other side"—Just this: that, their fears allayed, their hopes encouraged from any lower quarter, men would (as usual) turn away from the Fountain, to the cistern, of life. . . . That there are thousands who would forget God if they could but be assured of such a tolerable state of things beyond the grave as even this wherein we now live, is plainly to be anticipated from the fact that the doubts of so many in respect of religion concentrate themselves, now-a-days upon the question whether there is any life beyond the grave; a question which . . . does not immediately belong to religion at all. Satisfy such people, if you can, that they shall live, and what have they gained? A little comfort perhaps—but a comfort not from the highest source, and possibly gained too soon for their well-being. Does it bring them any nearer to God than they were before? Is he filling one cranny more of their hearts in consequence?

TW. chap. 94

God cannot by searching be found out, cannot be grasped by any mind, yet is ever before us, the One we can best know, the One we must know, the One we cannot help knowing. For his end in giving us being is that his humblest creature should at length possess himself, and be possessed by him.

WM. 29

God, Love of

"Don't you think God is sometimes better to us than we deserve?"

AN. 298

Who taught her that the glory of the Father's love lay in the inexorability of its demands, that it is of his deep mercy that no one can get out until he has paid the last penny.

DG

Every life is between two great fires of love of God; that is, so long as we do not give ourselves up right heartily to him, we fear the fire will burn us. And so it does when we go against its flames and not with them, refusing to burn with the same glorious fire with which God is always burning. When we try to put it out, or get away from it, then indeed it burns.

DG. 20

God's vengeance is as holy a thing as his love, yes, is love, for God is love and God is not vengeance.

HG. 63

Begin to love as God loves, and your grief will assuage; but for comfort wait his time.

HG. 115

Not only does he not claim perfect knowledge, but he disclaims it. He speaks once, at least, to his Father with an *if it be possible.* Those who believe omniscience essential to divinity, will therefore be driven to say that Christ was not divine. This will be their punishment for placing knowledge on a level with love.

MOL. 79

Love and pain seem so strangely one in this world, the wonder is how they will ever be parted. What God must feel like, with this world hanging on to him with all its pains and cries.

PF

If the man resists the burning of God, the consuming fire of Love, a terrible doom awaits him, and its day will come.

SI. 46

There will be danger—danger as everywhere; but he gives more grace. And if the man who has striven up the heights should yet fall from them into the deeps, is there not that fire of God, the consuming fire, which burns and destroys not?

SI. 116

It seems to him then that God does not care for him, and certainly he does not care for God. If he is still humble, he thinks that he is so bad that God cannot care for him. And he then believes for the time that God loves us only because and when and while we love him; instead of believing that God loves us always because he is our God, and that we live only by his love. Or he does not believe in a God at all, which is better.

SI. 172

The law comes to make us long for the needful grace—that is, for the divine condition, in which love is all, for God is Love.

SI. 193

Nor will God force any door to enter in. He may send a tempest about the house; the wind of his admonishment may burst doors and windows, yea, shake the house to its foundations; but not then, not so, will he enter. The door must be opened by the willing hand, ere the foot of Love will cross the threshold. He watches to see the door move from within. Every tempest is but an assault in the siege of love. The terror of God is but the other side of his love; it is love outside the house, that would be inside—love that knows the house is no house, only a place, until it enter—no home, but a tent, until the Eternal dwell there. *Things* must be cast out to make room for their souls—the eternal truths which in things find shape and show.

SII. 56

God is life, and the will-source of life. In the outflowing of that life, I know him; and when I am told that he is love, I see that if he were not love he would not, could not create. I know nothing deeper in him than love, nor believe there is in him anything deeper than love—nay, that there can be anything deeper than love. The being of God is love, therefore creation. I imagine that from all eternity he has been creating.

SII. 141

The unbeliever may easily imagine a better God than . . . common theology . . . offers him; but not the lovingest heart that ever beat can even reflect the length and breadth and depth and height of that love of God which shows itself in his Son—one, and of one mind, with himself.

SII. 143

God must love his creature that looks up to him with hungry eyes—hungry for life, for acknowledgment, for justice, for the possibilities of living that life which the making life has made him alive for the sake of living. The whole existence of a creature is a unit, an entirety of claim upon his Creator: just *therefore*, let him do with me as he will.

SII. 186

Oh the divine generosity that will grant us to be abashed and self-condemned before the Holy!—to come so nigh him as to see ourselves dark spots against his brightness! Verily we must be of his kind, else no show of him could make us feel small and ugly and unclean! Oh the love of the Father, that he should give us to compare ourselves with him, and be buried in humility and shame! To be rebuked before him is to be his.

SII. 205

The Lord did not die to provide a man with the wretched heaven he may invent for himself, or accept invented for him by others; he died to give him life, and bring him to the heaven of the Father's peace; the children must share in the essential bliss of the Father and the Son. This is and has been the Father's work from the beginning—to bring us into the home of his heart, where he shares the glories of life with the Living One, in whom was born life to light men back to the original life. This is our destiny; and however a man may refuse, he will find it hard to fight with God—useless to kick against the goads of his love.

SII. 261

God could not love, could not be love, without making things to love: Jesus has God to love; the love of the Son is responsive to the love of the Father.

SIII. 9

A man might flatter, or bribe, or coax a tyrant; but there is no refuge from the love of God; that love will, for very love, insist on the uttermost farthing.

SIII. 131

The love of the Father is a radiant perfection. Love and not self-love is lord of the universe.

SIII. 132

Such is the mercy of God that he will hold his children in the consuming fire of his distance until they pay the uttermost farthing, until they drop the purse of selfishness with all the dross that is in it, and rush home to the Father and the Son and the many brethren—rush inside the center of the life-giving fire whose outer circles burn.

SIII. 155

The love of God is the perfecting of every love. He is not the God of oblivion, but of eternal remembrance. There is no past with him.

SIII. 195

Nothing but the burning love of God can rid sin out of anywhere.

TW. 82

The love of God is so deep he can be satisfied with nothing less than getting as near as it is possible for the Father to draw nigh to his children—and that is into absolute contact of heart with heart, love with love, being with being.

WW. 12

I well remember feeling as a child that I did not care for God to love me if he did not love everybody: the kind of love I needed was love essential to my nature . . . the love therefore that all men needed, the love that belonged to their nature as the children of the Father, a love he could not give me except he gave it to all men.

WW. 37

God, Need for

It is this formless idea of something at hand that keeps men and women striving to tear from the bosom of the world the secret of their own hopes. How little they know that what they look for in reality is their God!

AF. chap. 26

When misery drives a man to call out to the source of his life—and I take the increasing outcry against existence as a sign of the growth of the race toward a sense of the need of regeneration—the answer, I think, will come in a quickening of his conscience.

HG. 6

The Lord knows what they need; they know only what they want. They want ease; he knows they need purity.

HG. 16

In how many souls has not the very thought of a real God waked a longing to be different, to be pure, to be right! The fact that this feeling is possible, that a soul can become dissatisfied with itself, and desire a change in itself, reveals God as an essential part of its being; for in itself the soul is aware that it cannot be what it would, what it ought—that it cannot set itself right: a need has been generated in the soul for which the soul can generate no supply; a presence higher than itself must have caused that need; a power greater than itself must supply it, for the soul knows its very need, its very lack, is of something greater than itself.

HG. 126

The primal need of the human soul is yet greater than this; the longing after righteousness is only one of the manifestations of it; the need itself is that of *existence not self-existent* for the consciousness of the presence of the causing Self-existent. It is the man's need of God.

HG. 127

Every true want, every genuine need, every God-created hunger, is a thing provided for in the idea of the universe; but no attempt to fill a void otherwise than the Heart of the Universe intended and intends, is or can be anything but a woe. God forgets none of his children—the naughty ones any more than the good.

HG. 149

The correlative of creation is search; that as God has *made* us, we must *find* him.

MOL. 22

God must do only the best, and man is greater and more needy than himself can know.

MOL. 114

Every generation must do its own seeking and its own finding. The fault of the fathers often is that they expect their finding to stand in place of their children's seeking—expect the children to receive that which has satisfied the need of their fathers upon their testimony; whereas rightly, their testimony is not ground for their children's belief, only for their children's search. That search is faith in the bud. No man can be sure until he has found for himself. All that is required of the faithful nature is a willingness to seek.

MOL. 126

In our ignorance lies a force of need, compelling us toward God.

MOL. 222

He who has God, has all things, after the fashion in which he who made them has them. To man, woman, and child, I say—if you are not content, it is because God is not with you, as you need him, not with you as he would be with you, as you *must* have him; for you need him as your body never needed food or air, need him as your soul never hungered after joy, or peace, or pleasure.

SII. 36

He that is made in the image of God must know him or be desolate. . . . Witness the dissatisfaction, yea desolation of my soul—wretched, alone, unfinished, without him.

SII. 61

Every need of God, lifting up the heart, is a seeking of God, is a begging for himself, is profoundest prayer, and the root and inspirer of all other prayer.

SII. 66

He knows little of himself who does not know that he is wretched, and miserable, and poor, and blind, and naked; but until he begins at least to suspect a need, how can he pray?

SII. 68

If you are in any trouble, try whether God will not help you: if you are in no need, why should you ask questions about prayer?

SII. 68

What if the main object in God's idea of prayer be the supplying of our great, our endless need—the need of himself?

SII. 72

Communion with God is the one need of the soul beyond all other need: prayer is the beginning of that communion, and some need is the motive of that prayer.

SII. 72

There could be no riches but for need. God himself is made rich by man's necessity. By that he is rich to give; through that we are rich by receiving.

SII. 76

It is God to whom every hunger, every aspiration, every desire, every longing of our nature is to be referred; he made all our needs—made us the creatures of a thousand necessities—and have we no claim on him? Nay, we have claims innumerable, infinite; and his one great claim on us is that we should claim our claims of him.

SII. 123

It is terrible to represent God as unrelated to us in the way of appeal to his righteousness. How should he be righteous without owing us anything? How would there be any right for the judge of all the earth to do if he owed nothing? Verily he owes us nothing that he does not pay like a God; but it is of the devil to imagine imperfection and disgrace in obligation. So far is God from thinking so that in every act of his being he lays himself under obligation to his creatures. Oh, the grandeur of his goodness, and righteousness, and fearless unselfishness! When doubt and dread invade, and the voice of love in the soul is dumb, what can please the Father of men better than to hear his child cry to him from whom he came, "Here I am, O God! You have made me: give me that which you have made me needing." The child's necessity, his weakness, his helplessness, are the strongest of all his claims.

SII. 184

A created need is a created claim. God is the origin of both need and supply, the father of our necessities, the abundant giver of the good things. Right gloriously he meets the claims of his child! The story of Jesus is the heart of his answer, not primarily to the prayers, but to the divine necessities of the children he has sent out into his universe.

SII. 185

When the soul, or heart, or spirit, or what you please to call that which is the man himself and not his body, sooner or later becomes aware that he needs someone above him, whom to obey, in whom to rest, from whom to seek deliverance from what in himself is despicable, disappointing, unworthy even of his own interest; when he is aware of an opposition in him, which is not harmony; that, while he hates it, there is yet present with him, and seeming to be himself, what sometimes he calls *the old Adam*, sometimes *the flesh*, sometimes *his lower nature*, sometimes *his evil self*; and sometimes recognizes as simply that part of his being where God is not; then indeed is the man in the region of truth, and beginning to come true in himself.

SIII. 76

I am saved—for God is light! My God, I come to you. That you should be yourself is enough for time and eternity, for my soul and all its endless need.

SIII. 167

You must be made miserable, that you may wake from your sleep to know that you need God. If you do not find him, endless life with the living (being) whom you bemoan would become and remain to you unendurable. The knowledge of your own heart will teach you this—not the knowledge you have, but the knowledge that is on its way to you through suffering. Then you will feel that existence itself is the prime of evils without the righteousness that is of God by faith.

SIII. 208

It is when we are most aware of the *factitude* of things that we are most aware of our need of God, and most able to trust in him. . . . The recognition of inexorable reality in any shape, or kind, or way, tends to rouse the soul to the yet more real, to its relations with higher and deeper existence. It is not the hysterical alone for whom the great dash of cold water is good. All who dream life instead of living it, require some similar shock.

WM. chap. 30

God, Presence of

And if we believe that God is everywhere, why should we not think him present even in the coincidences that sometimes seem so strange? For, if he be in the things that coincide, he must be in the coincidence of those things.

AN. chap. 30

Friend, you are close to God, infinitely closer than your imagination can represent to you; and if you do not know it, you are in the very essence a poor, foolish thing—whom God has not forgotten, though.

GW. 4

It is true that, being thus his offspring, God . . . cannot be far from any one of us: were we not in closest contact of creating and created, we could not exist; as we have in us no power to be, so have we none to continue being; but there is a closer contact still, as absolutely necessary to our well-being and highest existence as the other to our being at all, to the mere capacity of faring well or ill.

HG. 13

Blessed fact that he has made us so near him! that the scale of our being is so large, that we are completed only by his presence in it! that we are not men without him! that we can be one with our self-existent Creator! that we are not cut off from the original Infinite! that in him we must share infinitude, or be enslaved by the finite! The very patent of our royalty is, that not for a moment can we live our true life without the eternal life present in and with our spirits.

HG. 37

Without him at our unknown root, we cease to be. True, a dog cannot live without the presence of God; but I presume a dog may live a good dog-life without knowing the presence of his origin: man is dead if he know not the Power which is his cause, his deepest selfing self; the Presence which is not himself, and is nearer to him than himself; which is infinitely more himself, more his very being, than he is himself.

HG. 38

Though there be no distance with God, it looks like it to men.

MOL. 129

God who has made us can never be far from any man who draws the breath of life—nay, must be in him; not necessarily in his heart, as we say, but still in him.

SI. 92

My God, my God, why have you forsaken me? Never had it been so with him before. Never before had he been unable to see God beside him. Yet never was God nearer him than now. For never was Jesus more divine. He could not see, could not feel him near; and yet it is "*My* God" that he cries.

SI. 165

The next hour, the next moment, is as much beyond our grasp and as much in God's care, as that a hundred years away. Care for the next minute is just as foolish as care for the morrow, or for a day in the next thousand years—in neither can we do anything, in both God is doing everything. Those claims only of the morrow which have to be prepared today are of the duty of today: the moment which coincides with work to be done, is the moment to be minded; the next is nowhere until God has made it.

SII. 46

I appeal especially to all who keep house concerning the size of troubles that suffices to hide word and face of God.

SII. 54

There is a cry behind me, and a voice before; instincts of betterment tell me I must rise above my present self—perhaps even above all my possible self: I see not how to obey, how to carry them out! I am shut up in a world of consciousness, an unknown *I* in an unknown world: surely this world of my unwilled, unchosen, compelled existence, cannot be shut out from him, cannot be unknown to him, cannot be impenetrable, impermeable, unpresent to him from whom I am! nay, is it not his thinking in which I think? is it not by his consciousness that I am conscious? Whatever passes in me must be as naturally known to him as to me, and more thoroughly, even to infinite degrees. My thought must lie open to him: if he makes me think, how can I elude him in thinking? "If I should spread my wings toward the dawn, and sojourn at the last of the sea, even there your hand would lead me, and your right hand would hold me!" If he has determined the being, how shall any mode of that being be hidden from him? If I speak to him, if I utter words ever so low; if I but think words to him; nay, if I only think to him, surely he, my original, in whose life and will and no otherwise I now think concerning him, hears, and knows, and acknowledges! Then shall I not think to him?

SII. 64

No liveliest human imagination could supply adequate representation of what it would be to be left without a shadow of the presence of God. If God gave it, man could not understand it: he knows neither God nor himself in the way of the understanding. For not he who cares least about God was in this world ever left as God could leave him. I doubt if any man could continue following his wickedness from whom God had withdrawn.

SII. 110

For God is nigher to the man than is anything God has made: what can be closer than the making and the made? that which is, and that which is because the other is? that which wills, and that which answers, owing to the will, the heart, the desire of the other, its power to answer? What other relation imaginable could give claims to compare with those arising from such a relation?

SII. 186

The one bliss of the universe is the presence of God—which is simply God being to the man, and felt by the man as being, that which in his own nature he is—the indwelling power of his life. God must be to his creature what he is in himself, for it is by his essential being alone, that by which he *is*, that he can create. His presence is the unintermittent call and response of the creative to the created, of the father to the child.

SII. 227

He is not far from us at any moment.

SIII. 38

We go into the presence of the Son revealing the Father—into the presence of the Light of men. Our mediator is the Lord himself, the spirit of light, a mediator not sent by us to God to bring back his will, but come from God to bring us himself.

SIII. 47

The one only thing to make existence a good, the one thing to make it worth having, is just that there should be no film of separation between our life and the life of which ours is an outcome; that we should not only *know* that God is our life, but be aware, in some grand consciousness beyond anything imagination can present to us, of the presence of the making God, in the very process of continuing us the live things he has made us.

SIII. 250

Of all teachings that which presents a far distant God is the nearest to absurdity. Either there is none, or he is nearer to every one of us than our nearest consciousness of self. An unapproachable divinity is the veriest of monsters, the most horrible of human imaginations.

SG. 166

The Lord of Life is with you, and that is real company, even in dying, when no one else can be with you.

TW. 87

A man may see visions manifold, and believe them all; . . . something more is needed—he must have that presence of God in his soul of which the Son of Man spoke, saying, "If a man love me, he will keep my words; and my Father will love him, and we will come unto him, and make our abode with him."

WC. chap. 60

And all the time it was God near her that was making her unhappy. For as the Son of Man came not to send peace on the earth but a sword, so the first visit of God to the human soul is generally in a cloud of fear and doubt, rising from the soul itself at his approach. The sun is the cloud-dispeller, yet often he must look through a fog if he would visit the earth at all.

WM. chap. 33

It were a sad world indeed if God's presence were only interference, that is, miracle. The roundabout common ways of things are just as much his as the straight, miraculous ones—I incline to think more his, in the sense that they are plainly the ways he prefers. In all things that are, he is—present even in the evil we bring into the world, to foil it and bring good out of it.

WW. 49

God, Will of

Better be damned, doin' the will o' God, than saved doin' nothing!

AF

To know God, and not to do his will—that is eternal damnation.

The Christian World Pulpit

The kingdom of heaven is not come, even when God's will is our law: it is come when God's will is our will. While God's will is our law, we are but a kind of noble slaves; when his will is our will, we are free children.

DE. 374

"Do you think God cares to have me do his will? Is it anything to him?"

"I am sure of it. Why did he make you else? But it is not for the sake of being obeyed that he cares for it, but for the sake of serving you and making you blessed with his blessedness. He does not care about himself, but about you."

DE. 408

Whosoever is wide and free, and will do the will of God—not understand it, not care about it, not theorize about it, but do it—is a son of God. It is in the act that man stands up as a son of God. He may be ever such a philosopher, ever such a theologian, ever such a patriot or benevolent man; but it is only he who, in the act, in the doing of the thing, stands up before God, that is a son of God. That is the divine dignity: "My Father works hitherto, and I work." It is he who works that is the son of God.

GW. 126

For God's sake, do not cling to your own poor will. It is not worth having. It is a poor, miserable, degrading thing to fall down and worship the inclination of your own heart, which may have come from any devil, or from any accident of your birth, or from the weather, or from anything.

Take the will of God, eternal, pure, strong, living and true, the only good thing; take that, and Christ will be your brother. If we knew the glory of that, I believe we could even delight in going against the poor small things that we should like in ourselves, delight even in thwarting ourselves.

GW. 128

Strong is the man or woman whose eternal life subjects the individual liking to the perfect will. Such man, such woman, is free man, free woman.

HA. 275–76

God creates in the man the power to will his will.

It may cost God a suffering man can never know, to bring the man to the point at which he will will his will; but when he is brought to that point, and declares for the truth, that is, for the will of God, he becomes one with God, and the end of God in the man's creation, the end for which Jesus was born and died, is gained. The man is saved from his sins, and the universe flowers yet again in his redemption.

HG. 14

Until a man become the power of his own existence, become his own God, the sole thing necessary to his existing is the will of God; for the well-being and perfecting of that existence, the sole thing necessary is that the man should know his Maker present in him.

HG. 38

What he will do for you, he only knows. It may be you will never know what he will do, but only what he has done: it was too good for you to know except by receiving it. The moment you are capable of it, yours it will be.

HG. 115

Never can we know the majesty of the will of God concerning us except by understanding Jesus and the work the Father gave him to do.

ML. 21

Every effort of his children to rise above the invasion of evil in body or in mind is a pleasure to him. Few, I suppose, attain to this; but there is a better thing which to many, I trust, is easier—to say, your will be done.

MOL. 29

We lift our eyes to God; we bend no longer even to his will, but raise ourselves up toward his will, for his will has become our will, and that will is our sanctification.

MOL. 46

God has . . . put us just so far away from him that we can exercise the divine thing in us, our own will, in returning toward our source. Then we shall learn the fact that we are infinitely more great and blessed in being the outcome of a perfect self-constituting will, than we could be by the conversion of any imagined independence of origin into fact for us—a truth no man *can* understand, feel, or truly acknowledge, save in proportion as he has become one with his perfect origin, the will of God.

MOL. 54

The will of God is the absolutely free choice of the man; no perception of a unity such as cannot exist between independent wills, but only in unspeakable love and tenderness between the causing Will and the caused will, can yet have place.

MOL. 55

Those who cannot see how the human will should be free in dependence upon the will of God have not realized that the will of God made the will of man; that, when most it pants for freedom, the will of man is the child of the will of God, and therefore that there can be no natural opposition or strife between them. Nay, more, the whole labor of God is that the will of man should be free as his will is free—in the same way that his will is free—by the perfect love of the man for that which is true, harmonious, lawful, creative.

MOL. 55

It is one thing, and a good thing, to do for God's sake that which is not his will: it is another thing, and altogether a better thing—how much better, no words can tell—to do for God's sake that which is his will.

RF

If we are bound to search after what our Lord means—and he speaks that we may understand—we are at least equally bound to refuse any interpretation which seems to us unlike him, unworthy of him. . . . Some misapprehension . . . or some slavish adherence to old prejudices, may thus cause us to refuse the true interpretation, but we are nonetheless bound to refuse and wait for more light. To accept that as the will of our Lord which to us is inconsistent with what we have learned to worship in him already, is to introduce discord into that harmony whose end is to unite our hearts and make them whole.

SI. 68

To the Son of God the will of God is Life.

SI. 145

To put God to the question in any other way than by saying, What will you have me to do? is an attempt to compel God to declare himself, or to hasten his work.

SI. 147

The will of God should be done. Man should be free—not merely man as he thinks of himself, but man as God thinks of him. The divine idea shall be set free in the divine bosom; the man on earth shall see his angel face to face. He shall grow into the likeness of the divine thought, free not in his own fancy, but in absolute divine fact of being, as in God's idea. The great and beautiful and perfect will of God *must* be done.

SI. 160

I do not think it was our Lord's deepest trial when in the garden he prayed that the cup might pass from him, and prayed yet again that the will of the Father might be done. For that will was then present with him. He was living and acting in that will. But now the foreseen horror has come. He is drinking the dread cup, and the will has vanished from his eyes. Were that will visible in his suffering, his will could bow with tearful gladness under the shelter of its grandeur. But now his will is left alone to drink the cup of the will in torture. In the sickness of this agony, the will of Jesus arises perfect at last; and of itself, unsupported now, declares—a naked consciousness of misery hung in the waste darkness of the universe—declares for God, in defiance of pain, of death, of apathy, of self, of negation, of the blackness within and around it; calls aloud upon the vanished God.

SI. 168

This is the faith of the Son of God. God withdrew, as it were, that the perfect will of the Son might arise and go forth to find the will of the Father.

SI. 169

In every request, heart and soul and mind ought to supply the low accompaniment, "Your will be done"; but the making of any request brings us near to him.

SII. 75

The main debts whose payment God demands are those which lie at the root of all right, those we owe in mind, and soul, and being. Whatever in us can be or make an adversary, whatever could prevent us from doing the will of God, or from agreeing with our fellow—all must be yielded. Our every relation, both to God and our fellow, must be acknowledged heartily, met as a reality. Smaller debts, if any debt can be small, follow as a matter of course.

SII. 107

If we will but let our God and Father work his will with us, there can be no limit to his enlargement of our existence, to the flood of life with which he will overflow our consciousness. We have no conception of what life might be, of how vast the consciousness of which we could be made capable.

SII. 148

If we do the will of God, eternal life is ours—no mere continuity of existence, for that in itself is worthless as hell, but a being that is one with the essential Life, and so within his reach to fill with the abundant and endless outgoings of his love.

SII. 154

Obedience is the joining of the links of the eternal round. Obedience is but the other side of the creative will. Will is God's will, obedience is man's will; the two make one.

SII. 154

"Lo, I come to do your will, O God!" We, imperfect sons, shall learn to say the same words too: that we may grow capable and say them, and so enter into our birthright, yea, become partakers of the divine nature in its divinest element, that Son came to us—died for the slaying of our selfishness, the destruction of our mean hollow pride, the waking of our childhood.

SII. 187

We have to do with God who can, not with ourselves where we cannot; we have to do with the Will, with the Eternal Life of the Father of our spirits, and not with the being which we could not make, and which is his care. He is our care; we are his; our care is to will his will; his care, to give us all things. This is to deny ourselves.

SII. 217

We are not and cannot become true sons without our will willing his will, our doing following his making. It was the will of Jesus to be the thing God willed and meant him, that made him the true son of God.

SIII. 13

We can be sons and daughters . . . only by choosing God for the Father he is, and doing his will—yielding ourselves true sons to the absolute Father. Therein lies human bliss—only and essential.

SIII. 13

Come home with me, and sit with me on the throne of my obedience. Together we will do his will, and be glad with him, for his will is the only good.

SIII. 17

When a man truly and perfectly says with Jesus, and as Jesus said it, "Your will be done," he closes the everlasting life-circle; the life of the Father and the Son flows through him; he is a part of the divine organism. Then is the prayer of the Lord in him fulfilled: "I in them and you in me, that they made be made perfect in one."

SIII. 21

Before us . . . lies a bliss unspeakable, a bliss beyond the thought or invention of man, to every child who will fall in with the perfect imagination of the Father. His imagination is one with his creative will. The thing that God imagines, that thing exists.

SIII. 24

It is as if he said, "I ought to know what I say, for I have been from all eternity the Son of him from whom you issue, and whom you call your Father, but whom you will not have your Father; I know all he thinks and is; and I say this, that my perfect freedom, my pure individuality, rests on the fact that I have not another will than his."

SIII. 103

My will is all for his will, for his will is right. He is righteousness itself. His very being is love and equity and self-devotion, and he will have his children such as himself—creatures of love, of fairness, of self-devotion to him and their fellows.

SIII. 103

He gave man the power to thwart His will, that, by means of that same power, he might come at last to do His will in a higher kind and way than would otherwise have been possible to him.

SIII. 229

When the Lord gives you freedom and joy, use them in love and confidence. Be willing to fail in what you have set before you, and let the Lord work his own success—his acceptable and perfect will.

SF. 26

I think what he means by walking in the day, is simply doing the will of God.

SP

I will be after the will of the creating I; that he see and say with his whole being that to will the will of God in himself and for himself and concerning himself is the highest possible condition of a man.

TW. 76

When the Son of Man cried out, *Let this cup pass*, the Son of God in him could yet cry, *Let your will be done.*

TW. 86

We must never fear the will of God. . . . We are not right until we can pray heartily, not say submissively, "Your will be done!" We have not one interest, and God another. When we wish what he does not wish, we are not more against him than against our real selves. We are traitors to the human when we think anything but the will of God desirable, when we fear our very life.

WM

He shall do with me what he pleases; and I will help him!

WM. 35

Good and Evil

"Some people think it is not proper for a clergyman to dance. I mean to assert my freedom from any such law. If our Lord chose to represent, in his parable of the prodigal son, the joy in heaven over a repentant sinner by the figure of 'music and dancing,' I will hearken to him rather than to men, be they as good as they may."

For I had long thought that the way to make indifferent things bad, was for good people not to do them.

AN

It is dreadful not to be good, and to have bad ways inside one.

AN. chap. 5

Pleasure, obtained by wrong, is poison and horror. But it is not the pleasure that hurts; it is the wrong that is in it that hurts. The pleasure hurts only as it leads to more wrong.

AN. 153

I believe with all my heart that the true is the beautiful, and that nothing evil can be other than ugly. If it seems not so, it is in virtue of some good mingled with the evil, and not in the smallest degree in virtue of the evil.

AN. 155

If we, choosing, against our liking, do the right, go on so until we are enabled by doing it to see into the very loveliness and essence of the right, and know it to be altogether beautiful, and then at last never think of doing evil, but delight with our whole souls in doing the will of God, why then, do you not see, we combine the two, and we are free indeed, because we are acting like God out of the essence of our nature, knowing good and evil, and choosing the good with our whole hearts and delighting in it?

GW. 32–33

No evil can be cured in the race, except by its being cured in its individuals: tendency is not absolute evil; it is there that it may be resisted, not yielded to. There is no way of making three men right but by making right each one of the three; but a cure in one man who repents and turns is a beginning of the cure of the whole human race.

HG. 4

The one cure for any organism is to be set right—to have all its parts brought into harmony with each other; the one comfort is to know this cure in process. Rightness alone is cure. The return of the organism to its true self is its only possible ease. To free a man from suffering, he must be set right, put in health; and the health at the root of man's being, his rightness, is to be free from wrongness, that is, from sin. A man is right when there is no wrong in him. The wrong, the evil is in him; he must be set free from it. I do not mean set free from the sins he has done: that will follow; I mean the sins he is doing, or is capable of doing; the sins in his being which spoil his nature—the wrongness in him—the evil he consents to; the sin he is, which makes him do the sin he does.

HG. 5

There can be no deliverance but to come out of his evil dream into the glory of God.

HG. 7

It is the indwelling badness, ready to produce bad actions, that we need to be delivered from. Against this badness if a man will not strive, he is left to commit evil and reap the consequences. To be saved from these consequences would be no deliverance; it would be an immediate, ever deepening damnation. It is the evil in our being—no essential part of it, thank God!—the miserable fact that the very child of God does not care for his Father and will not obey him, causing us to desire wrongly, act wrongly, or, where we try not to act wrongly, yet making it impossible for us not to feel wrongly—this is what he came to deliver us from—not the things we have done, but the possibility of doing such things any more.

HG. 10

The man . . . who, instead of doing what he is told, broods speculating on the metaphysics of him who calls him to his work, stands leaning his back against the door by which the Lord would enter to help him. The moment he sets about putting straight the thing that is crooked—I mean doing right where he has been doing wrong—he withdraws from the entrance, gives way for the Master to come in.

HG. 21

The only true, the only possible preparation for the coming Lord, is to cease from doing evil and begin to do well—to send away sin. They must cleanse, not the streets of their cities, not their houses or their garments or even their persons, but their hearts and their doings.

HG. 26

When . . . a man comes to see that the very God must be his life, the heart of his consciousness; when he perceives that, rousing himself to put from him what is evil, and do the duty that lies at his door, he may fearlessly claim the help of him who "loved him into being," then his will immediately sides with his conscience; he begins to try to *be*; and—first thing toward being—to rid himself of what is antagonistic to all being, namely, *wrong*.

HG. 29

Multitudes will not even approach the appalling task, the labor and pain of *being*. God is doing his part, is undergoing the mighty toil of an age-long creation, endowing men with power to be; but few as yet are those who take up their part, who respond to the call of God, who will to be, who put forth a divine effort after real existence. To the many the spirit of the prophet cries, "Turn and change your way! The kingdom of heaven is near you. Let your King possess his own. Let God throne himself in you, that his liberty be your life, and you free men. That he may enter, clear the house for him. Send away the bad things out of it. Depart from evil, and do good. The duty that lies at your door, do it, be it great or small."

HG. 29

God knows good and evil, and, blessed be his name, chooses good.

HG. 33

Like him, his Son also chose good, and in that choice resisted all temptation to help his fellows otherwise than as their and his Father would. Instead of crushing the power of evil by divine force; instead of compelling justice and destroying the wicked; instead of making peace on the earth by the rule of a perfect prince; instead of gathering the children of Jerusalem under his wings whether they would or not, and saving them from the horrors that anguished his prophetic soul—he let evil work its will while it lived; he contented himself with the slow, unencouraging ways of help essential; making men good; casting out, not merely controlling Satan; carrying to their perfect issue on earth the old primeval principles because of which the Father honored him: "You have loved righteousness and hated iniquity; therefore God, even your God, has anointed you with the oil of gladness above your fellows."

HG. 33

No man . . . can be good without willing to be good, without setting himself against evil, without sending away sin. Other men have to send it away out of them; the Lord had to send it away from before him, that it should not enter into him. Therefore is the stand against sin common to the captain of salvation and the soldiers under him.

HG. 34

The one true end of all speech concerning holy things is—the persuading of the individual man to cease to do evil, to set himself to do well, to look to the Lord of his life to be on his side in the new struggle.

HG. 39

God forgets none of his children—the naughty ones any more than the good. Love and reward are for the good: love and correction for the bad. The bad ones will trouble the good, but shall do them no hurt.

HG. 149

The truth is this: he wants to make us in his own image, *choosing* the good, *refusing* the evil. How should he effect this if he were *always* moving us from within, as he does at divine intervals?

SI. 174

When the good man sees goodness, he thinks of his own evil: Jesus had no evil to think of, but neither does he think of his goodness; he delights in his Father's. "Why do you call me good? None is good except one, even God."

SII. 5

It is not to make us do all things right he cares, but to make us hunger and thirst after a righteousness possessing which we shall never need to think of what is or is not good, but shall refuse the evil and choose the good by a motion of the will which is at once necessity and choice. You see again he refers him immediately as before to his Father.

SII. 7

There is no half-way house of rest, where ungodliness may be dallied with, nor prove quite fatal.

SII. 114

Had I known good and evil, seeing them as you see them, then chosen the evil, and turned away from the good, I know not what I should not deserve; but you know it has ever been something good in the evil that has enticed my selfish heart—nor mine only, but that of all my kind.

SII. 191

We have done much that is evil, yea, evil is very deep in us, but we are not all evil, for we love righteousness; and are not you yourself, in your Son, the sacrifice for our sins, the atonement of our breach? You have made us subject to vanity, but have yourself taken your godlike share of the consequences. Could we ever have come to know good as you know it, except by passing through the sea of sin and the fire of cleansing?

SII. 191

The good man, conscious of his own evil and desiring no refuge but the purifying light, will chiefly rejoice that the exposure of evil makes for the victory of the truth, the kingdom of God and his Christ.

SIII. 243

Ignorant creatures who do not yet understand anything go about asking why God permits evil. *We* know why! It may be he could with a word cause evil to cease—but would that be to create good? It might make us good like oxen or harmless sheep, but would that be a goodness worthy of him who was made in the image of God? If a man ceased to be *capable* of evil, he must cease to be a man. What would the goodness be that could not help being good—that had no choice in the matter, but must be such because it was so made?

SF. 26

Satan said, "You shall be as gods, knowing good and evil." God says, "You shall be as gods, knowing good and evil, and choosing the good." For the sake of this, all the discipline of the world exists. God is teaching us to know good and evil in some real degree *as they are* and not as *they seem to the incomplete*, that we may learn to choose the good and refuse the evil.

SF. 26

If at last it should prove possible for a created being to see good and evil as they are, and choose the evil, then, and only then, there would, I presume, be nothing left for God but to set his foot upon him and crush him, as we crush a noxious insect.

SF. 26

God is deeper in us than our own life, yea, is the very center and cause of our life; therefore is the Life in us stronger than the Death, for the creating Good is stronger than the created Evil.

SF. 26

Middling people are shocked at the wickedness of the wicked; Gibbie, who knew both so well, was shocked only at the wickedness of the righteous. He never came quite to understand Mr. Sclater: the inconsistent never can be *understood.* That only which has absolute reason in it can be understood of man. There is a bewilderment about the very nature of evil which only he who made us capable of evil that we might be good, can comprehend.

SG. chap. 41

While the faults of a good man cannot be such evil things as the faults of a bad man, they are more blameworthy. . . . We must not confuse the guilt of the person with the abstract evil of the thing.

WM. 9

Evil was only through good; selfishness but a parasite on the tree of life.

WM. chap. 16

In all things that are, he is—present even in the evil we bring into the world, to foil it and bring good out of it.

WW. 49

The good of all evil is to make a way for love, which is essential good. Therefore evil exists, and will exist until love destroy and cast it out.

WW. 50

Goodness

We have got to be good, and if we will not willingly of ourselves, he will make us. It is what he made us for, and it ought to be the business of our lives.

The English Pulpit of Today

He came to make us good, and therein blessed children.

HG. 13

Emptiness is need of good; the emptiness that desires good is itself good.

HG. 128

It's damned hard to be good.

M

Mere acquaintance with a good man is a powerful antidote to evil.

MOL. 40

No God to help one to be good now! no God who cares whether one is good or not! if a God, then one who will not give his creature time enough to grow good, even if he is growing better, but will blot him out like a raindrop! Great God, forbid—if you are.

MOL. 218

"But if a body was never to do anything but what he knew to be good, he would have to live half his time doing nothing"—"How little you must have thought! Why, you don't seem even to know the good of the things you are constantly doing. Now don't mistake me. I don't mean you are good for doing them. It is a good thing to eat your breakfast, but you don't fancy it's very good of you to do it. The thing is good—not you. . . . There are a great many more good things than bad things to do."

PC. chap. 3

How many people would like to be good, if only they might be good without taking trouble about it! They do not like goodness well enough to hunger and thirst after it, or to sell all that they have that they may buy it; they will not falter at the gate of the kingdom of heaven; but they look with pleasure on this or that aerial castle of righteousness, and think it would be rather nice to live in! They do not know that it is goodness all the time that their very being is pining after, and that they are starving their nature of its necessary food.

PF. 298

Try not to feel good when you are not good, but cry to him who is good.

SI. 177

He did not care to hear himself called good. It was not of consequence to him. He was there to let men see the goodness of the Father in whom he gloried. For that he entered the weary dream of the world, in which the glory was so dulled and clouded. "You call *me* good! You should know my Father!"

SII. 4

When the good man sees goodness, he thinks of his own evil: Jesus had no evil to think of, but neither does he think of his goodness; he delights in his Father's. "Why do you call me good? None is good save one, even God."

SII. 5

The Lord's goodness is of the Father's goodness; because the Father is good the Son is good. When the word *good* enters the ears of the Son, his heart lifts it at once to his Father, the Father of all. His words contain no denial of goodness in himself: in his grand self-regard he was not the original of his goodness, neither did he care for his own goodness, except to be good: it was to him a matter of course. But for his Father's goodness, he would spend life, suffering, labor, death, to make that known! His other children must learn to give him his due, and love him as did the primal Son!

SII. 5

The Father was all in all to the Son, and the Son no more thought of his own goodness than an honest man thinks of his honesty.

SII. 5

The Lord cared neither for isolated truth nor for orphaned deed. It was truth in the inward parts, it was the good heart, the mother of good deeds, he cherished. It was the live, active, knowing, breathing good he came to further. He cared for no speculation in morals or religion.

SII. 6

It was good men he cared about, not notions of good things, or even good actions, save as the outcome of life, save as the bodies in which the primary live actions of love and will in the soul took shape and came forth. Could he by one word have set at rest all the questionings of philosophy as to the supreme good and the absolute truth, I venture to say that word he would not have uttered. But he would die to make men good and true.

SII. 6

There is one living good, in whom the good thing, and all good, is alive and ever operant. Ask me not about the good thing, but the good Person, the good Being, the origin of all good—who, because he is, can make good. He is the one live good, ready with his life to communicate living good, the power of being—and so doing—good, for he makes good itself to exist. It is not with this good thing and that good thing we have to do, but with that Power whence comes our power even to speak the word *good*. We have to do with him to whom no one can look without the need of being good waking up in his heart; to think about him is to begin to be good. To do a good thing is to do a good thing; to know God is to be good. It is not to make us do all things right he cares, but to make us hunger and thirst after a righteousness possessing which we shall never need to think of what is or is not good, but shall refuse the evil and choose the good by motion of the will which is at once necessity and choice.

SII. 7

"They are good"; that is "They are what I mean."

SIII. 251

God chooses to be good, else he would not be God: man must choose to be good, else he cannot be the son of God. Herein we see the grand love of the Father of men—that he gives them a part, and that a part necessary as his own, in the making of themselves. Thus, and thus only, by willing the good, can they become partakers of the divine nature.

SF

Had he had more of the wisdom of the serpent . . . he would perhaps have known that to try too hard to make people good is one way to make them worse; that the only way to make them good is to be good—remembering well the beam and the mote; that the time for speaking comes rarely, the time for being never departs.

SG. chap. 47

One of the great goods that come of having two parents, is that the one balances and rectifies the motions of the other. No one is good but God. No one holds the truth, or can hold it, in one and the same thought, but God. Our human life is often, at best, but an oscillation between the extremes which together make the truth.

SP. chap. 2

It does not make a thing good to call it good.

WM

She sometimes wished she were good; but there are thousands of wandering ghosts who would be good if they might without taking trouble; the kind of goodness they desire would not be worth a life to hold it.

WM. chap. 11

That those who are trying to be good are more continuously troubled than the indifferent, has for ages been a puzzle.

WM. 32

Gospel

The gospel is given to convince, not our understandings, but our hearts; that done, and never until then, our understandings will be free.

DG

Men, loving their sins, and feeling nothing of their dread hatefulness, have, consistently with their low condition, constantly taken this word concerning the Lord to mean that he came to save them from the punishment of their sins. The idea—the miserable fancy, rather—has terribly corrupted the preaching of the gospel. The message of the good news has not been truly delivered.

HG. 7

There is another important misapprehension of the words of the messengers of the good tidings—that they threaten us with punishment because of the sins we have committed, whereas their message is of forgiveness, not of vengeance; of deliverance, not of evil to come. Not for anything he has committed do they threaten a man with the outer darkness. Not for any or all of his sins that are past shall a man be condemned; not for the worst of them needs he dread remaining unforgiven. The sin he dwells in, the sin he will not come out of, is the sole ruin of a man.

HG. 9

Not seldom, what comes in the name of the gospel of Jesus Christ must seem, even to one not far from the kingdom of heaven, no good news at all. It does not draw him; it wakes in him not a single hope. He has no desire after what it offers him as redemption. The God it gives him news of is not one to whom he would draw nearer. But when such a man comes to see that the very God must be his life, the heart of his consciousness; when he perceives that, rousing himself to put from him what is evil, and do the duty that lies at his door, he may fearlessly claim the help of him who "loved him into being," then his will immediately sides with his conscience; he begins to try to *be*; and—first thing toward being—to rid himself of what is antagonistic to all being, namely, *wrong*. Multitudes will not even approach the appalling task, the labor and pain of *being*.

HG. 29

He is come to free us from everything that makes life less than bliss essential. No other could be a gospel worthy of the God of men.

HG. 66

The story of him who is himself the good news, the gospel of God, becomes not only more and more believable to his heart, but more and more ministrant to his life of conflict, and his assurance of a living Father who hears when his children cry. The gospel according to this or that expounder of it may repel him unspeakably; the gospel according to Jesus Christ attracts him supremely, and ever holds where it has drawn him.

HG. 67

No mere promise of deliverance from the consequences of sin would be any gospel to me. Less than the liberty of a holy heart, less than the freedom of the Lord himself, will never satisfy one human soul. Father, set me free in the glory of your will, so that I will only as you will. Your will be at once your perfection and mine. You alone are deliverance—absolute safety from every cause and kind of trouble that ever existed, anywhere now exists, or ever can exist in your universe.

HG. 68

Very different is the good news Jesus brings us from certain prevalent representations of the gospel, founded on the pagan notion that suffering is an offset for sin, and culminating in the vile assertion that the suffering of an innocent man, just because he is innocent, yea, perfect, is a satisfaction to the holy Father for the evil deeds of his children. As a theory concerning the atonement nothing could be worse, either intellectually, morally, or spiritually; announced as the gospel itself, as the good news of the kingdom of heaven, the idea is monstrous as any Chinese dragon. Such a so-called gospel is no gospel, however accepted as God sent by good men of a certain development. It is evil news, dwarfing, enslaving, maddening—news to the child-heart of the dreariest damnation. Doubtless some elements of the gospel are mixed up with it on most occasions of its announcement; none the more is it the message received from him. It can be good news only to such as are prudently willing to be delivered from a God they fear, but unable to accept the gospel of a perfect God, in whom to trust perfectly.

HG. 84

The good news of Jesus was just the news of the thoughts and ways of the Father in the midst of his family. He told them that the way men thought for themselves and their children was not the way God thought for himself and his children; that the kingdom of heaven was founded, and must at length show itself founded, on very different principles from those of the kingdoms and families of the world, meaning by the world that part of the Father's family which will not be ordered by him, will not even try to obey him.

HG. 84

All good news from heaven is of *truth*—essential truth, involving duty, and giving and promising help to the performance of it. There can be no good news for us men, except of uplifting love, and no one can be lifted up who will not rise. If God himself sought to raise his little ones without their consenting effort, they would drop from his foiled endeavor. He will carry us in his arms until we are able to walk; he will carry us in his arms when we are weary with walking; he will not carry us if we will not walk.

HG. 98

The Lord knew what trials, what tortures even, awaited his disciples after his death; he knew they would need every encouragement he could give them to keep their hearts strong, lest in some moment of dismay they should deny him. If they had denied him, where would our gospel be? If there are none able and ready to be crucified for him now, alas for the age to come! What a poor travesty of the good news of God will arrive at their doors!

HG. 150

"Come to me, all you who labor and are heavy laden, and I will give you rest." "I know the Father; come then to me, all you that labor and are heavy laden." He does not here call those who want to know the Father; his cry goes far beyond them; it reaches to the ends of the earth. He calls those who are weary; those who do not know that ignorance of the Father is the cause of all their labor and the heaviness of their burden.

HG. 165

"Come to me," he says, "and I will give you rest."

This is the Lord's own form of his gospel, more intensely personal and direct, at the same time of yet wider inclusion, than that which, at Nazareth, he appropriated from Isaiah; differing from it also in this, that it is interfused with strongest persuasion to the troubled to enter into and share his own eternal rest.

HG. 165

I do not see how the more phenomenal gospels are ever to be understood, save through a right perception of the relation in which the Lord stands to his Father, which relation is the main subject of the Gospel according to St. John.

HG. 171

Theologians have done more to hide the gospel of Christ than any of its adversaries. It was not for our understandings, but our will, that Christ came. He who does that which he sees, shall understand; he who is set upon understanding rather than doing, shall go on stumbling and mistaking and speaking foolishness. He has not that in him which can understand that kind. The gospel itself, and in it the parables of the truth, are to be understood only by those who walk by what they find. It is he that runs that shall read, and no other.

SII. 98

The Word is the Lord; the Lord is the gospel.

SIII. 166

In his Gospel (John) he gives us all *about* him, the message *concerning* him; now he tells us what in it makes it to himself and to us good news—tells us the very goodness of the good news. It is not now his own message about Jesus, but the soul of that message—that which makes it gospel—the news Jesus brought concerning the Father, and gave to the disciples as his message, for them to deliver to men. Throughout the story, Jesus, in all he does, and is, and says, is telling the news concerning his Father, which he was sent to give to John and his companions, that they might hand it on to their brothers; but here, in so many words, John tells us what he himself has heard from The Word—what in sum he has gathered from Jesus as the message he has to declare. He has received it in no systematic form; it is what a life, *the* life, what a man, *the* man, has taught him.

SIII. 166

"This then is the message," he says, "which we have heard of him, and declare to you, that God is light, and in him is no darkness at all." Ah, my heart, this is indeed the good news for you! This *is* a gospel! If God be light, what more, what else can I seek than God, than God himself!

SIII. 167

I love the light, and will not believe at the word of any man, or upon the conviction of any man, that that which seems to me darkness is in God. Where would the good news be if John said, "God is light, but you cannot see his light; you cannot tell, you have no notion, what light is; what God means by light, is not what you mean by light; what God calls light may be horrible darkness to you, for you are of another nature from him!" Where, I say, would be the good news of that?

SIII. 168

Greatness

The desire to be known of men is destructive to all true greatness; nor is there any honor worth calling honor but what comes from an unseen source. To be great is to seem small in the eyes of men.

DG. 11

Almost no community recognizes its great men until they are gone. The strongest influences are from their very nature of the most hidden working. They are deep out of sight.

DG. 11

There are thousands willing to do great things for one willing to do a small thing; but there never was any truly great thing that did not begin small.

WW. 60

In the human being humility and greatness are not only correlative, but are one and the same condition.

WW. 267

Growth

"Habits transmitted become instincts."

AF

I am not objecting to the amusement; only to cease to educate in order to amuse is to degenerate. Amusement is a good and sacred thing; but it is not on a par with education; and, indeed, if it does not in any way further the growth of the higher nature, it cannot be called good at all.

AN. 299

And the man has begun to be strong who has begun to know that, separated from life essential, that is, God, he is weakness itself, but of strength inexhaustible if he be one with his origin.

DG

The true way is difficult enough because of our unchildlikeness—uphill, steep, and difficult, but there is fresh life with every surmounted height, a purer air gained, more life for more climbing.

DG

. . . The path that is not the true one is not therefore an easy one. Uphill work is hard walking, but through a bog is worse.

DG

I want to help you to grow as beautiful as God meant you to be when he thought of you first.

ML. 80

He regards men not as they are merely, but as they shall be; not as they shall be merely, but as they are now growing, or capable of growing, toward that image after which he made them that they might grow to it.

SI. 36

All the growth of the Christian is the more and more life he is receiving. At first his religion may hardly be distinguishable from the mere prudent desire to save his soul: but at last he loses that very soul in the glory of love, and so saves it; self becomes but the cloud on which the white light of God divides into harmonies unspeakable.

SII. 144

Our souls shall be vessels ever growing, and ever as they grow, filled with the more and more life proceeding from the Father and the Son, from God the ordaining, and God the obedient.

SII. 154

. . . For the development of the divine nature in man, it is necessary that he should do something for God.

TW. 60

As a man advances more and more is required of him. A wrong thing in the good man becomes more and more wrong as he draws nearer to freedom from it.

WM

Nothing worth calling good can or ever will be started full grown. The essential of any good is life, and the very body of created life, and essential to it . . . is growth.

WW

God seems to take pleasure in working by degrees; the progress of the truth is as the permeation of leaven, or the growth of a seed: a multitude of successive small sacrifices may work more good in the world than many a large one. . . . It is the *Being* that is the precious thing. Being is the mother to all little Doings as well as the grown-up Deeds and the mighty heroic Sacrifice; and these little Doings, like the good children of the house, make the bliss of it.

WW. 4

This is indeed a divine law! There shall be no success to the man who is not willing to begin small. Small is strong, for it only can grow strong. Big at the outset is but bloated and weak.

WW. 60

Healing/Health

It is wonderful what the sickness which stupid men and women regard as the one evil thing, can do toward their redemption from an eternal slavery! True, they do not consciously desire any such redemption—far from it!—but there is another who does; and as their very existence is his, he gives them no choice in the matter.

DG. 44

. . . Health—physical, mental, moral, and spiritual—requires for its existence and continuance, work, often hard and bodily labor.

GC

Whatever the effect of illness may be upon the temper of some, it is most certainly an ally of the conscience.

MM

In this matter of healing, then, as in all the miracles, we find Jesus doing the works of the Father. God is our Savior: the Son of God comes healing the sick—doing that, I repeat, before our eyes, which the Father, for his own reasons, some of which I think I can see well enough, does from behind the veil of his creation and its laws. The cure comes by law, comes by the physician who brings the law to bear upon us; we awake, and lo! it is God the Savior. Every recovery is as much his work as the birth of a child; as much the work of the Father as if it had been wrought by the word of the Son before the eyes of the multitude.

MOL. 36

God will cure a man, will give him a fresh start of health and hope, and the man will be the better for it, even without having *yet* learned to thank him; but to behold the healer and acknowledge the outstretched hand of help, yet not to believe in the healer, is a terrible thing for the man.

MOL. 42

The Lord kept his personal healing for such as it would bring at once into some relation of heart and will with himself; whence arose his frequent demand of faith—a demand apparently always responded to: at the word, the flickering belief, the smoking flax, burst into a flame.

MOL. 42

The head, down-bent with sin, care, sorrow, pain, is uplifted; the groveling will sends its gaze heavenward; the earth is no more the one object of the aspiring spirit; we lift our eyes to God; we bend no longer even to his will, but raise ourselves up toward his will, for his will has become our will, and that will is our sanctification.

MOL. 46

Some keep in bed who have strength enough to get up and walk. There is a self-care and a self-pity, a laziness and conceit of incapacity, which are as unhealing for the body as they are unhealthy in the mind, corrupting all dignity and destroying all sympathy.

MOL. 55

Some sicknesses are to be cured with rest, others with labor.

MOL. 60

The fact that we may be ourselves to blame for our sufferings is no reason why we should not go to God to deliver us from them.

MOL. 61

Jesus did not cure all the ills in Judea. But those he did cure were at least real ills and real needs.

MOL. 111

He cannot be a healer only; he must be the very Lord of life—it may be of the universe.

MOL. 127

The Lord who made the universe—how *should* he show it but as the Healer did? He could not make the universe over again in the eyes of every man. If he did, the heart of the man could not hold the sight. He must reveal himself as the curing God—the God who set things which had gone wrong, right again: *that could* be done in the eyes of each individual man. This man may be he—the Messiah—Immanuel, God with us.

MOL. 128

These cures were like the healing granted to prayer in all ages—not that God is afar off, for he is closer to every man than his own conscious being is to his unconscious being—but that we receive the aid from the Unseen. Though there be no distance with God, it looks like it to men; and when Jesus cured thus, he cured with the same appearances which attended God's ordinary healing.

MOL. 129

The Lord could talk to his Father evermore in the forms of which words are but the shadows, nay, infinitely more, without forms at all, in the thoughts which are the souls of the forms. Why then needs he look up and sigh?—That the man, whose faith was in the merest nascent condition, might believe that whatever cure came to him from the hand of the healer, came from the hand of God.

MOL. 151

Jesus did not care to be believed in as the doer of the deed, save the deed itself were recognized as given him of the Father. If they saw him only, and not the Father through him, there was little gained indeed. The upward look and the sigh were surely the outward expression of the infrangible link which bound both the Lord and the man to the Father of all. He would lift the man's heart up to the source of every gift. No cure would be worthy gift without that: it might be an injury.

MOL. 152

Our Lord, I think, drew forth, encouraged, enticed into strength the feeble faith of the man. He brooded over him with his holy presence of love. He gave the faith time to grow. He cared more for his faith than his sight. He let him, as it were, watch him, feel him doing it, that he might know and believe. There is in this a peculiar resemblance to the ordinary modes God takes in healing men.

MOL. 153

All diseases that trouble humanity may well be regarded as inroads of the evil powers upon the palaces and temples of God, where only the Holy Spirit has a right to dwell; and to cast out such, is a marvel altogether as great as to expel the intruding forces to which the Jews attributed some of them.

MOL. 157

But we all need like healing. No man who does not yet love the truth with his whole being, who does not love God with all his heart and soul and strength and mind, and his neighbor as himself, is in his sound mind, or can act as a rational being, save more or less approximately. This is as true as it would be of us if possessed by other spirits than our own. Every word of unkindness, God help us! every unfair hard judgment, every trembling regard of the outward and fearless disregard of the inward life, is a siding with the spirit of evil against the spirit of good, with our lower and accidental selves, against our higher and essential—our true selves.

MOL. 182

Heart

For God's sake, do not cling to your own poor will. It is not worth having. It is a poor, miserable, degrading thing to fall down and worship the inclination of your own heart, which may have come from any devil, or from any accident of your birth, or from the weather, or from anything. Take the will of God, eternal, pure, strong, living and true, the only good thing; take that, and Christ will be your brother.

GW. 128

Outer and inner are one with him: the outermost sign is the revelation of the innermost heart.

MOL. 89

A faithful heart alone is capable of understanding the proof of the truest things. It is faith toward God which alone can lay hold of any of his facts.

MOL. 203

If God sees that heart corroded with the rust of cares, riddled into caverns and films by the worms of ambition and greed, then your heart is as God sees it, for God sees things as they are. And one day you will be compelled to see, nay, to *feel* your heart as God sees it; and to know that the cankered thing which you have within you, a prey to the vilest of diseases, is indeed the center of your being, your very heart.

SI. 122

The Lord cared neither for isolated truth nor for orphaned deed. It was truth in the inward parts, it was the good heart, the mother of good deeds, he cherished.

SII. 6

Tomorrow makes today's whole head sick, its whole heart faint.

SII. 49

As no Scripture is of private interpretation, so is there no feeling in a human heart which exists in that heart alone—which is not, in some form or degree, in every heart.

SII. 116

The heart that wants to do and think aright, the heart that seeks to worship him as no tyrant, but as the perfectly, absolutely righteous God, is the delight of the Father. To the heart that will not call that righteousness which it feels to be unjust, but clings to the skirt of his garment, and lifts pleading eyes to his countenance—to that heart he will lay open the riches of his being—riches which it has not entered that heart to conceive.

SII. 190

When our hearts turn to him, that is opening the door to him, that is holding up our mirror to him: then he comes in, not by our thought only, not in our idea only, but he comes himself, and of his own will—comes in as we could not take him, but as he can come and we receive him—enabled to receive by his very coming the one welcome guest of the whole universe.

SIII. 52

Home at last will do but the home of God's heart.

TW. 83

The roots of your heart go down beyond your knowledge—whole eternities beyond it—into the heart of God.

WW

. . . Whether the man knows it or not, his heart in its depths is ever crying out for God. Where the man does not know it, it is because the unfaithful Self, a would-be monarch, has usurped the consciousness.

WW

The cry of the human heart in all ages and in every moment is "Where is God and how shall I find him?"

WW. 5

You take it for granted that you know your own heart because you call it yours, but I say that your heart is a far deeper thing than you know or are capable of knowing. Its very nature is hid from you.

WW. 5

. . . The human heart has to go through much before it is able to house even a suspicion of the superabounding riches of the creating and saving God.

WW. 35

Heaven and Earth

Though so many of us now are ignorant what kind of home we need, what a home we are capable of having, we too shall inherit the earth with the Son eternal, doing with it as we would—willing with the will of the Father. To such a home as we now inhabit, only perfected, and perfectly beheld, we are traveling—never to reach it save by the obedience that makes us the children, therefore the heirs, of God.

HG. 58

The kingdom of heaven belongs to the poor; the meek shall inherit the earth. The earth as God sees it, as those to whom the kingdom of heaven belongs also see it, is good, all good, very good, fit for the meek to inherit; and one day they shall inherit it—not indeed as men of the world count inheritance, but as the Maker and Owner of the world has from the first counted it.

HG. 90

If we are the Lord's we possess the kingdom of heaven, and so inherit the earth. How many who call themselves by his name would have it otherwise: they would possess the earth and inherit the kingdom!

HG. 97

Two men are walking abroad together; to the one, the world yields thought after thought of delight; he sees heaven and earth embrace one another; he feels an indescribable presence over and in them; his joy will afterward, in the solitude of his chamber, break forth in song—to the other, oppressed with the thought of his poverty, or ruminating how to make much into more, the glory of the Lord is but a warm summer day; it enters in at no window of his soul; it offers him no gift; for, in the very temple of God, he looks for no God in it.

HG. 97

A heaven without human love it were inhuman, and yet more undivine, to desire; it ought not to be desired by any being made in the image of God.

HG. 108

Is not the prophecy on the groaning creation to have its fulfillment in the new heavens and the new earth, wherein dwells righteousness? Does not this involve its existence beyond what we call this world? Why should it not then involve immortality? Would it not be more like the king eternal, immortal, invisible, to know no life but the immortal? to create nothing that could die? to slay nothing but evil? "For he is not a God of the dead, but of the living; for all live for him."

HG. 226

The new man must have a new body with a new heaven and earth.

HG. 228

He will shake heaven and earth, that only the unshakeable may remain: he is a consuming fire, that only that which cannot be consumed may stand forth eternal.

SI. 31

Hard to let earth go, and take heaven instead? for eternal life, to let dead things drop? to turn his back on Mammon, and follow Jesus? lose his rich friends, and be of the Master's household? Let him say it was hard who does not know the Lord, who has never thirsted after righteousness, never longed for the life eternal!

SII. 13

For the only air of the soul, in which it can breathe and live, is the present God and the spirits of the just: that is our heaven, our home, our all-right place.

SII. 52

The heavens and the earth are around us that it may be possible for us to speak of the unseen by the seen; for the outermost husk of creation has correspondence with the deepest things of the Creator.

SIII. 31

I could persuade a man that heaven was the perfection of all he could desire around him, what would the man or the truth gain by it? If he knows the Lord, he will not trouble himself about heaven; if he does not know him, he will not be drawn to *him* by it. I would not care to persuade the feeble Christian that heaven was a place worth going to; I would rather persuade him that no spot in space, no hour in eternity is worth anything to one who remains such as he is.

SIII. 256

For my own part, I rejoice to think that there will be neither church nor chapel in the high countries; yea, that there will be nothing there called religion, and no law but the perfect law of liberty. For how should there be law or religion where every throb of the heart says *God*! where every song-throat is eager with thanksgiving! where such a tumult of glad waters is for ever bursting from beneath the throne of God, the tears of the gladness of the universe! Religion? Where will be the room for it, when the essence of every thought must be God? Law? What room will there be for law, when everything upon which law could lay a *shall not* will be too loathsome to think of?

SIII. 257

Heaven will be continuous touch with God. The very sense of being will in itself be bliss. For the sense of true life, there must be actual, conscious contact with the source of the life; therefore mere life—in itself, in its very essence good—good as the life of God which is our life—must be such bliss as, I think, will need the mitigation of the loftiest joys of communion with our blessed fellows; the mitigation of art in every shape, and of all combinations of arts; the mitigation of countless services to the incomplete, and hard toil for those who do not yet know their neighbor or their Father. The bliss of pure being will, I say, need these mitigations to render the intensity of it endurable by heart and brain.

SIII. 258

Whatever the place be like, one thing is certain, that there will be endless, infinite atonement, ever-growing love. Certain too it is that whatever the divinely human heart desires, it shall not desire in vain. The light which is God, and which is our inheritance because we are the children of God, insures these things. For the heart which desires is made thus to desire. God is; let the earth be glad, and the heaven, and the heaven of heavens! Whatever a father can do to make his children blessed, that will God do for his children. Let us, then, live in continual expectation, looking for the good things that God will give to men, being their Father and their everlasting Savior. If the things I have here come from him, and are so plainly but a beginning, shall I not take them as an earnest of the better to follow? How else can I regard them? For never, in the midst of the good things of this lovely world, have I felt quite at home in it. Never has it shown me things lovely or grand enough to satisfy me. It is not all I should like for a place to live in. It may be that my unsatisfaction comes from not having eyes open enough, or keen enough, to see and understand what he has given; but it matters little whether the cause lie in the world or in myself, both being incomplete: God is, and all is well.

SIII. 260

All that is needed to set the world right enough for me—and no empyrean heaven could be right for me without it—is, that I care for God as he cares for me; that my will and desires keep time and harmony with his music; that I have no thought that springs from myself apart from him; that my individuality have the freedom that belongs to it as born of his individuality, and be in no slavery to my body, or my ancestry, or my prejudices, or any impulse whatever from region unknown; that I be free by obedience to the law of my being, the live and live-making will by which life is life, and my life is myself.

SIII. 261

Hell

I would not favor a fiction to keep a whole world out of hell. The hell that a lie would keep any man out of is doubtless the very best place for him to go to. It is truth . . . that saves the world.

AN. chap. 9

The hell that a lie would keep any man out of is doubtless the very best place for him to go to.

AN. 144

Hell is God's and not the devil's. Hell is on the side of God and man, to free the child of God from the corruption of death. Not one soul will ever be redeemed from hell but by being saved from his sins, from the evil in him. If hell be needful to save him, hell will blaze, and the worm will writhe and bite, until he takes refuge in the will of the Father. "Salvation from hell" is salvation as conceived by such to whom hell and not evil is the terror. But if even for dread of hell a poor soul seek the Father, he will be heard of him in his terror, and taught of him to seek the immeasurably greater gift, will in the greater receive the less.

HG. 8

No man is safe from hell until he is free from his sins; but a man to whom his sins, that is, the evil things in him, are a burden, while he may indeed sometimes feel as if he were in hell, will soon have forgotten that ever he had any other hell to think of than that of his sinful condition. For to him his sins are hell; he would go to the other hell to be free of them; free of them, hell itself would be endurable to him.

HG. 8

Not one soul will ever be redeemed from hell but by being saved from his sins, from the evil in him.

HG. 9

Between death and the least movement of life there is a gulf wider than that fixed between the gates of heaven and the depths of hell.

MOL. 86

No, there is no escape. There is no heaven with a little of hell in it—no plan to retain this or that of the devil in our hearts or our pockets. Out Satan must go, every hair and feather!

SII. 103

When a man is true, if he were in hell he could not be miserable. He is right with himself because right with him whence he came.

SIII. 81

The one principle of hell is—I am my own. I am my own king and my own subject. *I* am the center from which go out my thoughts; *I* am the object and end of my thoughts; back upon *me* as the alpha and omega of life, my thoughts return. My own glory is, and ought to be, my chief care; my ambition, to gather the regards of men to the one center, myself. My pleasure is *my* pleasure. My kingdom is—as many as I can bring to acknowledge my greatness over them. My judgment is the faultless rule of things. My right is—what I desire. The more I am all in all to myself, the greater I am. The less I acknowledge debt or obligation to another; the more I close my eyes to the fact that I did not make myself; the more self-sufficing I feel or imagine myself—the greater I am. I will be free with the freedom that consists in doing whatever I am inclined to do, from whatever quarter may come the inclination. To do my own will so long as I feel anything to be my will, is to be free, is to live. To all these principles of hell, or of this world—they are the same thing, and it matters nothing whether they are asserted or defended so long as they are acted upon—the Lord, the King, gives the direct lie.

SIII. 102

Even the damned must at times become aware of what they are, and then surely a terrible though momentary hush must fall upon the forsaken regions.

SG. chap. 2

It is a human soul still, and wretched in the midst of all that whisky can do for it. From the pit of hell it cries out. So long as there is that which can sin, it is a man. And the prayer of misery carries its own justification, when the sober petitions of the self-righteous and the unkind are rejected. He who forgives not is not forgiven, and the prayer of the Pharisee is as the weary beating of the surf of hell, while the cry of a soul out of its fire sets the heartstrings of love trembling.

SG. chap. 6

Holy Spirit

"Seek first the kingdom of God and his righteousness, and all these things shall be added unto you?" Instead of doing so, we seek the things God has promised to look after for us, and refuse to seek the thing he wants us to seek—a thing that cannot be given us except we seek it. We profess to think Jesus the grandest and most glorious of men, and yet hardly care to be like him; and so when we are offered his Spirit, that is, his very nature within us, for the asking, we will hardly take the trouble to ask for it.

AN

That which is best he gives most plentifully, as is reason with him. Hence the quiet fullness of ordinary nature; hence the Spirit to them that ask it.

AN. chap. 3

Strange condition of despair into which the Spirit of God drives a man—a condition in which the Best alone is the Possible!

DE

The gift of the Spirit of God to make you think as God thinks, feel as God feels, judge as God judges, is just the one thing that is promised.

DO. 311

To what purpose is the Spirit of God promised to them that ask it, if not to help them order their way aright?

HG. 138

Whatever springs from any other source than the spirit that dwelt in Jesus, is of sin, and works to thwart the divine will.

M

He who asks *shall* receive—of the very best. One promise without reserve, and only one, because it includes all, remains: the promise of the Holy Spirit to them who ask it. He who has the Spirit of God, God himself, in him, has the Life in him, possesses the final cure of all ill, has in himself the answer to all possible prayer.

MOL. 114

The great heresy of the church of the present day is unbelief in this Spirit. The mass of the church does not believe that the Spirit has a revelation for every man individually.

SI. 54

The Spirit of God is the Spirit whose influence is known by its witnessing with our spirit.

SI. 92

Shall we dare to think that if we being evil know how to give good gifts to our children, God will not give us his own spirit when we come to ask him?

SI. 187

There is no unity but having the same spirit. There is but one spirit, that of truth.

SII. 129

To him who obeys, and thus opens the doors of his heart to receive the eternal gift, God gives the Spirit of his Son, the Spirit of himself, to be in him, and lead him to the understanding of all truth; that the true disciple shall thus always know what he ought to do, though not necessarily what another ought to do; that the Spirit of the Father and the Son enlightens by teaching righteousness.

SIII. 155

He who is willing to do the will of the Father shall know the truth of the teaching of Jesus. The spirit is "given to them that obey him."

SIII. 167

Honesty

Friends, if we be honest with ourselves, we shall be honest with each other.

ML. 71

The honesty in which a man can pride himself must be a small one, for more honesty will ever reveal more defect, while perfect honesty will never think of itself at all.

ML. 323

Hope

If you believe that the man Jesus Christ died and rose again, the whole thing is full of the dawn of an eternal morning, coming up beyond the hills of this life, and full of such hope as the highest imagination of the poet has not a glimmer of as yet.

The Christian World Pulpit

Do you hope for anything, friends? Thank God, that comes from your faith. No man that has not faith can hope.

The Christian World Pulpit

Is it not of the very essence of the Christian hope, that we shall be changed from much bad to all good?

HG. 109

Let the joy of your hope stream forth on your neighbors. Fold them round in that which makes you glad. Let your nature grow more expansive and communicative. Look like the man you are—a man who knows something very good. You believe yourself on the way to the heart of things: walk so, shine so, that all that see you shall want to go with you.

HG. 186

You who have light, show yourselves the sons and daughters of Light, of God, of Hope—the heirs of a great completeness. Freely let your light shine.

HG. 188

To object to Christianity as selfish is utter foolishness; Christianity alone gives any hope of deliverance from selfishness.

HG. 198

Those that hope little cannot grow much. To them the very glory of God must be a small thing, for their hope of it is so small as not to be worth rejoicing in.

HG. 218

To arouse the hope that there may be a God with a heart like our own is more for the humanity in us than to produce the absolute conviction that there is a being who made the heaven and the earth and the sea and the fountains of waters.

MOL. 197

Without the raising of the dead, without the rising of the Savior himself, Christianity would not have given what it could of *hope* for the future. Hope is not faith, but neither is faith sight; and if we have hope we are not miserable men.

MOL. 214

The future lies dark before us, with an infinite hope in the darkness. To be at peace concerning it on any other ground than the love of God, would be an absolute loss. Better fear and hope and prayer, than knowledge and peace without the prayer.

MOL. 221

There must be hope while there is existence; for where there is existence there must be God; and God is for ever good, nor can be other than good.

SII. 112

A man is nearer heaven when in deepest hell than just ere he begins to reap the reward of his doings—for he is in a condition to receive the smallest show of the life that is, as a boon unspeakable. All his years in the world he received the endless gifts of sun and air, earth and sea and human face divine, as things that came to him because that was their way, and there was no one to prevent them; now the poorest thinning of the darkness he would hail as men of old the glow of a descending angel; it would be as a messenger from God. Not that he would think of God! it takes long to think of God; but hope, not yet seeming hope, would begin to dawn in his bosom, and the thinner darkness would be as a cave of light, a refuge from the horrid self of which he used to be so proud.

SII. 112

However bad I may be, I am the child of God, and therein lies my blame. Ah, I would not lose my blame! in my blame lies my hope. It is the pledge of what I am, and what I am not; the pledge of what I am meant to be, what I shall one day be, the child of God in spirit and in truth.

SII. 120

Of all things let us avoid the false refuge of a weary collapse, a hopeless yielding to things as they are. It is the life in us that is discontented: we need more of what is discontented, not more of the cause of its discontent.

SII. 146

Humility

I think humiliation is a very different condition of mind from humility. Humiliation no man can desire: it is shame and torture. Humility is the true right condition of humanity—peaceful, divine. And yet a man may gladly welcome humiliation when it comes, if he finds that with a fierce shock and rude revulsion it has turned him right round, with his face away from pride, whither he was traveling and toward humility, however far away upon the horizon's verge she may sit waiting for him.

AN

A repentant sinner feels that he is making himself little when he prays to be made humble: the Christian philosopher sees such a glory and spiritual wealth in humility that it appears to him almost too much to pray for.

EA. 231–32

Knowing herself a nobody, she now first began to be a somebody.

ML. 368

Those who think their affairs too insignificant for God's regard, will justify themselves in lying crushed under their seeming ruin. Either we live in the heart of an eternal thought, or we are the product and sport of that which is lower than we.

WM. 45

Humility, the worship of the Ideal—that is, of the man Christ Jesus, is the only lifter-up of the head.

WW. 60

In the human being humility and greatness are not only correlative, but are one and the same condition.

WW. 267

Humor

The man had a redeeming sense of humor, though he did not know how to prize it, not believing it a gift of God.

SG. 15

Humor has its share even in religion—but oh, how few seem to understand its laws!

WW

It is not humor that is irreverent, but the mind that gives it the wrong turn. As we may be angry and not sin, so may we jest and not sin.

WW. 26

Hypocrisy

Half the misery in the world comes from trying to look, instead of trying to be, what one is not.

FS. 1

Trying to look what we ought to be is the beginning of hypocrisy.

HG. 180

Only when we cherish evil is there hypocrisy in hiding it.

HG. 184

What is hypocrisy? The desire to look better than you are; the hiding of things you do, because you would not be supposed to do them, because you would be ashamed to have them known where you are known. The doing of them is foul; the hiding of them, in order to appear better than you are, is fouler still.

SIII. 231

The man who does not live in his own consciousness as in the open heavens, is a hypocrite—and for most of us the question is, Are we growing less or more of such hypocrites? Are we ashamed of not having been open and clear? Are we fighting the evil thing which is our temptation to hypocrisy? The Lord has not a thought in him to be ashamed of before God and his universe, and he will not be content until he has us in the same liberty.

SIII. 231

We may trust God with our past as heartily as with our future. It will not hurt us so long as we do not try to hide things, so long as we are ready to bow our heads in hearty shame where it is fit we should be ashamed. For to be ashamed is a holy and blessed thing.

SIII. 238

Shame is a thing to shame only those who want to appear, not those who want to be. Shame is to shame those who want to pass their examination, not those who would get into the heart of things. In the name of God let us henceforth have nothing to be ashamed of, and be ready to meet any shame on its way to meet us. For to be humbly ashamed is to be plunged in the cleansing bath of the truth.

SIII. 238

Think what it must be for a man counting himself religious, orthodox, exemplary, to perceive suddenly that there was no religion in him, only love of self; no love of the right, only a great love of being in the right! What a discovery—that he was simply a hypocrite—one who loved to *appear*, and *was* not!

SIII. 239

What a horror will it not be to a vile man . . . when his eyes are opened to see himself as the pure see him, as God sees him! Imagine such a man waking all at once, not only to see the eyes of the universe fixed upon him with loathing astonishment, but to see himself at the same moment as those eyes see him.

SIII. 239

A man may loathe a thing in the abstract for years, and find at last that all the time he has been, in his own person, guilty of it. To carry a thing under our cloak caressingly, hides from us its identity with something that stands before us on the public pillory. Many a man might read this and assent to it, who cages in his own bosom a carrion bird that he never knows for what it is, because there are points of difference in its plumage from that of the bird he calls by an ugly name.

SIII. 240

A man may sink by such slow degrees that, long after he is a devil, he may go on being a good churchman or a good dissenter and thinking himself a good Christian.

SIII. 242

"O God," we think, "How terrible if it were I!" Just so terrible is it that it should be Judas. And have I not done things with the same germ in them, a germ which, brought to its evil perfection, would have shown itself the canker-worm, treachery? Except I love my neighbor as myself, I may one day betray him! Let us therefore be compassionate and humble, and hope for every man.

SIII. 242

Idolatry

. . . All hope or joy that does not turn its face upward, is an idolatry.

WM

The Living Life is the one power, the only that can, and he who puts his trust or hope in anything else whatever is a worshiper of idols.

WW. 50

Imagination

The imagination is an endless help toward faith, but it is no more faith than a dream of food will make us strong for the next day's work.

DG

It is God who gives you your mirror of imagination, and if you keep it clean, it will give back no shadow but of the truth.

PF. 29

We must not wonder things away into nonentity, but try to present them to ourselves after what fashion we are able—our shadows of the heavenly.

SIII. 5

Before us . . . lies a bliss unspeakable, a bliss beyond the thought or invention of man, to every child who will fall in with the perfect imagination of the Father. His imagination is one with his creative will. The thing that God imagines, that thing exists.

SIII. 24

Individuality

The philanthropist who regards the wrong as in the race, forgetting that the race is made up of conscious and wrong individuals, forgets also that wrong is always generated in and done by an individual; that the wrongness exists in the individual, and by him is passed over, as tendency, to the race; and that no evil can be cured in the race, except by its being cured in its individuals: tendency is not absolute evil; it is there that it may be resisted, not yielded to. There is no way of making three men right but by making right each one of the three; but a cure in one man who repents and turns is a beginning of the cure of the whole human race.

HG. 4

God gives in his children an analysis of himself, an analysis that will never be exhausted. It is the original God-idea of the individual man that will at length be given, without spot or blemish, into the arms of love.

HG. 110

Such . . . is the heart of the comfort the Lord will give those whose love is now making them mourn; and their present blessedness must be the expectation of the time when the true lover shall find the restored the same as the lost—with precious differences: the things that were not like the true self, gone or going; the things that were loveliest, lovelier still; the restored not merely more than the lost, but more the person lost than he or she that was lost. For the things which made him or her what he or she was, the things that rendered lovable, the things essential to the person, will be more present, because more developed.

HG. 110

He is the God of the individual man, or he could be no God of the race.

MOL. 28

Individual life is the life of the church.

MOL. 42

There is no massing of the people with him. In his behavior to men, just as in their relation to his Father, every man is alone with him.

MOL. 96

The whole divine treatment of man is that of a father to his children—only a father infinitely more a father than any man can be. Before him stands each, as much an individual child as if there were no one but him. The relation is awful in its singleness. Even when God deals with a nation as a nation, it is only as by this dealing the individual is aroused to a sense of his own wrong, that he can understand how the nation has sinned, or can turn himself to work a change. The nation cannot change save as its members change; and the few who begin the change are the elect of that nation.

MOL. 97

Before him stands each, as much an individual child as if there were no one but him. The relation is awful in its singleness.

MOL. 97

All communities are for the divine sake of individual life, for the sake of the love and truth that is in each heart, and is not cumulative—cannot be in two as one result. But all that is precious in the individual heart depends for existence on the relation the individual bears to other individuals: alone—how can he love? alone—where is his truth? It is for and by the individuals that the individual lives. A community is the true development of individual relations.

MOL. 98

The man, in virtue of standing alone in God, stands *with* his fellows, and receives from them divine influences without which he cannot be made perfect. It is in virtue of the living consciences of its individuals that a common conscience is possible to a nation.

MOL. 98

The Spirit of God speaks to the spirit of the man, and the providence of God arranges everything for the best good of the individual—counting the very hairs of his head.

MOL. 99

Our Lord would knit the bond between him and each man by arousing the man's individuality, which is, in deepest fact, his conscience.

MOL. 100

To assert one's individuality is not necessarily to be free: it *may* indeed be but the outcome of absolute slavery.

MOL. 122

Jesus *must* have hated anything like display. God's greatest work has never been done in crowds, but in closets; and when it works out from thence, it is not upon crowds, but upon individuals. A crowd is not a divine thing. It is not a body. Its atoms are not members one of another. A crowd is a chaos over which the Spirit of God has yet to move, ere each retires to his place to begin his harmonious work, and unite with all the rest in the organized chorus of the human creation. The crowd must be dispersed that the church may be formed.

MOL. 198

"Could you not give me some sign, or tell me something about you that never changes, or some other way to know you, or thing to know you by?"—"No, Curdie: that would be to keep you from knowing me. You must know me in quite another way from that. It would not be the least use to you or me either if I were to make you know me in that way. It would be but to know the sign of me—not to know me myself."

PC. chap. 7

The true name is one which expresses the character, the nature, the *meaning* of the person who bears it. It is the man's own symbol—his soul's picture, in a word—the sign which belongs to him and to no one else. Who can give a man this, his own name? God alone.

SI. 105

No one but God sees what the man is, or even, seeing what he is, could express in a name-word the sum and harmony of what he sees. To whom is this name given? To him that overcomes. When is it given? When he has overcome. Does God then not know what a man is going to become? As surely as he sees the oak which he put there lying in the heart of the acorn. Why then does he wait until the man has become by overcoming ere he settles what his name shall be? He does not wait; he knows his name from the first.

SI. 106

It is only when the man has become his name that God gives him the stone with the name on it, for then first can he understand what his name signifies. It is the blossom, the perfection, the completeness, that determines the name: and God foresees that from the first because he made it so: but the tree of the soul, before its blossom comes, cannot understand what blossom it is to bear and could not know what the word meant, which, in representing its own unarrived completeness, named itself. Such a name cannot be given until the man *is* the name. God's name for a man must be the expression of his own idea of the man, that being whom he had in his thought when he began to make the child, and whom he kept in his thought through the long process of creation that went to realize the idea. To tell the name is to seal the success—to say "In you also I am well pleased."

SI. 107

The name is one "which no man knows except he that receives it." Not only then has each man his individual relation to God, but each man has his peculiar relation to God. He is to God a peculiar being, made after his own fashion, and that of no one else. Hence he can worship God as no man else can worship him.

SI. 110

As the fir-tree lifts up itself with a far different need from the need of the palm-tree, so does each man stand before God, and lift up a different humanity to the common Father. And for each God has a different response. With every man he has a secret—the secret of the new name. In every man there is a loneliness, an inner chamber of peculiar life into which God only can enter. I say not it is *the innermost chamber*—but a chamber into which no brother, nay, no sister can come. From this it follows that there is a chamber also—(O God, humble and accept my speech)—a chamber in God himself, into which none can enter but the one, the individual, the peculiar man—out of which chamber that man has to bring revelation and strength for his brethren. This is that for which he was made—to reveal the secret things of the Father.

SI. 111

By his creation . . . each man is isolated with God: each, in respect of his peculiar making, can say, "*my* God"; each can come to him alone, and speak with him face to face, as a man speaks with his friend. There is no *massing* of men with God. When he speaks of gathered men, it is as a spiritual *body*, not a *mass*. For in a body every smallest portion is individual, and therefore capable of forming a part of the body.

SI. 112

Each has within him a secret of the Divinity; each is growing toward the revelation of that secret to himself, and so to the full reception, according to his measure, of the divine. Every moment that he is true to his true self, some new shine of the white stone breaks on his inward eye, some fresh channel is opened upward for the coming glory of the flower, the conscious offering of his whole being in beauty to the Maker. Each man, then, is in God's sight worth.

SI. 113

It is enough that God thinks about him. To be something to God—is not that praise enough? To be a thing that God cares for and would have complete for himself, because it is worth caring for—is not that life enough?

SI. 115

"God has cared to make me for himself," says the victor with the white stone, "and has called me that which I like best; for my own name must be what I would have it, seeing it is myself. What matter whether I be called a grass of the field, or an eagle of the air? a stone to build into his temple, or a Boanerges to wield his thunder? I am his; his idea, his making; perfect in my kind, yea, perfect in his sight; full of him, revealing him, alone with him. Let him call me what he will. The name shall be precious as my life. I seek no more."

SI. 115

Each will feel the sacredness and awe of his neighbor's dark and silent speech with his God. Each will regard the other as a prophet, and look to him for what the Lord has spoken.

SI. 116

The truth of every man is the perfected Christ in him. As Christ is the blossom of humanity, so the blossom of every man is the Christ perfected in him. The vital force of humanity working in him is Christ; he is his root—the generator and perfecter of his individuality.

SIII. 80

Every one of us is something that the other is not, and therefore knows something—it may be without knowing that he knows it—which no one else knows; and that it is every one's business, as one of the kingdom of light, and inheritor in it all, to give his portion to the rest; for we are one family, with God at the head and the heart of it, and Jesus Christ, our Elder Brother, teaching us of the Father, whom he only knows.

SIII. 255

Intellect

Intelligence is a consequence of love; nor is there any true intelligence without it.

AN. 478

There are many true things that cannot be seen with naked eye! The eye must be clothed and in its right mind first!

HA. 280

Instead of immediately obeying the Lord of life, the one condition upon which he can help them, and in itself the beginning of their deliverance, they set themselves to question their unenlightened intellects as to his plans for their deliverance—and not merely how he means to effect it, but how he can be able to effect it.

HG. 17

Incapable of understanding the first motions of freedom in themselves, they proceed to interpret the riches of his divine soul in terms of their own beggarly notions, to paraphrase his glorious verse into their own paltry commercial prose; and then, in the growing presumption of imagined success, to insist on their neighbors' acceptance of their distorted shadows of "the plan of salvation" as the truth of him in whom is no darkness, and the one condition of their acceptance with him.

HG. 18

They delay setting their foot on the stair which alone can lead them to the house of wisdom, until they shall have determined the material and mode of its construction. For the sake of knowing, they postpone that which alone can enable them to know, and substitute for the true understanding which lies beyond, a false persuasion that they already understand. They will not accept, that is, act upon, their highest privilege, that of obeying the Son of God. It is on them that do his will that the day dawns; to them the day-star arises in their hearts. Obedience is the soul of knowledge.

HG. 18

To cease to wonder is to fall plumb-down from the childlike to the commonplace—the most undivine of all moods intellectual. Our nature can never be at home among things that are not wonderful to us.

HG. 58

Faith in God will do more for the intellect at length than all the training of the schools.

MOL. 136 (note)

Our Lord had no design of constructing a system of truth in intellectual forms. . . . He spoke out of a region of realities which he knew could only be suggested—not represented—in the forms of intellect and speech. With vivid flashes of life and truth his words invade our darkness, rousing us with sharp stings of light to will our awaking, to arise from the dead and cry for the light which he can give, not in the lightning of words only, but in indwelling presence and power.

SI. 66

Our vision is so circumscribed, our theories are so small—the garment of them not large enough to wrap us in; our faith so continually fashions itself to the fit of our dwarf intellect, that there is endless room for rebellion against ourselves: we must not let our poor knowledge limit our not so poor intellect, our intellect limit our faith, our faith limit our divine hope; reason must humbly watch over all—reason, the candle of the Lord.

SII. 90

It is not intended by the speaker of the parables that any other should know intellectually what, known but intellectually, would be for his injury—what knowing intellectually he would imagine he had grasped, perhaps even appropriated. When the pilgrim of the truth comes on his journey to the region of the parable, he finds its interpretation. It is not a fruit or a jewel to be stored, but a well springing by the wayside.

SII. 99

To hold a thing with the intellect is not to believe it.

SII. 239

The uncertainty lies always in the intellectual region, never in the practical. What Paul cares about is plain enough to the true heart, however far from plain to the man whose desire to understand goes ahead of his obedience.

SIII. 43

The highest truth to the intellect, the abstract truth, is the relation in which man stands to the source of his being—his will to the will whence it became a will, his love to the love that kindled his power to love, his intellect to the intellect that lighted his.

SIII. 76

Oh the folly of any mind that would explain God before obeying him! That would map out the character of God instead of crying, Lord, what would you have me to do?

SIII. 115

Jesus is the creating and saving lord of our intellects as well as of our more precious hearts; nothing that he does not think, is worth thinking; no man can think as he thinks, except he be pure like him; no man can be pure like him, except he go with him, and learn from him.

SIII. 152

To teach your intellect what has to be learned by your whole being, what cannot be understood without the whole being, what it would do you no good to understand save you understood it in your whole being—if this be the province of any man, it is not mine. Let the dead bury their dead, and the dead teach their dead.

SIII. 226

Jew/Gentile

It was for the sake of the Gentiles as much as the Jews that Jesus came to the Jews first. For whatever glorious exceptions there were among the Gentiles, surpassing even similar among the Jews; and whatever the wide-spread refusal of the Jewish nation, he *could* not have been received among the Gentiles as among the Jews.

MOL. 134

It was not that God loved the Jews more than the Gentiles that he chose them first, but that he must begin somewhere: *why*, God himself knows, and perhaps has given us glimmerings.

MOL. 134

"It is not right to take the children's bread, and to cast it to dogs."

Terrible words! more dreadful far than any he ever spoke besides! Surely now she will depart in despair! But the Lord did not mean in them to speak *his* mind concerning the relation of Jew and Gentile; for not only do the future of his church and the teaching of his Spirit contradict it: but if he did mean what he said, then he acted as was unmeet, for he did cast a child's bread to a dog. No. He spoke as a Jew felt, that the elect Jews about him might begin to understand that in him is neither Jew nor Gentile, but all are brethren.

MOL. 135

Joy

It will take the utmost joy God can give, to let men know him; and what man, knowing him, would mind losing every other joy? Only what other joy could keep from entering where the God of joy already dwelt?

HG. 197

The whole history is a divine agony to give divine life to creatures. The outcome of that agony, the victory of that creative and again creative energy, will be radiant life, whereof joy unspeakable is the flower.

SII. 143

It is not selfish to be joyful.

SII. 227

What power could prevent him who sees the face of God from being joyful?—that bliss is his which lies behind all other bliss, without which no other bliss could ripen or last.

SII. 227

The love that is born in us is our salvation from selfishness. It is of the very essence of righteousness. Because a thing is joyful, it does not follow that I do it for the joy of it; yet when the joy is in others, the joy is pure. That *certain* joys should be joys, is the very denial of selfishness.

SII. 228

If the joy that alone makes life worth living, the joy that God is such as Christ, be a true thing in my heart, how can I but believe in the atonement of Jesus Christ? I believe it heartily, as God means it.

SIII. 158

(The Christian) does not take his joy from himself. He feels joy in himself, but it comes to him from others, not from himself—from God first, and from somebody, anybody, everybody next.

SIII. 223

It is not the contemplation of what God has made him; it is the being what God has made him, and the contemplation of what God himself is, and what he has made his fellows, that gives him his joy.

SIII. 224

Joy/Sorrow

They drank it in like sorrow, the only material out of which true joy can be fashioned.

DE

There is no evil in sorrow. True, it is not an essential good, a good in itself, like love; but it will mingle with any good thing, and is even so allied to good that it will open the door of the heart for any good. More of sorrowful than of joyful men are always standing about the everlasting doors that open into the presence of the Most High.

HG. 99

Joy is in its nature more divine than sorrow; for, although man must sorrow, and God share in his sorrow, yet in himself God is not sorrowful, and the "glad Creator" never made man for sorrow: it is but a stormy strait through which he must pass to his ocean of peace.

HG. 99

A man in sorrow is in general far nearer God than a man in joy. Gladness may make a man forget his thanksgiving; misery drives him to his prayers.

HG. 100

We *are* not yet, we are only *becoming*. The endless day will at length dawn whose every throbbing moment will heave our hearts Godward; we shall scarce need to lift them up: now, there are two doorkeepers to the house of prayer, and Sorrow is more on the alert to open than her grandson Joy.

HG. 100

To call a man *blessed* in his sorrow because of something to be given him, surely implies a something better than what he had before! True, the joy that is past may have been so great that the man might well feel blessed in the merest hope of its restoration; but would that be meaning enough for the word in the mouth of the Lord? That the interruption of his blessedness was but temporary would hardly be fit ground for calling the man *blessed* in that interruption. *Blessed* is a strong word, and in the mouth of Jesus means all it can mean.

HG. 104

Can his saying here mean less than, "Blessed are they that mourn, for they shall be comforted with a bliss well worth all the pain of the medicinal sorrow"? Besides, the benediction surely means that the man is blessed *because* of his condition of mourning, not in spite of it. His mourning is surely a part, at least, of the Lord's ground for congratulating him: is it not the present operative means whereby the consolation is growing possible? In a word, I do not think the Lord would be content to call a man blessed on the mere ground of his going to be restored to a former bliss by no means perfect; I think he congratulated the mourners upon the grief they were enduring, because he saw the excellent glory of the comfort that was drawing nigh; because he knew the immeasurably greater joy to which the sorrow was at once clearing the way and conducting the mourner. When I say *greater*, God forbid I should mean *other*! I mean the same bliss, divinely enlarged and divinely purified—passed again through the hands of the creative Perfection. The Lord knew all the history of love and loss; beheld throughout the universe the winged Love discrowning the skeleton Fear.

HG. 104

It is a joy profound as peace to know that God is determined . . . to have his children clean, clear, pure as very snow; is determined that not only shall they with his help make up for whatever wrong they have done, but at length be incapable, by eternal choice of good, under any temptation, of doing the thing that is not divine, the thing God would not do.

SII. 102

What power could prevent him who sees the face of God from being joyful?—that bliss is his which lies behind all other bliss, without which no other bliss could ripen or last.

SII. 127

Assuredly we are not to love God for the sake of what he can give us; nay, it is impossible to love him save because he is our God, and altogether good and beautiful; but neither may we forget what the Lord does not forget, that, in the end, when the truth is victorious, God will answer his creature in the joy of his heart. For what is joy but the harmony of the spirit! The good Father made his children to be joyful; only, ere they can enter into his joy, they must be like himself, ready to sacrifice joy to truth.

No promise of such joy is an appeal to selfishness.

SII. 226

When the Lord gives you freedom and joy, use them in love and confidence. Be willing to fail in what you have set before you, and let the Lord work his own success—his acceptable and perfect will.

SF. 26

Judge/Judgment

The man who can do a vile thing is incapable of seeing it as it is; and that ought to make us very doubtful of our own judgments of ourselves, especially if they be defensive judgments.

DG

We must not shrink, in fear of the judgment of men, from doing openly what we hold right; or at all acknowledge as a law-giver what calls itself Society, or harbor the least anxiety for its approval.

HG. 181

To God alone we live or die. Let us fall, as, thank him, we must, into his hands. Let him judge us. Posterity may be wiser than we; but posterity is not our judge.

MOL. 166

"We are both accountable to that being, if such there be, who has lighted in us the candle of judgment. To him alone we stand or fall. But there must be a final way of right, toward which every willing heart is led—and which no one can find who does not seek it."

MOL. 228

Lord! what a turning of things upside down there will be one day! What a setting of lasts first, and firsts last!

PF

Only to the child of God is true judgment possible.

SII. 135

God and not man is our judge.

SII. 213

The murderer and the unloving sit on the same bench before the judge of eternal truth.

TW

How many of the judgments we are told not to judge and yet do judge must make the angels of the judging and the judged turn and look at each other and smile a sad smile, ere they set themselves to forget that which so sorely needs to be forgotten.

TW. 89

How blessed a thing that God will judge us and man shall not! Where we see no difference, he sees ages of difference.

WW. 3

Like a man, and you will judge him with more or less fairness; dislike him, fairly or unfairly, and you cannot fail to judge him unjustly.

WW. 29

If anyone thinks that God will not search closely into things, I say there could not be such a God. He will see the uttermost farthing paid. His excuses are as just as his condemnations.

WW. 31

Justice/Injustice

Every gain of injustice is a loss to the world; for life consists neither in length of days nor in ease of body. Greed of life and wrong done to secure it, will never work anything but direct loss.

HG. 239

No one can be just without love.

ML. 170

The theological lie, that punishment is the satisfaction of justice.

PF

Man is not made for justice from his fellow, but for love, which is greater than justice, and by including supersedes justice. *Mere* justice is an impossibility, a fiction of analysis. It does not exist between man and man, save relatively to human *law*. Justice to be justice must be much more than justice.

SI. 225

Love is the law of our condition, without which we can no more render justice than a man can keep a straight line walking in the dark.

SI. 225

Because he is just, we are capable of knowing justice; it is because he is just, that we have the idea of justice so deeply embedded in us.

SIII. 110

Human justice may be a poor distortion of justice, a mere shadow of it; but the justice of God must be perfect.

SIII. 114

The justice of God is this . . . he gives every man, woman, child, and beast, everything that has being, *fair play*; he renders to every man according to his work; and therein lies his perfect mercy; for nothing else could be merciful to the man, and nothing but mercy could be fair to him. God does nothing of which any just man, the thing set fairly and fully before him so that he understood, would not say, "That is fair."

SIII. 115

The justice of God, forsooth, is his punishment of sin! A just man is one who cares, and tries, and always tries, to give fair play to everyone in everything. When we speak of the justice of God, let us see that we do mean justice! Punishment of the guilty may be involved in justice, but it does not constitute the justice of God one atom more than it would constitute the justice of a man.

SIII. 115

If it be said by any that God does a thing, and the thing seems to me unjust, then either I do not know what the thing is, or God does not do it.

SIII. 118

If God punish sin, it must be merciful to punish sin; and if God forgive sin, it must be just to forgive sin. We are required to forgive, with the argument that our Father forgives. It must, I say, be right to forgive. Every attribute of God must be infinite as himself. He cannot be sometimes merciful, and not always merciful. He cannot be just, and not always just. Mercy belongs to him, and needs no contrivance of theologic chicanery to justify it.

SIII. 119

Justice is not, never can be, satisfied by suffering—nay, cannot have any satisfaction in or from suffering.

SIII. 125

Justice requires that the wicked shall not go unpunished—that they, through the eye-opening power of pain, may come to see and do justice, may be brought to desire and make all possible amends, and so become just. Such punishment concerns justice in the deepest degree.

SIII. 127

When a man acknowledges the right he denied before; when he says to the wrong, "I abjure, I loathe you; I see now what you are; I could not see it before because I would not; God forgive me; make me clean, or let me die!" then justice, that is God, has conquered—and not until then.

SIII. 128

Justice . . . requires that sin should be put an end to; and not that only, but that it should be atoned for; and where punishment can do anything to this end, where it can help the sinner to know what he has been guilty of, where it can soften his heart to see his pride and wrong and cruelty, justice requires that punishment shall not be spared.

SIII. 129

Justice demands your punishment, because justice demands, and will have, the destruction of sin. Justice demands your punishment because it demands that your father should do his best for you. God, being the God of justice, that is of fair-play, and having made us what we are, apt to fall and capable of being raised again, is in himself bound to punish in order to deliver us—else is his relation to us poor beside that of an earthly father.

SIII. 132

God will be fair to you—so fair!—fair with the fairness of a father loving his own—who will have you clean, who will neither spare you any needful shame, nor leave you exposed to any that is not needful.

SIII. 238

While a satisfied justice is an unavoidable eternal event, a satisfied revenge is an eternal impossibility.

SIII. 244

If anyone thinks that God will not search closely into things, I say there could not be such a God. He will see the uttermost farthing paid. His excuses are as just as his condemnations.

WW. 31

Justice and Mercy

The grandest exercise of justice is mercy. . . . Confusion comes from the fancy that justice means *vengeance upon sin,* and not *the doing of what is right.* Justice can be at no strife with mercy, for not to do what is just would be most unmerciful.

EA. 150

I believe that justice and mercy are simply one and the same thing; without justice to the full there can be no mercy, and without mercy to the full there can be no justice; that such is the mercy of God that he will hold his children in the consuming fire of his distance until they pay the uttermost farthing, until they drop the purse of selfishness with all the dross that is in it, and rush home to the Father and the Son.

SIII. 55

There is *no* opposition, *no* strife whatever, between mercy and justice. Those who say justice means the punishing of sin, and mercy the not punishing of sin, and attribute both to God, would make a schism in the very idea of God.

SIII. 114

"How could he be a just God and not punish sin?"

"Mercy is a good and right thing," I answer, "and but for sin there could be no mercy. We are enjoined to forgive, to be merciful, to be as our Father in heaven. Two rights cannot possibly be opposed to each other. If God punish sin, it must be merciful to punish sin; and if God forgive sin, it must be just to forgive sin. We are required to forgive, with the argument that our Father forgives. It must, I say, be right to forgive. Every attribute of God must be infinite as himself. He cannot be sometimes merciful, and not always merciful. He cannot be just, and not always just. Mercy belongs to him, and needs no contrivance of theologic chicanery to justify it."

SIII. 119

God is absolutely just, and there is no deliverance from his justice, which is one with his mercy.

SIII. 146

Kingdom

The kingdom of heaven is not come, even when God's will is our law: it is come when God's will is our will. While God's will is our law, we are but a kind of noble slaves; when his will is our will, we are free children.

DE. bk. III. 12

"Repent, for the kingdom of heaven is at hand."

That kingdom had been at hand all his infancy, boyhood, and young manhood: he was in the world with his Father in his heart: that was the kingdom of heaven. Lonely man on the hillside, or boy the cynosure of doctor-eyes, his Father was everything to him: "Did you not know that I must be in my Father's things?"

HG. 40

The King of heaven came to offer them a share in his kingdom; but they were not poor in spirit, and the kingdom of heaven was not for them. Gladly would they have inherited the earth; but they were not meek, and the earth was for the lowly children of the perfect Father.

HG. 79

The oppressed of the Lord's time looked for a Messiah to set their nation free, and make it rich and strong; the oppressed of our time believe in money, knowledge, and the will of a people which needs but power to be in its turn the oppressor. The first words of the Lord on this occasion were: "Blessed are the poor in spirit, for theirs is the kingdom of heaven."

HG. 85

It is not the proud, it is not the greedy of distinction, it is not those who gather and hoard, not those who lay down the law to their neighbors, not those that condescend, any more than those that shrug the shoulder and shoot out the lip, that have any share in the kingdom of the Father. That kingdom has no relation with or resemblance to the kingdoms of this world, deals with no one thing that distinguishes their rulers, except to repudiate it.

HG. 86

The kingdom of God, the refuge of the oppressed, the golden age of the new world, the real Utopia, the newest yet oldest Atlantis, the home of the children, will not open its gates to the most miserable who would rise above his equal in misery, who looks down on any one more miserable than himself. It is the home of perfect brotherhood.

HG. 86

The poor, the beggars in spirit, the humble men of heart, the unambitious, the unselfish; those who never despise men, and never seek their praises; the lowly, who see nothing to admire in themselves, therefore cannot seek to be admired of others; the men who give themselves away—these are the freemen of the kingdom, these are the citizens of the new Jerusalem.

HG. 86

When a man says, I am low and worthless, then the gate of the kingdom begins to open to him, for there enter the true, and this man has begun to know the truth concerning himself.

HG. 87

The kingdom of heaven belongs to the poor; the meek shall inherit the earth.

HG. 90

He who does what his Lord tells him, is in the kingdom, if every feeling of heart or brain told him he was out.

ML

The kingdom comes not with observation, and the working of the leaven of its approach must be chiefly unseen. Like the creative energy itself, it works "in secret shadow, far from all men's sight."

MOL. 49

What is the kingdom of Christ? A rule of love, of truth—a rule of service. The king is the chief servant in it. "The kings of the earth have dominion: it shall not be so among you." "The Son of Man came to minister." "My Father works now, and I work." The great Workman is the great King, laboring for his own. So he that would be greatest among them, and come nearest to the King himself, must be the servant of all. It is *like king, like subject,* in the kingdom of heaven. No rule of force, as of one kind over another kind. It is the rule of *kind,* of *nature,* of deepest nature—of *God.* If, then, to enter into this kingdom we must become children, the spirit of children must be its pervading spirit throughout, from lowly subject to lowliest king.

SI. 14

"Whosoever shall humble himself as this little child, the same is greatest in the kingdom of heaven." Hence the sign that passes between king and subject. The subject kneels in homage to the kings of the earth: the heavenly King takes his subject in his arms. This is the sign of the kingdom between them. This is the all-pervading relation of the kingdom.

SI. 14

The kingdom he has given us cannot be moved, because it has nothing weak in it: it is of the eternal world, the world of being, of truth.

SI. 30

The kingdom must come in God's holy human way. Not by a stroke of grandeur, but by years of love, yea by centuries of seeming bafflement, by aeons of labor, must he grow into the hearts of the sons and daughters of his Father in heaven.

SI. 153

None can know how difficult it is to enter into the kingdom of heaven, but those who have tried—tried hard, and have not ceased to try. I care not to be told that one may pass at once into all possible sweetness of assurance; it is not assurance I desire, but the thing itself; not the certainty of eternal life, but eternal life.

SII. 32

It always was, always will be, hard to enter into the kingdom of heaven. It is hard even to believe that one must be born from above—must pass into a new and unknown consciousness.

SII. 32

Hard to believe in, this life, this kingdom of God, this simplicity of absolute existence, is hard to enter. How hard? As hard as the Master of salvation could find words to express the hardness: "If any man comes to me, and hates not . . . his own life also, he cannot be my disciple."

SII. 32

The true share, in the heavenly kingdom throughout, is not what you have to keep, but what you have to give away. The thing that is mine is the thing I have with the power to give it. The thing I have *no* power to give a share in, is nowise mine; the thing I cannot share with everyone, cannot be essentially my own.

SIII. 252

There are those who in their very first seeking of it are nearer to the kingdom of heaven than many who have for years believed themselves of it. In the former there is more of the mind of Jesus, and when he calls them they recognize him at once and go after him; while the others examine him from head to foot, and finding him not sufficiently like the Jesus of their conception, turn their backs and go to church or chapel or chamber to kneel before a vague form mingled of tradition and fancy.

TW. chap. 36

Kingship

They would have made him a king: he would make them poor in spirit, mighty in aspiration, all kings and priests unto God.

MOL. 240

Brothers, have you found our king? There he is, kissing little children and saying they are like God.

SI. 22

Where every man is a king, there and there only does the Lord care to reign, in the name of his Father.

SIII. 99

A king must rule over his own kind. Jesus is a king in virtue of no conquest, inheritance, or election, but in right of essential being; and he cares for no subjects but such as are his subjects in the same right. His subjects must be of his own kind, in their very nature and essence kings.

SIII. 100

He says, "I am a king, for I was born for the purpose, I came into the world with the object of bearing witness to the truth. Everyone that is of my kind, that is of the truth, hears my voice. He is a king like me, and makes one of my subjects."

SIII. 100

The Lord is a king because his life, the life of his thoughts, of his imagination, of his will, of every smallest action, is true—true first to God in that he is altogether his, true to himself in that he forgets himself altogether, and true to his fellows in that he will endure anything they do to him, nor cease declaring himself the son and messenger and likeness of God. They will kill him, but it matters not: the truth is as he says!

SIII. 101

Jesus is a king because his business is to bear witness to the truth. What truth? All truth; all verity of relation throughout the universe—first of all, that his Father is good, perfectly good; and that the crown and joy of life is to desire and do the will of the eternal source of will, and of all life.

SIII. 101

The one principle of hell is—"I am my own!"

SIII. 102

Kill me, but while I live I say, Such as I am he is. If I said I did not know him, I should be a liar. I fear nothing you can do to me. Shall the king who comes to say what is true, turn his back for fear of men? My Father is like me; I know it, and I say it. You do not like to hear it because you are not like him. I am low in your eyes which measure things by their show; therefore you say I blaspheme. I should blaspheme if I said he was such as anything you are capable of imagining him, for you love show, and power, and the praise of men. I do not, and God is like me. I came into the world to show him. I am a king because he sent me to bear witness to his truth, and I bear it.

SIII. 104

Kill me, and I will rise again. You can kill me, but you cannot hold me dead. Death is my servant; you are the slaves of Death because you will not be true, and let the truth make you free. Bound, and in your hands, I am free as God, for God is my Father. I know I shall suffer, suffer unto death, but if you knew my Father, you would not wonder that I am ready; you would be ready too. He is my strength. My Father is greater than I.

SIII. 104

The true king is the man who stands up a true man and speaks the truth, and will die but not lie. The robes of such a king may be rags or purple; it matters neither way. The rags are the more likely, but neither better nor worse than the robes. Then was the Lord dressed most royally when his robes were a jest, a mockery, a laughter.

SIII. 105

Knowledge

God would have us live. If we live we cannot but know; while all the knowledge in the universe could not make us live. Obedience is the road to all things. It is the only way to grow able to trust him. Love and faith and obedience are sides of the same prism.

DG. 4

All knowledge helps to the knowing of God by one who already knows him, inasmuch as there is nothing to be known but has its being in him.

DG. 29

Everything in the world is more or less misunderstood at first: we have to learn what it is, and come at length to see that it must be so, that it could not be otherwise. Then we know it; and we never know a thing *really* until we know it thus.

HG. 1

The tree of knowledge will never prove to man the tree of life. There is no law says, You will know; a thousand laws cry out, You will do right.

HG. 237

He who loves knowledge the most genuinely, will with the most patience wait for it until it can be had righteously.

HG. 238

As to knowledge, let justice guide your search and you will know the sooner. Do the will of God, and you shall know God, and he will open your eyes to look into the very heart of knowledge. Force your violent way, and gain knowledge, to miss truth.

HG. 239

We are often unable to tell people what they *need* to know, because they *want* to know something else.

L

Our Lord himself tells us in one case, at least, that he did not know, that only his Father knew. He could discern a necessary result in the future, but not the day or the hour thereof.

MOL. 79

Omniscience is a consequence, not an essential of the divine nature. God knows because he creates. The Father knows because he orders. The Son knows because he obeys. The knowledge of the Father must be perfect; such knowledge the Son neither needs nor desires. His sole care is to do the will of the Father. Herein lies his essential divinity.

MOL. 79

Not only does he not claim perfect knowledge, but he disclaims it. He speaks once, at least, to his Father with an *if it be possible*. Those who believe omniscience essential to divinity, will therefore be driven to say that Christ was not divine. This will be their punishment for placing knowledge on a level with love. No one who does so can worship in spirit and in truth, can lift up his heart in pure adoration. He will suppose he does, but his heaven will be in the clouds, not in the sky.

MOL. 79

I ask you to think how much God must know of which we know nothing.

SI. 127

When we want to know more, that more will be there for us.

SI. 195

That he did not in this world know everything, is plain from his own words, and from signs as well: I should scorn to imagine that ignorance touching his Godhead, that his Godhead could be hurt by what enhances his devotion. It enhances in my eyes the idea of his Godhead.

SIII. 196

We have no right to school ourselves to an imaginary duty. When we do not know, then what he lays on us is *not to know*, and to be content not to know.

WM

Laughter

"Blessed are you that weep now, for you shall laugh." Welcome words from the glad heart of the Savior! Do they not make our hearts burn within us?—They shall be comforted even to laughter!

HG. 150

The poor, the hungry, the weeping, the hated, the persecuted, are the powerful, the opulent, the merry, the loved, the victorious of God's kingdom—to be filled with good things, to laugh for very delight, to be honored and sought and cherished!

HG. 150

I wonder how many Christians there are who so thoroughly believe God made them that they can laugh in God's name; who understand that God invented laughter and gave it to his children.

MOL. 23

The Lord of gladness delights in the laughter of a merry heart.

MOL. 23

It is the heart that is not yet sure of its God that is afraid to laugh in his presence.

SG. chap. 23

Law

The law of the universe holds, and will hold, the name of the Father be praised: "Whatsoever a man sows, that shall he also reap." "They have sown the wind, and they shall reap the whirlwind." "He that sows to his flesh shall of the flesh reap corruption; but he that sows to the spirit shall of the spirit reap life everlasting." "Whosoever has, to him shall be given, and he shall have more abundance; but who has not, from him shall be taken away even what he has."

HG. 197

There is no law says, you shall know; a thousand laws cry out, you shall do right. These men are a law to themselves—and what a law!

HG. 237

Labor is a law of the universe, and is not an evil. Death is a law of this world at least, and is not an evil. Torture is the law of no world, but the hell of human invention. Labor and death are for the best good of those that labor and die; they are laws of life.

HG. 237

That God should bind himself in an iron net of his own laws—that his laws should bind him in any way, seeing they are just his nature in action—is sufficiently absurd; but that such laws should interfere with his deepest relation to his creatures, should be inconsistent with the highest consequences of that creation which alone gives occasion for those laws—that, in fact, the will of God should be at strife with the foregoing action of God, not to say with the very nature of God—that he should, with an unchangeable order of material causes and effects, cage in for ever the winged aspirations of the human will which he has made in the image of his own will, toward its natural air of freedom in his will, would be pronounced inconceivable, were it not that it has been conceived and uttered—conceived and uttered, however, only by minds to which the fact of this relation was, if at all present, then only in the vaguest and most incomplete form.

MOL. 106

We know so little of law that we cannot certainly say what would be an infringement of this or that law. That which at first sight appears as such, may be but the operating of a higher law which rightly dominates the other. It is the law, as we call it, that a stone should fall to the ground. A man may place his hand beneath the stone, and then, *if his hand be strong enough*, it is the law that the stone shall not fall to the ground. The law has been lawfully prevented from working its full end.

MOL. 227

A higher condition of harmony with law, may one day enable us to do things which must now *appear* an interruption of law.

MOL. 229

The immediate end of the commandments never was that men should succeed in obeying them, but that, finding they could not do that which yet must be done, finding the more they tried the more was required of them, they should be driven to the source of life and law—of their life and his law—to seek from him such reinforcement of life as should make the fulfillment of the law as possible, yea, as natural, as necessary.

SI. 11

The law itself is infinite, reaching to such delicacies of action, that the man who tries most will be the man most aware of defeat. We are not made for law, but for love. Love is law, because it is infinitely more than law. It is of an altogether higher region than law—is, in fact, the creator of law. Had it not been for love, not one of the *shall-nots* of the law would have been uttered.

SI. 190

Of what use then is the law? To lead us to Christ, the Truth—to waken in our minds a sense of what our deepest nature, the presence, namely, of God *in* us, requires of us—to let us know, in part by failure, that the purest effort of will of which we are capable cannot lift us up even to the abstaining from wrong to our neighbor.

SI. 191

In order to fulfill the commonest law... we must rise into a loftier region altogether, a region that is above law, because it is spirit and life and makes the law.

SI. 192

A law of God's nature is a way he would have us think of him; it is a necessary truth of all being. When a law of nature makes us see this; when we say, I understand that law; I see why it ought to be; it is just like God; then it rises, not to the dignity of a truth in itself, but to the truth of its own nature—namely, a revelation of character, nature, and will in God. It is a picture of something in God, a word that tells a fact about God, and is therefore far nearer being called a truth than anything below it.

SIII. 60

Law and Grace

We are not made for law, but for grace—or for faith, to use another word so much misused.

SI. 192

The law comes to make us long for the needful grace—that is, for the divine condition . . . in which love is all, for God is love.

SI. 193

Liberty

There is no such thing in the world as liberty, except under the law of liberty; that is, the acting according to the essential laws of our own being—not our feelings which go and come.

GW. 28

The one only liberty lies in obedience.

GW. 29

Only true lover of liberty is he, who will die to give it to his neighbor!

HG. 224

All liberty must of course consist in the realization of the ideal harmony between the creative will and the created life; in the correspondence of the creature's active being to the Creator's idea, which is his substantial soul. In other words, the creature's liberty is what his obedience to the law of his existence, the will of his maker, effects for him. The instant a soul moves counter to the will of its prime cause, the universe is its prison; it dashes against the walls of it, and the sweetest of its uplifting and sustaining forces at once become its manacles and fetters.

HG. 226

The creature's liberty is what his obedience to the law of his existence, the will of his maker, effects for him.

HG. 227

The liberty here intended, it may be unnecessary to say, is not that essential liberty—freedom from sin, but the completing of the redemption of the spirit by the redemption of the body, the perfecting of the greater by its necessary complement of the less.

HG. 228

Nothing is so pleasant to ordinary human nature as to know itself by its reflection from others. When it turns from these warped and broken mirrors to seek its reflection in the divine thought, then it is redeemed; then it beholds itself in the perfect law of liberty.

ML. 11

When a man is true, if he were in hell he could not be miserable. He is right with himself because right with him whence he came. To be right with God is to be right with the universe: one with the power, the love, the will of the mighty Father, the cherisher of joy, the Lord of laughter, whose are all glories, all hopes, who loves everything and hates nothing but selfishness.

SIII. 81

It is because we are not near enough to you to partake of your liberty that we want a liberty of our own different from yours.

WM. chap. 15

Life

In this loneliness of despair, life must find The Life.

DE

To make things real to us, is the end and the battle-cause of life.

DG. 1

God alone knows what life is enough for us to live, what life we shall find worth our while; and be sure he is laboring to make it as full, and lovely, and best in beauty, as it is possible for him to make it—only that depends on how much we make possible by believing he is what he is, and letting him have his own blessed way with us. If we do not trust him, and will not work with him, but are always thwarting him in his endeavors to make us alive, then we must be miserable; there is no help for it.

DG. 33

Every obedience is the opening of another door into the boundless universe of life.

HG. 145

Religion is no way of life, no show of life, no observance of any sort. It is neither the food nor the medicine of being. It is life essential.

ML

Whoever thinks of life as a something that could be without religion, is in deathly ignorance of both. Life and religion are one, or neither is anything.

ML

If I am made to live I ought not to be willing to cease. This unwillingness to cease—above all, this unwillingness to cease to love my own . . . may be in me the sign, may *well* be in me the sign that I am made to live.

MOL. 218

God does destroy; but not life. Its outer forms yield that it may grow, and growing pass into higher embodiments, in which it can grow yet more.

MOL. 258

To understand the words of our Lord is the business of life. For it is the main road to the understanding of The Word himself. And to receive him is to receive the Father, and so to have Life in ourselves. And Life, the higher, the deeper, the simpler, the original, is the business of life.

SI. 118

The poor idea of living forever, all that commonplace minds grasp at for eternal life—(is) its mere concomitant shadow, in itself not worth thinking about. When a man is . . . one with God, what should he do but live forever?

SII. 20

The man who for consciousness of well-being depends on anything but life, the life essential, is a slave; he hangs on what is less than himself.

SII. 35

Obedience is the one key of life

SII. 62

He has made us, but we have to be. All things were made *through* the Word, but that which was made *in* the Word was life, and that life is the light of men: they who live by this light, that is, live as Jesus lived—by obedience, namely, to the Father, have a share in their own making; the light becomes life in them; they are, in their lower way, alive with the life that was first born in Jesus, and through him has been born in them—by obedience they become one with the Godhead: "As many as received him, to them gave he power to become the sons of God." He does not *make* them the sons of God, but he gives them power to become the sons of God: in choosing and obeying the truth, man becomes the true son of the Father of lights.

SII. 126

He came to supply all our lack—from the root outward; for what is it we need but more life?

SII. 138

The Father has given to the Son to have life in himself; that life is our light. We know life only as light; it is the life in us that makes us see.

SII. 144

Life is the law, the food, the necessity of life. Life is everything. Many doubtless mistake the joy of life for life itself, and, longing after the joy, languish with a thirst at once poor and inextinguishable; but even that, thirst points to the one spring. These love self, not life, and self is but the shadow of life. When it is taken for life itself, and set as the man's center, it becomes a live death in the man, a devil he worships as his God: the worm of the death eternal he clasps to his bosom as his one joy.

SII. 145

Let us in all the troubles of life remember—that our one lack is life—that what we need is more life—more of the life-making presence in us making us more, and more largely, alive. When most oppressed, when most weary of life, as our unbelief would phrase it, let us bethink ourselves that it is in truth the inroad and presence of death we are weary of. When most inclined to sleep, let us rouse ourselves to live.

SII. 146

The consciousness of life is not life; it is only the outcome of life. The real life is that which is of and by itself—is life because it wills itself—which *is*, in the active, not the passive sense: this can only be God. But in us there ought to be a life correspondent to the life that is God's; in us also must be the life that wills itself—a life in so far resembling the self-existent life and partaking of its image, that it has a share in its own being. There is an original act possible to the man, which must initiate the reality of his existence. He must live in and by willing to live.

SII. 149

There is nothing for man worthy to be called life, but the life eternal—God's life, that is, after his degree shared by the man made to be eternal also. For he is in the image of God, intended to partake of the life of the Most High, to be alive as he is alive. Of this life the outcome and the light is righteousness, love, grace, truth; but the life itself is a thing that will not be defined, even as God will not be defined.

SII. 151

He who has it not cannot believe in it: How should death believe in life?

SII. 152

What the delight of the being, what the abundance of the life he came that we might have, we can never know until we have it.

SII. 154

The infinite God, the great one life, than whom is no other—only shadows, lovely shadows of him.

SII. 155

There is no joy belonging to human nature, as God made it, that shall not be enhanced a hundredfold to the man who gives up himself—though, in so doing, he may seem to be yielding the very essence of life.

SII. 225

As to what the life of God is in relation to us, we know that it is the causing life of everything that we call life—of everything that is; and in knowing this, we know something of that life, by the very forms of its force.

SIII. 7

We too must have life in ourselves. We too must, like the Life himself, live. We can live in no way but that in which Jesus lived, in which life was made in him. The way is, to give up our life. . . . Until then we are not alive; life is not made in us. The whole strife and labor and agony of the Son with every man is to get him to die as he died. All preaching that aims not at this is a building with wood and hay and stubble.

SIII. 20

Let us not trouble ourselves about the cause of our earthliness, except we know it to be some unrighteousness in us, but go at once to the Life.

SIII. 22

There is no life but that born of the life that the Word made in himself by doing your will, which life is the light of men. Through that light is born the life of men—the same life in them that came first into being in Jesus. As he laid down his life, so must men lay down their lives, that as he lives they may live also. That which was made in him was life, and the life is the light of men; and yet his own, to whom he was sent, *did not believe him.*

SIII. 24

The only perfect idea of life is—a unit, self-existent and creative. That is God, the only one. But to this idea, in its kind, must every life, to be complete as life, correspond.

TW. 58

Until we have the life in us, we shall never be at peace.

TW. 94

It is *being* that is the precious thing.

WW

Life and Death

Life is a constant sunrise, which death cannot interrupt, any more than the night can swallow up the sun. "God is not the God of the dead, but of the living; for all live unto him."

AN. 14

I think . . . of death as the first pulse of the new strength, shaking itself free from the old mouldy remnants of earth-garments, that it may begin in freedom the new life that grows out of the old. The caterpillar dies into the butterfly.

DE. bk. III, 8

"You have tasted of death now," said the Old Man. "Is it good?" "It is good," said Mossy. "It is better than life." "No," said the Old Man. "It is only more life."

GK

If there be a God, living or dying is all one—so it be what he pleases.

ML. 42

Between death and the least movement of life there is a gulf wider than that fixed between the gates of heaven and the depths of hell.

MOL. 86

O Death, where is your sting? O Grave, where is your victory? It is the inward life of truth that conquers the outward death of appearance; and nothing else, no revelation from without, could conquer it.

MOL. 189

His resurrection was all for others. That miracle was wrought in him, not for him.

MOL. 206

"I am the resurrection and the life: he that believes in me, though he were dead, yet shall he live!" The death of not believing in God—the God revealed in Jesus—is the only death.

MOL. 207

One main doubt and terror which drives men toward the revelation in Jesus, is this strange thing Death. How shall any man imagine he is complete in himself, and can do without a Father in heaven, when he knows that he knows neither the mystery whence he sprung by birth, nor the mystery to which he goes by death?

MOL. 214

If I am made to live I ought not to be willing to cease. This unwillingness to cease—above all, this unwillingness to cease to love my own . . . may be in me the sign, may *well* be in me the sign that I am made to live.

MOL. 218

If you are not, then this, like all other prayers, goes echoing through the soulless vaults of a waste universe, from the thought of which its peoples recoil in horror. Death, then, is genial, soul-begetting, and love-creating; and Life is nowhere, save in the imaginations of the children of the grave. Whence, then, oh! whence came those their imaginations? Death, you are not my father! Grave, you are not my mother! I come of another kind, nor shall you usurp dominion over me.

MOL. 219

"When that which is perfect is come, then that which is in part shall be done away." When the spirit of death is seen, the body of death vanishes from us. Death is God's angel of birth. We fear him. The dying stretches out loving hands of hope toward him. I do not believe that death is to the dying the dreadful thing it looks to the beholders. I think it is more like what the spirit may then be able to remember of its own birth as a child into this lower world, this porch of the heavenly.

MOL. 221

If we regard the miracles of our Lord as an epitome of the works of his Father, there must be room for what we call destruction.

In the grand process of existence, destruction is one of the phases of creation; for the inferior must ever be giving way for the growth of the superior: the husk must crumble and decay, that the seed may germinate and appear. As the whole creation passes on toward the sonship, death must ever be doing its sacred work about the lower regions, that life may ever arise triumphant, in its ascent toward the will of the Father.

MOL. 251

God does destroy; but not life. Its outer forms yield that it may grow, and growing pass into higher embodiments, in which it can grow yet more. That alone will be destroyed which has the law of death in itself—namely, sin. Sin is death, and death must be swallowed up of hell. Life, that is God, is the heart of things, and destruction must be destroyed. For this victory endless *forms* of life must yield—even the *form* of the life of the Son of God himself must yield upon the cross, that the life might arise a life-giving spirit; that his own words might be fulfilled—"For if I depart not, the Comforter will not come unto you."

MOL. 258

Everything is all right. It is life indeed for him to leave that a stone, which the Father had made a stone. It would be death to him to alter one word that he had spoken.

SI. 139

When a man tries to live by bread and not by the word that comes out of that heart of God, he may think he lives, but he begins to die or is dead. Our Lord says, "I can do without the life that comes of bread: without the life that comes of the word of my Father, I die indeed."

SI. 141

. . . When the agony of death was over, when the storm of the world died away behind his retiring spirit, and he entered the regions where there is only life, and therefore all that is not music is silence . . .

SI. 187

Our Lord says, "All live unto him." With him death is not. Your life sees our life, O Lord. All of whom *all* can be said, are present to you. You think about us, eternally more than we think about you. The little life that burns within the body of this death, glows unquenchable in your true-seeing eyes. If you did forget us for a moment, then indeed death would be. But unto you we live. The beloved pass from our sight, but they pass not from yours. This that we call death, is but a form in the eyes of men. It looks something final, an awful cessation, an utter change. It seems not probable that there is anything beyond. But if God could see us before we were, and make us after his ideal, that we shall have passed from the eyes of our friends can be no argument that he beholds us no longer.

SI. 234

It is a very small matter *to you* whether the man give you your right or not: it is life or death to you whether or not you give him his.

SII. 106

Low-sunk life imagines itself weary of life, but it is death, not life, it is weary of.

SII. 138

Life is the only reality; what men call death is but a shadow—a word for that which cannot be—a negation, owing the very idea of itself to that which it would deny.

SII. 144

But for life there could be no death. If God were not, there would not even be nothing. Not even nothingness preceded life. Nothingness owes its very idea to existence.

SII. 144

We who *are*, have nothing to do with death; our relations are alone with life. The thing that can mourn can mourn only from lack; it cannot mourn because of being, but because of not enough being.

SII. 145

He who has it not cannot believe in it: how should death believe in life, though all the birds of God are singing jubilant over the empty tomb?

SII. 152

God is life essential, eternal, and death cannot live in his sight; for death is corruption, and has no existence in itself, living only in the decay of the things of life.

SII. 163

If we do not die to ourselves, we cannot live to God, and he that does not live to God, is dead.

SIII. 96

Christ died to save us, not from suffering, but from ourselves; not from injustice, far less from justice, but from being unjust. He died that we might live—but live as he lives, by dying as he died who died to himself that he might live unto God.

SIII. 96

God is deeper in us than our own life, yea, is the very center and cause of our life; therefore is the Life in us stronger than the Death, for the creating Good is stronger than the created Evil.

SF. 26

We die daily. Happy those who daily come to life as well.

WC. chap. 22

. . . No one can be living a true life, to whom dying is a terror.

WM. 30

How little are we our own! Existence is decreed us; love and suffering are appointed us. We may resist, we may modify; but we cannot keep loving, and we cannot help dying.

WM. 35

Life Eternal

To see one divine fact is to stand face to face with essential eternal life.

SI. 29

The destructible must be burned out of it, or begin to be burned out of it, before it can *partake* of eternal life. When that is all burnt away and gone, then it has eternal life. Or rather, when the fire of eternal life has possessed a man, then the destructible is gone utterly, and he is pure.

SI. 45

To love God with all our heart, and soul, and strength, and mind, is to know God, and to know him is life eternal; that is the end of the whole saving matter; it is no human beginning, it is the grand end and eternal beginning of all things.

SII. 9

The immediate end of the commandments never was that men should succeed in obeying them, but that finding they could not do that which yet must be done, finding the more they tried the more was required of them, they should be driven to the source of life and law—of their life and his law—to seek from him such reinforcement of life as should make the fulfillment of the law as possible, yea, as natural, as necessary.

SII. 11

There was nothing like this in the law: was it not hard?—hard to let earth go, and take heaven instead? for eternal life, to let dead things drop?

SII. 13

The poor idea of living forever, all that commonplace minds grasp at for eternal life—(is) its mere concomitant shadow, in itself not worth thinking about. When a man is . . . one with God, what should he do but live forever?

SII. 20

When a man has eternal life, that is, when he is one with God, what should he do but live for ever? without oneness with God, the continuance of existence would be to me the all but unsurpassable curse—the unsurpassable itself being, a God other than the God I see in Jesus.

SII. 20

It is God himself come to meet the climbing youth, to take him by the hand, and lead him up his own stair, the only stair by which ascent can be made. He shows him the first step of it through the mist. His feet are heavy; they have golden shoes. To go up that stair, he must throw aside his shoes. He must walk bare-footed into life eternal.

SII. 20

Not all the merits of God and his Christ can give you eternal life; only God and his Christ can; and they cannot, would not if they could, without your keeping the commandments. The knowledge of the living God *is* eternal life. What have you to do with his merits? You have to know his being, himself.

SII. 29

They think *they can do without eternal life, if only they may live for ever!* Those who know what eternal life means count it the one terror to have to live on without it.

SII. 32

I care not to be told that one may pass at once into all possible sweetness of assurance; it is not assurance I desire, but the thing itself; not the certainty of eternal life, but eternal life.

SII. 33

It were a small boon indeed that God should forgive men, and not give himself. It would be but to give them back themselves; and less than God just as he is will not comfort men for the essential sorrow of their existence. Only God the gift can turn that sorrow into essential joy: Jesus came to give them God, who is eternal life.

SII. 44

The ignorant soul understands by this life eternal only an endless elongation of consciousness; what God means by it is a being like his own, a being beyond the attack of decay or death, a being so essential that it has no relation whatever to nothingness; a something which is, and can never go to that which is not, for with that it never had to do, but came out of the heart of Life, the heart of God, the fountain of being; an existence partaking of the divine nature, and having nothing in common, any more than the Eternal himself, with what can pass or cease.

SII. 151

Eternal life consists for man in absolute oneness with God and all divine modes of being, oneness with every phase of right and harmony. It consists in a love as deep as it is universal, as conscious as it is unspeakable; a love that can no more be reasoned about than life itself—a love whose presence is its all-sufficing proof and justification, whose absence is an annihilating defect: he who has it not cannot believe in it: how should death believe in life, though all the birds of God are singing jubilant over the empty tomb!

SII. 152

If we do the will of God, eternal life is ours—no mere continuity of existence, for that in itself is worthless as hell, but a being that is one with the essential life.

SII. 154

This is the life that was made *in* Jesus: "That which was made in him was life." This life, self-willed in Jesus, is the one thing that makes such life—the eternal life, the true life, possible—nay, imperative, essential, to every man, woman, and child, whom the Father has sent into the outer, that he may go back into the inner world, his heart.

SIII. 12

As the self-existent life of the Father has given us being, so the willed devotion of Jesus is his power to give us eternal life like his own—to enable us to do the same. There is no life for any man, other than the same kind that Jesus has; his disciple must live by the same absolute devotion of his will to the Father's; then is his life one with the life of the Father.

SIII. 12

Light

The world is not worse than it was. What we have to do is to let our light shine. Do you get any light? Let it shine. I do not mean, be an example to other people. You have no business to set yourselves up for an example. You have to be and to do, and that is letting the light shine. It now ought not to be possible to mistake a Christian for a man of the world.

The Christian World Pulpit

The lights of the world are live lights. The lamp that the Lord kindles is a lamp that can will to shine, a soul that must shine. Its true relation to the spirits around it—to God and its fellows—is its light.

HG. 177

"So have I lighted you, not that you may shine for yourselves, but that you may give light unto all. I have set you like a city on a hill, that the whole earth may see and share in your light. Shine therefore; so shine before men, that they may see your good things and glorify your Father for the light with which he has lighted you. Take heed to your light that it be such, that it so shine, that in you men may see the Father—may see your works so good, so plainly his, that they recognize his presence in you, and thank him for you."

HG. 177

God alone is the light, and our light is the shining of his will in our lives. If our light shine at all, it must be, it can be only in showing the Father; nothing is light that does not bear him witness.

HG. 178

The man that sees the glory of God would turn sick at the thought of glorifying his own self, whose one only possible glory is to shine with the glory of God. When a man tries to shine from the self that is not one with God and filled with his light, he is but making ready for his own gathering contempt. The man who, like his Lord, seeks not his own, but the will of him who sent him, he alone shines.

HG. 178

Need I say that to let our light shine is to be just, honorable, true, courteous, more careful over the claim of our neighbor than our own, as knowing ourselves in danger of overlooking it, and not bound to insist on every claim of our own!

HG. 179

The outshining of any human light must be obedience to truth recognized as such; our first show of light as the Lord's disciples must be in doing the things he tells us.

HG. 179

He who goes about his everyday duty as the work the Father has given him to do is he who lets his light shine. But such a man will not be content with this: he must yet let his light shine.

HG. 182

If anyone, hearing the injunction to let his light shine, makes himself shine instead, it is because the light is not in him!

HG. 184

There may be those . . . who, having some, or imagining they have much light, yet have not enough to know the duty of letting it shine on their neighbors. The Lord would have his men so alive with his light that it should forever go flashing from each to all, and all, with eternal response, keep glorifying the Father.

HG. 186

You who have light, show yourselves the sons and daughters of Light, of God, of Hope—the heirs of a great completeness. Freely let your light shine.

HG. 188

Let your light out freely, that men may see it, but not that men may see you. If I do anything, not because it has to be done, not because God would have it so, not that I may do right, not because it is honest, not that I love the thing, not that I may be true to my Lord, not that the truth may be recognized as truth and as his, but that I may be seen as the doer, that I may be praised of men, that I may gain repute or fame; be the thing itself ever so good, I may look to men for my reward, for there is none for me with the Father.

HG. 189

Our light must shine in cheerfulness, in joy, yea, where a man has the gift, in merriment; in freedom from care save for one another, in interest in the things of others, in fearlessness and tenderness, in courtesy and graciousness. In our anger and indignation, specially, must our light shine. But we must give no quarter to the most shadowy thought of how this or that will look.

HG. 201

As at the first God said, "Let there be light," so the work of God is still to give light to the world, and Jesus must work his work, and *be* the light of the world—light in all its degrees and kinds, reaching into every corner where work may be done, arousing sleepy hearts, and opening blind eyes.

MOL. 62

A man had said, "I am the light of the world," and lo! here was the light of the world. The words had been vague as a dark form in darkness, but now the thing itself had invaded his innermost soul.

MOL. 64

What a divine *invention*, what a mighty gift of God is this very common thing—these eyes to see with—that light which enlightens the world, this sight which is the result of both.

MOL. 67

Such is the Father of lights who enlightens the world and every man that comes into it. Every pulsation of light on every brain is from him. Every feeling of law and order is from him. Every hint of right, every desire after the true, whatever we call aspiration, all longing for the light, every perception that this is true, that that ought to be done, is from the Father of lights. His infinite and varied light gathered into one point—for how shall we speak at all of these things if we do not speak in figures?—concentrated and embodied in Jesus, became *the* light of the world. For the light is no longer only diffused, but in him man "beholds the light *and whence it flows.*"

MOL. 67

Not merely is our chamber enlightened, but we see the lamp. And so we turn again to God, the Father of lights, yea even of The Light of the World. Henceforth we know that all the light wherever diffused has its center in God, as the light that enlightened the blind man flowed from its center in Jesus. In other words, we have a glimmering, faint, human perception of the absolute glory. We know what God is in recognizing him as our God.

MOL. 68

Where, when, or how the inner spiritual light passes into or generates outward physical light, who can tell? This border-land, this touching of what we call mind and matter, is the region of miracles—of material creation, I might have said, which is *the* great—I suspect, the *only* miracle.

MOL. 279

Nothing blinds so much as light, and their very glory might well render him unable to distinguish plainly the familiar features of *The* Son of Man.

SII. 165

The one only thing truly to reconcile all differences is, to walk in the light.

SII. 261

The life of Jesus is the light of men, revealing to them the Father.

SIII. 20

Light is not enough; light is for the sake of life. We too must have life in ourselves. We too must, like the Life himself, live. We can live in no way but that in which Jesus lived, in which life was made in him. That way is, to give up our life. This is the one supreme action of life possible to us for the making of life in ourselves. Christ did it of himself, and so became light to us, that we might be able to do it in ourselves, after him, and through his originating act. We must do it ourselves, I say. The help that he has given and gives, the light and the spirit-working of the Lord, the spirit, in our hearts, is all in order that we may, as we must, do it ourselves. Until then we are not alive; life is not made in us.

SIII. 20

It is no reflected light we see, but the glory of God shining *in*, shining out of, shining in and from the face of Christ, the glory of the Father, one with the Son.

SIII. 47

This *is* a gospel! If God be light, what more, what else can I seek than God, than God himself!

SIII. 167

Whatever seems to me darkness, that I will not believe of my God. If I should mistake, and call that darkness which is light, will he not reveal the matter to me, setting it in the light that lights every man, showing me that I saw but the husk of the thing, not the kernel? Will he not break open the shell for me, and let the truth of it, his thought, stream out upon me?

SIII. 167

He will not let it hurt me to mistake the light for darkness, while I take not the darkness for light. The one comes from blindness of the intellect, the other from blindness of heart and will. I love the light, and will not believe at the word of any man, or upon the conviction of any man, that that which seems to me darkness is in God.

SIII. 168

Where would the good news be if John said, "God is light, but you cannot see his light; you cannot tell, you have no notion, what light is; what God means by light, is not what you mean by light; what God calls light may be horrible darkness to you, for you are of another nature from him!" Where, I say, would be the good news of that?

SIII. 168

To say that what our deepest conscience calls darkness may be light to God, is blasphemy; to say light in God and light in man are of differing kinds, is to speak against the spirit of light.

SIII. 169

God is light far beyond what we can see, but what we mean by light, God means by light; and what is light to God is light to us, or would be light to us if we saw it, and will be light to us when we do see it.

SIII. 169

God means us to be jubilant in the fact that he is light—that he is what his children, made in his image, mean when they say *light*; that what in him is dark to them, is dark by excellent glory, by too much cause of jubilation; that, however dark it may be to their eyes, it is light even as they mean it, light for their eyes and souls and hearts to take in the moment they are enough of eyes, enough of souls, enough of hearts, to receive it in its very being.

SIII. 169

Living Light, you will not have me believe anything dark of you! you will have me so sure of you as to dare to say that is not of God which I see dark, see unlike the Master! If I am not honest enough, if the eye in me be not single enough to see your light, you will punish me, I thank you, and purge my eyes from their darkness, that they may let the light in, and so I become an inheritor, with your other children, of that light which is your Godhead, and makes your creatures need to worship you. "In your light we shall see light."

SIII. 169

All men will not, in our present imperfection, see the same light; but light is light notwithstanding, and what each does see, is his safety if he obeys it. In proportion as we have the image of Christ mirrored in us, we shall know what is and is not light. But never will anything prove to be light that is not of the same kind with that which we mean by light, with that in a thing which makes us call it light. The darkness yet left in us makes us sometimes doubt of a thing whether it be light or darkness; but when the eye is single, the whole body will be full of light.

SIII. 170

To fear the light is to be untrue, or at least it comes of untruth. No being, for himself or for another, needs fear the light of God. Nothing can be in light inimical to our nature, which is of God, or to anything in us that is worthy. All fear of the light, all dread lest there should be something dangerous in it, comes of the darkness still in those of us who do not love the truth with all our hearts; it will vanish as we are more and more interpenetrated with the light.

SIII. 170

Come to God, then, my brother, my sister, with all your desires and instincts, all your lofty ideals, all your longing for purity and unselfishness, all your yearning to love and be true, all your aspirations after self-forgetfulness and child-life in the breath of the Father; come to him with all your weaknesses, all your shames, all your futilities; with all your helplessness over your own thoughts; with all your failure, yea, with the sick sense of having missed the tide of true affairs; come to him with all your doubts, fears, dishonesties, meannesses, paltrinesses, misjudgments, wearinesses, disappointments, and stalenesses: be sure he will take you and all your miserable brood, whether of draggle-winged angels, or covert-seeking snakes, into his care, the angels for life, the snakes for death, and you for liberty in his limitless heart! For he is light, and in him is no darkness at all. If he were a king, a governor; if the name that described him were *The Almighty*, you might well doubt whether there could be light enough in him for you and your darkness; but he is your Father, and more your Father than the word can mean in any lips but his who said, "my Father and your Father, my God and your God"; and such a father *is* light, an infinite, perfect light.

SIII. 172

If he were any less or any other than he is, and you could yet go on growing, you must at length come to the point where you would be dissatisfied with him; but he is light, and in him is no darkness at all. If anything seem to be in him that you cannot be content with, be sure that the ripening of your love to your fellows and to him, the source of your being, will make you at length know that anything else than just what he is would have been to you an endless loss.

SIII. 173

Everyone who has not yet come to the light is not necessarily keeping his face turned away from it. We dare not say that this or that man would not have come to the light had he seen it; we do not know that he will not come to the light the moment he does see it. God gives every man time. There is a light that lightens sage and savage, but the glory of God in the face of Jesus may not have shined on this sage or that savage.

SIII. 176

Light is my inheritance through him whose life is the light of men, to wake in them the life of their Father in heaven. Loved be the Lord who in himself generated that life which is the light of men!

SIII. 262

God, like his body, the light, is all about us, and prefers to shine in upon us sideways. We could not endure the power of his vertical glory.

WW. 13

Light and Darkness

There is sometimes an advantage in the dark; you do not see how dangerous the way is. We sometimes take the darkness about us for the source of all our difficulties, but that may be a great mistake.

DG. 20

Light unshared is darkness. To be light indeed, it must shine out. It is of the very essence of light, that it is for others. The thing is true of the spiritual as of the physical light—of the truth as of its type.

HG. 176

In the darkness each soul is alone; in the light the souls are a family.

HG. 177

If it does not shine, it is darkness. In the darkness which a man takes for light, he will thrust at the heart of the Lord himself.

HG. 182

If . . . light being my pleasure, I do it that the light may shine, and that men may know *the* Light, the Father of lights, I do well; but if I do it that I may be seen shining, that the light may be noted as emanating from me and not from another, then am I of those that seek glory of men and worship Satan; the light that through me may possibly illuminate others, will, in me and for me, be darkness.

HG. 190

Your conscience does not trouble you? Take heed that the light that is in you be not darkness.

HG. 242

Let us then arise in God-born strength every time that we feel the darkness closing, or become aware that it has closed around us, and say, "I am of the Light and not of the Darkness."

SI. 177

God in the dark can make a man thirst for the light, who never in the light sought but the dark. The cells of the prison may differ in degree of darkness; but they are all alike in this, that not a door opens but to payment. There is no day but the will of God, and he who is of the night cannot be for ever allowed to roam the day; unfelt, unprized, the light must be taken from him, that he may know what the darkness is. When the darkness is perfect, when he is totally without the light he has spent the light in slaying, then will he know darkness.

SII. 108

Whatever seems to me darkness, that I will not believe of my God. If I should mistake, and call that darkness which is light, will he not reveal the matter to me, setting it in the light that lights every man, showing me that I saw but the husk of the thing, not the kernel? Will he not break open the shell for me, and let the truth of it, his thought, stream out upon me? He will not let it hurt me to mistake the light for darkness, while I take not the darkness for light. The one comes from blindness of the intellect, the other from blindness of heart and will.

SIII. 167

It is true, the light of God may be so bright that we see nothing; but that is not darkness, it is infinite hope of light.

SIII. 168

To say that what our deepest conscience calls darkness may be light to God, is blasphemy; to say light in God and light in man are of differing kinds, is to speak against the spirit of light.

SIII. 169

God is light far beyond what we can see, but what we mean by light, God means by light; and what is light to God is light to us, or would be light to us if we saw it, and will be light to us when we do see it.

SIII. 169

"In your light we shall see light."

All men will not, in our present imperfection, see the same light; but light is light notwithstanding, and what each does see, is his safety if he obeys it. In proportion as we have the image of Christ mirrored in us, we shall know what is and is not light. But never will anything prove to be light that is not of the same kind with that which we mean by light, with that in a thing which makes us call it light. The darkness yet left in us makes us sometimes doubt of a thing whether it be light or darkness; but when the eye is single, the whole body will be full of light.

SIII. 170

To fear the light is to be untrue, or at least it comes of untruth. No being, for himself or for another, needs fear the light of God. Nothing can be in light inimical to our nature, which is of God, or to anything in us that is worthy. All fear of the light, all dread lest there should be something dangerous in it, comes of the darkness still in those of us who do not love the truth with all our hearts; it will vanish as we are more and more interpenetrated with the light.

SIII. 170

Be not afraid to build upon the rock Christ, as if your holy imagination might build too high and heavy for that rock, and it must give way and crumble beneath the weight of your divine idea. Let no one persuade you that there is in him a little darkness, because of something he has said which his creature interprets into darkness. The interpretation is the work of the enemy—a handful of tares of darkness sown in the light. Neither let your cowardly conscience receive any word as light because another calls it light, while it looks to you dark. Say either the thing is not what it seems, or God never said or did it. But, of all evils, to misinterpret what God does, and then say the thing as interpreted must be right because God does it, is of the devil.

SIII. 173

Do not try to believe anything that affects you as darkness. Even if you mistake and refuse something true thereby, you will do less wrong to Christ by such a refusal than you would by accepting as his what you can see only as darkness. It is impossible you are seeing a true, a real thing—seeing it as it is, I mean—if it looks to you darkness. But let your words be few, lest you say with your tongue what you will afterward repent with your heart. Above all things believe in the light, that it is what you call light, though the darkness in you may give you cause at a time to doubt whether you are verily seeing the light.

SIII. 174

God is light indeed, but there *is* darkness; darkness is death, and men are in it.

Yes; darkness is death, but not death to him that comes out of it.

SIII. 174

No man is condemned for anything he has done; he is condemned for continuing to do wrong. He is condemned for not coming out of the darkness, for not coming to the light, the living God, who sent the light, his Son, into the world to guide him home.

SIII. 175

Choosing evil, clinging to evil, loving the darkness because it suits with their deeds, therefore turning their backs on the inbreaking light, how can they but be condemned—if God be true, if he be light, and darkness be alien to him! Whatever of honesty is in man, whatever of judgment is left in the world, must allow that their condemnation is in the very nature of things, that it must rest on them and abide.

SIII. 175

The condemnation is of those who, having seen Jesus, refuse to come to him, or pretend to come to him but do not the things he says. They have all sorts of excuses at hand; but as soon as a man begins to make excuse, the time has come when he might be doing that from which he excuses himself. How many are there not who, believing there is something somewhere with the claim of light upon them, go on and on to get more out of the darkness! This consciousness, all neglected by them, gives broad ground for the expostulation of the Lord—"You will not come to me that you might have life!"

SIII. 177

To recognize that we are to blame, is to say that we ought to be better, that we are able to do right if we will. We are able to turn our faces to the light, and come out of the darkness; the Lord will see to our growth.

SIII. 190

To say a man might disobey and be none the worse, would be to say that *no* may be *yes*, and light sometimes darkness; it would be to say that the will of God is not man's bliss.

SIII. 192

Concealment is darkness; misunderstanding is a fog.

SIII. 237

All things are God's, not as being in his power—that of course—but as coming from him. The darkness itself becomes light around him when we think that verily he has created the darkness, for there could have been no darkness but for the light.

SIII. 251

The darkness knows neither the light nor itself; only the light knows itself and the darkness also. None but God hates evil and understands it.

WM. chap. 39

Love

It is not good at all . . . to do everything for those you love, and not give them a share in the doing. It's not kind. It's making too much of yourself, my child.

AB. 110–11

Love makes everything lovely: hate concentrates itself on the one thing hated.

AF. vol. 2, chap. 10

Every man in love shows better than he is, though, thank God, not better than he is meant to become.

AF. 271

And we are nowhere told to love everybody alike, only to love every one who comes within our reach as ourselves.

AN. 230

Love is the opener as well as closer of eyes.

DG

Love is the true revealer of secrets, because it makes one with the object regarded.

DO. 117

Surely then inasmuch as man is made in the image of God, nothing less than a love in the image of God's love, all-embracing, quietly excusing, heartily commending, can constitute the blessedness of man; a love not insensible to that which is foreign to it, but overcoming it with good.

DO. 213

Opinion is often the very death of love. Love aright, and you will come to think aright; and those who think aright must think the same. In the meantime, it matters nothing. The thing that does matter is that whereto we have attained, by that we should walk.

DO. 293

As the love of him who is love, transcends ours as the heavens are higher than the earth, so must he desire in his child infinitely more than the most jealous love of the best mother can desire in hers. He would have him rid of all discontent, all fear, all grudging, all bitterness in word or thought, all gauging and measuring of his own with a different rod from that he would apply to another's. He will have no curling of the lip; no indifference in him to the man whose service in any form he uses; no desire to excel another, no contentment at gaining by his loss. He will not have him receive the smallest service without gratitude; would not hear from him a tone to jar the heart of another, a word to make it ache, be the ache ever so transient.

HG. 12

There can be no good news for us men, except of uplifting love, and no one can be lifted up who will not rise.

HG. 98

To understand is not more wonderful than to love.

L. 57

If I turned from every show of love lest it should be feigned, how was I ever to find the real love which must be somewhere in every world?

L. 123

Real love is obedience and all things beside. The Lord's own devotion was that which burns up the letter with the consuming fire of love, fulfilling and setting it aside. High love needs no letter to guide it. Doubtless the letter is all that weak faith is capable of, and it is well for those who keep it! But it is ill for those who do not outgrow and forget it! Forget it, I say, *by outgrowing it.* The Lord cared little for the letter of his own commands; he cared all for the spirit, for that was life.

MOL. 94

Love indeed is the highest in all truth; and the pressure of a hand, a kiss, the caress of a child, will do more to save sometimes, than the wisest argument, even rightly understood.

PF

It is by loving and not by being loved that one can come nearest to the soul of another.

PH. chap. 23

To love only those that love us, is, as the Lord has taught us, but a pinched and sneaking way of loving.

RS. 71

Love is one, and love is changeless.

SI. 27

Nothing is inexorable but love. Love which will yield to prayer is imperfect and poor. Nor is it then the love that yields, but its alloy. . . . For love loves unto purity.

SI. 27

Love has ever in view the absolute loveliness of that which it beholds. Where loveliness is incomplete, and love cannot love its fill of loving, it spends itself to make more lovely, that it may love more. . . .

SI. 27

. . . All that is not beautiful in the beloved, all that comes between and is not of love's kind, must be destroyed. And our God is a consuming fire.

SI. 28

Love is divine, and then most divine when it loves according to *needs* and not according to *merits.*

SI. 79

Where a man does not love, the not-loving must seem rational. For no one loves because he sees why, but because he loves.

SI. 202

Let a man once love, and all those difficulties which appeared opposed to love, will just be so many arguments for loving.

SI. 203

The love that enlarges not its borders, that is not ever spreading and including, and deepening, will contract, shrivel, decay, die.

SI. 208

Nor will God force any door to enter in. He may send a tempest about the house; the wind of his admonishment may burst doors and windows, yea, shake the house to its foundations; but not then, no so, will he enter. The door must be opened by the willing hand, ere the foot of Love will cross the threshold. He watches to see the door move from within. Every tempest is but an assault in the siege of love. The terror of God is but the other side of his love; it is love outside, that would be inside—love that knows the house is no house, only a place, until it enter.

SII. 56

Must not the glory of existence be endlessly redoubled in the infinite love of the creature—for all love is infinite—to the infinite God, the great one life, than whom is no other—only shadows, lovely shadows of him!

SII. 155

In the main we love because we cannot help it. There is no merit in it: How should there be in any love? But neither is it selfish. There are many who confound righteousness with merit, and think there is nothing righteous where there is nothing meritorious. "If it makes you happy to love," they say, "where is your merit? It is only selfishness." There is no merit, I reply, yet the love that is born in us is our salvation from selfishness. It is of the very essence of righteousness. . . . That *certain* joys should be joys, is the very denial of selfishness. The man would be a demoniacally selfish man, whom Love itself did not make joyful.

SII. 228

The bond of the universe, the chain that holds it together, the one active unity, the harmony of things, the negation of difference, the reconciliation of all forms, all shows, all wandering desires, all returning loves; the fact at the root of every vision, revealing that "love is the only good in the world."

SIII. 18

I love the one God seen in the face of Jesus Christ.

SIII. 161

"He never said, 'You must all think the same way!' But he did say 'You must all love one another, and not fight!'"

SF. 5

God is love, and Love is that which is, and was, and shall be for evermore—boundless, unconditioned, self-existent, creative! "Truly," he said to himself, "God is love, and God is all and in all! He is not abstraction; he is the one eternal Individual God! In him love evermore breaks forth anew into fresh personality—in every new consciousness, in every new child of the one creating Father. In every burning heart, in everything that hopes and fears and is, Love is the creative presence, the center, the course of life, yea Life itself, yea, God himself!"

SF. 166–67

The best things are the commonest, but the highest types and the best combinations of them are the rarest. There is more love in the world than anything else, for instance; but the best love and the individual in whom love is supreme are the rarest of all things.

SG. chap. 8

He was . . . one who did not make the common miserable blunder of taking the shadow cast by love—the desire, namely, to be loved—for love itself; his love was a vertical sun, and his own shadow was under his feet. . . . But do not mistake me through confounding, on the other hand, the desire to be loved—which is neither wrong nor noble, any more than hunger is either wrong or noble—and the delight in being loved, to be devoid of which a man must be lost in an immeasurably deeper, in an evil, ruinous, yea, a fiendish selfishness.

SG. chap. 59

The man who thoroughly loves God and his neighbor is the only man who will love a woman ideally—who can love her with the love God thought of between them when he made man male and female. The man, I repeat, who loves God with his very life, and his neighbor as Christ loves him, is the man who alone is capable of grand, perfect, glorious love to any woman.

SG. 416

The glorification of the Son of God is the glorification of the human race, for the glory of God is the glory of man, and that glory is love!

SP

If he is severe, it is with the severity of love that will speak only the truth.

SP. 284

To explain to him who loves not, is but to give him the more plentiful material for misinterpretation.

TW. 347

For a man may see visions manifold, and believe them all; and yet his faith shall not save him; something more is needed—he must have that presence of God in his soul, of which the Son of Man spoke, saying: "If a man love me, he will keep my words; and my Father will love him, and we will come unto him, and make our abode with him." God in him he will be able to love for very love's sake; God not in him his best love will die into selfishness.

WC. 419

A love can never be lost. It is a possession.

WM

Love without religion is the plucked rose. Religion without love—there is no such thing. Religion is the bush that bears all the roses; for religion is the natural condition of man in relation to the eternal facts, that is, the truths, of his own being. To live is to love; there is no life but love. What shape the love puts on, depends on the persons between whom is the relation. The poorest love with religion, is better, because truer, therefore more lasting, more genuine, more endowed with the possibility of persistence—that is, of infinite development, than the most passionate devotion between man and woman without it.

WM. 202–3

Love and Hate

Hate keeps its object present even more than the opposite passion. Love makes everything lovely; hate concentrates itself on the one thing hated.

AF. 192

Contempt is murder committed by the intellect, as hatred is murder committed by the heart.

DE

Charity having life in itself, is the opposite and destroyer of contempt as well as of hatred.

DE

A moral, that is, a human, a spiritual being, must either be God, or one with God. This truth begins to reveal itself when the man begins to feel that he cannot cast out the thing he hates, cannot be the thing he loves. That he hates thus, that he loves thus, is because God is in him, but he finds he has not enough of God.

HG. 127

Love, not hate, is deepest in what Love "loved into being."

L. 94

We need God to keep us from hating. Great in goodness, yea absolutely good, God must be, to have a right to make us—to compel our existence, and decree its laws!

WM. 35

Mammon

To let our light shine, we must take care that we have no respect for riches: if we have none, there is no fear of our showing any. To treat the poor man with less attention or cordiality than the rich is to show ourselves the servants of Mammon.

HG. 180

The most futile of all human endeavors is to serve God and Mammon. The man who makes the endeavor betrays his Master in the temple and kisses him in the garden; takes advantage of him in the shop, and offers him "divine service!" on Sunday. His very churchgoing is but a further service of Mammon!

HG. 181

The man to whom business is one thing and religion another is not a disciple. If he refuses to harmonize them by making his business religion, he has already chosen Mammon; if he thinks not to settle the question, it is settled.

HG. 181

If you are poor, then look not on your purse when it is empty. He who desires more than God wills him to have, is also a servant of mammon, for he trusts in what God has made, and not in God himself. He who laments what God has taken from him, he is a servant of Mammon. He who for care can not pray, is a servant of Mammon.

PF. 34

There was nothing like this in the law: Was it not hard?—Hard to let earth go, and take heaven instead? For eternal life, to let dead things drop? To turn his back on Mammon, and follow Jesus? Lose his rich friends, and be of the Master's household? Let him say it was hard who does not know the Lord, who has never thirsted after righteousness, never longed for the life eternal!

SII. 13

Either you do not believe the word the Lord spoke—that, if we seek first the kingdom of God and his righteousness, all things needful will be added to us; or what he undertakes does not satisfy you; it is not enough; you want more; you prefer the offers of Mammon. You are nowise anxious to be saved from the too-much that is a snare; you want what you call a fortune—the freedom of the world.

SII. 256

Mammon, the most contemptible of deities, is the most worshiped, both outside and in the house of God: to many of the religious rich, . . . the great damning revelation will be their behavior to the poor to whom they thought themselves very kind.

SIII. 240

He had a great respect for money and much overrated its value as a means of doing even what he called good: religious people generally do.

SG. chap. 39

"See how, even in the services of the church, as they call them, they will accumulate gorgeousness and cost. Had I my way, . . . I would never have any vessel used in the Eucharist but wooden platters and wooden cups."

"But are we not to serve him with our best?" said my wife.

"Yes, with our very hearts and souls, with our absolute being. But all external things should be in harmony with the spirit of his revelation. And if God chose that his Son should visit the earth in homely fashion, in homely fashion likewise should be everything that enforces and commemorates that revelation. All church-form should be on the other side from show and expense. Let the money go to build decent houses for God's poor, not to give them his holy bread and wine out of silver and gold and precious stones—stealing from the significance of the content by the meretricious grandeur of the [container]. I would send all the church-plate to fight the devil with his own weapons in our overcrowded cities, and in our villages where the husbandmen are housed like swine, by giving them room to be clean, and decent air from heaven to breathe. When the people find the clergy thus in earnest, they will follow them fast enough, and the money will come in like salt and oil upon the sacrifice."

SP. 51–52

Man

It takes a long time, and, what is more, a true heart, to know anybody. There are people that belong to the same family through the whole of a long life, and yet do not know each other to the very end.

The Christian World Pulpit

To let things be as they in reality are, and act with truth in respect of them, is to be a man.

DG. 24

The world's man, its great, its successful, its honorable man, is he who may have and do what he pleases, whose strength lies in money and the praise of men; the greatest in the kingdom of heaven is the man who is humblest and serves his fellows the most.

HG. 85

For what is a lamp or a man lighted? For them that need light, therefore for all. A candle is not lighted for itself; neither is a man. The light that serves self only is no true light; its one virtue is that it will soon go out. The bushel needs to be lighted, but not by being put over the lamp. The man's own soul needs to be lighted, but light for itself only, light covered by the bushel, is darkness whether to soul or bushel.

HG. 176

That which is within a man, not that which lies beyond his vision, is the main factor in what is about to befall him.

L. 81

The man to whom virtue is but the ornament of character, something over and above, not essential to it, is not yet a man.

ML. 61

There is hardly a limit to the knowledge and sympathy a man may have in respect to the finest things, and yet be a fool.

MM

A man may be a poet even, and speak with the tongue of an angel, and yet be a very bad fool.

MM

There is no massing of the people with him. In his behavior to men, just as in their relation to his Father, every man is alone with him.

MOL. 96

Every generation must do its own seeking and its own finding. The fault of the fathers often is that they expect their finding to stand in place of their children's seeking—expect the children to receive that which has satisfied the need of their fathers upon their testimony; whereas rightly, their testimony is not ground for their children's belief, only for their children's search. That search is faith in the bud. No man can be sure until he has found for himself. All that is required of the faithful nature is a willingness to seek.

MOL. 126

An evil man is sometimes cowed in the presence of a good man.

MOL. 180

A beast does not know that he is a beast, and the nearer a man gets to being a beast the less he knows it.

PC. chap. 8

"Perhaps some people can see things other people can't see."

PG. 158

As the fir-tree lifts up itself with a far different need from the need of the palm-tree, so does each man stand before God, and lift up a different humanity to the common Father. And for each God has a different response. With every man he has a secret—the secret of the new name. In every man there is a loneliness, an inner chamber of peculiar life into which God only can enter. I say not it is *the innermost chamber*—but a chamber into which no brother, nay, no sister can come.

SI. 111

There is no massing of men with God. When he speaks of gathered men, it is as a spiritual *body*, not as a *mass*.

SI. 112

Each man, then, is in God's sight worth. Life and action, thought and intent, are sacred. And what an end lies before us! To have a consciousness of our own ideal being flashed into us from the thought of God! Surely for this may well give way all our paltry self-consciousnesses, our self-admirations and self-worships!

SI. 113

Man's first business is, "What does God want me to do?" not "What will God do if I do so and so?"

SI. 148

Man thinks his consciousness is himself; whereas his life consists in the inbreathing of God, and the consciousness of the universe of truth. To have himself, to know himself, to enjoy himself, he calls life; whereas, if he would forget himself, tenfold would be his life in God and his neighbors.

SI. 214

The region of man's life is a spiritual region. God, his friends, his neighbors, his brothers all, is the wide world in which alone his spirit can find room. Himself is his dungeon.

SI. 215

He is made for the All, for God, who is the All, is his life. And the essential joy of his life lies abroad in the liberty of the All.

SI. 215

The number of fools not yet acknowledging the first condition of manhood nowise alters the fact that he who *has* begun to recognize duty and acknowledge the facts of his being, is but a tottering child on the path of life. He is on the path: he is as wise as at the time he can be; the Father's arms are stretched out to receive him; but he is not therefore a wonderful being; not therefore a model of wisdom; not at all the admirable creature his largely remaining folly would, in his worst moments (that is, when he feels best) persuade him to think himself; he is just one of God's poor creatures.

SII. 19

To make a man happy as a lark, *might be* to do him grievous wrong: to make a man wake, rise, look up, turn, is worth the life and death of the Son of the Eternal.

SII. 26

Our vision is so circumscribed, our theories are so small—the garment of them not large enough to wrap us in; our faith so continually fashions itself to the fit of our dwarf intellect, that there is endless room for rebellion against ourselves: we must not let our poor knowledge limit our not so poor intellect, our intellect limit our faith, our faith limit our divine hope; reason must humbly watch over all—reason, the candle of the Lord.

SII. 90

The man himself must turn against himself, and so be for himself. If nothing else will do, then hell-fire; if less will do, whatever brings repentance and self-repudiation, is God's repayment.

SII. 95

Man finds it hard to get what he wants, because he does not want the best; God finds it hard to give, because he would give the best, and man will not take it.

SII. 142

The true man trusts in a strength which is not his, and which he does not feel, does not even always desire.

SII. 148

When a man is, with his whole nature, loving and willing the truth, he is then a live truth. But this he has not originated in himself. He has seen it and striven for it, but not originated it. The one originating, living, visible truth, embracing all truths in all relations, is Jesus Christ. He is true: He is the live Truth.

SIII. 79

Every human being is like a facet cut in the great diamond to which I may dare liken the father of him who likens his kingdom to a pearl. Every man, woman, child—for the incomplete also is his, and in its very incompleteness reveals him as a progressive worker in his creation—is a revealer of God.

SIII. 253

We do not half appreciate the benefits to the race that spring from honest dullness. The *clever* people are the ruin of everything.

TW. 7

For the greatest fool and rascal in creation there is yet a worse condition, and that is not to know it, but think himself a respectable man.

TW. 58

No one knows what a poor creature he is but the man who makes it his business to be true.

WM

To be true to a man in any way is to help him.

WW

Man/Woman

The Maker of men alone understands his awful mystery between the man and woman. But without it, frightful indeed as are some of its results, assuredly the world he has made would burst its binding rings and fly asunder in shards, leaving his spirit nothing to enter, no time to work his lovely will.

PF. 27

"What do you think the first duty of married people, Mercy—to each other I mean," he said.

"To be always what they look," answered Mercy.

"Yes, but I mean actively: What is it their first duty to do toward each other?"

"I can't answer that without thinking."

"Is it not each to help the other to do the will of God?"

"I would say yes, if I were sure I really meant it."

"You will mean it one day."

"Are you sure God will teach me?"

"I think he cares more to do that than anything else."

"More than to save us?"

"What is saving but taking us out of the dark into the light? There is no salvation but to know God and grow like him."

WM. 301

Meekness

The earth as God sees it, as those to whom the kingdom of heaven belongs also see it, is good, all good, very good, fit for the meek to inherit; and one day they shall inherit it—not indeed as men of the world count inheritance, but as the Maker and Owner of the world has from the first counted it. So different are the two ways of inheriting, that one of the meek may be heartily enjoying his possession, while one of the proud is selfishly walling him out from the spot in it he loves best.

HG. 90

The meek are those that do not assert themselves, do not defend themselves, never dream of avenging themselves, or of returning aught but good for evil. They do not imagine it their business to take care of themselves.

HG. 90

The meek man may indeed take much thought, but it will not be for himself. He never builds an exclusive wall, shuts any honest neighbor out. He will not always serve the wish, but always the good of his neighbor. His service must be true service. Self shall be no umpire in affair of his. Man's consciousness of himself is but a shadow: the meek man's self always vanishes in the light of a real presence.

HG. 90

Because the man is meek, his eye is single; he sees things as God sees them, as he would have his child see them: to confront creation with pure eyes is to possess it.

HG. 91

We cannot see the world as God means it, save in proportion as our souls are meek. In meekness only are we its inheritors. Meekness alone makes the spiritual retina pure to receive God's things as they are, mingling with them neither imperfection nor impurity of its own. A thing so beheld that it conveys to me the divine thought issuing in its form, is mine; by nothing but its mediation between God and my life can anything be mine.

HG. 93

In the soul of the meek, the earth remains an endless possession—his because he who made it is his—his as nothing but his Maker could ever be the creature's. He has the earth by his divine relation to him who sent it forth from him as a tree sends out its leaves. To inherit the earth is to grow ever more alive to the presence, in it and in all its parts, of him who is the life of men.

HG. 94

Mercy

Mercy cannot get in where mercy goes not out. The outgoing makes way for the incoming. God takes the part of humanity against the man. The man must treat men as he would have God treat him.

HG. 140

The demand for mercy is far from being for the sake only of the man who needs his neighbor's mercy; it is greatly more for the sake of the man who must show the mercy. It is a small thing to a man whether or not his neighbor be merciful to him; it is life or death to him whether or not he be merciful to his neighbor.

HG. 141

The greatest mercy that can be shown to man is to make him merciful; therefore, if he will not be merciful, the mercy of God must compel him thereto. In the parable of the king taking account of his servants, he delivers the unmerciful debtor to the tormentors, "until he should pay all that was due unto him." The king had forgiven his debtor, but as the debtor refuses to pass on the forgiveness to his neighbor—the only way to make a return in kind—the king withdraws his forgiveness.

HG. 141

If we forgive not men their trespasses, our trespasses remain. For how can God in any sense forgive, remit, or send away the sin which a man insists on retaining? Unmerciful, we must be given up to the tormentors until we learn to be merciful.

HG. 141

God is merciful: we must be merciful. There is no blessedness except in being such as God; it would be altogether unmerciful to leave us unmerciful.

HG. 141

The reward of the merciful is, that by their mercy they are rendered capable of receiving the mercy of God—yea, God himself, who is Mercy.

HG. 141

The reward of mercy is not often of this world; the merciful do not often receive mercy in return from their fellows; perhaps they do not often receive much gratitude. Nonetheless, being the children of their Father in heaven, will they go on to show mercy, even to their enemies. They must give like God, and like God be blessed in giving.

HG. 146

This losing of things is of the mercy of God: it comes to teach us to let them go.

SII. 54

Miracles

God will not give us little things to spoil our appetite for great things. He will never be content until we are one with him as he is one with Christ. God will not give us signs and wonders and these inferior things; for be sure God's common and usual way is far better than this miraculous way, as we call it: because, if it were all miracle, then we would make it all common.

The Christian World Pulpit

I do not believe in miracles in the sense that there is anything done against the laws of nature; when I say laws of nature, I mean the nature of God—God is he who made nature. I believe everything is done by the nature of God, and therefore I can believe anything the most wonderful if it be according to the nature of God. I find in the New Testament no miracle that I cannot believe; they seem to me just the right thing, just the natural, simple thing. I do not know how, but there is a good deal to be learned yet before we can venture to say it cannot be, of any one of those wonders which our Savior wrought.

The Christian World Pulpit

To know God as the beginning and end, the root and cause, the giver, the enabler, the love and joy and perfect good, the present one existence in all things and degrees and conditions, is life. And faith, in its simplest, truest, mightiest form, is—to do his will in the one thing revealing itself at the moment as duty. The faith that works miracles is an inferior faith to this—and not what the old theologians call a saving faith.

DG. 1

Those who would not believe without signs and wonders could never believe worthily with any number of them, and none should be given them! His mighty works were to rouse the love and strengthen the faith of the meek and lowly in heart, of such as were ready to come to the light, and show that they were of the light.

HG. 73

The Lord never did mighty work in proof of his mission; to help a growing faith in himself and his Father, he would do anything! He healed those whom healing would deeper heal—those in whom suffering had so far done its work that its removal also would carry it on. To the Nazarenes he would not manifest his power; they were not in a condition to get good from such manifestation: it would but confirm their present arrogance and ambition. Wonderful works can only nourish a faith already existent; to him who believes without it, a miracle *may* be granted.

HG. 74

In Nazareth, because of unbelief, the Lord could only lay his hands on a few sick folk; in the rest was none of that leaning toward the truth, which alone can make room for the help of a miracle.

HG. 75

The Lord could easily have satisfied the Nazarenes that he was the Messiah: they would but have hardened into the nucleus of an army for the subjugation of the world. To a warfare with their own sins, to the subjugation of their doing and desiring to the will of the great Father, all the miracles in his power would never have persuaded them. A true convincement is not possible to hearts and minds like theirs.

HG. 79

It needs no great power of faith to believe in the miracles—for true faith is a power, not a mere yielding. There are far harder things to believe than the miracles. For a man is not required to believe in them save as believing in Jesus.

MOL. 2

The works that his Father does so widely, so grandly that they transcend the vision of men, the Son must do briefly and sharply before their very eyes.

This, I think, is the true nature of the miracles, an epitome of God's processes in nature beheld in immediate connection with their source—a source as yet lost to the eyes and too often to the hearts of men in the far-receding gradations of continuous law. That men might see the will of God at work, Jesus did the works of his Father thus.

MOL. 3

In the name of him who delighted to say "My Father is greater than I," I will say that his miracles in bread and in wine were far less grand and less beautiful than the works of the Father they represented, in making the corn to grow in the valleys, and the grapes to drink the sunlight on the hillsides of the world, with all their infinitudes of tender gradation and delicate mystery of birth. But the Son of the Father be praised, who, as it were, condensed these mysteries before us, and let us see the precious gifts coming at once from gracious hands—hands that love could kiss and nails could wound.

MOL. 4

There are some . . . who would perhaps find it more possible to accept the New Testament story if the miracles did not stand in the way. But perhaps, again, it would be easier for them to accept both if they could once look into the true heart of these miracles. So long as they regard only the surface of them, they will, most likely, see in them only a violation of the laws of nature: when they behold the heart of them, they will recognize there at least a possible fulfillment of her deepest laws.

MOL. 4

What in the hands of the Father are the mighty motions and progresses and conquests of life, in the hands of the Son are miracles. I do not myself believe that he valued the working of these miracles as he valued the utterance of the truth in words; but all that he did had the one root, *obedience*, in which alone can any son be free.

MOL. 6

What is the highest obedience? Simply a following of the Father—a doing of what the Father does. Every true father wills that his child should be as he is in his deepest love, in his highest hope. All that Jesus does is of his Father. What we see in the Son is of the Father. What his works mean concerning him, they mean concerning the Father.

MOL. 6

To him who can thank God with free heart for his good wine, there is a glad significance in the fact that our Lord's first miracle was this turning of water into wine. It is a true symbol of what he has done for the world in glorifying all things. With his divine alchemy he turns not only water into wine, but common things into radiant mysteries, yea, every meal into a Eucharist, and the sepulchre into an outgoing gate. I do not mean that he makes any change in the things or ways of God, but a mighty change in the hearts and eyes of men, so that God's facts and God's meanings become their faiths and their hopes.

MOL. 18

That the wine should be his first miracle, and that the feeding of the multitudes should be the only other creative miracle, will also suggest many thoughts in connection with the symbol he has left us of his relation to his brethren. In the wine and the bread of the Eucharist, he reminds us how utterly he has given, is giving himself for the gladness and the strength of his Father's children. Yea, more; for in that he is the radiation of the Father's glory, this bread and wine is the symbol of how utterly the Father gives himself to his children, how earnestly he would have them partakers of his own being. If Jesus was the Son of the Father, is it hard to believe that he should give men bread and wine?

MOL. 19

It is possible to see a miracle, and not believe in it; while many of those who saw a miracle of our Lord believed in the miracle, and yet did not believe in him.

MOL. 23

God will cure a man, will give him a fresh start of health and hope, and the man will be the better for it, even without having *yet* learned to thank him; but to behold the healer and acknowledge the outstretched hand of help, yet not to believe in the healer, is a terrible thing for the man.

MOL. 42

The miracles were for the persons on whom they passed. To the spectators they were something, it is true; but they were of unspeakable value to, and of endless influence upon their subjects. The true mode in which they reached others was through the healed themselves.

MOL. 66

In this miracle as in all the rest, Jesus did in little the great work of the Father; for how many more are they to whom God has given the marvel of vision than those blind whom the Lord enlightened!

MOL. 66

"God does not even cure everyone who asks him. And so with the other things you say are good to pray for."

Jesus did not cure all the ills in Judea. But those he did cure were at least real ills and real needs.

MOL. 111

Why did you not pray the Father? Why do you want always to *see*? The door of prayer has been open ever since God made man in his own image; why are signs and wonders necessary to your faith?

MOL. 124

The order of creation, the goings on of life, were ceaselessly flowing from the very heart of the Father: Why should they seek signs and wonders differing from common things only in being uncommon? In essence there was no difference. Uncommonness is not excellence, even as commonness is not inferiority. The sign, the wonder is, in fact, the lower thing, granted only because of men's hardness of heart and slowness to believe—in itself of inferior nature to God's chosen way. Yet, if signs and wonders could help them, have them they should, for neither were they at variance with the holy laws of life and faithfulness: they were but less usual utterances of the same.

MOL. 125

It was not good for men to see too many miracles. They would feast their eyes, and then cease to wonder or think. The miracle, which would be all, and quite dissociated from religion, with many of them, would cease to be wonderful, would become a common thing with most. Yea, some would cease to believe that it had been.

MOL. 198

A wonder is a poor thing for faith after all; and the miracle could be only a wonder in the eyes of those who had not prayed for it, and could not give thanks for it; who did not feel that in it they were partakers of the love of God.

MOL. 198

We know so little of law that we cannot certainly say what would be an infringement of this or that law. That which at first sight appears as such, may be but the operating of a higher law which rightly dominates the other. It is the law, as we call it, that a stone should fall to the ground. A man may place his hand beneath the stone, and then, *if his hand be strong enough*, it is the law that the stone shall not fall to the ground. The law has been lawfully prevented from working its full end. In similar ways, God might stop the working of one law by the intervention of another. Such intervention, if not understood by us, would be what we call a miracle.

MOL. 217

In our ignorance likewise lies the room for the development of the simple will, as well as the necessity for arousing it. Hence this ignorance is but the shell of faith.

In this, as in all his miracles, our Lord *shows* in one instance what his Father is ever doing without showing it.

Even the report of this is the best news we can have from the *other* world—as we call it.

MOL. 222

In similar ways, God might stop the working of one law by the intervention of another. Such intervention, if not understood by us, would be what we call a miracle.

MOL. 227

Possibly a different condition of the earth, producible according to law, might cause everything to fly off from its surface instead of seeking it. The question is whether or not we can believe that the usual laws might be set aside by laws including higher principles and wider operations.

MOL. 227

Our Lord in all his dominion over nature, set forth only the complete man—man as God means him one day to be. Why should he not know where the fishes were? or even make them come at his will?

MOL. 230

Some of these miracles were the natural result of a physical nature perfect from the indwelling of a perfect soul, whose unity with the Life of all things and in all things was absolute—in a word, whose sonship was perfect.

MOL. 231

If in the human form God thus visited his people, he would naturally show himself Lord over their circumstances. He will not lord it over their minds, for such lordship is to him abhorrent: they themselves must see and rejoice in acknowledging the lordship which makes them free. There was no grand display, only the simple doing of what at the time was needful. Some say it is a higher thing to believe of him that he took things just as they were, and led the revealing life without the aid of wonders. On any theory this is just what he did as far as his own life was concerned.

MOL. 231

He had no ambition to show himself the best of men. He comes to reveal the Father. He will work even wonders to the end, for the sake of those who could not believe as he did and had to be taught it. No miracle was needful for himself: he saw the root of the matter—the care of God.

MOL. 231

Men must believe in the great works of the Father through the little works of the Son: all that he showed was little to what God was doing. They had to be helped to see that it was God who did such things as often as they were done. He it is who causes the corn to grow for man. He gives every fish that a man eats. Even if things are terrible yet they are God's, and the Lord will still the storm for their faith in him—tame a storm, as a man might tame a wild beast—for his Father measures the waters in the hollow of his hand, and men are miserable not to know it.

MOL. 232

If he was the Son of God, the bread might as well grow in his hands as the corn in the fields. It is, I repeat, only a doing in condensed form, hence one more easily associated with its real source, of that which God is for ever doing more widely, more slowly, and with more detail both of fundamental wonder and of circumstantial loveliness.

MOL. 236

Happy are they who demand a good reason, and yet can believe a wonder!

MOL. 236

Either God is all in all, or he is nothing. Either Jesus is the Son of the Father, or he did no miracle. Either the miracles are fact, or I lose—not my faith in this man—but certain outward signs of truths which these very signs have aided me to discover and understand and see in themselves.

MOL. 245

That God will never alter his laws, I fully admit and uphold, for they are the outcome of his truth and fact; but that he might not act in ways unrecognizable by us as consistent with those laws, I have yet to see reason ere I believe.

MOL. 247

A present God manages the direction of those laws, even as a man, in his inferior way, works out his own will in the midst and by means of those laws. Shall God create that which shall fetter and limit and enslave himself? What should his laws, as known to us, be but the active mode in which he embodies certain truths—that mode also the outcome of his own nature? If so, they must be always capable of falling in with any, if not of effecting every, expression of his will.

MOL. 248

If we regard the miracles of our Lord as an epitome of the works of his Father, there must be room for what we call destruction.

MOL. 251

The essential truth of God it must be that creates its own visual image in the sun that enlightens the world: when man who is the image of God is filled with the presence of the eternal, he too, in virtue of his divine nature thus for the moment ripened to glory, radiates light from his very person. Where, when, or how the inner spiritual light passes into or generates outward physical light, who can tell? This borderland, this touching of what we call mind and matter, is the region of miracles—of material creation, I might have said, which is *the* great—I suspect, the *only* miracle.

MOL. 278

A man will hear but what he can hear, will see but what he can see, and, telling the story again, can tell but what he laid hold of, what he seemed to himself to understand. His effort to reproduce the impression made upon his mind will, as well as the impression itself, be liable to numberless altering, modifying, even, in a measure, discomposing influences. But it does not, therefore, follow that the reproduction is false.

SI. 131

The Father said, That is a stone. The Son would not say, That is a loaf. No one creative *fiat* shall contradict another. The Father and the Son are of one mind. The Lord could hunger, could starve, but would not change into another thing what his Father had made one thing. There was no such change in the feeding of the multitudes. The fish and the bread were fish and bread before. . . . There was in these miracles, and I think in all, only a hastening of appearances: the doing of that in a day, which may ordinarily take a thousand years, for with God time is not what it is with us. He makes it. . . . Nor does it render the process one whit more miraculous. Indeed, the wonder of the growing corn is to me greater than the wonder of feeding the thousands. It is easier to understand the creative power going forth at once—immediately—than through the countless, the lovely, the seemingly forsaken wonders of the cornfield.

SI. 138

A mere marvel is practically soon forgotten, and long before it is forgotten, many minds have begun to doubt the senses, their own even, which communicated it. Inward sight alone can convince of truth; signs and wonders never. No number of signs can do more than convey a probability that he who shows them knows that of which he speaks. They cannot convey the truth. But the vision of the truth itself, in the knowledge of itself, a something altogether beyond the region of signs and wonders, is the power of God, is salvation. This vision was in the Lord's face and form to the pure in heart who were able to see God; but not in his signs and wonders to those who sought after such.

SI. 152

The miracles of Jesus were the ordinary works of his Father, wrought small and swift that we might take them in.

SII. 44

That God cannot interfere to modify his plans, interfere without the change of a single law of his world, is to me absurd. If we can change, God can change, else is he less free than we—his plans, I say, not principles, not ends: God himself forbid!

SII. 81

As in all his miracles Jesus did only in miniature what his Father does ever in the great—in far wider, more elaborate, and beautiful ways, I will adduce from them an instance of answer to prayer.

SII. 81

Poor, indeed, was the making of the wine in the earthen pots of stone, compared with its making in the lovely growth of the vine with its clusters of swelling grapes.

SII. 81

The question is not at present, however, of removing mountains, a thing that will one day be simple to us, but of waking and rising from the dead *now*.

SIII. 21

Second causes are God's as much as first, and Christ made use of them as his Father's way. It were a sad world indeed if God's presence were only interference, that is, miracle.

WW. 49

The roundabout common ways of things are just as much his as the straight, miraculous ones—I incline to think more his, in the sense that they are plainly the ways he prefers.

WW. 49

Money

It is better to trust in work than in money; God never buys anything, and is forever at work.

DG. 22

That to fear poverty was the same thing as to love money, for that both came of lack of faith in the living God!

PF

Money is not Mammon; it is God's invention; it is good and the gift of God. But for money and the need of it, there would not be half the friendship in the world. It is powerful for good when divinely used. Give it plenty of air, and it is sweet as the hawthorn; shut it up, and it cankers and breeds worms. Like all the best gifts of God, like the air and the water, it must have motion and change and shakings asunder; like the earth itself, like the heart and mind of man, it must be broken and turned, not heaped together and neglected. It is an angel of mercy, whose wings are full of balm and dews and refreshings; but when you lay hold of him, pluck his pinions, pen him in a yard, and fall down and worship him—then, with the blessed vengeance of his master, he deals plague and confusion and terror, to stay the idolatry.

PF. 32

How would you not spend your money for the Lord, if he needed it at your hand! He does need it; for he that spends it upon the least of his fellows, spends it upon his Lord. To hold fast upon God with one hand, and open wide the other to your neighbor—that is religion; that is the Law and the Prophets, and the true way to all better things that are yet to come. Lord, defend us from Mammon. Hold your temple against his foul invasion. Purify our money with your air, and your sun, that it may be our slave, and you our Master. Amen.

PF. 35

Money is the power of this world—a power for defeat and failure to him who holds it—a weakness to be overcome ere a man can be strong; yet many decent people fancy it a power of the world to come! It is indeed a little power, as food and drink, as bodily strength, as the winds and the waves are powers; but it is no mighty thing for the redemption of men; yea, to the redemption of those who have it, it is the saddest obstruction.

SII. 16

The Master had repudiated money that he might do the will of his Father; and the disciple must be as his master. Had he done as the Master told him, he would soon have come to understand. Obedience is the opener of eyes.

SII. 19

Bring him a true heart, an obedient hand: he has given his life-blood for that; but your money—he neither needs it nor cares for it.

SII. 27

It is not the rich man only who is under the dominion of things; they too are slaves who, having no money, are unhappy from the lack of it. The man who is ever digging his grave is little better than he who already lies mouldering in it. The money the one has, the money the other would have, is in each the cause of an eternal stupidity. To the one as to the other comes the word, *"How is it that you do not understand?"*

SII. 39

Not merely shall we not love money, or trust in it, or seek it as the business of life, but, whether we have it or have it not, we must never think of it as a windfall from the tree of event or the cloud of circumstance, but as the gift of God.

SII. 216

He had a great respect for money, and much overrated its value as a means of doing even what *he* called good: religious people generally do—with a most un-Christian dullness. We are not told that the Master made the smallest use of money for his end.

SG. 278

Think of money as Christ thought of it, not otherwise; for no other way is true, however it may recommend itself to good men.

WM

The first thing in regard to money is to prevent it from doing harm.

WW. 4

What we too often count righteous care, but our Lord calls the care of the world, consumes the life of the heart as surely as the love of money.

WW. 23

Mortality/Immortality

It is not a belief in immortality that will deliver a man from the woes of humanity, but faith in the God of life, the Father of lights, the God of all consolation and comfort.

TW. 94

Dissociate immortality from the living Immortality, and it is not a thing to be desired.

WC. chap. 58

Mourning

Grief, then, sorrow, pain of heart, mourning, is no partition-wall between man and God. So far is it from opposing any obstacle to the passage of God's light into man's soul, that the Lord congratulates them that mourn.

HG. 99

The promise to them that mourn is not *the kingdom of heaven*, but that their mourning shall be ended, that they shall be comforted. To mourn is not to fight with evil; it is only to miss that which is good. It is not an essential heavenly condition, like poorness of spirit or meekness. No man will carry his mourning with him into heaven—or, if he does, it will speedily be turned either into joy, or into what will result in joy, namely redemptive action.

HG. 101

Mourning is a canker-bitten blossom on the rose-tree of love. Is there any mourning worthy the name that has not love for its root? Men mourn because they love. Love is the life out of which are fashioned all the natural feelings, every emotion of man. Love modeled by faith is hope; love shaped by wrong is anger—verily anger, though pure of sin; love invaded by loss is grief.

HG. 101

The garment of mourning is oftenest a winding-sheet; the loss of the loved by death is the main cause of the mourning of the world.

HG. 101

Assuredly they who mourn for their sins will be gloriously comforted, but certainly such also as are bowed down with any grief.

HG. 111

Nature

The birds grew silent, because their history laid hold on them, compelling them to turn their words into deeds, and keep eggs warm, and hunt for worms.

AF. vol.1, chap. 32

Should not man and nature go together in this world which was made for man—not for science, but for man?

AN. 68

To the man of God, all nature will be but changeful reflections of the face of God.

DO. 256

What was his place of prayer? Not the temple, but the mountain-top. Where does he find symbols whereby to speak of what goes on in the mind and before the face of his Father in heaven? Not in the temple; not in its rites; not on its altars; not in its Holy of Holies; he finds them in the world and its lovely-lowly facts; on the roadside, in the field, in the vineyard, in the garden, in the house; in the family, and the commonest of its affairs—the lighting of the lamp, the leavening of the meal, the neighbor's borrowing, the losing of the coin, the straying of the sheep. Even in the unlovely facts also of the world which he turns to holy use, such as the unjust judge, the false steward, the faithless laborers, he ignores the temple.

HG. 51

As the commonest things in nature are the most lovely, so the commonest agencies in humanity are the most powerful.

MOL. 48

Nature is brimful of symbolic and analogical parallels to the goings and comings, the growth and the changes of the highest nature in man. It could not be otherwise. For not only did they issue from the same thought, but the one is made for the other. Nature as an outer garment for man, or a living house, rather, for man to lie in. So likewise must all the works of him who did the works of the Father bear the same mark of the original of all.

MOL. 153

The wonder of the growing corn is to me greater than the wonder of feeding the thousands. It is easier to understand the creative power going forth at once—immediately—than through the countless, the lovely, the seemingly forsaken wonders of the cornfield.

SI. 138

That which cannot be shaken shall remain. That which is immortal in God shall remain in man. The death that is in them shall be consumed. It is the law of nature—that is, the law of God—that all that is destructible shall be destroyed.

SII. 44

The body of man does not exist for the sake of its hidden secrets; its hidden secrets exist for the sake of its outside—

for the face and the form in which dwells revelation: its outside is the deepest of it. So Nature as well exists primarily for her face, her look, her appeals to the heart and the imagination, her simple service to human need, and not for the secrets to be discovered in her and turned to man's farther use.

SII. 196

What in the name of God is our knowledge of the elements of the atmosphere to our knowledge of the elements of nature? What are its oxygen, its hydrogen, its nitrogen, its carbonic acid, its ozone, and all the possible rest, to the blowing of the wind on our faces? What is the analysis of water to the babble of a running stream? What is any knowledge of things to the heart, beside its child-play with the Eternal!

SII. 196

By an infinite decomposition we should know nothing more of what a thing really is, for, the moment we decompose it, it ceases to be, and all its meaning is vanished. Infinitely more than astronomy even, which destroys nothing, can do for us, is done by the mere aspect and changes of the vault over our heads. Think for a moment what would be our idea of greatness, of God, of infinitude, of aspiration, if, instead of a blue, far withdrawn, light-spangled firmament, we were born and reared under a flat white ceiling! I would not be supposed to depreciate the labors of science, but I say its discoveries are unspeakably less precious than the merest gifts of nature, those which, from morning to midnight, we take unthinking from her hands. One day, I trust, we shall be able to enter into their secrets from within them—by natural contact between our heart and theirs. When we are one with God we may well understand in an hour things that no man of science, prosecuting his investigations from the surface with all the aids that keenest human intellect can supply, would reach in the longest lifetime.

SII. 197

A law of God's nature is a way he would have us think of him; it is a necessary truth of all being. When a law of nature makes us see this; when we say, I understand that law; I see why it ought to be; it is just like God; then it rises, not to the dignity of a truth in itself, but to the truth of its own nature—namely, a revelation of character, nature, and will in God. It is a picture of something in God, a word that tells a fact about God, and is therefore far nearer being called a truth than anything below it.

SIII. 60

I believe that every fact in nature is a revelation of God, is there such as it is because God is such as he is; and I suspect that all its facts impress us so that we learn God unconsciously.

SIII. 61

How should we imagine what we may of God, without the firmament over our heads, a visible sphere, yet a formless infinitude! What idea could we have of God without the sky? The truth of the sky is what it makes us feel of the God that sent it out to our eyes.

SIII. 61

The truth of the flower is, not the facts about it, be they correct as ideal science itself, but the shining, glowing, gladdening, patient thing throned on its stalk—the compeller of smile and tear.

SIII. 65

Is oxygen-and-hydrogen the divine idea of water? Or has God put the two together only that man might separate and find them out? He allows his child to pull his toys to pieces: but were they made that he might pull them to pieces? He were a child not to be envied for whom his inglorious father would make toys to such an end! A school-examiner might see therein the best use of a toy, but not a father! Find for us what in the constitution of the two gases makes them fit and capable to be thus honored in forming the lovely thing, and you will give us a revelation about more than water, namely about the God who made oxygen and hydrogen. There is no water in oxygen, no water in hydrogen; it comes bubbling fresh from the imagination of the living God, rushing from under the great white throne of the glacier. The very thought of it makes one gasp with an elemental joy no metaphysician can analyze. The water itself, that dances and sings, and slakes the wonderful thirst—symbol and picture of that draught for which the woman of Samaria made her prayer to Jesus—this lovely thing itself, whose very wetness is a delight to every inch of the human body in its embrace—this live thing which, if I might, I would have running through my room, yea, babbling along my table—this water is its own self its own truth, and is therein a truth of God. Let him who would know the truth of the Maker, become sorely athirst, and drink of the brook by the way—then lift up his heart—not at that moment to the Maker of oxygen and hydrogen, but to the Inventor and Mediator of thirst and water, that man might foresee a little of what his soul may find in God.

SIII. 67

Wherever, in anything that God has made, in the glory of it, be it sky or flower or human face, we see the glory of God, there a true imagination is beholding a truth of God.

SIII. 69

If the flowers were not perishable, we should cease to contemplate their beauty, either blinded by the passion for hoarding the bodies of them, or dulled by the hebetude of commonplaceness that the constant presence of them would occasion. To compare great things with small, the flowers wither, the bubbles break, the clouds and sunsets pass, for the very same holy reason (in the degree of its application to them) for which the Lord withdrew from his disciples and ascended again to his Father—that the Comforter, the Spirit of Truth, the Soul of things, might come to them and abide with them, and so, the Son return, and the Father be revealed. The flower is not its loveliness, and its loveliness we must love, else we shall only treat them as flower-greedy children, who gather and gather, and fill hands and baskets from a mere desire of acquisition.

SP. chap. 19

"If it were not for the outside world, we should have no inside world to understand things by. Least of all could we understand God without these millions of sights and sounds and scents and motions, weaving their endless harmonies. They come out from his heart to let us know a little of what is in it!"

WM. 214

How many things are there in the world in which the wisest of us can ill descry the hand of God! Who not knowing could read the lily in its bulb, the great oak in the pebble-like acorn? God's beginnings do not *look* like his endings, but they *are* like; the oak *is* in the acorn, though we cannot see it.

WW. 43

Neighbor

When God comes to a man, man looks round for his neighbor. When man departed from God in the Garden of Eden, the only man in the world ceased to be the friend of the only woman in the world; and, instead of seeking to bear her burden, became her accuser to God, in whom he saw only the Judge, unable to perceive that the infinite love of the Father had come to punish him in tenderness and grace. But when God in Jesus comes back to men, brothers and sisters spread forth their arms to embrace each other, and so to embrace him. This is, when he is born again in our souls.

AN

Nothing . . . so much as humble ministration to your neighbors, will help you to that perfect love of God which casts out fear; nothing but the love of God—that God revealed in Christ—will make you able to love your neighbor aright; and the Spirit of God, which alone gives might for any good, will by these loves, which are life, strengthen you at last to believe in the light even in the midst of darkness; to hold the resolution formed in health when sickness has altered the appearance of everything around you; and to feel tenderly toward your fellow, even when you yourself are plunged in dejection or racked with pain.

AN. 386

Nothing helps many, perhaps all, to believe in God so much as the active practical love of the neighbor. If he who loves not his brother whom he has seen, can still love God whom he has not seen, then he who loves his brother must find it the easier to love God.

DG. 27

Be just to your neighbor that you may love him.

HG. 30

Among his relations with his neighbor, infinitely precious, comparison with his neighbor has no place. Which is the greater is of no account. He would not choose to be less than his neighbor; he would choose his neighbor to be greater than he. He looks up to every man. Otherwise gifted than he, his neighbor is more than he. All come from the one mighty Father.

HG. 88

The thought of standing higher in the favor of God than his brother would make him miserable. He would lift every brother to the embrace of the Father. Blessed are the poor in spirit, for they are of the same spirit as God, and of nature the kingdom of heaven is theirs.

HG. 89

The evil a man does to his neighbor shall do his neighbor no harm, shall work indeed for his good; but he himself will have to mourn for his doing. A sore injury to himself, it is to his neighbor a cause of jubilation—not for the evil the man does to himself—over that there is sorrow in heaven—but for the good it occasions his neighbor.

HG. 149

The part of philanthropist is indeed a dangerous one; and the man who would do his neighbor good must first study how not to do him evil and must begin by pulling the beam out of his own eye.

L. 71

To love our brother is to worship the Consuming Fire.

SI. 32

No man who will not forgive his neighbor, can believe that God is willing, yea wanting, to forgive *him*.

SI. 84

Each will feel the sacredness and awe of his neighbor's dark and silent speech with his God. Each will regard the other as a prophet, and look to him for what the Lord has spoken. Each, as a high priest returning from his Holy of Holies, will bring from his communion some glad tidings, some gospel of truth, which, when spoken, his neighbors shall receive and understand. Each will behold in the other a marvel of revelation, a present son or daughter of the Most High, come forth from him to reveal him afresh. In God each will draw nigh to each.

SI. 116

If a man keeps the law, I know he is a lover of his neighbor. But he is not a lover because he keeps the law: he keeps the law because he is a lover. No heart will be content with the law for love. The law cannot fulfill love.

SI. 190

It is impossible to keep the law toward one's neighbor except one loves him.

SI. 190

To refuse our neighbor love, is to do him the greatest wrong. . . . In order to fulfill the commonest law, I repeat, we must rise into a loftier region altogether, a region that is above law, because it is spirit and life and makes the law: in order to keep the law toward our neighbor, we must love our neighbor.

SI. 192

"Who is my neighbor?" said the lawyer. And the Lord taught him that every one to whom he could be or for whom he could do anything was his neighbor; therefore, that each of the race, as he comes within the touch of one tentacle of our nature, is our neighbor.

SI. 193

When we want to know more, that more will be there for us. Not every man, for instance, finds his neighbor in need of help, and he would gladly hasten the slow results of opportunity by true thinking.

SI. 195

The man who will love his neighbor can do so by no immediately operative exercise of the will. It is the man fulfilled of God from whom he came and by whom he is, who alone can as himself love his neighbor who came from God too and is by God too.

SI. 196

It *is* possible to love our neighbor as ourselves. Our Lord *never* spoke hyperbolically, although, indeed, that is the supposition on which many unconsciously interpret his words, in order to be able to persuade themselves that they believe them. We may see that it is possible before we attain to it; for our perceptions of truth are always in advance of our condition. True, no man can see it perfectly until he is it; but we must see it, that we may be it. A man who knows that he does not yet love his neighbor as himself may believe in such a condition, may even see that there is no other goal of human perfection, nothing else to which the universe is speeding, propelled by the Father's will.

SI. 197

No man can love his neighbor *merely* because the Lord says so. The Lord says so because it is right and necessary and natural, and the man wants to feel it thus right and necessary and natural.

SI. 199

A man must not choose his neighbor; he must take the neighbor that God sends him. In him, whoever he be, lies, hidden or revealed, a beautiful brother. The neighbor is just the man who is next to you at the moment, the man with whom any business has brought you in contact.

SI. 210

This love of our neighbor is the only door out of the dungeon of self, where we mope and mow, striking sparks, and rubbing phosphorescences out of the walls, and blowing our own breath in our own nostrils, instead of issuing to the fair sunlight of God, the sweet winds of the universe.

SI. 214

The one bliss, next to the love of God, is the love of our neighbor. If any say, "You love because it makes you blessed," I deny it: "We are blessed, I say, because we love." No one could attain to the bliss of loving his neighbor who was selfish and sought that bliss from love of himself. Love is unselfishness. In the main we love because we cannot help it.

SII. 227

Except I love my neighbor as myself, I may one day betray him! Let us therefore be compassionate and humble, and hope for every man.

SIII. 242

There was a time when I could not understand that he who loved not his brother was a murderer: now I see it to be no figure of speech, but, in the realities of man's moral and spiritual nature, an absolute simple fact. The murderer and the unloving sit on the same bench before the judge of eternal truth. The man who loves not his brother I do not say is at this moment capable of killing him, but if the natural working of his unlove be not checked, he will assuredly become capable of killing him. Until we love our brother—yes until we love our enemy, who is yet our brother—we contain within ourselves the undeveloped germ of murder.

TW. 341

Our business is not to protect ourselves from our neighbor's wrong, but our neighbor from our wrong. This is to slay evil; the other is to make it multiply.

WM. 46

New Birth

The change that must pass in him more than equals a new creation, inasmuch as it is a higher creation. But its necessity is involved in a former creation; and thence we have a right to ask help of our Creator, for he requires of us what he has created us unable to effect without him. Nay, nay!—could we do anything without him, it were a thing to leave undone.

HG. 37

Cure for any ill in me or about me there is none, but to become the son of God I was born to be. Until such I am, until Christ is born in me, until I am revealed a son of God, pain and trouble will endure—and God grant they may! Call this presumption, and I can only widen my assertion: until you yourself are the son of God you were born to be, you will never find life a good thing.

SII. 135

"But how can God bring this about in me?"—Let him do it and perhaps you will know.

SIII. 226

Obedience

With an obedient mind one learns the rights of things fast enough; for it is the law of the universe, and to obey is to understand.

AB. 175

You have been very careful in reading your Bible and going to church, and doing this or that thing which you think belongs to religion; but have you been doing the thing Christ told you? If you do that, I do not care whatever else you do; you cannot be wrong then.

The Christian World Pulpit

"Do this," and he does it. It is obedience, friends, that is faith; it is doing that thing which you, let me say, even only suppose to be the will of God; for if you are wrong, and do it because you think it is his will, he will set you right. It is the turning of the eye to the light; it is the sending of the feet into the path that is required, putting the hands to do the things which the conscience says ought to be done.

The Christian World Pulpit

Faith is the trying of the things unseen—the putting of them to the test; and whatever your doubts and fears are, try God by obedience, and then you will get help to carry you on. Less than that will not do.

The Christian World Pulpit

Obedience is the road to all things. It is the only way to grow able to trust him. Love and faith and obedience are sides of the same prism.

DG. 9

Obedience is the one condition of progress.

DO. 289

Obedience is the grandest thing in the world to begin with. Yes, and we shall end with it too. I do not think the time will ever come when we shall not have something to do, because we are told to do it without knowing why.

DO. 307

The one only liberty lies in obedience.

GW. 29

Men would understand: they do not care to *obey*—understand where it is impossible they should understand save by obeying.

HG. 17

Instead of immediately obeying the Lord of life, the one condition upon which he can help them, and in itself the beginning of their deliverance, they set themselves to question their unenlightened intellects as to his plans for their deliverance—and not merely how he means to effect it, but how he can be able to effect it.

HG. 17

Upon obedience our energy must be spent; understanding will follow.

HG. 19

Obedience is the soul of knowledge.

HG. 19

By obedience, I intend no kind of obedience to man, or submission to authority claimed by man or community of men. I mean obedience to the will of the Father, however revealed in our conscience.

HG. 19

Until a man begins to obey, the light that is in him is darkness.

HG. 19

Every obedience is the opening of another door into the boundless universe of life.

HG. 145

"Our Lord speaks of many coming up to his door confident of admission, whom yet he sends from him. Faith is obedience, not confidence."

ML

The whole secret is to do the thing the Master tells you: then you will understand what he tells you.

MM

Our Lord delays the cure . . . with no further speech. The man knows nothing about him, and he makes no demand upon his faith, except that of obedience. He gives him something to do at once. He will find him again by and by. The man obeys, takes up his bed, and walks.

MOL. 58

Obedience is the only service.

MOL. 93

Real love is obedience and all things beside.

MOL. 94

All shapes of argument must be employed to arouse the slumbering will of men. Even the obedience that comes of the lowest fear is a first step toward an infinitely higher condition than that of the most perfect nature created incapable of sin.

MOL. 252

It is not obedience alone that our Lord will have, but obedience to the *truth*, that is, to the Light of the World, truth beheld and known.

SI. 11

Nothing but the obedience of the Son, the obedience unto the death, the absolute *doing* of the will of God because it was the truth, could redeem the prisoner, the widow, the orphan.

SI. 158

It is a beautiful thing to obey the rightful source of a command: it is a more beautiful thing to worship the radiant source of our light, and it is for the sake of obedient vision that our Lord commands us. For then our heart meets his: we see God.

SI. 200

A time comes to every man when he must obey, or make such refusal—*and know it.*

SII. 15

Obedience is the opener of eyes.

SII. 19

None can know how difficult it is to enter into the kingdom of heaven, but those who have tried—tried hard, and have not ceased to try.

SII. 32

Obedience is the one key of life.

SII. 62

Obedience is the joining of the links of the eternal round. Obedience is but the other side of the creative will. Will is God's will, obedience is man's will; the two make one.

SII. 154

It is the one terrible heresy of the church, that it has always been presenting something else than obedience as faith in Christ.

SII. 243

Get up, and do something the Master tells you; so make yourself his disciple at once. Instead of asking yourself whether you believe or not, ask yourself whether you have this day done one thing because he said, Do it, or once abstained because he said, Do not do it.

SII. 244

It is simply absurd to say you believe, or even want to believe, in him, if you do not anything he tells you.

SII. 245

We must learn to obey him in everything, and so must begin somewhere: let it be at once, and in the very next thing that lies at the door of our conscience! O fools and slow of heart, if you think of nothing but Christ, and do not set yourselves to do his words! you but build your houses on the sand.

SII. 245

It is to the man who is trying to live, to the man who is obedient to the word of the Master, that the word of the Master unfolds itself.

SII. 245

He says the man that does not do the things he tells him, builds his house to fall in utter ruin.

SII. 246

Obedience is not perfection, but trying.

SII. 249

Correctest notions without obedience are worthless.

SII. 249

The whole secret of progress is the doing of the thing we know. There is no other way of progress in the spiritual life; no other way of progress in the understanding of that life: only as we do, can we know.

SII. 253

Oh the folly of any mind that would explain God before obeying him! that would map out the character of God, instead of crying, Lord, what would you have me to do?

SIII. 115

To put off obeying him until we find a credible theory concerning him is to set aside the potion we know it our duty to drink, for the study of the various schools of therapy.

SIII. 152

Obey the truth, I say, and let theory wait. Theory may spring from life, but never life from theory.

SIII. 152

To him who obeys, and thus opens the door of his heart to receive the eternal gift, God gives the Spirit of his Son.

SIII. 155

Every man must read the Word for himself. One may read it in one shape, another in another: all will be right if it be indeed the Word they read, and they read it by the lamp of obedience.

SIII. 167

He who is willing to do the will of the Father shall know the truth of the teaching of Jesus. The spirit is "given to them that obey him."

SIII. 167

How many are there not who seem capable of anything for the sake of the church or Christianity, except the one thing its Lord cares about—that they should do what he tells them. He would deliver them from themselves, into the liberty of the sons of God, make them his brothers: they leave him to vaunt their church.

SIII. 188

To say a man might disobey and be none the worse, would be to say that *no* may be *yes*, and light sometimes darkness; it would be to say that the will of God is not man's bliss.

SIII. 192

Let patience have her perfect work. Statue under the chisel of the sculptor, stand steady to the blows of his mallet. Clay on the wheel, let the fingers of the divine potter model you at their will. Obey the Father's slightest word: hear the Brother who knows you and died for you.

SIII. 227

Your hand be on the latch to open the door at his first knock. If you open the door and not see him, do not say he did not knock, but understand that he is there, and wants you to go out to him. It may be he has something for you to do for him. Go and do it, and perhaps you will return with a new prayer, to find a new window in your soul.

SIII. 227

He only who obeys him, does or can know him; he who obeys him cannot fail to know him.

SG

By obeying one learns how to obey.

SG. 334

The reason why you do not trust him more is that you obey him so little. If you would only ask what God would have you to do, you would soon find your confidence growing.

SP

Impressed as I am with the truth of his nature, the absolute devotion of his life, and the essential might of his being, I yet obey not [Christ], I shall not only deserve to perish, but in that very refusal draw ruin upon my head.

TW

When will men understand that it is neither thought nor talk, neither sorrow for sin nor love of holiness that is required of them, but obedience! To *be* and to *obey* are one.

WM

The only way to know what is true is to do what is true.

WW. 129

Old Age

I am now getting old—faster and faster. I cannot help my gray hairs, nor the wrinkles that gather so slowly yet ruthlessly; no, nor the quaver that will come in my voice, nor the sense of being feeble in the knees, even when I walk only across the floor of my study. But I have not got used to age yet. I do not *feel* one atom older than I did at three-and-twenty. Nay, to tell all the truth, I feel a good deal younger. For then I only felt that a man had to take up his cross; whereas now I feel that a man has to follow him; and that makes an unspeakable difference. When my voice quavers, I feel that it is mine and not mine; that it just belongs to me like my watch, which does not go well now, though it went well thirty years ago—not more than a minute out in a month. And when I feel my knees shake, I think of them with a kind of pity, as I used to think of an old mare of my father's of which I was very fond when I was a lad, and which bore me across many a field and over many a fence, but which at last came to have the same weakness in her knees that I have in mine; and she knew it too, and took care of them, and so of herself, in a wise equine fashion. These things are not me—or *I*, if the grammarians like it better (I always feel a strife between doing as the scholar does and doing as other people do); they are not me, I say; I *have* them—and, please God, shall soon have better. For it is not a pleasant thing for a young man, or a young woman either, I venture to say, to have an old voice, and a wrinkled face, and weak knees, and gray hair, or no hair at all. And if any moral Philistine, as our queer German brothers over the Northern fish-pond would call him, say that this is all rubbish, for that we *are* old. I would answer; "Of all children how can the children of God be old?"

AN. 2

Oneness

Oneness with God is the end of all this order of things. When that is attained, God only knows in what glorious regions of life and labor he will place us, able to do greater things than the Lord himself did when he was on earth.

DG. 25

It is only where a man is at one with God that he can do the right thing or take the right way. Whatever springs from any other source than the spirit that dwelt in Jesus, is of sin, and works to thwart the divine will.

M. 53

Although . . . every man stands alone in God, I yet say two or many can meet in God as they cannot meet save in God; nay, that only in God can two or many truly meet; only as they recognize their oneness with God can they become one with each other.

MOL. 99

When a man has eternal life, that is, when he is one with God, what should he do but live forever? without oneness with God, the continuance of existence would be to me the all but unsurpassable curse—the unsurpassable itself being, a God other than the God I see in Jesus.

SII. 20

There can be no unity, no delight of love, no harmony, no good in being, where there is but one. Two at least are needed for oneness; and the greater the number of individuals, the greater, the lovelier, the richer, the diviner is the possible unity.

SII. 141

The self-existent God is that other by whose will we live; so the links of the unity must already exist, and can but require to be brought together. For the link in our being wherewith to close the circle of immortal oneness with the Father, we must of course search the deepest of man's nature: there only, in all assurance, can it be found. And there we do find it.

SII. 153

If we do the will of God, eternal life is ours—no mere continuity of existence, for that in itself is worthless as hell, but a being that is one with the essential life.

SII. 154

Nothing is but good but the will of God; nothing noble enough for the desire of the heart of man but oneness with the eternal. For this God must make him yield his very being, that he may enter in and dwell with him.

SII. 194

The doing of the will of God is the way to oneness with God, which alone is salvation.

SII. 249

God and man together, the vital energy flowing unchecked from the Creator into his creature—that is the salvation of the creature.

SII. 250

For of no onehood comes unity; there can be no oneness where there is only one. For the very beginnings of unity there must be two. Without Christ, therefore, there could be no universe. The reconciliation wrought by Jesus is not the primary source of unity, of safety to the world; that reconciliation was the necessary working out of the eternal antecedent fact, the fact making itself potent upon the rest of the family—that God and Christ are one, are Father and Son, the Father loving the Son as only the Father can love, the Son loving the Father as only the Son can love.

SIII. 18–19

The prayer of the Lord for unity between men and the Father and himself, springs from the eternal need of love.

SIII. 19

When a man truly and perfectly says with Jesus, and as Jesus said it, "Your will be done," he closes the everlasting life-circle; the life of the Father and the Son flows through him; he is a part of the divine organism. Then is the prayer of the Lord in him fulfilled: "I in them and you in me, that they made be made perfect in one."

SIII. 21

Salvation lies in being one with Christ, even as the branch is one with the vine.

WM

God is not shut up in heaven, neither is there one law of life there and another here; I desire more life here, and shall have it, for what is needful for this world is to be had in this world. In proportion as I become one with God, I shall have it.

WM. 22

Opinion

Those who seek God with their faces hardly turned toward him, who, instead of beholding the Father in the Son, take the stupidest opinions concerning him and his ways from men who, if they have themselves ever known him, have never taught him from their own knowledge of him, but from the dogmas of others, go wandering about in dark mountains, or through marsh, spending their strength in avoiding precipices and bog-holes, sighing and mourning over their sins instead of leaving them behind and fleeing to the Father, whom to know is eternal life.

DG. 6

Opinion is often the very death of love. Love aright, and you will come to think aright; and those who think aright must think the same. In the meantime, it matters nothing. The thing that does matter is that whereto we have attained, by that we should walk.

DO

It is only as they help us toward God, that our opinions are worth a straw; and every necessary change in them must be to more truth, to greater uplifting power.

DO. 295

The opinion of the wisest man, if he does not do the things he reads, is not worth a rush. He may be partly right, but you have no reason to trust him.

MM

Truth in the inward parts is a power not an opinion.

PF. 264

If a man care more for opinion than for life, it is not worth any other man's while to persuade him to renounce the opinions he happens to entertain; he would but put other opinions in the same place of honor—a place which can *belong* to no opinion whatever: it matters nothing what such a man may or may not believe, for he is not a true man. By holding with a school he supposes to be right, he but bolsters himself up with the worst of all unbelief—opinion calling itself faith—unbelief calling itself religion.

SII. 231

For him who is in earnest about the will of God, it is of endless consequence that he should think rightly of God. He cannot come close to him, cannot truly know his will, while his notion of him is in any point that of a false god. The thing shows itself absurd. If such a man seem to himself to be giving up even his former assurance of salvation, in yielding such ideas of God as are unworthy of God, he must nonetheless, if he will be true, if he would enter into life, take up that cross also. He will come to see that he must follow *no* doctrine, but in true as word of man could state it, but the living Truth, the Master himself.

SII. 231

Whatever be your *opinions* on the greatest of all subjects, is it well that the impression with regard to Christianity made upon your generation, should be that of your opinions, and not of something beyond opinion? Is Christianity capable of being represented by opinion, even the best? If it were, how many of us are such as God would choose to represent his thoughts and intents by our opinions concerning them? Who is there of his friends whom any thoughtful man would depute to represent his thoughts to his fellows? If you answer, "The opinions I hold and by which I represent Christianity, are those of the Bible," I reply, that none can understand, still less represent, the opinions of another, but such as are of the same mind with him—certainly none who mistake his whole scope and intent so far as in supposing *opinion* to be the object of any writer in the Bible.

SII. 238

Except the light of the knowledge of the glory of God in the face of Christ Jesus make a man sick of his opinions, he may hold them to doomsday for me; for no opinion, I repeat, is Christianity, and no preaching of any plan of salvation is the preaching of the glorious gospel of the living God. Even if your plan, your theories, were absolutely true, the holding of them with sincerity, the trusting in this or that about Christ, or in anything he did or could do, the trusting in anything but himself, his own living self, is a delusion.

SII. 241

When I say *truth*, I do not mean *opinion*: to treat opinion as if that were truth, is grievously to wrong the truth.

SIII. 107

Opinion, right or wrong, will do nothing to save him. I would that he thought no more about this or any other opinion, but set himself to do the work of the Master.

SIII. 139

Let a man do right, nor trouble himself about worthless opinion; the less he heeds tongues, the less difficult will he find it to love men.

SIII. 235

He had a good opinion of himself—on what grounds I do not know; but he was rich. . . . I doubt if there is any more certain soil for growing a good opinion of oneself. Certainly, the more you try to raise one by doing what is right and worth doing, the less you succeed.

WM. 6

Others

It is not by driving away our brother that we can be alone with God.

AF. vol. 2, chap. 12

To find God in others is better than to grow *solely* in the discovery of him in ourselves, if indeed the latter were possible.

EA. 227

It is a fundamental necessity of the kingdom of heaven, impossible as it must seem to all outside it, that each shall count other better than himself; it is the natural condition of the man God made, in relation to the other men

God has made. Man is made, not to contemplate himself, but to behold in others the Beauty of the Father. A man who lives to meditate upon and worship himself, is in the slime of hell.

HA. 77

The man who does not house self has room to be his real self—God's eternal idea of him. He lives eternally; in virtue of the creative power present in him with momently unimpeded creature, he *is.* How should there be in him one thought of ruling or commanding or surpassing! He can imagine no bliss, no good in being greater than someone else. He is unable to wish himself other than he is, except more what God made him for, which is indeed the highest willing of the will of God. His brother's well-being is essential to his bliss.

HG. 89

What a sweet color the divine light takes to itself in courtesy, whose perfection is the recognition of every man as a temple of the living God.

HG. 183

In thinking lovingly about others, we think healthily about ourselves.

MM. 495

Nowhere in the divine arrangements is my gain another's loss.

MOL. 56

We are as God made us.—No, I will not say that: I will say rather, I am as God is making me, and I shall one day be as he has made me. Meantime I know that he will have me love my enemy tenfold more than now I love my friend.

PF. 29

It is by loving and not by being loved that one can come nearest to the soul of another.

PH. chap. 23

He gives himself to us—shall not we give ourselves to him? Shall we not give ourselves to each other whom he loves?

SI. 21

Otherness is the essential ground of affection.

SI. 201

The man who loves his fellow is infinitely more alive than he whose endeavor is to exalt himself above him.

SII. 146

The true disciple shall . . . always know what he ought to do, though not necessarily what another ought to do.

SII. 155

Every man who tries to obey the Master is my brother, whether he counts me such or not, and I revere him; but dare I give quarter to what I see to be a lie because my brother believes it? The lie is not of God, whoever may hold it.

SIII. 150

Do not heed much if men mock you and speak lies of you, or in goodwill defend you unworthily. Heed not much if even the righteous turn their backs upon you. Only take heed that you tun not from them.

SIII. 228

Are you willing to be made glad that you were wrong when you thought others were wrong?

SIII. 236

Every one of us is something that the other is not, and therefore knows something—it may be without knowing that he knows it—which no one else knows; and that it is every one's business, as one of the kingdom of light, and inheritor in it all, to give his portion to the rest; for we are one family, with God at the head and heart of it, and Jesus Christ, our Elder Brother, teaching us of the Father, whom he only knows.

SIII. 255

The man or woman who opposes the heart's desire of another, except in aid of righteousness, is a servant of Satan.

WM. 35

Respect and graciousness from each to each is of the very essence of Christianity, independently of rank, or possession or relations. . . . The man who thinks of the homage due to him, and not of the homage owing by him, is essentially rude.

WM. 54

Patience

One of the principal parts of faith is patience, and that the setting of wrong things right is so far from easy that not even God can do it all at once. But time is nothing to him who sees the end from the beginning; he does not grudge thousands of years of labor. The things he cares to do for us require our cooperation, and that makes the great difficulty: we are such poor fellow workers with him! All that seems to deny his presence and labor only, necessitates a larger theory of that presence and labor.

WW. 53

Peace/Peacemakers

We can never be at peace until we have performed the highest duty of all—until we have arisen, and gone to our Father.

DE

If God be at peace, why should not I be?

DG. 10

Those that are on their way to see God, those who are growing pure in heart through hunger and thirst after righteousness, are indeed the children of God; but specially the Lord calls those his children who, on their way home, are peacemakers in the traveling company; for, surely, those in any family are specially the children, who make peace with and among the rest.

HG. 132

His eldest Son, his very likeness, was the first of the family peacemakers. Preaching peace to them that were afar off and them that were nigh, he stood undefended in the turbulent crowd of his fellows, and it was only over his dead body that his brothers began to come together in the peace that will not be broken. He rose again from the dead; his peace-making brothers, like himself, are dying unto sin; and not yet have the evil children made their Father hate, or their Elder Brother flinch.

HG. 134

One thing is plain—that we must love the strife-maker; another is nearly as plain—that, if we do not love him, we must leave him alone; for without love there can be no peace-making, and words will but occasion more strife. To be kind neither hurts nor compromises. Kindness has many phases, and the fitting form of it may avoid offense, and must avoid untruth.

HG. 138

Whatever our relation, then, with any peace-breaker, our mercy must ever be within call; and it may help us against an indignation too strong to be pure, to remember that when any man is reviled for righteousness' sake, then is he blessed.

HG. 139

Peace is for those who *do* the truth not those who opine it. The true man troubled by intellectual doubt, is so troubled unto further health and growth. Let him be alive and hopeful, above all obedient, and he will be able to wait for the deeper content which must follow with completer insight.

PF. 264

You say, "Lord I believe: help mine unbelief," but when he says, "Leave everything behind you, and be as I am toward God, and you shall have peace and rest."

SII. 257

Let us be at peace, because peace is at the heart of things—peace and utter satisfaction between the Father and the Son—in which peace they call us to share; in which peace they promise that at length, when they have their good way with us, we shall share.

SIII. 23

Perfection

Unhappy men were we, if God were the God of the perfected only, and not of the growing, the becoming! "Blessed are they," says the Lord concerning the not yet pure, "which do hunger and thirst after righteousness, for they shall be filled." Filled with righteousness, they are pure; pure, they shall see God.

HG. 124

Nothing is required of man that is not first in God. It is because God is perfect that we are required to be perfect.

SI. 9

That no keeping but a perfect one will satisfy God, I hold with all my heart and strength; but that there is none else he cares for, is one of the lies of the enemy. What father is not pleased with the first tottering attempt of his little one to walk? What father would be satisfied with anything but the manly step of the full-grown son?

SII. 10

Perfection—the thing the commonplace Christian thinks he can best do without—the thing the elect hungers after with an eternal hunger. Perfection, the perfection of the Father, is eternal life.

SII. 12

To gain the perfection he desired, the one thing lacking was, that he should sell all that he had, give it to the poor, and follow the Lord! Could this be all that lay between him and entering into life? God only knows what the victory of such an obedience might at once have wrought in him! Much, much more would be necessary before perfection was reached, but certainly the next step, to sell and follow, would have been the step into life: had he taken it, in the very act would have been born in him that whose essence and vitality is eternal life, needing but process to develop it not the glorious consciousness of oneness with The Life.

SII. 12

"I do not want to be perfect, I am content to be saved." Such as he do not care for being perfect as their Father in heaven is perfect, but for being what they call *saved.* They little think that without perfection there is no salvation—perfection is salvation: they are one.

SII. 25

There is a great difference between *I wish I was* and *I should like to be*—as much as between a grumble and a prayer. To be content is not to be satisfied. No one ought to be satisfied with the imperfect.

TW

The nearer perfection a character is, the louder is the cry of conscience at the appearance of fault; and, on the other hand, the worst criminals have had the easiest minds.

TW. 32

Poems

Preacher's Repentance

O Lord, I have been talking to the
people;
Thought's wheels have round me
whirled a fiery zone,
And the recoil of my word's airy ripple
My heart unheedful has puffed up
and blown.
Therefore I cast myself before thee
prone:
Lay cool hands on my burning
brain and press
From my weak heart the swelling
emptiness.

DS. Jan 31

Deeds

I would go near thee—but I cannot
press
Into thy presence—it helps not to
presume.
Thy doors are deeds.

DS. May 16

Prayer

My prayers, my God, flow from
what I am not;
I think thy answers make me what I
am,
Like weary waves thought follows
upon thought,
But the still depth beneath is all
thine own,
And there thou mov'st in paths to us
unknown.
Out of strange strife thy peace is
strangely wrought;
If the lion in us pray—thou answer-
est the lamb.

DS. May 26

The house is not for me

The house is not for me—it is for
Him.
His royal thoughts require many a
stair,
Many a tower, many an outlook fair
Of which I have no thought.

DS. July 16

Hoarding

In holy things may be unholy greed.
Thou giv'st a glimpse of many a
lovely thing
Not to be stored for use in any
mind,
But only for the present spiritual
need.
The holiest bread, if hoarded, soon
will breed
The mammon-moth, the having-
pride . . .

DS. Aug. 7

The day's first job

With every morn my life afresh
must break
The crust of self, gathered about me
fresh.

DS. Oct. 10

Obstinate illusion

Have pity on us for the look of
things,
When blank denial stares us in the face.
Although the serpent mask have
lied before
It fascinates the bird.

DS. Nov. 3

The rules of Conversation

Only no word of mine must ever
foster
The self that in a brother's bosom
gnaws;
I may not fondle failing, nor the
boaster
Encourage with the breath of my
applause.

DS. Nov. 9

Lord, loosen in me the hold of visible things;
Help me to walk by faith and not by
sight;
I would, through thickest veils and
coverings,
See into the chambers of the living
light.
Lord, in the land of things that swell
and seem,
Help me to walk by the other light
supreme,
Which shows Thy facts behind
man's vaguely hinting
dream.

DS. 99

Noontide Hymn

I love Thy skies, Thy sunny mists,
Thy fields, Thy mountains hoar,
Thy wind that bloweth where it
lists—
Thy will, I love it more.

I love Thy hidden truth to seek
All round, in sea, on shore;
The arts whereby like gods we
speak—
Thy will to me is more.

I love Thy men and women, Lord,
The children round Thy door;
Calm thoughts that inward strength
afford—
Thy will than these is more.

But when Thy will my life doth hold
Thine to the very core,
The world, which that same will
doth mould,
I love, then, ten times more!

PI. 319

In Thee lies hid my unknown heart,
In Thee my perfect mind;
In all my joys, my Lord, Thou art
The deeper joy behind.

PI. 381

The Giver

To give a thing and take again
Is counted meanness among men;
To take away what once is given
Cannot then be the way of heaven!

But human hearts are crumbly
stuff,
And never, never love enough,
Therefore God takes and, with a
smile,
Puts our best things away a while.

Thereon some weep, some rave,
some scorn,
Some wish they never had been
born;
Some humble grow at last and still,

And then God gives them what they
will.

PII. 128

Love Is Strength

Love alone is great in might,
Makes the heavy burden light,
Smooths rough ways to weary feet,
Makes the bitter morsel sweet:
Love alone is strength!

Might that is not born of Love
Is not Might born from above,
Has its birthplace down below
Where they neither reap nor sow;
Love alone is strength!

Love is stronger than all force,
Is its own eternal source;
Might is always in decay,
Love grows fresher every day:
Love alone is strength!

Little ones, no ill can chance;
Fear ye not, but sing and dance;
Though the high-heaved heaven
should fall
God is plenty for us all:
God is Love and Strength!

PII. 130–31

The man who was lord of fate,
Born in an ox's stall,
Was great because He was much too
great
To care about greatness at all.

Ever and only He sought
The will of His Father good;
Never of what was high He thought,
But of what His Father would.

You long to be great; you try;
You feel yourself smaller still:
In the name of God let ambition
die;
Let Him make you what He will.

Who does the truth, is one
With the living Truth above;
Be God's obedient little son,
Let ambition die in love.

PII. 178

Rondel

I do not know Thy final will,
It is too good for me to know:
Thou willest that I mercy show,
That I take heed and do no ill,
That I the needy warm and fill,
Nor stones at any sinner throw;
But I know not Thy final will—
It is too good for me to know.

I know Thy love unspeakable—
For love's sake able to send woe!
To find Thine own Thou lost
didst go,
And wouldst for men Thy blood yet
spill!—
How should I know Thy final will,
Godwise too good for me to
know!

PII. 336

Possession(s)

God lets men have their playthings, like the children they are, that they may learn to distinguish them from true possessions. If they are not learning that, he takes them from them, and tries the other way: for lack of them and its misery, they will perhaps seek the true!

DG. 1

Things go wrong because men have such absurd and impossible notions about *possession*. They are always trying to possess, to call their own, things which it is impossible from their very nature, ever to possess or make their own.

DG. 77

"All things are mine, therefore they are yours"? Oh, for his liberty among the things of the Father! Only by knowing them the things of our Father can we escape enslaving ourselves to them. Through the false, the infernal idea of *having*, of *possessing* them, we make them our tyrants, make the relation between them and us an evil thing.

HG. 54

The man who, by the exclusion of others from the space he calls his, would grasp any portion of the earth as his own, befools himself in the attempt. The very bread he has swallowed cannot so in any real sense be his.

HG. 92

The man so dull as to insist that a thing is his because he has brought it and paid for it, had better bethink himself that not all the combined forces of law, justice, and good-will can keep it his; while even death cannot take the world from the man who possesses it as alone the Maker of him and it cares that he should possess it. This man leaves it, but carries it with him; that man carries with him only its loss.

HG. 93

The more things men seek, the more varied the things they imagine they need, the more are they subject to vanity—all the forms of which may be summed in the word "disappointment." He who would not house with disappointment must seek the incorruptible, the true. He must break the bondage of havings and shows; of rumors, and praises, and pretenses, and selfish pleasures. He must come out of the false into the real; out of the darkness into the light; out of the bondage of corruption into the glorious liberty of the children of God. To bring men to break with corruption, the gulf of the inane yawns before them. Aghast in soul, they cry, "Vanity of vanities! all is vanity!" and beyond the abyss begin to espy the eternal world of truth.

HG. 212

Nor does the lesson apply to those only who worship Mammon: . . . it applies to those equally who in any way worship the transitory; who seek the praise of men more than the praise of God; who would make a show in the world by wealth, by taste, by intellect, by power, by art, by genius of any kind, and so would gather golden opinions to be treasured in a storehouse of earth. Nor to such only, but surely to those as well whose pleasures are of a more evidently transitory nature still, such as the pleasures of the senses in every direction—whether lawfully or unlawfully indulged, if the joy of being is centered in them—do these words bear terrible warning. For the hurt lies not in this—that these pleasures are false like the deceptions of magic, for such they are not: . . . nor yet in this—that they pass away and leave a fierce disappointment behind: that is only so much the better; but the hurt lies in this—that the immortal, the infinite, created in the image of the everlasting God, is housed with the fading and the corrupting, and clings to them as its good—clings to them until it is infected and interpenetrated with their proper diseases, which assume in it a form more terrible in proportion to the superiority of its kind.

SI. 123

He thought to gain a thing by a doing, when the very thing desired was *a being*: he would have that as a possession which must possess him.

SII. 6

A man is in bondage to whatever he cannot part with that is less than himself. He could have taken his possessions from him by an exercise of his own will, but there would have been little good in that; he wished to do it by the exercise of the young man's will: that would be a victory indeed for both! So would he enter into freedom and life, delivered from the bondage of Mammon by the lovely will of the Lord in him, one with his own. By the putting forth of the divine energy in him, he would escape the corruption that is in the world through lust—that is, the desire or pleasure of *having*.

SII. 14

It is God himself come to meet the climbing youth, to take him by the hand, and lead him up his own stair, the only stair by which ascent can be made. He shows him the first step of it through the mist. His feet are heavy; they have golden shoes. To go up that stair he must throw aside his shoes. He must walk bare-footed into life eternal. Rather than so, rather than stride free-limbed up the everlasting stair to the bosom of the Father, he will keep his precious shoes! It is better to drag them about on the earth, than part with them for a world where they are useless!

SII. 20

Although never can man be saved without being freed from his possessions, it is yet only *hard*, not *impossible*, for a rich man to enter into the kingdom of God.

SII. 21

We, too, dull our understandings with trifles, fill the heavenly spaces with phantoms, waste the heavenly time with hurry. When I trouble myself over a trifle, even a trifle confessed—the loss of some little article, say—spurring my memory, and hunting the house, not from immediate need, but from dislike of loss; when a book has been borrowed of me and not returned, and I have forgotten the borrower, and fret over the missing volume.

SII. 33

Possessions are *things*, and *things* in general, save as affording matter of conquest and means of spiritual annexation, are very ready to prove inimical to the better life. The man, who for consciousness of well-being depends upon anything but life, the life essential, is a slave; he hangs on what is less than himself. He is not perfect, who, deprived of everything, would not sit down calmly content, aware of a well-being untouched; for nonetheless would he be possessor of all things, the child of the Eternal.

SII. 34

... *Things* are given us—this body, first of things—that through them we may be trained both to independence and true possession of them. We must possess them; they must not possess us. Their use is to mediate—as shapes and manifestations in lower kind of the things that are unseen, that is, in themselves unseeable, the things that belong, not to the world of speech, but the world of silence, not to the world of showing, but the world of being, the world that cannot be shaken, and must remain. These things unseen take form in the things of time and space—not that they may exist, for they exist in and from eternal Godhead, but that their being may be known to those in training for the eternal; these things unseen the sons and daughters of God must possess. But instead of reaching out after them, they grasp at their forms, regard the things seen as the things to be possessed, fall in love with the bodies instead of the souls of them.

SII. 35

He who has God, has all things, after the fashion in which he who made them has them.

SII. 36

Things can never be really possessed by the man who cannot do without them.

SII. 36

It is imperative on us to get rid of the tyranny of *things*.

SII. 37

When a man begins to abstain, then first he recognizes the strength of his passion; it may be, when a man has not a thing left, he will begin to know what a necessity he had made of things: and if then he begin to contend with them, to cast out of his soul what Death has torn from his hands, then first will he know the full passion of possession, the slavery of prizing the worthless part of the precious.

SII. 37

It is not by possessing we live, but by life we possess. . . . Thus death may give a new opportunity—with some hope for the multitude counting themselves Christians, who are possessed by things as by a legion of devils: who stand well in their church: whose lives are regarded as stainless; who are kind, friendly, give largely, believe in the redemption of Jesus, talk of the world and the church, yet whose care all the time is to heap up, to make much into more, to add house to house and field to field, burying themselves deeper and deeper in the ash-heap of *Things*.

SII. 39

Because of possession the young man had not a suspicion of the grandeur of the call with which Jesus honored him. He thought he was hardly dealt with to be offered a patent of heaven's nobility—he was so very rich! *Things* filled his heart; things blocked up his windows; things barricaded his door, so that the very God could not enter. His soul was not empty, swept, and garnished, but crowded with meanest idols, among which his spirit crept about upon its knees, wasting on them the gazes that belonged to his fellows and his Master.

SII. 47

If it be *things* that slay you, what matter whether things you have, or things you have not?

SII. 48

Is it not time I lost a few things when I care for them so unreasonably? This losing of things is of the mercy of God: it comes to teach us to let them go. Or have I forgotten a thought that came to me, which seemed of the truth? . . . I keep trying and trying to call it back, feeling a poor man until that thought be recovered—to be far more lost, perhaps, in a note-book, into which I shall never look again to find it! I forget that it is live things God cares about.

SII. 54

Naturally capable, he had already made of himself rather a dull fellow; for when a man spends his energy on appearing to have, he is all the time destroying what he has, and therein the very means of becoming what he desires to seem. If he gains his end his success is his punishment.

SG. chap. 50

Nothing is so deadening to the divine as an habitual dealing with the outsides of holy things.

TW. chap. 74

Happily for our blessedness, the joy of possession soon palls.

WC. chap. 11

All is man's only *because* it is God's. The true possession of anything is to see and feel in it what God made it for; and the uplifting of the soul by that knowledge, is the joy of true having.

WM

"Did you ever think of the origin of the word *Avarice?*"—"No"—"It comes—at least it seems to me to come—from the same root as the verb *have.* It is the desire to call *things* ours—the desire of company which is not of our kind—company such as, if small enough, you would put in your pocket and carry about with you. We call the holding in the hand, or the house, or the pocket, or the power, *having*: but things so held cannot really be *had*; *having* is but an illusion in regard to *things.* It is only what we can be *with* what we really possess—that is, what is of our kind, from God to the lowest animal partaking of humanity."

WM. chap. 32

The Lord had no land of his own. he did not care to have it, any more than the twelve legions of angels he would not pray for. His pupils must not care for things he did not care for.

WM. 32

God only can be ours perfectly; nothing called property can be ours at all.

WM. 32

Things are ours that we may use them for all—sometimes that we may sacrifice them. God had but one precious thing, and he gave that!

WM. 46

Poverty

The men who are aware of their own essential poverty; not the men who are poor in friends, poor in influence, poor in acquirements, poor in money, but those who are poor in spirit, who *feel themselves poor creatures*; who know nothing to be pleased with themselves for, and desire nothing to make them think well of themselves; who know that they need much to make their life worth living, to make their existence a good thing, to make them fit to live; these humble ones are the poor whom the Lord calls blessed.

HG. 87

When a man says, I am low and worthless, then the gate of the kingdom begins to open to him, for there enter the true, and this man has begun to know the truth concerning himself. Whatever such a man has attained to, he straight-way forgets; it is part of him and behind him; his business is with what he has not, with the things that lie above and before him.

HG. 87

The man who is proud of anything he thinks he has reached, has not reached it. He is but proud of himself, and imagining a cause for his pride. If he had reached, he would already have begun to forget. He who delights in contemplating whereto he has attained, is not merely sliding back; he is already in the dirt of self-satisfaction. The gate of the kingdom is closed, and he outside.

HG. 87

The child who, clinging to his Father, dares not think he has in any sense attained while as yet he is not as his Father—his Father's heart, his Father's heaven is his natural home. To find himself thinking of himself as above his fellows would be to that child a shuddering terror; his universe would contract around him, his ideal wither on its throne. The least motion of self-satisfaction, the first thought of placing himself in the forefront of estimation, would be to him a flash from the nether abyss. God is his life and his lord. That his Father should be content with him must be all his care.

HG. 88

That to fear poverty was the same thing as to love money, for that both came of lack of faith in the living God!

PF

Our Lord never mentions poverty as one of the obstructions to his kingdom, neither has it ever proved such; riches, cares, and desires he does mention.

WW

Power

To have what we want is riches, but to be able to do without is power.

DG. 1

It was not his power, however, but his glory, that Jesus showed forth in the miracle. His power could not be hidden, but it was a poor thing beside his glory. Yea, power in itself is a poor thing. If it could stand alone, which it cannot, it would be a horror. No amount of lonely power could create. It is the love that is at the root of power, the power of power, which alone can create. What then was this his glory? What was it that made him glorious? It was that, like his Father, he ministered to the wants of men. Had they not needed the wine, not for the sake of whatever show of his power would he have made it. The concurrence of man's need and his love made it possible for that glory to shine forth.

MOL. 19

In every man the power by which he does the commonest things is the power of God. The power is not *of* us. Our power does it; but we do not make the power.

MOL. 54

Truth in the inward parts is a power not an opinion.

PF. 264

Such power was his, not to take care of himself, but to work the work of him that sent him. Such power was his not even to honor his Father save as his Father chose to be honored, who is far more honored in the ordinary way of common wonders, than in the extraordinary way of miracles. Because it was God's business to take care of him, his to do what the Father told him to do. To make that stone bread would be to take the care out of the Father's hands, and turn the divinest thing in the universe into the merest commonplace of self-preservation.

SI. 137

Where power dwells, there is no force; where the spirit-Lord is, there is liberty.

SIII. 54

Man bows down before a power that can account for him, a power to whom he is no mystery as he is to himself.

SIII. 77

He gave man the power to thwart his will, that, by means of that same power, he might come at last to do his will in a higher kind and way than would otherwise have been possible to him.

SIII. 229

Praise

We must lay no value on the praise of men, or in any way seek it. We must honor no man because of intellect, fame, or success.

HG. 181

What! seek the praise of men for being fair to our own brothers and sisters? What! seek the praise of God for laying our hearts at the feet of him to whom we utterly belong? There is no pride so mean—and all pride is absolutely, essentially mean—as the pride of being holier than our fellow, except the pride of being holy. Such imagined holiness is foulness.

HG. 192

With the praise or blame of men we have nought to do. Their blame may be a good thing, their praise cannot be. But the worst sort of the praise of men is the praise we give ourselves. We must do nothing to be seen of ourselves. We must seek no approbation even, but that of God, else we shut the door of the kingdom from the outside. His approbation will but quicken our sense of unworthiness.

HG. 192

The man, then, who does right, and seeks no praise from men, while he merits nothing, shall be rewarded by his Father, and his reward will be right precious to him.

HG. 200

We must let our light shine, make our faith, our hope, our love, manifest—that men may praise, not us for shining, but the Father for creating the light.

HG. 200

No man with faith, hope, love, alive in his soul, could make the divine possessions a show to gain for himself the admiration of men: not the less must they appear in our words, in our looks, in our carriage—above all, in honorable, unselfish, hospitable, helpful deeds.

HG. 200

From the faintest thought of the praise of men, we must turn away. No man can be the disciple of Christ and desire fame. To desire fame is ignoble; it is a beggarly greed. In the noble mind, it is the more of an infirmity. There is no aspiration in it—nothing but ambition. It is simply selfishness that would be proud if it could. Fame is the applause of the many, and the judgment of the many is foolish; therefore the greater the fame, the more is the foolishness that swells it, and the worse is the foolishness that longs after it.

HG. 201

The praise of God never falls wrong, therefore never does any one harm. The Lord even implies we ought to seek it.

MOL. 142

Prayer

A prayer may do a body good when it's not quite the kind to be altogether acceptable to the mind of the Almighty. But I doubt that his ear is closed for any prayer that goes up his way.

AF. 284

"Amen. There is no prayer in the universe as that. It means everything best and most beautiful. Your will, O God, evermore be done."

AN. 494

It seemed natural to pray; it seemed to come of itself: that could not be except it was first natural for God to hear.

DE

The chosen agonize after the light; stretch out their hands to God; stir up themselves to lay hold upon God!

DG

One ought not to be miserable about another as if God had forgotten him—only to pray and be ready.

DG

When we pray to God, it seems it puts it in God's power to make use of us for the carrying out of the thing we pray for; we don't know how, but so it seems to be; and God can work through us without our knowing how.

DG. 226

Gladness may make a man forget his thanksgiving; misery drives him to his prayers.

HG. 100

One thing is clear in regard to every trouble—that the natural way with it is straight to the Father's knee. The Father is father *for* his children, else why did he make himself their father?

HG. 115

What it would not be well for God to give before a man had asked for it, it may be not only well, but best, to give when he has asked. I believe that the first half of our training is up to the asking point; after that the treatment has a grand new element in it. For God can give when a man is in the fit condition to receive it, what he cannot give before because the man cannot receive it.

MOL. 108

A man cannot receive except another will give; no more can a man give if another will not receive; he can only offer. Doubtless, God works on every man, else he *could* have no divine tendency at all; there would be no *thither* for him to turn his face toward; there could be at best but a sense of want. But the moment the man has given in to God—to use a homely phrase—the spirit for which he prays can work in him all *with* him, not now (as it *appeared* then) *against* him.

MOL. 109

We shall have nothing which we ourselves, when capable of judging and choosing with open eyes to its true relation to ourselves, would not wish and choose to have. If God should give otherwise, it must be as a healing punishment of inordinate and hurtful desire.

MOL. 110

Not my will but your will. For he will know that God gives only the best.

MOL. 111

The man who has prayed most is, I suspect, the least doubtful whether God hears prayer now as Jesus heard it then.

MOL. 113

In our imperfect condition both of faith and of understanding, the whole question of asking and receiving must necessarily be surrounded with mist and the possibility of mistake. It can be successfully encountered only by the man who for himself asks and hopes. It lies in too lofty regions and involves too many unknown conditions to be reduced to formulas of ours; for God must do only the best, and man is greater and more needy than himself can know.

MOL. 114

If we allow that prayer may in any case be heard for the man himself, it almost follows that it must be heard for others. It cannot well be in accordance with the spirit of Christianity, whose essential expression lies in the sacrifice of its founder, that a man should be heard only when he prays for himself.

MOL. 116

When a man prays for his fellow man, for wife or child, mother or father, sister or brother or friend, the connection between the two is so close in God, that the blessing begged may well flow to the end of the prayer. Such a one then is, in his poor, far-off way, an advocate with the Father, like his master, Jesus Christ, The Righteous. He takes his friend into the presence with him, or if not into the presence, he leaves him with but the veil between them, and they touch through the veil.

MOL. 119

The door of prayer has been open ever since God made man in his own image.

MOL. 124

If ever there was a Man such as we read about here, then he who prays for his friends shall be heard of God. I do not say he shall have whatever he asks for. God forbid. But he shall be heard. And the man who does not see the good of that, knows nothing of the good of prayer; can, I fear, as yet, only pray for himself, when most he fancies he is praying for his friend.

MOL. 154

Often, indeed, when men suppose they are concerned for the well-beloved, they are only concerned about what they shall do without them. Let them pray for themselves instead, for that will be the truer prayer.

MOL. 155

All prayer is assuredly heard: What evil matter is it that it should be answered only in the right time and right way? The prayer argues a need—that need will be supplied. One day is with the Lord as a thousand years, and a thousand years as one day. All who have prayed shall one day justify God and say—Your answer is beyond my prayer, as your thoughts and your ways are beyond my thoughts and my ways.

MOL. 155

I take prayer and fasting to indicate a condition of mind elevated above the cares of the world and the pleasures of the senses, in close communion with the God of life.

MOL. 179

"And Jesus lifted up his eyes, and said, Father, I thank you that you have heard me. And I knew that you hear me always: but because of the people which stand by I said it, that they may believe that you have sent me." So might they believe that the work was God's, that he was doing the will of God, and that they might trust in the God whose will was such as this. He claimed the presence of God in what he did, that by the open claim and the mighty deed following it they might see that the Father justified what the Son said, and might receive him and all that he did as the manifestation of the Father.

MOL. 212

God of justice, you know how hard it is for us, and you will be fair to us. We have seen no visions; we have never heard the voice of your Son, of whom those tales, so dear to us, have come down the ages; we have to fight on in much darkness of spirit and of mind, both from the ignorance we cannot help, and from the fault we could have helped; we inherit blindness from the error of our fathers; and when fear, or the dread of shame, or the pains of death, come upon us like a wall, and you appear nowhere, either in our hearts, or in the outer universe; we cannot tell whether the things we seemed to do in your name, were not mere hypocrisies, and our very life is but a gulf of darkness. We cry aloud, and our despair is as a fire in our bones to make us cry; but to all our crying and listening, there seems neither hearing nor answer in the boundless waste. You who know yourself God, who know yourself that for which we groan, you whom Jesus called Father, we appeal to you, not as we imagine you, but as you see yourself as Jesus knows you, to your very self we cry—help us, O Cause of us! O you from whom alone we are this weakness, through whom alone we can become strength, help us—be our Father. We ask for nothing beyond what your Son has told us to ask. We beg for no signs or wonders, but for your breath upon our souls. Your spirit in our hearts. We pray for no cloven tongues of fire—for no mighty rousing of brain or imagination; but we do with all our power of prayer, pray for your spirit; we do not even pray to know that it is given to us; let us, if it so pleases you, remain in doubt of the gift for years to come—but lead us thereby. Knowing ourselves only as poor and feeble, aware only of ordinary and common movements of mind and soul, may we yet be possessed by the spirit of God, led by his will in ours. For all things in a man, even those that seem to him the commonest and least uplifted, are the creation of your heart, and by the lowly doors of our wavering judgment, dull imagination, lukewarm love, and palsied will, you can enter and glorify all. Give us patience because our hope is in you, not in ourselves. Work your will in us, and our prayers are ended, Amen.

PF. 129

Questions imply answers. He has put the questions in my heart; he holds the answers in his. I will seek them from him. I will wait, but not until I have knocked. I will be patient, but not until

I have asked. I will seek until I find. He has something for me. My prayer shall go up unto the God of my life.

SI. 52

What a man likes best *may* be God's will, may be the voice of the Spirit striving *with* his spirit, not against it; and if, as I have said, it be not so—if the thing he asks is not according to his will—there is that consuming fire. The danger lies, not in asking from God what is not good, nor even in hoping to receive it from him, but in not asking him, in not having him of our council.

SI. 57

I doubt if a man *can* ask anything from God that is bad.

SI. 58

"In everything, by prayer and supplication, with thanksgiving, let your requests be made known to God." For this *everything*, nothing is too small. That it should trouble us is enough.

SI. 61

With every haunting trouble then, great or small, the loss of thousands or the lack of a shilling, go to God, and appeal to him, the God of your life, to deliver you, his child, from that which is unlike him, therefore does not belong to you, but is antagonistic to your nature. If your trouble is such that you cannot appeal to him, the more need you should appeal to him!

SII. 55

Everything difficult indicates something more than our theory of life yet embraces, checks some tendency to abandon the strait path, leaving open only the way ahead. But there is a reality of being in which all things are easy and plain—oneness, that is, with the Lord of Life; to pray for this is the first thing; and to the point of this prayer every difficulty hedges and directs us.

SII. 58

A truth, a necessity of God's own willed nature, is enough to set up against a whole army of appearances. It looks as if he did not hear you: never mind; he does.

SII. 59

Those who cry to God are his own chosen—plain in the fact that they cry to him. He has made and appointed them to cry: they do cry: will he not hear them? They exist that they may pray; he has chosen them that they may choose him; he has called them that they may call him—that there may be such communion, such interchange as belongs to their being and the being of their Father.

SII. 60

If, seeing we live not by our will, we live by another will, then is there reason, and then only can there be reason in prayer.

SII. 62

If there be a God, and I am his creature, there may be, there should be, there must be some communication open between him and me. If any one allow a God, but one scarce good enough to care about his creatures, I will yield him that it were foolish to pray to such a God; but the notion that, with all the good impulses in us, we are the offspring of a cold-hearted devil, is so horrible in its inconsistency, that I would ask that man what hideous and cold-hearted disregard to the truth makes him capable of the supposition! To such a one God's terrors, or, if not his terrors, then God's sorrows yet will speak; the divine something in him will love, and the love be left moaning.

SII. 62

If I find that I can neither rule the world in which I live nor my own thoughts or desires; that I cannot quiet my passions, order my likings, determine my ends, will my growth, forget when I would, or recall what I forget; that I cannot love where I would, or hate where I would; that I am not king over myself; that I cannot supply my own needs, do not even always know which of my seeming needs are to be supplied, and which treated as imposters; if, in a word, my own being is everyway too much for me; if I can neither understand it, be satisfied with it, nor better it—may it not well give me pause—the pause that ends in prayer?

SII. 63

Shall I not tell him my troubles—how he, even he, has troubled me by making me?—how unfit I am to be that which I am?—that my being is not to me a good thing yet?—that I need a law that shall account to me for it in righteousness—reveal to me how I am to make it a good—how I am to *be* a good and not an evil?

SII. 65

If I speak to him, if I utter words ever so low; if I but think words to him; nay, if I only think to him, surely he, my original, in whose life and will and no otherwise I now think concerning him, hears, and knows, and acknowledges!

SII. 65

If it be reasonable for me to cry thus, if I cannot but cry, it is reasonable that God should hear, he cannot but hear. A being that could not hear or would not answer prayer, could not be God.

SII. 66

Every need of God, lifting up the heart, is a seeking of God, is a begging for himself, is profoundest prayer, and the root and inspirer of all other prayer.

SII. 66

Reader, if you are in any trouble, try whether God will not help you: if you are in no need, why should you ask questions about prayer? True, he knows little of himself who does not know that he is wretched, and miserable, and poor, and blind, and naked; but until he begins at least to suspect a need, how can he pray?

SII. 68

That God should as a loving father listen, hear, consider, and deal with the request after the perfect tenderness of his heart, is to me enough; it is little that I should go without what I pray for.

SII. 71

Communion with God is the one need of the soul beyond all other need; prayer is the beginning of that communion, and some need is the motive of that prayer. Our wants are for the sake of our coming into communion with God, our eternal need.

SII. 72

"But if God is so good as you represent him, and if he knows all that we need, and better far than we do ourselves, why should it be necessary to ask him for anything?" I answer, What if he knows prayer to be the thing we need first and most?

SII. 72

What if the main object in God's idea of prayer be the supplying of our great, our endless need—the need of himself?

SII. 72

Communion, a talking with God, a coming-to-one with him, which is the sole end of prayer, yea, of existence itself in its infinite phases. We must ask that we may receive; but that we should receive what we ask in respect of our lower needs, is not God's end in making us pray, for he could give us everything without that: to bring his child to his knee, God withholds that man may ask.

SII. 73

In regard . . . to the high necessities of our nature, it is in order that he may be able to give that God requires us to ask—requires by driving us to it—by shutting us up to prayer. For how can he give into the soul of a man what it needs, while that soul cannot receive it? The ripeness for receiving is the asking.

SII. 73

When the soul is hungry for the light, for the truth—when its hunger has waked its higher energies, thoroughly roused the will, and brought the soul into its highest condition, that of action, its only fitness for receiving the things of God, that action is prayer.

SII. 73

Sometimes to one praying will come the feeling . . . "Were it not better to abstain? If this thing be good, will he not give it me? Would he not be better pleased if I left it altogether to him?" It comes, I think, of a lack of faith and childlikeness . . . it may even come of ambition after spiritual distinction.

SII. 74

In every request, heart and soul and mind ought to supply the low accompaniment, "Your will be done"; but the making of any request brings us near to him.

SII. 75

Anything large enough for a wish to light upon, is large enough to hang a prayer upon: the thought of him to whom that prayer goes will purify and correct the desire.

SII. 75

To say, "Father, I should like this or that," would be enough at once, if the wish were bad, to make us know it and turn from it. Such prayer about things must of necessity help to bring the mind into true and simple relation with him; to make us remember his will even when we do not see what that will is. Surely it is better and more trusting to tell him all without fear or anxiety. Was it not thus the Lord carried himself toward his Father when he said, "If it be possible, let this cup pass from me"? But there was something he cared for more than his own fear—his Father's will: "Nevertheless, not my will, but yours be done." There is no apprehension that God might be displeased with him for saying what he would like, and not leaving it all to his Father. Neither did he regard his Father's plans as necessarily so fixed that they could not be altered to his prayer.

SII. 75

The true son-faith is that which comes with boldness, fearless of the Father doing anything but what is right fatherly, patient, and full of lovingkindness. We must not think to please him by any asceticism even of the spirit; we must speak straight out to him. The true child will not fear, but lay bare his wishes to the perfect Father. The Father may will otherwise, but his grace will be enough for the child.

SII. 75

As to any notion of prevailing by entreaty over an unwilling God, that is heathenish, and belongs to such as think him a hard master, or one like the unjust judge. What so quenching to prayer as the notion of unwillingness in the ear that hears! And when prayer is dull, what makes it flow like the thought that God is waiting to give, wants to give us everything! "Let us therefore come boldly to the throne of grace, that we may obtain mercy, and find grace to help in time of need."

SII. 76

"How should any design of the All-wise be altered in response to prayer of ours? How are we to believe such a thing?" By reflecting that he is the all-wise, who sees before him, and will not block his path.

SII. 77

What stupidity of perfection would that be which left no margin about God's work, no room for change of plan upon change of fact—yea, even the mighty change that, behold now at length, his child is praying! See the freedom of God in his sunsets—never a second like one of the foregone!—in his moons and skies—in the ever-changing solid earth!—all moving by no dead law, but in the harmony of the vital law of liberty, God's creative perfection—all ordered from within. A divine perfection that were indeed, where was no liberty! where there could be but one way of a thing!

SII. 78

I may move my arm as I please: shall God be unable so to move his? If but for himself, God might well desire no change, but he is God for the sake of his growing creatures; all his making and doing is for them, and change is the necessity of their very existence.

SII. 79

If you say he has made things to go, set them going, and left them—then I say, If his machine interfered with his answering the prayer of a single child, he would sweep it from him—not to bring back chaos, but to make room for his child.

SII. 80

We must remember that God is not occupied with a grand toy of worlds and suns and planets, of attractions and repulsions, of agglomerations and crystallizations, of forces and waves; that these but constitute a portion of his workshops and tools for the bringing out of righteous men and women to fill his house of love withal.

SII. 80

That God cannot interfere to modify his plans, interfere without the change of a single law of his world, is to me absurd. If we can change, God can change, else is he less free than we—his plans, I say, not principles, not ends: God himself forbid!—change them after divine fashion, above our fashions as the heavens are higher than the earth.

SII. 81

At the prayer of his mother, he made room in his plans for the thing she desired. It was not his wish then to work a miracle, but if his mother wished it, he would. He did for his mother what for his own part he would rather have left alone. Not always did he do as his mother would have him; but this was a case in which he could do so, for it would interfere nowise with the will of his Father. . . . The Son, then, could change his intent and spoil nothing: so, I say, can the Father; for the Son does nothing but what he sees the Father do.

SII. 82

If we believe that God is the one unselfish, the one good being in the universe, and that his one design with his children is to make them perfect as he is perfect; if we believe that he not only would once give, but is always giving himself to us for our life; if we believe—which once I heard a bishop decline to acknowledge—that God does his best for *every* man; if also we believe that God knows every man's needs, and will, for love's sake, not spare one pang that may serve to purify the soul of one of his children; if we believe all this, how can we think he will in any sort alter his way with one because another prays for him? The prayer would arise from nothing in the person prayed for; why should it initiate a change in God's dealing with him?

SII. 84

Yet and yet, there is, there must be some genuine, essential good and power in the prayer of one man for another to the Maker of both—and that just because their Maker is perfect, not less than very God.

SII. 85

If God has made us to love like himself, and like himself long to help; if there are for whom we, like him, would give our lives to lift them from the evil gulf of their ungodliness; if the love in us would, for the very easing of the love he kindled, gift another—like himself who chooses and cherishes even the love that pains him; if, in the midst of a sore need to bless, to give, to help, we are aware of an utter impotence; if the fire burns and cannot out; and if all our hope for ourselves lies in God—what is there for us, what can we think of, what do, but go to God?

SII. 85

There can be no need for which he has no supply. The best argument that he has help, is that we have need. If I can be helped through my friend, I think God will take the thing up, and do what I cannot do—help my friend that I may be helped—perhaps help me to help him. You see, in praying for another we pray for ourselves—for the relief of the needs of our love; it is not prayer for another alone, and thus it comes under the former kind. Would God give us love, the root of power, in us, and leave that love, whereby he himself creates, altogether helpless in us? May he not at least expedite something for our prayers? Where he could not alter, he could perhaps expedite, in view of some help we might then be able to give. If he desires that we should work with him, that work surely helps him!

SII. 86

One way is clear: the prayer will react upon the mind that prays, its light will grow, will shine the brighter, and draw and enlighten the more. But there must be more in the thing. Prayer in its perfect idea being a rising up into the will of the Eternal, may not the help of the Father become one with the prayer of the child, and for the prayer of him he holds in his arms, go forth from him who wills not yet to be lifted to his embrace? To his bosom God himself cannot bring his children at once, and not at all except through his own suffering and theirs. But will not any good parent find some way of granting the prayer of the child who comes to him, saying, "Papa, this is my brother's birthday: I have nothing to give him, and I do love him so! could you give me something to give him, or give him something for me?"

SII. 88

And why should the good of anyone depend on the prayer of another? I can only answer with the return question, "Why should my love be powerless to help another?"

SII. 88

If *in* God we live and move and have our being; if the very possibility of loving lies in this, that we exist in and by the live air of love, namely God himself, we must in this very fact be nearer to each other than by any bodily proximity or interchange of help; and if prayer is like a pulse that sets this atmosphere in motion, we must then by prayer come closer to each other than are the parts of our body by their complex nerve-telegraphy. Surely, in the Eternal, hearts are never parted! surely, through the Eternal, a heart that loves and seeks the good of another, must hold that other within reach! Surely the system of things would not be complete in relation to the best thing in it—love itself, if love had no help in prayer. If I love and cannot help, does not my heart move me to ask him to help who loves and can?—him without whom life would be to me nothing, without whom I should neither love nor care to pray!—will he answer, "Child, do not trouble me; I am already doing all I can"? If such answer came, who that loved would not be content to be nowhere in the matter? But how if the eternal, limitless Love, the unspeakable, self-forgetting God-devotion, which, demanding all, gives all, should say, "Child, I have been doing all I could; but now you are come, I shall be able to do more! here is a corner for you, my little one: push at this thing to get it out of the way"! How if he should answer, "Pray on, my child; I am hearing you; it goes through me in help to him. We are of one mind about it; I help and you help. I shall have you all safe home with me by and by! There is no fear, only we must work, and not lose heart. Go, and let your light so shine before men that they may see your good things, and glorify me by knowing that I am light and no darkness"!

SII. 89

There are some who would argue for prayer, not on the ground of any possible answer to be looked for, but because of the good to be gained in the spiritual attitude of the mind in praying. There are those even who, not believing in any ear to hear, any heart to answer, will yet pray. They say it does them good; they pray to nothing at all, but they get spiritual benefit.

SII. 91

So needful is prayer to the soul that the mere attitude of it may encourage a good mood. Verily to pray to that which is not, is in logic a folly; yet the good that, they say, comes of it, may rebuke the worse folly of their unbelief, for it indicates that prayer is natural, and how could it be natural if inconsistent with the very mode of our being? Theirs is a better way than that of those who, believing there is a God, but not believing that he will give any answer to their prayers, yet pray to him; that is more foolish and more immoral than praying to the No-god. Whatever the God be to whom they pray, their prayer is a mockery of him, of themselves, of the truth.

SII. 91

Prayer does react in good upon the praying soul, irrespective of answer. But to pray for the sake of the prayer, and without regard to there being no one to hear, would to me indicate a nature not merely illogical but morally false, did I not suspect a vague undetected apprehension of a Something diffused through the All of existence, and some sort of shadowiest communion therewith.

SII. 91

There is a communion with God that asks for nothing, yet asks for everything. This last is the very essence of prayer, though not petition. It is possible for a man, not indeed to believe in God, but to believe that there is a God, and yet not desire to enter into communion with him; but he that prays and does not faint will come to recognize that to talk with God is more than to have all prayers granted—that it is the end of all prayer, granted or refused. And he who seeks the Father more than anything he can give, is likely to have what he asks, for he is not likely to ask amiss.

SII. 92

Even such as ask amiss may sometimes have their prayers answered. The Father will never give the child a stone that asks for bread; but I am not sure that he will never give the child a stone that asks for a stone. If the Father says, "My child, that is a stone; it is no bread"; and the child answers, "I am sure it is bread; I want it"; may it not be well he should try his bread?

SII. 92

No prayer for any revenge that would gratify the selfishness of our nature, a thing to be burned out of us by the fire of God, needs think to be heard. Be sure, when the Lord prayed his Father to forgive those who crucified him, he uttered his own wish and his Father's will at once: God will never punish according to the abstract abomination of sin, as if men knew what they were doing. "Vengeance is mine," he says: with a right understanding of it, we might as well pray for God's vengeance as for his forgiveness; that vengeance is, to destroy the sin—to make the sinner abjure and hate it; nor is there any satisfaction in a vengeance that seeks or effects less.

SII. 95

If any prayers are offered against us; if the vengeance of God be cried out for, because of some wrong you or I have done, God grant us his vengeance! Let us not think that we shall get off!

SII. 95

God will avenge his own elect. He is not delaying; he is at work for you. Only you must pray, and not faint. Ask, ask; it shall be given you. Seek most the best things; to ask for the best things is to have them; the seed of them is in you, or you could not ask for them.

SII. 96

From whatever quarter come our troubles, whether from the world outside or the world inside, still let us pray. In his own right way, the only way that could satisfy us, for we are of his kind, will God answer our prayers with help. He will avenge us of our adversaries, and that speedily.

SII. 96

"More life!" is the unconscious prayer of all creation, groaning and travailing for the redemption of its lord, the Son who is not yet a Son.

SII. 139

Never wait for fitter time or place to talk to him. To wait until you go to church, or to your closet, is to make *him* wait. He will listen as you walk in the lane or the crowded street, on the common or in the place of shining concourse.

SIII. 227

So thinking, she began to pray to what dim, distorted reflection of God there was in her mind. They alone pray to the real God, the Maker of the heart that prays, who know his Son Jesus. If our prayers were heard only in accordance with the idea of God to which we seem to ourselves to pray, how miserably would our infinite wants be met! But every honest cry, even if sent into the deaf ear of an idol, passes on to the ears of the unknown God, the heart of the unknown Father.

SG. chap. 29

She never imagined that words were necessary; she believed that God knew her every thought, and that the moment she lifted up her heart, it entered into communion with him; but the very sound of the words she spoke seemed to make her feel nearer to the Man who being the eternal Son of the Father, yet had ears to hear and lips to speak, like herself. To talk to him aloud, also kept her thoughts together, helped her to feel the fact of the things she contemplated as well as the reality of his presence.

SG. 178

If our prayers were heard only in accordance with the idea of God to which we seem to ourselves to pray, how miserable would our infinite wants be met! But every honest cry, even if sent into the deaf ear of an idol, passes on to the ears of the unknown God, the heart of the unknown Father.

SG. 194

"In every thing let your requests be made known unto God."

"I sometimes feel as if I would not ask him for anything, but just let him give me what he likes. . . ."

"Not to ask may seem to you a more submissive way, but I don't think it is so childlike. It seems to me far better to say, 'O Lord, I should like this or that, but I would rather not have it if you do not like it also.' Such prayer brings us into conscious and immediate relations with God. Remember, our thoughts are then passing to him, sent by our will into his mind. Our Lord taught us to pray always and not get tired of it. God, however poor creatures we may be, would have us talk to him, for then he can speak to us better than when we turn no face to him."

TW. 448

"O God!" I cried and that was all. But what are the prayers of the whole universe more than expansions of that one cry? It is not what God can give us, but God that we want.

WC. chap. 59

Don't fancy you are doing God any service by praying to him. He likes you to pray to him because he loves you, and wants you to love him. And whatever you do, don't go saying a lot of words you don't mean. If you think you ought to pray, say your Lord's Prayer and be done with it.

WC. 149

Our prayers must rise that our thoughts may follow them.

WM

We are not right until we can pray heartily, not say submissively, "Your will be done!" We have not one interest, and God another.

WM

"If ever I prayed, mother, I certainly have not given it up"—"Ever prayed, Ian! When a mere child you prayed like an aged Christian!"—"Ah, mother, that was a sad pity! I asked for things of which I felt no need. I was a hypocrite. I ought to have prayed like a little child."

WM. chap. 7

When we are one with our life, so that no prayer can be denied, there will be no end to the lovely possibilities.

WM. 22

And if there was a good deal of superstition mingled with her prayer, the main thing in it was genuine that is, the love that prompted it; and if God heard only perfect prayers, how could he be the prayer-hearing God?

WM. 33

Prayer Answers

There's no knowing what God can do nor yet what best of reasons he has for not doing it sooner! When we think he's letting the time go by and doing nothing, he may just be doing all things.

DG. 226

What he will do for you, he only knows. It may be you will never know what he will do, but only what he has done: it was too good for you to know except by receiving it. The moment you are capable of it, it will be yours.

HG. 115

"What then is the good of praying, if it is not to go by what I want?" I can only answer, "You have to learn, and it may be by a hard road."

MOL. 110

Not my will but yours. For he will know that God gives only the best.

MOL. 111

God has not to satisfy the judgment of men as they are, but as they will be and must be, having learned the high and perfectly honest and grand way of things which is his will.

MOL. 112

The man who has prayed most is, I suspect, the least doubtful whether God hears prayer now as Jesus heard it then.

MOL. 113

I do believe that the Spirit of God, after widening its channels for nearly nineteen hundred years, can flow in greater plenty and richness now. Hence the answers to prayer must not only not be of quite the same character as then, but they must be better, coming yet closer to the heart of the need, whether known as such by him who prays, or not. But the change lies in man's power of reception, for God is always the same to his children. Only, being infinite, he must speak to them and act for them in the endless diversity which their growth and change render necessary. Thus only they can receive of his fullness who is all in all and unchangeable.

MOL. 113

He who asks *shall* receive—of the very best. One promise without reserve, and only one, because it includes all, remains: the promise of the Holy Spirit to them who ask it. He who has the Spirit of God, God himself, in him, has the Life in him, possesses the final cure of all ill, has in himself the answer to all possible prayer.

MOL. 114

All prayer is assuredly heard: What evil matter is it that it should be answered only in the right time and right way? The prayer argues a need—that need will be supplied. One day is with the Lord as a thousand years, and a thousand years as one day. All who have prayed shall one day justify God and say—Your answer is beyond my prayer, as your thoughts and your ways are beyond my thoughts and my ways.

MOL. 155

The God to whom we pray is nearer to us than the very prayer ere it leaves the heart; hence his answers may well come to us through the channel of our own thoughts.

PF

It is not love that grants a boon unwillingly; still less is it love that answers a prayer to the wrong and hurt of him who prays. Love is one, and love is changeless.

SI. 27

Why should the question admit of doubt? We know that the wind blows; why should we not know that God answers prayer? I reply, What if God does not care to have you know it at second hand? What if there would be no good in that? There is some testimony on record, and perhaps there might be much were it not that, having to do with things so immediately personal, and generally so delicate, answers to prayer would naturally not often be talked about; but no testimony concerning the thing can well be conclusive; for, like a reported miracle, there is always some way to daff it; and besides, the conviction to be got that way is of little value: it avails nothing to know the thing by the best of evidence.

SII. 66

A being that could not hear or would not answer prayer, could not be God.

SII. 66

God may hear all prayers that ever were offered to him, and a man may believe that he does, nor be one whit the better for it, so long as God has no prayers of his to hear, he no answers to receive from God. Nothing in this quarter will ever be gained by investigation. Reader, if you are in any trouble, try whether God will not help you; if you are in no need, why should you ask questions about prayer? True, he knows little of himself who does not know that he is wretched, and miserable, and poor, and blind, and naked; but until he begins at least to suspect a need, how can he pray?

SII. 68

A God capable of being so moved in one direction or another, is a God not worth believing in—could not be the God believed in by Jesus Christ—and he said he knew.

SII. 68

A God that should fail to hear, receive, attend to one single prayer, the feeblest or worst, I cannot believe in; but a God that would grant every request of every man or every company of men, would be an evil God—that is no God, but a demon.

SII. 68

That God should hang in the thought-atmosphere like a windmill, waiting until men enough should combine and send out prayer in sufficient force to turn his outspread arms, is an idea too absurd. God waits to be gracious, not to be tempted. A man capable of proposing such a test, could have in his mind no worthy representative idea of a God, and might well disbelieve in any. It is better to disbelieve than believe in God unworthy.

SII. 69

I want to believe in God. I want to know that there is a God that answers prayer, that I may believe in him. There was a time when I believed in him. I prayed to him in great and sore trouble of heart and mind, and he did not hear me. I have not prayed since.

How do you know that he did not hear you?

He did not give me what I asked, though the weal of my soul hung on it.

In your judgment. Perhaps he knew better.

I am the worse for his refusal. I would have believed in him if he had heard me.

Until the next desire came which he would not grant, and then you would have turned your God away. A desirable believer you would have made! A worthy brother to him who thought nothing fit to give the Father less than his all! You would accept of him no decision against your desire! That ungranted, there was no God, or not a good one!

SII. 69

God has not to consider his children only at the moment of their prayer. Should he be willing to give a man the thing he knows he would afterwards wish he had not given him? If a man be not fit to be refused, if he be not ready to be treated with love's severity, what he wishes may perhaps be given him in order that he may wish it had not been given him; but barely to give a man what he wants because he wants it, and without farther purpose of his good, would be to let a poor ignorant child take his fate into his own hands—the cruelty of a devil. Yet is every prayer heard; and the real soul of the prayer may require, for its real answer, that it should not be granted in the form in which it is requested.

SII. 70

If you knew God, you would leave that to him. He is not mocked, and he will not mock. But he knows you better than you know yourself, and would keep you from fooling yourself. He will not deal with you as the child of a day, but as the child of eternal ages. You shall be satisfied, if you will but let him have his way with the creature he has made. The question is between your will and the will of God.

SII. 70

He is not one of those who give readiest what they prize least. He does not care to give anything but his best, or that which will prepare for it. Not many years may pass before you confess, "You are a God who hears prayer, and gives a better answer." You may come to see that the desire of your deepest heart would have been frustrated by having what seemed its embodiment then. That God should as a loving Father listen, hear, consider, and deal with the request after the perfect tenderness of his heart, is to me enough; it is little that I should go without what I pray for.

SII. 70

To hear is not necessarily to grant—God forbid! but to hear is necessarily to attend to—sometimes as necessarily to refuse.

SII. 71

If it be granted that any answer which did not come of love, and was not from the final satisfaction of him who prayed, would be unworthy of God; that it is the part of love and knowledge to watch over the wayward, ignorant child; then the trouble of seemingly unanswered prayers begins to abate, and a lovely hope and comfort takes its place in the child-like soul.

SII. 71

If we have God, we can do without the answer to any prayer.

SII. 72

What if the main object in God's idea of prayer be the supplying of our great, our endless need—the need of himself? What if the good of all our smaller and lower needs lies in this, that they help to drive us to God?

SII. 72

We shall be refused our prayer if that be better; but what is good our Father will give us with divine good will. The Lord spoke his parable "to the end that they ought always to pray, *and not to faint*."

SII. 76

In many cases, the prayer, far more than the opportunity of answering it, is God's end.

SII. 78

"How should any design of the All-wise be altered in response to prayer of ours!" How are we to believe such a thing?

By reflecting that he is the All-wise, who sees before him, and will not block his path. Such objection springs from poorest idea of God in relation to us. It supposes him to have cares and plans and intentions concerning our part of creation, irrespective of us. What is the whole system of things for, but our education? Does God care for suns and planets and satellites, for divine mathematics and ordered harmonies, more than for his children? I venture to say he cares more for oxen than for those. He lays no plans irrespective of his children; and, his design being that they shall be free, active, live things, he sees that space be kept for them: they need room to struggle out of their chrysalis, to undergo the change that comes with the waking will, and to enter upon the divine sports and labors of children in the house and domain of their Father. Surely he may keep his plans in a measure unfixed, waiting the free desire of the individual soul! Is not the design of the first course of his children's education just to bring them to the point where they shall pray? and shall his system appointed to that end be then found hard and fast, tooth-fitted and inelastic, as if informed of no live causing soul, but an unselfknowing force—so that he cannot answer the prayer because of the system which has its existence for the sake of the prayer?

SII. 79

If the fitness of answering prayer lies in the praying of him who prays: the attitude necessary to reception does not belong to those *for* whom prayer is made, but to him *by* whom it is made.

SII. 83

We must not tie God to our measures of time, or think he has forgotten that prayer even which, apparently unanswered, we have forgotten.

SII. 88

It may be that the answer to prayer will come in a shape that seems a refusal. It may come even in an increase of that from which we seek deliverance.

SII. 90

Such as ask amiss may sometimes have their prayers answered. The Father will never give the child a stone that asks for bread; but I am not sure that he will never give the child a stone that asks for a stone. If the Father says, "My child, that is a stone; it is no bread," and the child answers, "I am sure it is bread; I want it," may it not be well that he should try his "bread"?

SII. 92

Perhaps, indeed, the better the gift we pray for, the more time is necessary to its arrival.

SII. 93

He may delay because it would not be safe to give us at once what we ask: we are not ready for it. To give ere we could truly receive, would be to destroy the very heart and hope of prayer, to cease to be our Father. The delay itself may work to bring us nearer to our help, to increase the desire, perfect the prayer, and ripen the receptive condition.

SII. 93

God loses no time, though the answer may not be immediate.

SII. 93

To give us the spiritual gift we desire, God may have to begin far back in our spirit, in regions unknown to us, and do much work that we can be aware of only in the results; for our consciousness is to the extent of our being but as the flame of the volcano to the world-gulf whence it issues; in the gulf of our unknown being God works behind our consciousness.

SII. 94

With his holy influence, with his own presence (the one thing for which most earnestly we cry) he may be approaching our consciousness from behind, coming forward through regions of our darkness into our light, long before we begin to be aware that he is answering our request—has answered it, and is visiting his child.

SII. 94

God does not put off like the unrighteous judge; he does not delay until irritated by the prayers of the needy; he will hear while they are yet speaking; yea, before they call he will answer.

SII. 94

"Vengeance is mine," he says: with a right understanding of it, we might as well pray for God's vengeance as for his forgiveness; that vengeance is, to destroy the sin—to make the sinner abjure and hate it; nor is there any satisfaction in a vengeance that seeks or effects less. The man himself must turn against himself, and so be for himself. If nothing else will do, then hell-fire; if less will do, whatever brings repentance and self-repudiation, is God's repayment. Friends, if any prayers are offered against us; if the vengeance of God be cried out for, because of some wrong you or I have done, God grant us his vengeance! Let us not think that we shall get off!

SII. 95

All things are possible with God, but all things are not easy.

SII. 139

No answer will do for him but the answer that God only can give; for who but God can justify God's ways to his creature?

SII. 177

If a child cry, "I want the darkness," and complain that he will not give it, yet he will not give it. He gives what his child needs—often by refusing what he asks. If his child say, "I will not be good; I prefer to die; let me die!" his dealing with that child will be as if he said—"No; I have the right to content you, not giving you your own will but mine, which is your one good. You shall not die; you shall live to thank me that I would not hear your prayer. You know what you ask, but not what you refuse."

SIII. 171

There are good things God must delay giving until his child has a pocket to hold them—until he gets his child to make that pocket. He must first make him fit to receive and to have. There is no part of our nature that shall not be satisfied—and that not by lessening it, but by enlarging it to embrace an ever-enlarging enough.

SIII. 172

If God were not only to hear our prayers, as he does ever and always, but to answer them as we want them answered, he would not be God our Savior, but the ministering genius of our destruction.

WW. 49

Pride

No good ever comes of pride, for it is the meanest of mean things, and no one but he who is full of it thinks it grand.

MM

His pride was bitterly wounded. Would it had been mortally! But pride seems in some natures to thrive upon wounds, as in others does love.

PF. 265

I learned that it is better, a thousand-fold, for a proud man to fall and be humbled, than to hold up his head in his pride and fancied innocence. I learned that he that will be a hero, will barely be a man; that he that will be nothing but a doer of his work, is sure of his manhood.

PH. 166

If the good man does not cast out his pride, it will sink him lower than the bad man's, for it will degenerate into a worse pride than that of any bad man.

WM. 5

Pride is the ruin of dignity, for it is a worshiping of self, and that involves a continuous sinking.

WW

Punishment

The horrible thing is being bad, and all punishment is help to deliver us from that, nor will punishment cease until we have ceased to be bad.

DG

The mission of Jesus was from the same source and with the same object as the punishment of our sins. He came to work along with our punishment. He came to side with it, and set us free from our sins.

HG. 8

The theological lie, that punishment is the satisfaction of justice.

PF

Ignorance may be at once a punishment and a kindness: all punishment is kindness, and the best of which the man at the time is capable: "Because you will not do, you shall not see; but it would be worse for you if you did see, not being of the disposition to do." Such are punished in having the way closed before them; they punish themselves; their own doing results as it cannot but result on them.

SII. 100

God puts a seal upon the will of man; that seal is either his great punishment, or his mighty favor: "You love the darkness, stay in the darkness."

SII. 101

The punishment of the wrongdoer makes no atonement for the wrong done.

SIII. 112

"How could he be a just God and not punish sin?"

SIII. 119

Punishment is *nowise* an *offset* to sin. Foolish people sometimes, in a tone of self-gratulatory pity, will say, "If I have sinned I have suffered." Yes, verily, but what of that? What merit is there in it? Even had you laid the suffering upon yourself, what did that do to make up for the wrong? That you may have bettered by your suffering is well for you, but what atonement is there in the suffering? The notion is a false one altogether.

SIII. 121

Punishment, deserved suffering, is no equipoise to sin. It is no use laying it in the other scale. It will not move it a hair's breadth. Suffering weighs nothing at all against sin. It is not of the same kind, not under the same laws, any more than mind and matter. We say a man deserves punishment; but when we forgive and do not punish him, we do not *always* feel that we have done wrong; neither when we do punish him do we feel that any amends has been made for his wrongdoing. If it were an offset to wrong, then God would be bound to punish for the sake of the punishment; but he cannot be, for he forgives. Then it is not for the sake of the punishment, as a thing that in itself ought to be done, but for the sake of something else, as a means to an end, that God punishes. It is not directly for justice, else how could he show mercy, for that would involve injustice?

SIII. 121

Punishment . . . is not the thing required of God, but the absolute destruction of sin. What better is the world, what better is the sinner, what better is God, what better is the truth, that the sinner should suffer—continue suffering to all eternity? Would there be less sin in the universe? Would there be any making-up for sin? Would it show God justified in doing what he knew would bring sin into the world, justified in making creatures who he knew would sin? What setting-right would come of the sinner's suffering? If justice demand it, if suffering be the equivalent for sin, then the sinner must suffer, then God is bound to exact his suffering, and not pardon; and so the making of man was a tyrannical deed, a creative cruelty. But grant that the sinner has deserved to suffer, no amount of suffering is any atonement for his sin. To suffer to all eternity could not make up for one unjust word. Does that mean, then, that for an unjust word I deserve to suffer to all eternity? The unjust word is an eternally evil thing; nothing but God in my heart can cleanse me from the evil that uttered it; but does it follow that I saw the evil of what I did so perfectly, that eternal punishment for it would be just? Sorrow and confession and self-abasing love will make up for the evil word; suffering will not. For evil in the abstract, nothing can be done. It is eternally evil. But I may be saved from it by learning to loathe it, to hate it, to shrink from it with an eternal avoidance.

SIII. 123

The only vengeance worth having on sin is to make the sinner himself its executioner. Sin and punishment are in no antagonism to each other in man, any more than pardon and punishment are in God; they can perfectly co-exist. The one naturally follows the other, punishment being born of sin, because evil exists only by the life of good, and has no life of its own, being in itself death.

SIII. 124

If sin must be kept alive, then hell must be kept alive; but while I regard the smallest sin as infinitely loathsome, I do not believe that any being, never good enough to see the essential ugliness of sin, could sin so as to *deserve* such punishment. I am not now, however, dealing with the question of the duration of punishment, but with the idea of punishment itself; and would only say in passing, that the notion that a creature born imperfect, nay, born with impulses to evil not of his own generating, and which he could not help having, a creature to whom the true face of God was never presented, and by whom it never could have been seen, should be thus condemned, is as loathsome a lie against God as could find place in heart too undeveloped to understand what justice is, and too low to look up into the face of Jesus.

SIII. 126

When a man loathes himself, he has begun to be saved. Punishment tends to this result.

SIII. 127

Punishment is for the sake of amendment and atonement. God is bound by his love to punish sin in order to deliver his creature; he is bound by his justice to destroy sin in his creation. Love is justice—is the fulfilling of the law, for God as well as for his children.

SIII. 127

It is no pleasure to God, as it so often is to us, to see the wicked suffer. To regard any suffering with satisfaction, save it be sympathetically with its curative quality, comes of evil, is inhuman because undivine, is a thing God is incapable of. His nature is always to forgive, and just because he forgives, he punishes.

SIII. 131

Jesus did not die to save us from punishment; he was called Jesus because he should save his people from their sins.

SIII. 133

If we were punished for every fault, there would be no end, no respite; we should have no quiet wherein to repent; but God passes by all he can. He passes by and forgets a thousand sins, yea, tens of thousands, forgiving them all—only we must begin to be good, begin to do evil no more. He who refuses must be punished and punished—punished through all the ages—punished until he gives way, yields, and comes to the light, that his deeds may be seen by himself to be what they are, and be by himself reproved, and the Father at last have his child again.

SIII. 179

There are three conceivable kinds of punishment—first, that of mere retribution, which I take to be entirely and only human—therefore, indeed, more properly inhuman, for that which is not divine is not essential to humanity, and is of evil, and an intrusion upon the human; second, that which works repentance; and third, that which refines and purifies, working for holiness. But the punishment that falls on whom the Lord loves because they have repented, is a very different thing from the punishment that falls on those whom he loves indeed but cannot forgive because they hold fast by their sins.

SIII. 180

The severest punishment that can be inflicted upon the wrongdoer is simply to let him know what he is; for his nature is of God, and the deepest in him is the divine.

SIII. 244

Purgatory

You may have sent him into a hotter purgatory, and at the same time made it shorter for him. We know nothing but that God is righteous.

E. 184

One of the painful things in the dogma of the endless loss of the wicked is that it leaves no room for the righteous to make up to them for the wrongs they did them in this life. For the righteous do the wicked far more wrong than they think—the righteous being all the time, in reality, the wealthy, and the wicked the poor. But it is a blessed word, that there are first that shall be last, and last that shall be first. . . . Is there not the might of love, and all eternity for it to work in, to set things right?

TW. 309

Heartily he loves you, heartily he hates the evil in you—so heartily that he will even cast you into the fire to burn you clean. By making you clean he will give you rest.

TW. 342

Purity

The Lord knows what they need; they know only what they want. They want ease; he knows they need purity. Their very existence is an evil, of which, but for his resolve to purify them, their Maker must rid his universe. How can he keep in his sight a foul presence? Must the Creator send forth his virtue to hold alive a thing that will be evil—a thing that ought not to be, that has no claim but to cease? The Lord himself would not live save with an existence absolutely good.

HG. 16

He cannot make himself pure, but he can leave that which is impure; he can spread out the "defiled, discolored web" of his life before the bleaching sun of righteousness; he cannot save himself, but he can let the Lord save him.

HG. 21

He who saw God, who sees him now, who always did and always will see him, says, "Be pure, and you also shall see him."

HG. 117

None but the pure in heart see God; only the growing-pure hope to see him.

HG. 120

"What is it, then, to be pure in heart?"

I answer, It is not necessary to define this purity, or to have in the mind any clear form of it. For even to know perfectly, were that possible, what purity of heart is, would not be to be pure in heart.

HG. 122

Though you do not know any definition of purity, you know enough to begin to be pure. You do not know what a man is, but you know how to make his acquaintance—perhaps even how to gain his friendship. Your brain does not know what purity is; your heart has some acquaintance with purity itself. Your brain is seeking to know what it is, may even obstruct your heart in bettering its friendship with it. To know what purity is, a man must already be pure; but he who can put the question already knows enough of purity, I repeat, to begin to become pure.

HG. 122

If you care to see God, be pure.

HG. 123

If you will not be pure, you will grow more and more impure; and instead of seeing God, will at length find yourself face to face with a vast inane—a vast inane, yet filled full of one inhabitant, that devouring monster, your own false self. If for this neither do you care, I tell you there is a Power that will not have it so; a Love that will make you care by the consequences of not caring.

HG. 123

You who seek purity, and would have your fellow men also seek it, spend not your labor on the stony ground of their intellect, endeavoring to explain what purity is; give their imagination the one pure man; call up their conscience to witness against their own deeds; urge upon them the grand resolve to be pure.

HG. 123

If this moment you determine to start for purity, your conscience will at once tell you where to begin. If you reply, "My conscience says nothing definite," I answer, "You are but playing with your conscience. Determine, and it will speak."

HG. 123

With the first endeavor of a soul toward her, Purity will begin to draw nigh, calling for admittance; and never will a man have to pause in the divine toil, asking what next is required of him; the demands of the indwelling Purity will ever be in front of his slow-laboring obedience.

HG. 124

Unhappy men were we, if God were the God of the perfected only, and not of the growing, the becoming! "Blessed are they," says the Lord, concerning the not yet pure, "which do hunger and thirst after righteousness, for they shall be filled." Filled with righteousness, they are pure; pure, they shall see God.

HG. 124

A great purity of soul is needful in him who would master the powers of evil.

MOL. 179

It is the nature of God, so terribly pure that it destroys all that is not pure as fire, which demands like purity in our worship. He will have purity. It is not that the fire will burn us if we do not worship thus; but that the fire will burn us until we worship thus; yea, will go on burning within us after all that is foreign to it has yielded to its force, no longer with pain and consuming, but as the highest consciousness of life, the presence of God.

SI. 31

Can it be any comfort to them to be told that God loves them so that he will burn them clean? . . . They do not want to be clean, and they cannot bear to be tortured.

SI. 38

The man who loves God, and is not yet pure, courts the burning of God. Nor is it always torture. The fire shows itself sometimes only as light—still it will be fire of purifying. The consuming fire is just the original, the active form of Purity, that which makes pure, that which is indeed Love, the creative energy of God. Without purity there can be as no creation so no persistence. That which is not pure is corruptible, and corruption cannot inherit incorruption.

SI. 46

The notion that the salvation of Jesus is a salvation from the consequences of our sins, is a false, mean, low notion. The salvation of Christ is salvation from the smallest tendency or leaning to sin. It is a deliverance into the pure air of God's ways of thinking and feeling. It is a salvation that makes the heart pure, with the will and choice of the heart to be pure. To such a heart, sin is disgusting. It sees a thing as it is—that is, as God sees it, for God sees everything as it is.

SIII. 132

Redemption

The human race groans for deliverance: How much does the race know that its redemption lies in becoming one with the Father, and partaking of his glory? Here and there one of the race knows it—which is indeed a pledge for the race—but the race cannot be said to know its own lack, or to have even a far-off notion of what alone can stay its groaning.

HG. 207

Nothing but the obedience of the Son, the obedience unto the death, the absolute *doing* of the will of God because it was the truth, could redeem the prisoner, the widow, the orphan.

SI. 158

As the world must be redeemed in a few men to begin with, so the soul is redeemed in a few of its thoughts and works and ways to begin with: it takes a long time to finish the new creation of this redemption.

SII. 131

If God be defeated, he must destroy—that is, he must withdraw life. How can he go on sending forth his life into irreclaimable souls, to keep sin alive in them throughout the ages of eternity? But then, I say, no atonement would be made for the wrongs they have done; God remains defeated, for he has created that which sinned, and which would not repent and make up for its sin. But those who believe that God will thus be defeated by many souls, must surely be of those who do not believe he cares enough to do his very best for them. He *is* their Father; he had power to make them out of himself, separate from himself, and capable of being one with him; surely he will somehow save and keep them! Not the power of sin itself can close *all* the channels between creating and created.

SIII. 130

I believe that no hell will be lacking which would help the just mercy of God to redeem his children.

SIII. 155

There are powers to be born, creations to be perfected, sinners to be redeemed through the ministry of pain, that could be born, perfected, redeemed, in no other way.

WM

See what it cost him to redeem the world! He did not find that easy, or to be done in a moment without pain or toil. Yea, awfully omnipotent is God. For he wills, effects and perfects the thing which, because of the bad in us, he has to carry out in suffering and sorrow, his own and his Son's.

WW. 23

Religion

There is one kind of religion in which the more devoted a man is, the fewer proselytes he makes: the worship of himself.

AF. vol. 2, chap. 1

What religion is there in being convinced of a future state? Is that to worship God? It is no more religion than the belief that the sun will rise tomorrow is religion. It may be a source of happiness to those who could not believe it before, but it is not religion.

AN. chap. 15

It is God and man, and that is real religion. It is not this observation and that observation; it is my soul and his soul, and then my hands to do his will. That is real religion.

The Christian World Pulpit

You have been very careful in reading your Bible and going to church, and doing this or that thing which you think belongs to religion; but have you been doing the thing Christ told you? If you do that, I do not care whatever else you do; you cannot be wrong then.

The Christian World Pulpit

Religion is simply the way home to the Father.

DG. 6

Religion itself, in the hearts of the unreal, is a dead thing; what seems life in it is the vermiculate life of a corpse.

HG. 192

It is much easier to persuade men that God cares for certain observances, than that he cares for simple honesty and truth and gentleness and lovingkindness.

M

Religion is no way of life, no show of life, no observance of any sort. It is neither the food nor the medicine of being. It is life essential.

ML

Whoever thinks of life as a something that could be without religion, is in deathly ignorance of both. Life and religion are one, or neither is anything.

ML

A great part of our irreligion springs from our disbelief in the humanity of God.

MOL. 265

The worst heresy, next to that of dividing religion and righteousness, is to divide the Father from the Son—in thought or feeling or action or intent; to represent the Son as doing that which the Father does not himself do. Jesus did nothing but what the Father did and does.

SII. 143

It is those who know only and respect the outsides of religion, such as never speak or think of God but as *the Almighty* or *Providence*, who will say of the man who would go close up to God, and speak to him out of the deepest in the nature he has made, "he is irreverent." To utter the name of God in the drama—highest of human arts, is with such men blasphemy. They pay court to God, not love him; they treat him as one far away, not as the one whose bosom is the only home.

SII. 180

. . . Willing his own being in the will of the only I AM. This is the rounding, recreating, unifying of the man. This is religion; and all that gathers not with this, scatters abroad.

TW. 66

Love without religion is the plucked rose. Religion without love—there is no such thing. Religion is the bush that bears all the roses; for religion is the natural condition of man in relation to the eternal facts, that is the truths, of his own being. To live is to love; there is no life but love. What shape the love puts on, depends on the persons between whom is the relation. The poorest love with religion, is better, because truer, therefore more lasting, more genuine, more endowed with the possibility of persistence—that is, of infinite development, than the most passionate devotion between man and woman without it.

WM. 202–3

Repentance

"God *will* have his creatures good. They cannot escape him."

"Then a man may put off repentance as long as he pleases."

"Certainly he may—at least as long as he can—but it is a fearful thing to try issues with God."

E. 98

Son of our Father, help us to do what you say, and so with you die unto sin, that we may rise to the sonship for which we were created. Help us to repent even to the sending away of our sins.

HG. 22

The change must be one of will and conduct—a radical change of life on the part of the man: he must repent—that is, change his mind—not to a different opinion, not even to a mere betterment of his conduct—not to anything less than a sending away of his sins.

HG. 26

"Bring forth therefore fruits meet for repentance": is not this the same as, "Repent unto the sending away of your sins"?

HG. 28

The message of John to his countrymen was then, and is yet, the one message to the world: "Send away your sins, for the kingdom of heaven is near." Some of us—I cannot say *all*, for I do not know—who have already repented, who have long ago begun to send away our sins, need fresh repentance every day—how many times a day, God only knows.

HG. 31

We are so ready to get upon some path that seems to run parallel with the narrow way, and then take no note of its divergence! What is there of us when we discover that we are out of the way but to bethink ourselves and turn? By those "who need no repentance," the Lord may have meant such as had repented perfectly, had sent away all their sins, and were now with him in his Father's house; also such as have never sinned, and such as no longer turn aside for any temptation.

HG. 31

John baptized unto repentance because those to whom he was sent had to repent. They must bethink themselves, and send away the sin that was in them. But had there been a man aware of no sin in him, but aware that life would be no life were not sin kept out of him, that man would have been right in receiving the baptism of John unto the continuous dismission of the sin ever wanting to enter in at his door. The object of the baptism was the sending away of sin; its object was repentance only where necessary to, only as introducing, as resulting in that. He to whom John was not sent, he whom he did not call, he who needed no repentance, was baptized for the same object, to the same conflict for the same end—the banishment of sin from the dominions of his Father—and that first by his own sternest repudiation of it in himself. Thence came his victory in the wilderness: he would have his Father's way, not his own. Could he be less fitted to receive the baptism of John, that the object of it was no new thing with him, who had been about it from the beginning, yea, from all eternity? *We* shall be about it, I presume, to all eternity.

HG. 36

Although repentance comes because God pardons—yet the man becomes aware of the pardon only in the repentance; so it is only when the man has become his name that God gives him the stone with the name upon it, for then first can he understand what his name signifies.

SI. 107

To make a man happy as a lark, *might be* to do him grievous wrong; to make a man wake, rise, look up, turn, is worth the life and death of the Son of the Eternal.

SII. 26

Repentance is the first pressure of the bosom of God.

SII. 113

If we were punished for every fault, there would be no end, no respite; we should have no quiet wherein to repent; but God passes by all he can. He passes by and forgets a thousand sins, yea, tens of thousands, forgiving them all—only we must begin to be good, begin to do evil no more. He who refuses must be punished and punished—punished through all the ages—punished until he gives way, yields, and comes to the light, that his deeds may be seen by himself to be what they are, and be by himself reproved, and the Father at last have his child again. For the man who in this world resists to the full, there may be, perhaps, a whole age or era in the history of the universe during which his sin shall not be forgiven; but *never* can it be forgiven until he repents. How can they who will not repent be forgiven, save in the sense that God does and will do all he can to make them repent? Who knows but such sin may need for its cure the continuous punishment of an aeon?

SIII. 179

The heavenly order goes upon other principles than ours, and there are first that shall be last, and last that shall be first. Only, at the root of all human bliss lies repentance.

TW. 47

She had not learned that the look of things as you go, is not their look when you turn to go back; that with your attitude their mood will have altered. Nature is like a lobster-pot: she lets you easily go on, but not easily return.

WM. chap. 33

Evil cannot be destroyed without repentance.

WW. 49

Resurrection

His resurrection was all for others. That miracle was wrought in him, not for him.

MOL. 206

Without the rising of the Savior himself, Christianity would not have given what it could of *hope* for the future. Hope is not faith, but neither is faith sight; and if we have hope we are not miserable men.

MOL. 214

What better sign of immortality than the raising of the dead could God give? He cannot, however, be always raising the dead before our eyes; for then the holiness of death's ends would be a failure. We need death; only it shall be undone once and again for a time, that we may know it is not what it seems to us.

MOL. 219

In Christ we have an ever-growing revelation. He is the resurrection and the life. As we know him we know our future.

In our ignorance lies a force of need, compelling us toward God.

MOL. 222

The works of the Lord he himself represents as given him of the Father: it matters little whether we speak of his resurrection as a miracle wrought by himself, or wrought in him by the Father. If he was one with the Father, the question cannot be argued, seeing that Jesus apart from the Father is not a conceivable idea. It is only natural that he who had power to call from the grave the body which had lain there for four days, should have power over the body he had himself laid down, to take it again with reanimating possession.

MOL. 260

If Christ be risen, then is the grave of humanity itself empty. We have risen with him, and death has henceforth no dominion over us. Of every dead man and woman it may be said: He—she—is not here, but is risen and gone before us. Ever since the Lord lay down in the tomb, and behold it was but a couch whence he arose refreshed, we may say of every brother: He is not dead but sleeping. He too is alive and shall arise from his sleep.

MOL. 268

The way to the tomb may be hard, as it was for him; but we who look on, see the hardness and not the help; we see the suffering but not the sustaining: that is known only to the dying and God. They can tell us little of this, and nothing of the glad safety beyond.

MOL. 268

Not to believe in mutual recognition beyond, seems to me a far more reprehensible unbelief than that in the resurrection itself. I can well understand how a man should not believe in any life after death. I will confess that although probabilities are for it, *appearances* are against it. But that a man, still more a woman, should believe in the resurrection of the very same body of Jesus, who took pains that his friends should recognize him therein; that they should regard his resurrection as their one ground for the hope of their own uprising, and yet not believe that friend shall embrace friend in the mansions prepared for them, is to me astounding. Such a shadowy resumption of life I should count unworthy of the name of resurrection.

MOL. 269

What seemed to the disciples the final acme of disappointment and grief, the vanishing of his body itself, was in reality the first sign of the dawn of an illimitable joy. He was not there because he had risen.

MOL. 271

Shall God call himself the God of the dead, of those who were alive once, but whom he either could not or would not keep alive?

SI. 233

"And wherefore should he not be so far the God of the dead, if during the time allotted to them here, he was the faithful God of the living?" What God-like relation can the ever-living, life-giving, changeless God hold to creatures who partake not of his life, who have death at the very core of their being, are not worth their Maker's keeping alive?

SI. 234

A man's material body will be to his consciousness at death no more than the old garment he throws aside at night, intending to put on a new and a better in the morning.

SI. 237

Yet not the less is the doctrine of the resurrection gladdening as the sound of the silver trumpet of its visions, needful as the very breath of life to our longing souls. Let us know what it means, and we shall see that it is thus precious.

SI. 238

Our God is an unveiling, a revealing God. He will raise you from the dead, that I may behold you; that that which vanished from the earth may again stand forth, looking out of the same eyes of eternal love and truth, holding out the same mighty hand of brotherhood, the same delicate and gentle, yet strong hand of sisterhood, to me, this me that knew you and loved you in the days gone by.

SI. 242

The God of the resurrection is awake all the time, watching his sleeping men and women, even as a mother who watches her sleeping baby, only with larger eyes and more full of love than hers; and so, you know not how, all at once you know that you are what you are; that there is a world that wants you outside of you, and a God that wants you inside of you; you rise from the death of sleep, not by your own power, for you know nothing about it; God put his hand over your eyes, and you were dead; he lifted his hand and breathed light on you, and you rose from the dead, thanked the God that raised you up, and went forth to do your work. From darkness to light; from blindness to seeing; from knowing nothing to looking abroad on the mighty world; from helpless submission to willing obedience—is not this a resurrection indeed?

SP

It is for the sake of the resurrection that death exists.

SP

To come out of the ugly into the beautiful; out of the mean and selfish into the noble and loving; out of the paltry into the great; out of the false into the true; out of the filthy into the clean; out of the commonplace into the glorious; out of the corruption of disease into the fine vigor and gracious movements of health; in a word, out of evil into good—is not this a resurrection indeed—*the* resurrection of all, the resurrection of Life?

SP

Yea, every time that a man passes from resentment to forgiveness, from cruelty to compassion, from harshness to tenderness, from indifference to carefulness, from selfishness to honesty, from honesty to generosity, from generosity to love—a resurrection, the bursting of a fresh bud of life out of the grave of evil, gladdens the eye of the Father watching his children.

SP

Reward

That men may be drawn to taste and see and understand, the Lord associates reward with righteousness.

HG. 142

God's rewards are always in kind. "I am your Father; be my children, and I will be your Father."

HG. 145

Righteousness can never fail of perfect reward.

HG. 145

The idea of merit is nowise essential to that of reward. Jesus tells us that the lord who finds his servant faithful will make him sit down to meat, and come forth and serve him; he says likewise, "When you have done all, say we are unprofitable servants; we have done only that which it was our duty to do."

HG. 145

A sense of merit is the most sneaking shape that self-satisfaction can assume. God's reward lies closed in all well-doing: the doer of right grows better and humbler, and comes nearer to God's heart as nearer to his likeness; grows more capable of God's own blessedness, and of inheriting the kingdoms of heaven and earth.

HG. 145

To be made greater than one's fellows is the offered reward of hell, and involves no greatness; to be made greater than one's self is the divine reward, and involves a real greatness.

HG. 146

A man might be set above all his fellows, to be but so much less than he was before; a man cannot be raised a hair's breadth above himself without rising nearer to God. The reward itself, then, is righteousness; and the man who was righteous for the sake of such reward, knowing what it was, would be righteous for the sake of righteousness—which yet, however, would not be perfection.

HG. 146

The Lord not only promises the greatest possible reward; he tells his disciples the worst they have to expect. He not only shows them the fair countries to which they are bound; he tells them the truth of the rough weather and the hardships of the way. He will not have them choose in ignorance. At the same time he strengthens them to meet coming difficulty by instructing them in its real nature.

HG. 147

They must not imagine, because they are the servants of his Father, that therefore they shall find their work easy; they shall only find the reward great. Neither will he have them fancy, when evil comes upon them, that something unforeseen, unprovided for, has befallen them. It is just then, on the contrary, that their reward comes nigh: when men revile them and persecute them, then they may know that they are blessed.

HG. 147

Love and reward are for the good: love and correction for the bad. The bad ones will trouble the good, but shall do them no hurt.

HG. 149

Those whom our Lord felicitates are all the children of one family; and everything that can be called blessed or blessing comes of the same righteousness. If a disciple be blessed because of any one thing, every other blessing is either his, or on the way to become his; for he is on the way to receive the very righteousness of God.

HG. 151

If you say, "No one ought to do right for the sake of reward," I go further and say, "No man *can* do right for the sake of reward. A man may do a thing indifferent, he may do a thing wrong, for the sake of reward; but a thing in itself right, done for reward, would, in the very doing, cease to be right." At the same time, if a man does right, he cannot escape being rewarded for it; and to refuse the reward would be to refuse life, and foil the creative love. The whole question is of the kind of reward expected.

HG. 195

My fit wages may be pain, sorrow, humiliation of soul: I stretch out my hands to receive them. Your reward will be to lift me out of the mire of self-love, and bring me nearer to yourself and your children: welcome, divinest of good things! Your highest reward is your purest gift; you did make me for it from the first; you, the eternal life, have been laboring still to fit me for receiving it—the vision, the knowledge, the possession of yourself. I can seek but what you wait and watch to give: I would be such into whom your love can flow.

HG. 198

Rich and Poor

God knows it is hard for the rich man to enter into the kingdom of heaven; but the rich man does sometimes enter in; for God has made it possible. And the greater the victory, when it is the rich man that overcomes the world. It is easier for the poor man to enter the kingdom, yet many of the poor have failed to enter in, and the greater is the disgrace of their defeat. For the poor have more done for them, as far as outward things go, in the way of salvation, than the rich, and have a beatitude all to themselves besides.

AN

We are rich or poor according to what we are, not what we have.

DE

Although never can man be saved without being freed from his possessions, it is yet only *hard*, not impossible, *for a rich man to enter into the kingdom of God.*

SII. 21

A condition of things, in which it would be easy for a rich man to enter into the kingdom of heaven, is to me inconceivable. There is no kingdom of this world into which a rich man may not easily enter—in which, if he be but rich enough, he may not be the first. A kingdom into which it would be easy for a rich man to enter could be no kingdom of heaven.

SII. 22

Why should the rich fare differently from other people in respect of the world to come? They do not perceive that the law is they *shall* fare like other people, whereas they want to fare as rich people.

SI. 22

The rich man does not by any necessity of things belong to the kingdom of Satan, but into that kingdom he is especially welcome, whereas into the kingdom of heaven he will be just as welcome as another man.

SII. 22

It is not the rich man only who is under the dominion of things; they too are slaves who, having no money, are unhappy from the lack of it. . . .

The money the one has, the money the other would have, is in each the cause of an eternal stupidity.

SII. 39

The rich man who held his *things* lightly, nor let them nestle in his heart; who was a channel and no cistern; who was ever and always forsaking his money—starts, in the new world, side by side with the man who accepted, not hated, his poverty. Each will say, "I am free!"

SII. 52

It is pitiable to be wretched—and that I venture to suspect, the rich are oftener than the poor.

WM. 87

Rich/Riches

To have what we want is riches, but to be able to do without is power.

DG. 1

But with God all things are possible: he can save even the rich!

L. 207

A condition of things in which it would be easy for a rich man to enter into the kingdom of heaven is to me inconceivable. There is no kingdom of this world into which a rich man may not easily enter—in which, if he be but rich enough, he may not be the first: a kingdom into which it would be easy for a rich man to enter could be no kingdom of heaven.

SII. 22

What riches and fancied religion, with the self-sufficiency they generate between them, can make man or woman capable of, is appalling . . . to many of the religious rich in that day, the great damning revelation will be their behavior to the poor to whom they thought themselves very kind.

SIII. 240

I am proud of a race whose social relations are the last upon which they will retrench, whose latest yielded pleasure is their hospitality. It is a common feeling that only the *well-to-do* have a right to be hospitable. The ideal flower of hospitality is almost unknown to the rich; it can hardly be grown save in the gardens of the poor; it is one of their beatitudes.

WM. chap. 16

It takes a good many disgraceful things to bring a rich man to outward disgrace.

WM. 179

He . . . has always been rich, and accustomed to have his own way! I begin to think one punishment of making money in a wrong manner is to be prosperous in it!

WM. 339

It must be one of the punishments of riches that they make the sight of poverty so disagreeable! To luxury, poverty is a living reproach.

WM. 353

The Righteous

There is no liberty but in doing right. There is no freedom but in living out of the deeps of our nature—not out of the surface.

The English Pulpit of Today

There is no wrong man can do but is a thwarting of the living Right.

ML. 42

The righteous do the wicked far more wrong than they think—the righteous being all the time, in reality, the wealthy, and the wicked the poor. But it is a blessed word that there are first that shall be last, and last that shall be first.

TW. 42

A man who would pull out even a mote from his brother's eye, must first pull out the beam from his own eye, must be righteous against his own selfishness. That is the only way to wound the root of evil.

WM

The Father cannot bear rudeness in his children any more than wrong.

WW

Righteousness

It is God we want, not heaven; his righteousness not an imputed one, for our own possession; remission, not letting off.

DG

It is only Righteousness that has a right to secrecy, and does not want it. Evil has no right to secrecy, alone intensely desires it, and rages at being foiled of it; for when its deeds come to the light, even Evil has righteousness enough left to be ashamed of some of them.

DG. 35

Is power or love the making might of the universe? He who answers this question aright possesses the key to all righteous questions.

EA. 79

The one cure for any organism is to be set right—to have all its parts brought into harmony with each other; the one comfort is to know this cure in process. Rightness alone is cure. The return of the organism to its true self is its only possible ease.

HG. 5

As much as either is it common sense that a man should look for and expect the help of his Father in the endeavor. Alone, he might labor to all eternity and not succeed. He who has not made himself cannot set himself right without him who made him. But his Maker is in him, and is his strength.

HG. 20

To love righteousness is to make it grow, not to avenge it; and to win for righteousness the true victory, he, as well as his brethren, had to send away evil.

HG. 34

We must, by a full act of the will, give ourselves altogether to righteousness. We must make it the business of our lives to send away sin, and do the will of the Father. That is my work as much as the work of any man who must repent ere he can begin. I will not be left out when you call men to be pure as our Father is pure.

HG. 39

Every being that can, must devote himself to righteousness. To be right is no adjunct of completeness; it is the ground and foundation of existence.

HG. 40

Long ere the Lord appeared, ever since man was on the earth, nay, surely, from the very beginning, was his Spirit at work in it for righteousness; in the fullness of time he came in his own human person, to fulfill all righteousness. He came to his own of the same mind with himself, who hungered and thirsted after righteousness. They should be fulfilled of righteousness!

HG. 124

To hunger and thirst after anything implies a sore personal need, a strong desire, a passion for that thing. Those that hunger and thirst after righteousness seek with their whole nature the design of that nature. Nothing less will give them satisfaction; that alone will set them at ease. They long to be delivered from their sins, to send them away, to be clean and blessed by their absence—in a word, to become men, God's men; for, sin gone, all the rest is good.

HG. 125

Love is the father of righteousness. It could not be, and could not be hungered after, but for love. The lord of righteousness himself could not live without Love, without the Father in him. Every heart was created for, and can live no otherwise than in and upon love eternal, perfect, pure, unchanging; and love necessitates righteousness.

HG. 126

Weakness cannot know itself weak. It is a little strength that longs for more; it is infant righteousness that hungers after righteousness.

HG. 127

To every soul dissatisfied with itself comes this word, at once rousing and consoling, from the Power that lives and makes him live—that in his hungering and thirsting he is blessed, for he shall be filled. His hungering and thirsting is the divine pledge of the divine meal. The more he hungers and thirsts, the more blessed is he; the more room is there in him to receive that which God is yet more eager to give than he to have. It is the miserable emptiness that makes a man hunger and thirst; and as the body, so the soul hungers after what belongs to its nature.

HG. 127

A man hungers and thirsts after righteousness because his nature needs it—needs it because it was made for it; his soul desires its own.

HG. 128

Even if the hunger after righteousness should in part spring from a desire after self-respect, it is not therefore *all* false. A man could not even be ashamed of himself, without some "feeling sense" of the beauty of rightness. By divine degrees the man will at length grow sick of himself, and desire righteousness with a pure hunger—just as a man longs to eat that which is good, nor thinks of the strength it will restore.

HG. 128

To be filled with righteousness will be to forget even righteousness itself in the bliss of being righteous, that is, a child of God. The thought of righteousness will vanish in the fact of righteousness. When a creature is just what he is meant to be, what only he is fit to be; when, therefore, he is truly himself, he never thinks what he is. He *is* that thing; why think about it? It is no longer outside of him that he should contemplate or desire it.

HG. 129

God made man, and woke in him the hunger for righteousness; the Lord came to enlarge and rouse this hunger. The first and lasting effect of his words must be to make the hungering and thirsting long yet more. If their passion grow to a despairing sense of the unattainable, a hopelessness of ever gaining that without which life were worthless, let them remember that the Lord congratulates the hungry and thirsty, so sure does he know them of being one day satisfied. Their hunger is a precious thing to have, nonetheless that it were a bad thing to retain unappeased. It springs from the lack but also from the love of good, and its presence makes it possible to supply the lack. Happy, then, you pining souls!

HG. 129

If your hunger seems long in being filled, it is well it should seem long. But what if your righteousness tarry because your hunger after it is not eager? There are who sit long at the table because their desire is slow; they eat as who should say, We need no food. In things spiritual, increasing desire is the sign that satisfaction is drawing nearer.

HG. 130

Fear not, you hungering and thirsting; you shall have righteousness enough, though none to spare—none to spare, yet enough to overflow upon every man.

HG. 130

Hear another like word of the Lord. He assures us that the Father hears the cries of his elect—of those whom he seeks to worship him because they worship in spirit and in truth. "Shall not God avenge his own elect," he says, "which cry day and night unto him?" Now what can God's elect have to keep on crying for, night and day, but righteousness? He allows that God seems to put off answering them, but assures us he will answer them speedily. Even now he must be busy answering their prayers; increasing hunger is the best possible indication that he is doing so. For some divine reason it is well they should not yet know in themselves that he is answering their prayers; but the day must come when we shall be righteous even as he is righteous; when no word of his will miss being understood because of our lack of righteousness;

when no unrighteousness shall hide from our eyes the face of the Father.

HG. 131

It is the part of the enemy of righteousness to increase the difficulties in the way of becoming righteous, and to diminish those in the way of seeming righteous. Jesus desires no righteousness for the pride of being righteous, any more than for advantage to be gained by it; therefore, while requiring such purity as the man, beforehand, is unable to imagine, he gives him all the encouragement he can.

HG. 144

Men cannot be righteous without love; to love a righteous man is the best, the only way to learn righteousness; the Lord gives us himself to love, and promises his closest friendship to them that overcome.

HG. 145

So long as the constitution of that universe remains, so long as the world continues to be made by God, righteousness can never fail of perfect reward.

HG. 145

Only take heed that you do not your righteousness before men, to be seen of them.

HG. 188

Righteousness does not demand creation; it is Love, not Righteousness, that cannot live alone. The creature must already be, ere Righteousness can put in a claim. But, hearts and souls there, Love itself, which created for love and joy, presses the demand of Righteousness first.

HG. 196

A righteousness that created misery in order to uphold itself would be a righteousness that was unrighteous. God will die for righteousness, but never create for a joyless righteousness.

HG. 196

Or are you so well satisfied with what you are, that you have never sought eternal life, never hungered and thirsted after the righteousness of God, the perfection of your being? If this latter be your condition, then be comforted; the Master does not require of you to sell what you have and give to the poor. *You* follow him! *You* go with him to preach good tidings!—you who care not for righteousness! You are not one whose company is desirable to the Master. Be comforted, I say: he does not want you; he will not ask you to open your purse for him; you may give or withhold: it is nothing to him.

SII. 26

Christ is our righteousness, not that we should escape punishment, still less escape being righteous, but as the live potent creator of righteousness in us, so that we, with our wills receiving his spirit, shall like him resist unto blood, striving against sin; shall know in ourselves, as he knows, what a lovely thing is righteousness, what a mean, ugly, unnatural thing is unrighteousness. He *is* our righteousness, and that righteousness is no fiction, no pretense, no imputation.

SII. 104

One thing that tends to keep men from seeing righteousness and unrighteousness as they are, is, that they have been told many things are righteous and unrighteous, which are neither the one nor the other. Righteousness is just fairness—from God to man, from man to God and to man; it is giving every one his due—his large mighty due. He is righteous, and no one else, who does this.

SII. 104

Any system which tends to persuade men that there is any salvation but that of becoming righteous even as Jesus is righteous; that a man can be made good, as a good dog is good, without his own willed share in the making; that a man is saved by having his sins hidden under a robe of imputed righteousness—that system, so far as this tendency, is of the devil and not of God. Thank God, not even error shall injure the true of heart; it is not wickedness. They grow in the truth, and as love casts out fear, so truth casts out falsehood.

SII. 104

The true child, the righteous man, will trust absolutely, against all appearances, the God who has created in him the love of righteousness.

SII. 199

To impute the righteousness of one to another, is simply to act a falsehood; to call the faith of a man his righteousness is simply to speak the truth. Was it not righteous in Abraham to obey God?

SII. 213

You must be made miserable, that you may wake from your sleep to know that you need God. If you do not find him, endless life with the living whom you bemoan would become and remain to you unendurable. The knowledge of your own heart will teach you this—not the knowledge you have, but the knowledge that is on its way to you through suffering. Then you will feel that existence itself is the prime of evils, without *the righteousness which is of God by faith.*

SIII. 208

What does the apostle mean by the righteousness that is of God by faith? He means the same righteousness Christ had by his faith in God, the same righteousness God himself has.

SIII. 209

"He has made him to be sin for us who knew no sin, that we might be made the righteousness of God in him"; "He gave him to be treated like a sinner, killed and cast out of his own vineyard by his husbandmen, that we might in him be made righteous like God." As the antithesis stands it is rhetorically correct. But if the former half means, "he made him to be treated as if he were a sinner," then the latter half should, in logical precision, mean, "that we might be treated as if we were righteous."

"That is just what Paul does mean," insist not a few. "He means that Jesus was treated by God as if he were a sinner, our sins being imputed to him, in order that we might be treated as if we were righteous, his righteousness being imputed to us."

That is, that, by a sort of legal fiction, Jesus was treated as what he was not, in order that we might be treated as what we are not. This is the best device, according to the prevailing theology, that the God of truth, the God of mercy, whose glory is that he is just to men by forgiving their sins, could fall upon for saving his creatures!

SIII. 209

They say first, God must punish the sinner, for justice requires it; then they say he does not punish the sinner, but punishes a perfectly righteous man instead, attributes his righteousness to the sinner, and so continues just. Was there ever such a confusion, such an inversion of right and wrong! Justice *could not* treat a righteous man as an unrighteous; neither, if justice required the punishment of sin, *could* justice let the sinner go unpunished. To lay the pain upon the righteous in the name of justice is simply monstrous. No wonder unbelief is rampant. Believe in Moloch if you will, but call him Moloch, not Justice. Be sure that the thing that God gives, the righteousness that is of God is a real thing, and not a contemptible legalism. Pray God I have no righteousness imputed to me. Let me be regarded as the sinner I am; for nothing will serve my need but to be made a righteous man, one that will no more sin.

SIII. 212

The apostle says that a certain thing was imputed to Abraham for righteousness; or, as the revised version has it, "reckoned unto him": What was it that was thus imputed to Abraham? The righteousness of another? God forbid! It was his own faith. The faith of Abraham is reckoned to him for righteousness.

SIII. 213

Abraham was unjust in many things, and by no means a righteous man. True; he was not a righteous man in any complete sense; his righteousness would never have satisfied Paul; neither, you may be sure, did it satisfy Abraham; but his faith was nevertheless righteousness, and if it had not been counted to him for righteousness, there would have been falsehood somewhere, for such faith as Abraham's *is righteousness.* It was no mere intellectual recognition of the existence of a God, which is consistent with the deepest atheism; it was that faith which is one with action: "He went out, not knowing whither he went." The very act of believing in God after such fashion that, when the time of action comes, the man will obey God, is the highest act, the deepest, loftiest righteousness of which man is capable, is at the root of all other righteousness, and the spirit of it will work until the man is perfect.

SIII. 214

While faith in God is the first duty, and may therefore well be called righteousness in the man in whom it is operative, even though it be imperfect, there is more reason than this why it should be counted to a man for righteousness. It is the one spiritual act which brings the man into contact with the original creative power, able to help him in every endeavor after righteousness, and ensure his progress to perfection. The man who exercises it may therefore also well be called a righteous man, however far from complete in righteousness.

SIII. 215

To the man who has no faith in God, faith in God cannot look like righteousness; neither can he know that it is creative of all other righteousness toward equal and inferior lives: he cannot know that it is not merely the beginning of righteousness, but the germ of life, the active potency whence life-righteousness grows. It is not like some single separate act of righteousness; it is the action of the whole man, turning to good from evil—turning his back on all that is opposed to righteousness, and starting on a road on which he cannot stop, in which he must go on growing more and more righteous, discovering more and more what righteousness is, and more and more what is unrighteous in himself.

SIII. 216

The Bible never deals with impossibilities, never demands of any man at any given moment a righteousness of which at that moment he is incapable; neither does it lay upon any man any other law than that of perfect righteousness. It demands of him righteousness; when he yields that righteousness of which he is capable, content for the moment, it goes on to demand more: the common sense of the Bible is lovely.

SIII. 216

If a man is to be blamed for not choosing righteousness, for not turning to the light, for not coming out of the darkness, then the man who does choose and turn and come out, is to be justified in his deed, and declared to be righteous. He is not yet thoroughly righteous, but is growing in and toward righteousness. He needs creative God, and time for will and effort. Not yet quite righteous, he cannot yet act quite righteously, for only the man in whom the image of God is perfected can live perfectly. Born into the world without righteousness, he cannot see, he cannot know, he is not in touch with perfect righteousness, and it would be the deepest injustice to demand of him, with a penalty, at any given moment, more than he knows how to yield; but it is the highest love constantly to demand of him perfect righteousness as what he must attain to.

SIII. 217

With what life and possibility is in him, he must keep turning to righteousness and abjuring iniquity, ever aiming at the righteousness of God. Such an obedient faith is most justly and fairly, being all that God himself can require of the man, called by God righteousness in the man. It would not be enough for the righteousness of God, or Jesus, or any perfected saint, because they are capable of perfect righteousness.

SIII. 217

The righteousness of Abraham was not to compare with the righteousness of Paul. He did not fight with himself for righteousness, as did Paul—not because he was better than Paul and therefore did not need to fight, but because his idea of what was required of him was not within sight of that of Paul; yet was he righteous in the same way as Paul was righteous: he had begun to be righteous, and God called his righteousness righteousness, for faith is righteousness. His faith was an act recognizing God as his law, and that is not a partial act, but an all-embracing and all-determining action. A single righteous deed toward one's fellow could hardly be imputed to a man as righteousness. A man who is not trying after righteousness may yet do many a righteous act: they will not be forgotten to him, neither will they be imputed to him as righteousness. Abraham's action of obedient faith was righteousness nonetheless that his righteousness was far behind Paul's. Abraham started at the beginning of the long, slow, disappointing preparation of the Jewish people; Paul started at its close, with the story of Jesus behind him. Both believed, obeying God, and therefore both were righteous.

SIII. 219

What, then, is the righteousness which is of God by faith? It is simply the thing that God wants every man to be, wrought out in him by constant obedient contact with God himself. It is not an attribute either of God or man, but a fact of character in God and in man. It is God's righteousness wrought out in us, so that as he is righteous we too are righteous. It does not consist in obeying this or that law; not even the keeping of every law, so that no hair's-breadth did we run counter to one of them, would be righteousness. To be righteous is to be such a heart, soul, mind, and will, as, without regard to law, would recoil with horror from the lightest possible breach of any law. It is to be so in love with what is fair and right as to make it impossible for a man to do anything that is less than absolutely righteous. It is not the love of righteousness in the abstract that makes anyone righteous, but such a love of fairplay toward everyone with whom we come into contact, that anything less than the fulfilling, with a clear joy, of our divine relation to him or her, is impossible. For the righteousness of God goes far beyond mere deeds, and requires of us love and helping mercy as our highest obligation and justice to our fellow men—those of them too who have done nothing for us, those even who have done us wrong. Our relations with others, God first and then our neighbor in order and degree, must one day become, as in true nature they are, the gladness of our being; and nothing then will ever appear good for us, that is not in harmony with those blessed relations. Every thought will not merely be just, but will be just because it is something more, because it is live and true.

SIII. 220

The righteousness which is of God by faith in the source, the prime of that righteousness, is then just the same kind of thing as God's righteousness, differing only as the created differs from the creating. The righteousness of him who does the will of his Father in heaven, is the righteousness of Jesus Christ, is God's own righteousness. The righteousness which is of God by faith in God, is God's righteousness. The man who has this righteousness, thinks about things as God thinks about them, loves the things that God loves, cares for nothing that God does not care about.

SIII. 222

The man with God's righteousness does not love a thing merely because it is right, but loves the very rightness in it. He not only loves a thought, but he loves the man in his thinking that thought; he loves the thought alive in the man. He does not take his joy from himself. He feels joy in himself, but it comes to him from others, not from himself—from God first, and from somebody, anybody, everybody next.

SIII. 223

For our encouragement to fight on, he tells us that those that hunger and thirst after righteousness shall be filled, that they shall become as righteous as the spirit of the Father and the Son in them can make them desire.

SIII. 231

It often seems to those in earnest about the right as if all things conspired to prevent their progress. This, of course, is but an appearance, arising in part from this, that the pilgrim must be headed back from the side-paths into which he is constantly wandering.

TW. chap. 36

Rights

It is a very small matter *to you* whether the man give you your rights or not; it is life or death to you whether or not you give him his.

SII. 106

We are the clay, it is true, but *his* clay, but spiritual clay, live clay, with needs and desires—and *rights*; we are clay, but clay worth the Son of God's dying for, that it might learn to consent to be shaped unto honor.

SII. 182

God has given us rights. Out of him we have nothing; but, created by him, come forth from him, we have even rights toward him—ah, never, never *against* him! his whole desire and labor is to make us capable of claiming, and induce us to claim of him the things whose rights he bestowed in creating us. No claim had we to be created: that involves an absurdity; but, being made, we have claims on him who made us: our needs are our claims.

SII. 183

We can deserve from him nothing at all, in the sense of any right proceeding from ourselves. All our rights are such as the bounty of love inconceivable has glorified our being with—bestowed for the one only purpose of giving the satisfaction, the fulfillment of the same—rights so deep, so high, so delicate, that their satisfaction cannot be given until we desire it—yea long for it with our deepest desire. The giver of them came to men, lived with men, and died by the hands of men, that they might possess these rights abundantly: more not God could do to fulfill his part—save indeed what he is doing still every hour, every moment, for every individual. Our rights are rights with God himself at the heart of them. He could recall them if he pleased, but only by recalling us, by making us cease. While we exist, by the being that is ours, they are ours. If he could not fulfill our rights to us—because we would not have them, that is—if he could not make us such as to care for these rights which he has given us out of the very depth of his creative being, I think he would have to uncreate us. But as to deserving, that is absurd: he had to die in the endeavor to make us listen and receive.

SII. 192

Lest it should be possible that any unchildlike soul might, in arrogance and ignorance, think to stand upon his rights *against* God, and demand of him this or that after the will of the flesh, I will lay before such a possible one some of the things to which he has a right, yea, perhaps has first of all a right to, from the God of his life, because of the beginning he has given him—because of the divine germ that is in him. He has a claim on God, then, a divine claim, for any pain, want, disappointment, or misery, that would help to show him to himself as the fool he is; he has a claim to be punished to the last scorpion of the whip, to be spared not one pang that may urge him toward repentance; yea, he has a claim to be sent out into the outer darkness, whether what we call hell, or something speechlessly worse, if nothing less will do. He has a claim to be compelled to repent; to be hedged in on every side; to have one after another of the strong, sharp-toothed sheepdogs of the great shepherd sent after him, to thwart him in any desire, foil him in any plan, frustrate him of any hope, until he come to see at length that nothing will ease his pain, nothing make life a thing worth having, but the presence of the living God within him; that nothing is good but the will of God; nothing noble enough for the desire of the heart of man but oneness with the eternal. For this God must make him yield his very being, that he may enter in and dwell with him.

SII. 193

He who teaches his neighbor to insist on his rights, is not a teacher of righteousness.

WM

Sacrifice(s)

We should never wish our children or friends to do what we would not do ourselves if we were in their position. We must accept righteous sacrifices as well as make them.

PC. chap. 1

What Jesus did, was what the Father is always doing; the suffering he endured was that of the Father from the foundation of the world, reaching its climax in the person of his Son. God provides the sacrifice; the sacrifice is himself. He is always, and has ever been, sacrificing himself to and for his creatures. It lies in the very essence of his creation of them.

SII. 142

God accepted men's sacrifices until he could get them to see—and with how many has he yet not succeeded, in the church and out of it!—that he does not care for such things.

SIII. 139

To believe in a vicarious sacrifice, is to think to take refuge with the Son from the righteousness of the Father; to take refuge with his work instead of with the Son himself; to take refuge with a theory of that work instead of the work itself; to shelter behind a false quirk of law instead of nestling in the eternal heart of the unchangeable and righteous Father, who is merciful in that he renders to every man according to his work, and compels their obedience, nor admits judicial quibble or subterfuge. God will never let a man off with any fault. He must have him clean.

SIII. 147

We sacrifice to God!—it is God who has sacrificed his own Son to us; there was no way else of getting the gift of himself into our hearts.

SIII. 158

Jesus sacrificed himself to his Father and the children to bring them together—all the love on the side of the

Father and the Son, all the selfishness on the side of the children.

SIII. 158

Thousands that are capable of great sacrifices are yet not capable of the little ones which are all that are required of them.

WW

God seems to take pleasure in working by degrees; the progress of the truth is as the permeation of leaven, or the growth of a seed; a multitude of successive small sacrifices may work more good in the world than many a larger one.

WW

It is the *Being* that is the precious thing. Being is the mother to all little Doings as well as the grown-up Deeds and the mighty heroic Sacrifice; and these little Doings, like the good children of the house, make the bliss of it.

WW. 4

Salvation

"Nothing but Christ himself, your lord and friend and brother, not all the doctrines about him, even if every one of them were true, can save you."

DG

Just in proportion as a man is saved, will he do the work of God's world aright—the whole design of it being this—to rear a beautiful holy family for himself, the Father in heaven, and for each other his children.

DG. 25

The world is his nursery for his upper rooms—for a higher and nobler state of being—a state which can be developed only by the doing of the will of God. Any state that could be otherwise developed would be nothing worth. Through that alone can we be filled with him as our conscious life, and that is salvation.

DG. 25

To save a man from his sins is to say to him, in sense perfect and eternal, "Rise up and walk. Be at liberty in your essential being. Be free as the Son of God is free." To do this for us, Jesus was born, and remains born to all the ages.

HG. 6

He cannot make himself pure, but he can leave that which is impure; he can spread out the "defiled, discolored web" of his life before the bleaching sun of righteousness; he cannot save himself, but he can let the Lord save him.

HG. 21

God and man must combine for salvation from sin, and the same word, here and elsewhere translated *remission*, seems to be employed in the New Testament for the share of either in the great deliverance.

HG. 23

What did Jesus come into the world to do? The will of God in saving his people from their sins—not from the punishment of their sins, that blessed aid to repentance, but from their sins themselves, the paltry as well as the heinous, the venial as well as the loathsome. His whole work was and is to send away sin—to banish it from the earth, yea, to cast it into the abyss of nonexistence behind the back of God. His was the holy war; he came carrying it into our world; he resisted unto blood; the soldiers that followed him he taught and trained to resist also unto blood, striving against sin; so he became the captain of their salvation, and they, freed themselves, fought and suffered for others.

HG. 35

The only merit that could live before God is the merit of Jesus—who of himself, at once, untaught, unimplored, laid himself aside, and turned to the Father, refusing his life save in the Father. Like God, of himself he chose righteousness, and so merited to sit on the throne of God. In the same spirit he gave himself afterward to his Father' s children, and merited the power to transfuse the life-redeeming energy of his spirit into theirs: made perfect, he became the author of eternal salvation unto all them that obey him.

HG. 199

No man can ever save his soul. God only can do that.

You can glorify him by giving yourself up heart and soul and body and life to his Son. Then you shall *be* saved. That you must leave to *him*, and *do what he tells you.*

M. 53

The whole trouble is that we won't let God help us.

ML. 114

God is our Savior.

MOL. 36

To see one divine fact is to stand face to face with essential eternal life. For this vision of truth God has been working for ages of ages. For this simple condition, this apex of life, upon which a man wonders like a child that he cannot make other men see as he sees, the whole labor of God's science, history, poetry . . . was evolving truth upon truth in lovely vision, in torturing law, never lying, never repenting; and for this will the patience of God labor while there is yet a human soul whose eyes have not been opened, whose child-heart has not yet been born in him. For this one condition of humanity, this simple beholding, has all the outthinking of God flowed in forms innumerable and changeful from the foundation of the world; and for this, too, has the divine destruction been going forth; that his life might be our life, that in us, too, might dwell that same consuming fire which is essential love.

SI. 29

While men take part *with* their sins, while they feel as if, separated from their sins, they would be no longer themselves, how can they understand that the lightning word is a Savior—that word which pierces to the dividing between the man and the evil, which will slay the sin and give life to the sinner? Can it be any comfort to them to be told that God loves them so that he will burn them clean?

SI. 37

Instead of so knowing Christ that they have him in them saving them, they lie wasting themselves in soul-sickening self-examination as to whether they are believers, whether they are really trusting in the atonement, whether they are truly sorry for their sins—the way to madness of the brain, and despair of the heart.

SI. 244

"I cannot be perfect; it is hopeless; and he does not expect it."—It would be more honest if he said, "I do not want to be perfect; I am content to be saved." Such as he do not care for being perfect as their Father in heaven is perfect, but for being what they call *saved*. They little think that without perfection there is no salvation—that perfection is salvation.

SII. 25

If they are not righteous even as he is righteous, they are not saved, whatever be their gladness or their content; they are but on the way to be saved.

SII. 33

Let any tell me of peace and content, yea, joy unspeakable, as the instant result of the new birth; I deny no such statement, refuse no such testimony; all I care to say is, that, if by salvation they mean less than absolute oneness with God, I count it no salvation, neither would be content with it if it included every joy in the heaven of their best imagining.

SII. 33

He is God our Savior; it is because God is our Savior that Jesus is our Savior.

SII. 143

Men . . . would rather receive salvation from God than God their salvation.

SII. 178

Blessed be God, the one result for all who so draw nigh to him will be—to see him plainly, surely right, the perfect Savior, the profoundest refuge even from the wrongs of their own being, yea, nearer to them always than any wrong they could commit; so seeing him, they will abhor themselves, and rejoice in him.

SII. 206

When you say that, to be saved, a man must hold this or that, then are you leaving the living God and his will, and putting trust in some notion about him or his will.

SII. 240

There is but one plan of salvation, and that is to believe in the Lord Jesus Christ; that is, to take him for what he is—our master, and his words as if he meant them, which assuredly he did. To do his words is to enter into vital relation with him, to obey him is the only way to be one with him. The relation between him and us is an absolute one; it can nohow begin to *live* but in obedience: it *is* obedience.

SII. 246

The doing of the will of God is the way to oneness with God, which alone is salvation.

SII. 249

Well do I know it is faith that saves us—but not faith in any work of God—it is faith in God himself.

SII. 250

If I did not believe God as good as the tenderest human heart, the fairest, the purest, the most unselfish human heart could imagine him, yea, an infinitude better, higher than we as the heavens are higher than the earth—believe it, not as a proposition, or even as a thing I was convinced of, but with the responsive condition and being of my whole nature; if I did not feel every fiber of heart and brain and body safe with him because he is the Father who made me that I am—I would not be saved, for this faith is salvation; it is God and the man one.

SII. 250

The working out of this our salvation must be pain, and the handing of it down to them that are below must ever be in pain; but the eternal form of the will of God in and for us, is intensity of bliss.

SIII. 14

The notion that the salvation of Jesus is a salvation from the consequences of our sins, is a false, mean, low notion. The salvation of Christ is salvation from the smallest tendency or leaning to sin. It is a deliverance into the pure air of God's ways of thinking and feeling. It is a salvation that makes the heart pure, with the will and choice of the heart to be pure. To such a heart, sin is disgusting. It sees a thing as it is—that is, as God sees it, for God sees everything as it is. The soul thus saved would rather sink into the flames of hell than steal into heaven and skulk there under the shadow of an imputed righteousness. No soul is saved that would not prefer hell to sin. Jesus did not die to save us from punishment; he was called Jesus because he should save his people from their sins.

SIII. 132

A man must say, "I have sinned, and deserve to be tortured to all eternity. But Christ has paid my debts, by being punished instead of me. Therefore he is my Savior. I am now bound by gratitude to him to turn away from evil."

SIII. 143

I am saved—for God is light! My God, I come to you. That you should be yourself is enough for time and eternity, for my soul and all its endless need.

SIII. 167

He is God our Savior. Jesus is our Savior because God is our Savior. He is the God of comfort and consolation. He will soothe and satisfy his children better than any mother her infant. The only thing he will not give them is—leave to stay in the dark.

SIII. 171

Let him do it, and perhaps you will know; if you never know, yet there it will be. Help him to do it, or he cannot do it. He originates the possibility of your being his son, his daughter; he makes you able to will it, but you must will it. If he is not doing it in you—that is, if you have as yet prevented him from beginning, why should I tell you, even if I knew the process, how he would do what you will not let him do? Why should you know? What claim have you to know? But indeed how should you be able to know? For it must deal with deeper and higher things than you *can* know anything of until the work is at least begun. Perhaps if you approved of the plans of the glad Creator, you would allow him to make of you something divine! To teach our intellect what has to be learned by your whole being, what cannot be understood without the whole being, what it would do you no good to understand save you understood it in your whole being—if this be the province of any man, it is not mine.

SIII. 226

For the sake of your father and the first-born among many brethren to whom we belong, for the sake of those he has given us to love the most dearly, let patience have her perfect work. Statue under the chisel of the sculptor, stand steady to the blows of his mallet. Clay on the wheel, let the fingers of the divine potter model you at their will. Obey the Father's lightest word; hear the Brother who knows you, and died for you; beat down your sin, and trample it to death.

SIII. 227

Brother, when you sit at home in your house, which is the temple of the Lord, open all your windows to breathe the air of his approach; set the watcher on your turret, that he may listen out into the dark for the sound of his coming, and your hand be on the latch to open the door at his first knock. Should you open the door and not see him, do not say he did not knock, but understand that he is there, and wants you to go out to him. It may be he has something for you to do for him. Go and do it, and perhaps you will return with a new prayer, to find a new window in your soul.

SIII. 227

Any salvation short of God is no salvation at all.

WM

Salvation lies in being one with Christ, even as the branch is one with the vine.

WM

I am sometimes almost terrified at the scope of the demands made upon me, at the perfection of the self-abandonment required of me; yet outside of such absoluteness can be no salvation.

WM. 22

Science

To inquire into what God has made is the main function of the imagination. It is aroused by facts, is nourished by facts, seeks for higher and yet higher laws in those facts; but refuses to regard science as the sole interpreter of nature, or the laws of science as the only region of discovery.

DO. 2

Alas for the science that will sacrifice the law of righteousness but to behold a law of sequence!

HG. 237

If a man tells me that science says God is not a likely being, I answer, Probably not—such as you, who have given your keen, admirable, enviable powers to the observation of outer things only, are capable of supposing him; but that the God I mean may not be the very heart of the lovely order you see so much better than I, you have given me no reason to fear. My God may be above and beyond and in all that.

MOL. 36

Human science cannot discover God; or human science is but the backward undoing of the tapestry-web of God's science, works with its back to him, and is always leaving him—his intent, that is, his perfected work—behind it, always going farther and farther away from the point where his work culminates in revelation. Doubtless it thus makes some small intellectual approach to him, but at best it can come only to his back; science will never find the fact of God.

SIII. 62

Analysis is well, as death is well; analysis is death, not life. It discovers a little of the way God walks to his ends, but in so doing it forgets and leaves the end itself behind. I do not say the man of science does so, but the very process of his work is such a leaving of God's ends behind.

SIII. 63

Ask a man of mere science, what is the truth of a flower: he will pull it to pieces, show you its parts, explain how they operate, how they minister each to the life of the flower; he will tell you what changes are wrought in it by scientific cultivation; where it lives originally, where it can live; the effects upon it of another climate; what part the insects bear in its varieties—and doubtless many more facts about it. Ask the poet what is the truth of the flower, and he will answer: "Why, the flower itself, the perfect flower, and what it cannot help saying to him who has ears to hear it." The truth of the flower is, not the facts about it, be they correct as ideal science itself, but the shining, glowing, gladdening, patient thing throned on its stalk—the compeller of smile and tear from child and prophet.

The man of science laughs at this, because he is only a man of science, and does not know what it means; but the poet and the child care as little for his laughter as the birds of God, as Dante calls the angels, for his treatise on aerostation. The children of God must always be mocked by the children of the world, whether in the church or out of it—children with sharp ears and eyes, but dull hearts. Those that hold love the only good in the world, understand and smile at the world's children, and can do very well without anything they have got to tell them. In the higher state to which their love is leading them, they will speedily outstrip the men of science, for they have that which is at the root of science, that for the revealing of which God's science exists.

SIII. 64

God's science in the flower exists for the existence of the flower in its relation to his children. If we understand, if we are at one with, if we love the flower, we have that for which the science is there, that which alone can equip us for true search into the means and ways by which the divine idea of the flower was wrought out to be presented to us. The idea of God *is* the flower; his idea is not the botany of the flower. Its botany is but a thing of ways and means—of canvas and color and brush in relation to the picture in the painter's brain. The mere intellect can never find out that which owes its being to the heart supreme. The relation of the intellect to that which is born of the heart is an unreal except it be a humble one. The idea of God, I repeat, is the flower. He thought it; invented its means; sent it, a gift of himself, to the eyes and hearts of his children.

SIII. 65

What shall it profit a man to know all things, and lose the bliss, the consciousness of well-being, which alone can give value to his knowledge?

SIII. 65

Seeing God

Each and all must one day be seen and known in the light. Well for those who are humble enough and true enough not to shrink from the exposure of even their faults and sins—who hate them so much themselves that they would have them have no quarter.

DG. 36

The cry of the deepest in man has always been to see God.

HG. 117

He who saw God, who sees him now, who always did and always will see him, says, "Be pure, and you also shall see him." To see God was the Lord's own, eternal, one happiness; therefore he knew that the essential bliss of the creature is to behold the face of the Creator.

HG. 117

All that the creature needs to see or know, all that the creature can see or know, is the face of him from whom he came. Not seeing and knowing it, he will never be at rest; seeing and knowing it, his existence will yet indeed be a mystery to him and an awe, but no more a dismay.

HG. 118

None but the pure in heart see God; only the growing-pure hope to see him. Even those who saw the Lord, the express image of his person, did not see God. They only saw Jesus—and then but the outside Jesus, or a little more. They were not pure in heart; they saw him and did not see him. They saw him with their eyes, but not with those eyes which alone can see God. Those were not born in them yet.

HG. 119

Our very senses, filled with the things of our passing sojourn, combine to cast discredit on the existence of any world for the sake of which we are furnished with an inner eye, an eternal ear. But had we once seen God face to face, should we not be always and forever sure of him? we have had but glimpses of the Father.

HG. 120

If we had seen God face to face, but had again become impure of heart—if such a fearful thought be a possible idea—we should then no more believe that we had ever beheld him. A sin-clouded soul could never recall the vision whose essential verity was its only possible proof.

HG. 120

Neither the eyes of the resurrection-body, nor the eyes of unembodied spirits can see God; only the eyes of that eternal something that is of the very essence of God, the thought-eyes, the truth-eyes, the love-eyes, can see him. It is not because we are created and he uncreated, it is not because of any difference involved in that difference of all differences, that we cannot see him. If he pleased to take a shape, and that shape were presented to us, and we saw that shape, we should not therefore be seeing God. Even if we knew it was a shape of God—call it even God himself our eyes rested upon; if we had been told the fact and believed the report; yet, if we did not see the *Godness*, were not capable of recognizing him, so as without the report to know the vision him, we should not be seeing God, we should only be seeing the tabernacle in which for the moment he dwelt. In other words, not seeing what in the form made it a form fit for him to take, we should not be seeing a presence which could only be God.

HG. 120

To see God is to stand on the highest point of created being. Not until we see God—no partial and passing embodiment of him, but the abiding presence—do we stand upon our own mountaintop, the height of the existence God has given us, and up to which he is leading us. That there we should stand, is the end of our creation.

HG. 121

Nor shall we ever see, that is, know, God perfectly. We shall indeed never absolutely know man or woman or child; but we may know God as we never can know human being—as we never can know ourselves. We not only may, but we must so know him, and it can never be until we are pure in heart. Then shall we know him with the infinitude of an ever-growing knowledge.

HG. 122

If you care to see God, be pure.

HG. 123

To see the Father is the cry of every child-heart in the universe of the Father—is the need, where not the cry, of every living soul.

HG. 164

God knows how things look to us both far off and near; he also can see them so when he pleases. What they look to him is what they are: we cannot see them so, but we see them as he meant us to see them, therefore truly, according to the measure of the created.

M. 49

Having seen him, in his absence we understand him better. That we might know him he came; that we might go to him he went.

SII. 189

Seeing God, Job forgets all he wanted to say, and he thought he would say if he could but see him.

SII. 203

Job had his desire: he saw the face of God—and abhorred himself in dust and ashes. He sought justification; he found self-abhorrence.

SII. 205

No man has ever seen God in any outward, visible, close-fitting form of his own: he is revealed in no shape save that of his Son.

SIII. 34

Multitudes of men have with their mind's, or rather their heart's eye, seen more or less of God; and perhaps every man might have and ought to have seen something of him. We cannot follow God into his infinitesimal intensities of spiritual operation, any more than into the atomic life-potencies that lie deep beyond the eye of the microscope: God may be working in the heart of a savage, in a way that no wisdom of his wisest, humblest child can see, or imagine that it sees.

SIII. 34

Many who have never beheld the face of God, may yet have caught a glimpse of the hem of his garment; many who have never seen his shape, may yet have seen the vastness of his shadow; thousands who have never felt the warmth of its fold, have yet been startled by

> No face: only the sight
> Of a sweepy garment vast and
> white.

SIII. 34

We do not yet see God as he is—and that must be because we do not yet really understand Jesus—do not see the glory of God in his face. God is just like him.

SF. 17

God, like his body, the light, is all about us, and prefers to shine in on us sideways. We could not endure the power of his vertical glory. No mortal man can see God and live; and he who loves not his brother whom he has seen, shall not love his God whom he has not seen.

WW. 13

[We must] seek the sweet enablings of the living light to see things as they are—as God sees them, who never is wrong because he has no selfishness, but is the living Love and the living Truth, without whom there would be no love and no truth.

WW. 53

Self

There is one kind of religion in which the more devoted a man is, the fewer proselytes he makes: the worship of himself.

AF. 151

It was no use asking myself why I should be jealous: there the ugly thing was. So I went and told God I was ashamed, and begged him to deliver me from the evil, because his was the kingdom and the power and the glory. And he took my part against myself, for he waits to be gracious.

AN. 191

All self-will is madness.

AN. 277

Self, I repeat, is as full of worms as it can hold, and is the damnedest friend a man can have.

DG. 37

When self is first it simply makes devils of us.

DG. 668

Self is a quicksand; God is the only rock.

HA. 242

The being of which we are conscious is not our full self; the extent of our consciousness of our self is no measure of our self; our consciousness is infinitely less than we; while God is more necessary even to that poor consciousness of self than our self-consciousness is necessary to our humanity.

HG. 38

No crying will make him comfort your selfishness. He will not render you incapable of loving truly. He despises neither your love, though mingled with selfishness, nor your suffering that springs from both; he will disentangle your selfishness from your love, and cast it into the fire. His cure for your selfishness at once and your suffering is to make you love more—and more truly; not with the love of love, but with the love of the person whose lost love you moan about. For the love of love is the love of yourself.

HG. 115

The injunction is not to hide what you do from others, but to hide it from yourself. The Master would have you not plume yourself upon it, not cherish the thought that you have done it, or confer with yourself in satisfaction over it. You must not count it to your praise. A man must not desire to be satisfied with himself. His right hand must not seek the praise of his left hand. His doing must not invite his after-thinking. The right hand must let the thing done go, as a thing done with. We must meditate nothing either as a fine thing for us to do, or a fine thing for us to have done. We must not imagine any merit in us: it would be to love a lie, for we can have none; there is no such thing possible.

HG. 190

What a hell of horror, I thought, to wander alone, a bare existence never going out of itself, never widening its life in another life, but, bound with the cords of its poor peculiarities, lying an eternal prisoner in the dungeon of its own being!

L. 83

Dignity is such a delicate thing!

L. 121

You must follow the truth, and, in that pursuit, the less one thinks about himself, the pursuer, the better.

MM. 45

Self-forgetfulness in the reaching out after that which is essential to us is the healthiest of mental conditions. One has to look to his way, to his deeds, to his conduct—not to himself.

MM. 45

Like most men, he was so well satisfied with himself that he saw no occasion to take trouble to be anything better than he was. Never suspecting what a noble creature he was meant to be, he never saw what a poor creature he was.

MM. 157

No man's dignity is affected by what another does to him, but only by what he does, or would like to do, himself.

MM. 222

Our feelings, especially where a wretched self is concerned, are notably illogical.

PF

He ceased thinking, gave way to the feeling that God dealt hardly with him, and sat stupidly indulging a sense of grievance—with self-pity, than which there is scarce one more childish or enfeebling in the whole circle of the emotions.

PF. 53

I learned that it was not myself but only my shadow that I had lost. I learned that it is better . . . for a proud man to fall and be humbled than to hold up his head in pride and fancied innocence. I learned that he that will be a hero, will barely be a man; that he that will be nothing but a doer of his work, is sure of his manhood.

PH. chap. 22

The fear of God will cause a man to flee, not from him, but from himself; not from him, but to him, the Father of himself, in terror lest he should do him wrong or his neighbor wrong.

SI. 32

The wrath will consume what they *call* themselves; so that the selves God made shall appear, coming out with tenfold consciousness of being, and bringing with them all that made the blessedness of the life the men tried to lead without God. They will know that now first are they fully themselves. The avaricious, weary, selfish, suspicious old man shall have passed away. The young, ever young self, will remain. That which they *thought* themselves shall have vanished: that which they *felt* themselves, though they misjudged their own feelings, shall remain—remain glorified in repentant hope. For that which cannot be shaken shall remain. That which is immortal in God shall remain in man. The death that is in them shall be consumed.

SI. 44

When a man gives up self, his past sins will no longer oppress him. It is enough for the good of life that God lives, that the All-perfect exists, and that we can behold him.

SI. 94

"God has cared to make me for himself," says the victor with the white stone, "and has called me that which I like best; for my own name must be what I would have it, seeing it is myself. What matter whether I be called a grass of the field, or an eagle of the air? a stone to build into his temple, or a Boanerges to wield his thunder? I am his; his idea, his making; perfect in my kind, yea, perfect in his sight; full of him, revealing him, alone with him. Let him call me what he will. The name shall be precious as my life. I seek no more."

SI. 115

The true self is that which can look Jesus in the face, and say *My Lord.*

SI. 171

This love of our neighbor is the only door out of the dungeon of self, where we mope and mow, striking sparks, and rubbing phosphorescences out of the walls, and blowing our own breath in our own nostrils, instead of issuing to the fair sunlight of God, the sweet winds of the universe.

SI. 214

Man thinks his consciousness is himself; whereas his life consists in the inbreathing of God, and the consciousness of the universe of truth. To have himself, to know himself, to enjoy himself, he calls life; whereas, if he would forget himself, tenfold would be his life in God and his neighbors.

SI. 214

The region of man's life is a spiritual region. God, his friends, his neighbors, his brothers all, is the wide world in which alone his spirit can find room. Himself is his dungeon.

SI. 215

A man is in bondage to whatever he cannot part with that is less than himself.

SII. 14

Are you so well satisfied with what you are, that you have never sought eternal life, never hungered and thirsted after the righteousness of God, the perfection of your being?

SII. 26

Witness the dissatisfaction, yea desolation of my soul—wretched, alone, unfinished, without him. It cannot act from itself, save in God; acting from what seems itself without God, is no action at all, it is a mere yielding to impulse. All within is disorder and spasm. There is a cry behind me, and a voice before; instincts of betterment tell me I must rise above my present self—perhaps even above all my possible self: I see not how to obey, how to carry them out! I am shut up in a world of consciousness, an unknown I in an unknown world: surely this world of my unwilled, unchosen, compelled existence, cannot be shut out from him, cannot be unknown to him, cannot be impenetrable, impermeable, unpresent to him from whom I am?

SII. 61

There is endless room for rebellion against ourselves.

SII. 90

The man himself must turn against himself, and so be for himself. If nothing else will do, then hell-fire; if less will do, whatever brings repentance and self-repudiation, is God's repayment.

SII. 95

The misery would be not merely the absence of all being other than his own self, but the fearful, endless, unavoidable presence of that self. Without the correction, the reflection, the support of other presences, being is not merely unsafe, it is a horror—for anyone but God, who is his own being.

SII. 111

It is the lovely creatures God has made all around us, in them giving us himself, that, until we know him, save us from the frenzy of aloneness—for that aloneness is Self, Self, Self. The man who minds only himself must at last go mad if God did not interfere.

SII. 111

Will the soul that could not believe in God, with all his lovely world around testifying of him, believe when shut in the prison of its own lonely, weary all-and-nothing? It would for a time try to believe that it was indeed nothing, a mere glow of the setting sun on a cloud of dust, a paltry dream that dreamed itself—then, ah, if only the dream might dream that it was no more! that would be the one thing to hope for. Self-loathing, and that for no sin, from no repentance, from no vision of better, would begin and grow and grow; and to what it might not come no soul can tell—of essential, original misery, uncompromising self-disgust! Only, then, if a being be capable of self-disgust, is there not some room for hope.

SII. 111

If God once get a willing hold, if with but one finger he touch the man's self, swift as possibility will he draw him from the darkness into the light.

SII. 114

To the heart of God, the one and only goal of the human race—the refuge and home of all and each, he must set out and go, or the last glimmer of humanity will die from him.

SII. 114

Many doubtless mistake the joy of life for life itself; and, longing after the joy, languish with a thirst at once poor and inextinguishable; but even that thirst points to the one spring. These love self, not life, and self is but the shadow of life. When it is taken for life itself, and set as the man's center, it becomes a live death in the man, a devil he worships as his god; the worm of the death eternal he clasps to his bosom as his one joy!

SII. 145

We are made for love, not for self. Our neighbor is our refuge; *self* is our demon-foe.

SII. 155

Self, accepted as the law of self, is the one demon-enemy of life; God is the only Savior from it, and from all that is not God, for God is life, and all that is not God is death. Life is the destruction of death, of all that kills, of all that is of death's kind.

SII. 163

The soul God made is thus hungering, though the selfish, usurping self, which is its consciousness, is hungering only after low and selfish things, ever trying, but in vain, to fill its mean, narrow content, with husks too poor for its poverty-stricken desires. For even that most degraded chamber of the soul which is the temple of the deified Self, cannot be filled with less than God; even the usurping Self must be miserable until it cease to look at itself in the mirror of Satan, and open the door of its innermost closet to the God who means to dwell there, and make peace.

SII. 194

Blessedest gift is self-contempt, when the giver of it is the visible glory of the Living One. For there to see is to partake; to be able to behold that glory is to live; to turn from and against self is to begin to be pure of heart.

SII. 205

Not every man deserves for his sins to be punished everlastingly from the presence of the Lord; and that the best of men, when he sees the face of God, will know himself vile. God is just, and will never deal with the sinner as if he were capable of sinning the pure sin; yet if the best man be not delivered from himself, that self will sink him into Tophet.

SII. 206

The first thing in all progress is to leave something behind; to follow him is to leave one's self behind. "If any man would come after me, let him deny himself."

SII. 211

I will allow that the mere effort of will . . . may add to the man's power over his lower nature; but in that very nature it is God who must rule and not the man, however well he may mean. From a man's rule of himself, in smallest opposition, however devout, to the law of his being, arises the huge danger of nourishing, by the pride of self-conquest, a far worse than even the unchained animal self—the demoniac self.

SII. 212

True victory over self is the victory of God in the man, not of the man alone. It is not subjugation that is enough, but subjugation by God. In whatever man does without God, he must fail miserably—or succeed more miserably. No portion of a man can rule another, for God, not the man, created it, and the part is greater than the whole.

SII. 212

The diseased satisfaction which some minds feel in laying burdens on themselves, is a pampering, little as they may suspect it, of the most dangerous appetite of that self which they think they are mortifying.

SII. 212

Verily it is not to thwart or tease the poor self Jesus tells us. That was not the purpose for which God gave it to us! He tells us we must leave it altogether—yield it, deny it, refuse it, lose it: thus only shall we save it, thus only have a share in our own being.

SII. 213

The self is given to us that we may sacrifice it; it is ours that we like Christ may have somewhat to offer—not that we should torment it, but that we should deny it; not that we should cross it, but that we should abandon it utterly: then it can no more be vexed.

SII. 214

We must refuse, abandon, deny self altogether as a ruling, or determining, or originating element in us. It is to be no longer the regent of our action. We are no more to think, "What should I like to do?" but "What would the Living One have me do?"

SII. 214

It is not selfish to take that which God has made us to desire; neither are we very good to yield it—we should only be very bad not to do so, when he would take it from us; but to yield it heartily, without a struggle or regret, is not merely to deny the Self a thing it would like, but to deny the Self itself, to refuse and abandon it. The Self is God's making—only it must be the "slave of Christ," that the Son may make it also the free son of the same Father; it must receive all from him—not as from nowhere; as well as the deeper soul, it must follow him, not its own desires. It must not be its own law; Christ must be its law.

SII. 214

The time will come when it shall be so possessed, so enlarged, so idealized, by the indwelling God, who is its deeper, its deepest self, that there will be no longer any enforced denial of it needful: it has been finally denied and refused and sent into its own obedient place; it has learned to receive with thankfulness, to demand nothing; to turn no more upon its own center, or any more think to minister to its own good.

SII. 215

To deny oneself then, is to act no more from the standing-ground of self; to allow no private communication, no passing influence between the self and the will; not to let the right hand know what the left hand does. No grasping or seeking, no hungering of the individual, shall give motion to the will; no desire to be conscious of worthiness shall order the life; no ambition whatever shall be a motive of action; no wish to surpass another be allowed a moment's respite from death; no longing after the praise of men influence a single throb of the heart. To deny the self is to shrink from no dispraise or condemnation or contempt of the community, or circle, or country, which is against the mind of the Living one; for no love or entreaty of father or mother, wife or child, friend or lover, to turn aside from following him, but forsake them all as any ruling or ordering power in our lives; we must do nothing to please them that would not first be pleasing to him. Right deeds, and not the judgment thereupon; true words, and not what reception they may have, shall be our care.

SII. 215

Self, I have not to consult you, but him whose idea is the soul of you, and of which as yet you are all unworthy. I have to do, not with you, but with the source of you, by whom it is that any moment you exist—the Causing of you, not the caused you. You may be my consciousness, but you are not my being. If you were, what a poor, miserable, dingy, weak wretch I should be! but my life is hid with Christ in God, whence it came, and whither it is returning—with you certainly, but as an obedient servant, not a master. Submit, or I will cast you from me, and pray to have another consciousness given me. For God is more to me than my consciousness of myself. He is my life; you are only so much of it as my poor half-made being can grasp—as much of it as I can now know at once.

SII. 217

Because I have fooled and spoiled you, treated you as if you were indeed my own self, you have dwindled yourself and have lessened me, until I am ashamed of my self. If I were to mind what you say, I should soon be sick of you; even now I am ever and anon disgusted with your paltry, mean face, which I meet at every turn. No! let me have the company of the Perfect One, not of you! of my Elder Brother, the Living One! I will not make a friend of the mere shadow of my own being!

SII. 217

Good-bye, Self! I deny you, and will do my best every day to leave you behind me.

SII. 218

We must be jealous for God against ourselves, and look well to the cunning and deceitful Self—ever cunning and deceitful until it is informed of God—until it is thoroughly and utterly denied, and God is to it also All-in-all—until we have left it quite empty of our will and our regard, and God has come into it, and made it.

SII. 220

Although the idea of the denial of self is an entire and absolute one, yet the thing has to be done *daily*: we must keep on denying. It is a deeper and harder thing than any sole effort of most Herculean will may finally effect. For indeed the will itself is not pure, is not free, until the Self is absolutely denied.

SII. 222

Is there not many a Christian who, having *begun* to deny himself, yet spends much strength in the vain and evil endeavor to accommodate matters between Christ and the dear Self—seeking to save that which so he must certainly lose—in how different a way from that in which the Master would have him lose it!

SII. 222

It is one thing to have the loved self devoured of hell in hate and horror and disappointment; another to yield it to conscious possession by the living God himself, who will raise it then first and only to its true individuality, freedom, and life. With its cause within it, then, indeed, it shall be saved!—how then should it but live!

SII. 222

Here is the promise to those who will leave all and follow him: "*Whoever shall lose his life, for my sake, the same shall save it*"—in St. Matthew, "*find it.*" What speech of men or angels will serve to shadow the dimly glorious hope! To lose ourselves in the salvation of God's heart! to be no longer any care to ourselves, but know God taking divinest care of us, his own! to be and feel just a resting-place for the divine love—a branch of the tree of life for the dove to alight upon and fold its wings! to be an open air of love, a thoroughfare for the thoughts of God and all holy creatures! to know one's self by the reflex action of endless brotherly presence—yearning after nothing from any, but ever pouring out love by the natural motion of the spirit! to revel in the hundredfold of everything good we may have had to leave for his sake—above all, in the unsought love of those who love us as we love them—circling us round, bathing us in bliss—never reached after, every received, ever welcomed, altogether and divinely precious! to know that God and we mean the same thing, that we are in the secret, the child's secret of existence, that we are pleasing in the eyes and to the heart of the Father! to live nestling at his knee, climbing to his bosom, blessed in the mere and simple being which is one with God, and is the outgoing of his will, justifying the being by the very facts of the being, by its awareness of itself as bliss!—what a self is this to receive again from him for that we left, forsook, refused! We left it paltry, low, mean; he took up the poor cinder of a consciousness, carried it back to the workshop of his spirit, made it a true thing, radiant, clear, fit for eternal companying and indwelling, and restored it to our having and holding for ever!

SII. 223

To yield self is to give up grasping at things in their second causes, as men call them, but which are merely God's means, and to receive them direct from their source—to take them seeing whence they come, and not as if they came from nowhere, because no one appears presenting them. The careless soul receives the Father's gifts as if it were a way things had of dropping into his hand.

SII. 225

There is no joy belonging to human nature, as God made it, that shall not be enhanced a hundredfold to the man who gives up himself—though, in so doing, he may seem to be yielding the very essence of life.

SII. 225

When (a man) is aware of an opposition in him, which is not harmony: that, while he hates it, there is yet present with him, and seeming to be himself, what sometimes he calls *the old Adam*, sometimes *the flesh*, sometimes *his lower nature*, sometimes *his evil self*; and sometimes recognizes as simply that part of his being where God is not; then indeed is the man in the region of truth, and beginning to come true in himself.

SIII. 77

When a man is true, if he were in hell he could not be miserable. He is right with himself because right with him whence he came.

SIII. 81

For the one principle of hell is—"I am my own. I am my own king and my own subject. I am the center from which go out my thoughts; I am the object and end of my thoughts; back upon *me* as the alpha and omega of life, my thoughts return. My own glory is, and ought to be, my chief care; my ambition, to gather the regards of men to the one center, myself. My pleasure is *my* pleasure. My kingdom is—as many as I can bring to acknowledge my greatness over them. My judgment is the faultless rule of things. My right is—what I desire. The more I am all in all to myself, the greater I am. The less I acknowledge debt or obligation to another; the more I close my eyes to the fact that I did not make myself; the more self-sufficing I feel or imagine myself—the greater I am. I will be free with the freedom that consists in doing whatever I am inclined to do, from whatever quarter may come the inclination. To do my own will so long as I feel anything to be my will, is to be free, is to live." To all these principles of hell, or of this world—they are the same things, and it matters nothing whether they are asserted or defended so long as they are acted upon—the Lord, the King, gives the direct lie.

SIII. 102

The only terrible, or at least the supremely terrible revelation is that of a man to himself. What a horror will it not be to a vile man—more than all to a man whose pleasure has been enhanced by the suffering of others—a man that knew himself such as men of ordinary morals would turn from with disgust, but who has hitherto had no insight into what he is—what a horror will it not be to him when his eyes are opened to see himself as the pure see him, as God sees him! Imagine such a man waking all at once, not only to see the eyes of the universe fixed upon him with loathing astonishment, but to see himself at the same moment as those eyes see him! What a waking!—into the full blaze of fact and consciousness, of truth and violation!

To know my deed, 'twere best not know myself!

SIII. 239

What springs from my self and not from God is evil; it is a perversion of something of God's.

SIII. 262

"One thing I dare to hope—that at the first temptation to show-off, I shall be made aware of my danger, and have the grace given me to pull up. . . . I know I shall make many blunders and do the things very badly; but failure itself will help to save me from conceit—will keep me, I hope, from thinking of myself, at all, enabling me to leave myself in God's hands, willing to fail if he please."

SF. 313

Vain were the fancy, by treatise or sermon or poem or tale, to persuade a man to forget himself. He cannot if he would. Sooner will he forget the presence of a raging tooth. There is no forgetting of ourselves but in the finding of our deeper, our true self—God's idea of us when he devised us—the Christ in us. Nothing but that self can displace the false, greedy, whining self, of which most of us are so fond and proud. And that self no man can find for himself . . . "but as many as received him, to them gave he power to become the sons of God."

SG. chap. 24

The things that come out of a man are they that defile him, and to get rid of them a man must go into himself, be a convict, and scrub the floor of his cell.

SG. chap. 40

When people seek advice it is too often in the hope of finding the adviser side with their second familiar self instead of their awful first self of which they know so little.

TW. chap. 54

"But does a man owe nothing to himself?" "Nothing that I know of. I am under no obligation to myself. How can I divide myself and say that the one half of me is indebted to the other? To my mind, it is a mere fiction of speech"—"But whence, then, should such a fiction arise?"—"From the dim sense of a real obligation, I suspect—the object of which is mistaken. I suspect it really springs from our relation to the unknown God, so vaguely felt that a false form is readily accepted for its embodiment."

WC. chap. 42

What is a called man's love for himself, is not love; it is but a fantastic resemblance of love. . . . A man cannot love himself. . . . I sickened at the sight of myself: How could I ever get rid of the demon? The same instant I saw the one escape: I must offer it back to its source—commit it to the One who had made it. I must live no more from it, but from the source of it; seek to know nothing more of it than he gave me to know by his presence therein. . . . What flashes of self-consciousness might cross me, should be God's gift, not of my seeking, and offered again to him in ever new self-sacrifice. Alas! Alas! This I saw then, and this I yet see; but oh, how far am I still from the divine annihilation! The only comfort is, God is, and I am his, else I should not be at all.

WC. 416–17

I began to learn that it was impossible to live for oneself even, save in the presence of others—then, alas, fearfully possible. Evil was only through good; selfishness but a parasite on the tree of life.

WM. chap. 16

There is no spectre so terrible as the unsuspected spectre of a man's own self.

WM. 26

No one knows what a poor creature he is but the man who makes it his business to be true. The only mistake worse than thinking well of himself, is for a man to think God takes no interest in him.

WM. 198

The demon-man is uppermost, not Christ-man. He is down in the crying heart, and the demon-man—that is the self that worships itself—is trampling on the heart and smothering it up in the rubbish of ambitions, lusts, and cares.

WW

Whether the man knows it or not, his heart in its depths is ever crying out for God. Where the man does not know it, it is because the unfaithful Self, a would-be monarch, has usurped the consciousness.

WW. 5

Selfishness

There is no interpreter of right with stronger convictions than selfishness.

DG. 37

The faith of Jesus in his God and Father is, even now, setting me free from my one horror, selfishness; making my life an unspeakable boon to me, letting me know its roots in the eternal and perfect; giving me such love to my fellow, that I trust at last to love him as Christ has loved me.

PF. 211

Every reward held out by Christ is a pure thing; nor can it enter the soul save as a death to selfishness.

SII. 226

It may be deep selfishness to refuse to be happy. Is there selfishness in the Lord's seeing of the travail of his soul and being satisfied? Selfishness consists in taking the bliss from another; to find one's bliss in the bliss of another is not selfishness. Joy is not selfishness, and the greater the joy thus reaped, the farther is that joy removed from selfishness.

SII. 227

As by the law is the knowledge of sin, so by love is selfishness rampantly roused—to be at last like death, swallowed up in victory—the victory of the ideal self that dwells in God.

WM. 38

Service

To serve is the highest, noblest calling in creation. For even the Son of Man came not to be ministered unto, but to minister, yea, with himself.

AN

Obedience is the only service.

MOL. 93

Whosoever gives a cup of cold water to a little one, refreshes the heart of the Father. To do as God does, is to receive God; to do a service to one of his children is to receive the Father.

SI. 6

As soon as even service is done for the honor and not for the service-sake, the doer is that moment outside the kingdom.

SI. 16

The last act of our Lord in thus commending his spirit at the close of his life, was only a summing up of what he had been doing all his life. He had been offering this sacrifice, the sacrifice of himself, all the years, and in thus sacrificing he had lived the divine life. Every morning when he went out ere it was day, every evening when he lingered on the night-lapt mountain after his friends were gone, he was offering himself to his Father in the communion of loving words, of high thoughts, of speechless feelings; and, between, he turned to do the same thing in deed, namely, in loving word, in helping thought, in healing action toward his fellows; for the way to worship God while the daylight lasts is to work; the service of God, the only "divine service," is the helping of our fellows.

SI. 183

Learning Christ, we are not only sorry for what we have done wrong, we not only turn from it and hate it, but we become able to serve both God and man with an infinitely high and true service, a soul-service. We are able to offer our whole being to God to whom by deepest right it belongs.

SIII. 159

Until our small services are sweet with divine affection, our great ones, if such we are capable of, will never have the true Christian flavor about them.

SG

True and genuine service may be rendered to the living God; and for the development of the divine nature in man, it is necessary that he should do something for God. Nor is it hard to discover how; for God is in every creature that he has made, and in their needs he is needy, and in all their afflictions he is afflicted.

TW. 60

God is the one great servant of all, and that the only way to serve him is to be a fellow servant with him—to be, say, a nurse in his nursery, and tend this or that lonely, this or that rickety child of his.

WW. 4

Sin

All wickedness tends to destroy individuality and declining natures assimilate as they sink.

AF. vol. 3, chap. 4

There are no sins for which there is less reason or less excuse than small ones. In no sense are they worth committing.

DG. 15

"The ways of transgressors are always hard in the end. Happy they who find them hard in the beginning."

GC

The Lord never came to deliver men from the consequences of their sins while yet those sins remained: that would be to cast out of window the medicine of cure while yet the man lay sick; to go dead against the very laws of being.

HG. 7

His present, his live sins—those pervading his thoughts and ruling his conduct; the sins he keeps doing, and will not give up; the sins he is called to abandon, and clings to; the same sins which are the cause of his misery, though he may not know it—these are they for which he is even now condemned.

HG. 9

Our wrong deeds are our dead works; our evil thoughts are our live sins. These, the essential opposites of faith and love, the sins that dwell and work in us, are the sins for which Jesus came to deliver us.

HG. 11

One master-sin is at the root of all the rest. It is no individual action, or anything that comes of mood, or passion; it is the nonrecognition by the man, and consequent inactivity in him, of the highest of all relations, that relation which is the root and first essential condition of every other true relation of or in the human soul. It is the absence in the man of harmony with the being whose thought is the man's existence, whose word is the man's power of thought.

HG. 13

Any honest soul may understand this much, however—for it is a thing we may of ourselves judge to be right—that the Lord cannot save a man from his sins while he holds to his sins.

HG. 20

The Lord is not unreasonable; he requires no high motives where such could not yet exist. He does not say, "You must be sorry for your sins, or you need not come to me": to be sorry for his sins a man must love God and man, and love is the very thing that has to be developed in him.

HG. 20

God and man must combine for salvation from sin, and the same word, here and elsewhere translated *remission*, seems to be employed in the New Testament for the share of either in the great deliverance.

HG. 23

Both God and man send away sins, but in the one case God sends away the sins of the man, and in the other the man sends away his own sins.

HG. 25

They could not rid themselves of their sins, but they could set about sending them away; they could quarrel with them, and proceed to turn them out of the house: the Lord was on his way to do his part in their final banishment.

HG. 28

When a man breaks with his sins, then the wind of the Lord's fan will blow them away, the fire of the Lord's heart will consume them.

HG. 28

He is against sin: in so far as, and while, they and sin are one, he is against them—against their desires, their aims, their fears, and their hopes and thus he is altogether and always *for them.*

SI. 38

The man whose deeds are evil, fears the burning. But the burning will not come the less that he fears it or denies it. Escape is hopeless. For Love is inexorable. Our God is a consuming fire. He shall not come out until he has paid the uttermost farthing.

SI. 46

He loves the sinner so much that he cannot forgive him in any other way than by banishing from his bosom the demon that possesses him, by lifting him out of that mire of his iniquity.

SI. 85

Every sin meets with its due fate—inexorable expulsion from the paradise of God's Humanity.

SI. 85

Sin cannot be deep as life, for you are the life; and sorrow and pain go deeper than sin, for they reach to the divine in us: you can suffer, though you will not sin. To see men suffer might make us shun evil, but it never could make us hate it. We might see thereby that you hate sin, but we never could see that you love the sinner. Chastise us, we pray you, in lovingkindness, and we shall not faint.

SII. 191

Not every man deserves for his sins to be punished everlastingly from the presence of the Lord; and that for the best of men, when he sees the face of God, will know himself vile. God is just, and will never deal with the sinner as if he were capable of sinning the pure sin; yet if the best man be not delivered from himself, that self will sink him into Tophet.

SII. 206

No man will be condemned for any sin that is past; that, if he be condemned, it will be because he would not come to the light when the light came to him; because he would not cease to do evil and learn to do well; because he hid his unbelief in the garment of a false faith, and would not obey; because he imputed to himself a righteousness that was not his; because he preferred imagining himself a worthy person, to confessing himself everywhere in the wrong, and repenting. We may be sure also of this, that, if a man becomes the disciple of Christ, he will not leave him in ignorance as to what he has to believe; he shall know the truth of everything it is needful for him to understand. If we do what he tells us, his light will go up in our hearts. Until then we could not understand even if he explained to us.

SII. 251

If God would not punish sin, or if he did it for anything but love, he would not be the Father of Jesus Christ, the God who works as Jesus wrought.

SIII. 9

Punishment is *nowise* an *offset* to sin.

SIII. 121

Primarily, God is not bound to *punish* sin; he is bound to *destroy* sin. If he were not the Maker, he might not be bound to destroy sin—I do not know; but seeing he has created creatures who have sinned, and therefore sin has, by the creating act of God, come into the world, God is, in his own righteousness, bound to destroy sin.

SIII. 122

God does destroy sin; he is always destroying sin. In him I trust that he is destroying sin in me. He is always saving the sinner from his sins, and that is destroying sin. But vengeance on the sinner, the law of a tooth for a tooth, is not in the heart of God, neither in his hand. If the sinner and the sin in him, are the concrete object of the divine wrath, then indeed there can be no mercy. Then indeed there will be an end put to sin by the destruction of the sin and the sinner together. But thus would no atonement be wrought—nothing be done to make up for the wrong God has allowed to come into being by creating man. There must be an atonement, a making-up, a bringing together—an atonement which, I say, cannot be made except by the man who has sinned.

SIII. 122

The only vengeance worth having on sin is to make the sinner himself its executioner.

SIII. 124

Sin and suffering are not natural opposites; the opposite of evil is good, not suffering; the opposite of sin is not suffering, but righteousness.

SIII. 124

The notion that the salvation of Jesus is a salvation from the consequences of our sins is a false, mean, low notion.... Jesus did not die to save us from punishment; he was called Jesus because he should save his people from their sins.

SIII. 133

I believe that no man is ever condemned for any sin except one—that he will not leave his sins and come out of them, and be the child of him who is his Father.

SIII. 154

Sense of sin is not inspiration, though it may lie not far from the temple door. It is indeed an opener of the eyes, but upon home defilement, not upon heavenly truth.

SIII. 160

"All manner of sin and blasphemy," the Lord said, "shall be forgiven unto men; but the blasphemy against the spirit shall not be forgiven." God speaks, as it were, in this manner: "I forgive you everything. Not a word more shall be said about your sins—only come out of them; come out of the darkness of your exile; come into the light of your home, of your birthright, and do evil no more."

SIII. 177

As soon as a man begins to make excuse, the time has come when he might be doing that from which he excuses himself.

SIII. 177

The one thing that cannot be forgiven is the sin of choosing to be evil, of refusing deliverance. It is impossible to forgive that. It would be to take part in it.

SIII. 178

If a man refuse to come out of his sin, he must suffer the vengeance of a love that would be no love if it left him there.

SIII. 179

Whatever is not of faith is sin; it is a stream cut off—a stream that cuts itself off from its source, and thinks to run on without it.

SIII. 262

Think not about your sin so as to make it either less or greater in your own eyes. Bring it to Jesus and let him show you how vile a thing it is. And leave it to him to judge you, sure that he will judge you justly; extenuating nothing, for he has to cleanse you utterly; and yet forgetting no smallest excuse that may cover the amazement of your guilt or witness for you that not with open eyes did you do the deed. . . . But again, I say, let it be Christ who excuses you. He will do it to more purpose than you, and will not wrong your soul by excusing you a hair too much, or your heart by excusing you a hair too little.

TW. chap. 67

He knows he put me where I was sure to sin; he will not condemn me because I have sinned; he leaves me to do that myself.

WM

Slavery

While God's will is our law, we are but a kind of noble slaves; when his will is our will, we are free children.

DG. bk. III. 12

A man is in bondage to whatever he cannot part with that is less than himself.

SI. 14

The man who for consciousness of well-being depends on anything but life, the life essential, is a slave; he hangs on what is less than himself. He is not perfect who, deprived of every *thing*, would not sit down calmly content, aware of a well-being untouched; for nonetheless would he be possessor of all things, the child of the Eternal.

SII. 35

When a man begins to abstain, then first he recognizes the strength of his passion; it may be, when a man has not a thing left, he will begin to know what a necessity he had made of things; and if then he begin to contend with them, to cast out of his soul what Death has torn from his hands, then first will he know the full passion of possession, the slavery of prizing the worthless part of the precious.

SII. 37

Never soul was set free without being made to feel its slavery; nothing but itself can enslave a soul, nothing without itself free it.

SII. 38

But it is not the rich man only who is under the dominion of things; they too are slaves who, having no money, are unhappy from the lack of it.

SII. 39

Whoever will live must cease to be a slave and become a child of God. There is no half-way house of rest, where ungodliness may be dallied with, nor prove quite fatal.

SII. 114

Christ is the way out, and the way in: the way from slavery, conscious or unconscious, into liberty; the way from the unhomeliness of things to the home we desire but do not know; the way from the stormy skirts of the Father's garments to the peace of his bosom.

SII. 210

No amount of slavery to sin can keep a man from being as much the slave of God as God chooses in his mercy to make him. It is his sin makes him a slave instead of a child. His slavery to sin is his ruin; his slavery to God is his only hope. God indeed does not love slavery; he hates it; he will have children, not slaves.

SIII. 85

Whoever will not do what God desires of him, is a slave whom God can compel to do it, however he may bear with him. He who, knowing this, or fearing punishment, obeys God, is still a slave, but a slave who comes within hearing of the voice of his master.

SIII. 86

There are, however, far higher than he, who yet are but slaves. Those to whom God is not all in all, are slaves. They may not commit great sins; they may be trying to do right; but so long as they *serve* God, as they call it, from duty, and do not know him as their Father, the joy of their being, they are slaves—good slaves, but slaves. If they did not try to do their duty, they would be bad slaves. They are by no means so slavish as those that serve from fear, but they are slaves; and because they are but slaves, they can fulfill no righteousness, can do no duty perfectly, but must ever be trying after it wearily and in pain, knowing well that if they stop trying, they are lost.

SIII. 86

The real slave is he who does not seek to be a child; who does not desire to end his slavery; who looks upon the claim of the child as presumption; who cleaves to the traditional authorized service of forms and ceremonies, and does not know the will of him who made the seven stars and Orion, much less cares to obey it; who never lifts up his heart to cry, "Father, what would you have me to do?" Such are continually betraying their slavery by their complaints.

SIII. 87

The slaves of sin rarely grumble at that slavery; it is their slavery to God they grumble at; of that alone they complain—of the painful messengers he sends to deliver them from their slavery both to sin and to himself.

SIII. 88

Whether they deny God, or mock him by acknowledging and not heeding him, or treat him as an arbitrary, formal monarch; whether, taking no trouble to find out what pleases him, they do dull things for his service he cares nothing about, or try to propitiate him by assuming with strenuous effort some yoke the Son never wore, and never called on them to wear, they are slaves, and not the less slaves that they are slaves to God; they are so thoroughly slaves, that they do not care to get out of their slavery by becoming sons and daughters, by finding the good of life where alone it can or could lie.

SIII. 89

They desire to be free with another kind of freedom than that with which God is free; unknowing, they seek a more complete slavery.

SIII. 90

There is, in truth, no midway between absolute harmony with the Father and the condition of slaves—submissive or rebellious. If the latter, their very rebellion is by the strength of the Father in them.

SIII. 90

The very protest of the rebel against slavery, comes at once of the truth of God in him, which he cannot all cast from him, and of a slavery too low to love truth—a meanness that will take all and acknowledge nothing, as if his very being was a disgrace to him. The liberty of the God that would have his creature free, is in contest with the slavery of the creature who would cut his own stem from his root that he might call it his own and love it; who rejoices in his own consciousness, instead of the life of that consciousness; who poises himself on the tottering wall of his own being, instead of the rock on which that being is built.

SIII. 91

God cannot have slaves about him always. You must give up your slavery, and be set free from it. That is what I am here for. If I make you free, you shall be free indeed; for I can make you free only by making you what you were meant to be, sons like myself. That is how alone the Son can work. But it is you who must become sons; you must will it, and I am here to help you.

SIII. 94

Yourselves are your slavery. That is the darkness which you have loved rather than the light. You have given honor to yourselves, and not to the Father; you have sought honor from men, and not from the Father! Therefore, even in the house of your Father, you have been but sojourning slaves.

SIII. 94

Sleep

Little as we think of it, God has us in his hands far more than any mother has her little child of a week old. You cannot help going to sleep; he makes you. You do not know what sleep is a bit, with all the philosophy you can bring to bear upon it; you, so busy all the day, are still, when asleep—like death, and anybody might kill you. There you lie, passive, helpless, but not forgotten. If it were not for this sleep—that is, the bodily silence—we should all go mad. You know that sleeplessness is the first step to madness. If there never be a silence in the soul, and a man goes on always with his own thoughts and schemes and endeavors, it brings about a moral and a spiritual madness.

The Christian World Pulpit

It may be said of the body in regard of sleep as well as in regard of death, "It is sown in weakness, it is raised in power. . . ." No one can deny the power of the wearied body to paralyze the soul; but I have a correlate theory which I love, and which I expect to find true—that, while the body wearies the mind, it is the mind that restores vigor to the body, and then, like the man who has built him a stately palace, rejoices to dwell in it. I believe that, if there be a living, conscious love at the heart of the universe, the mind, in the quiescence of its consciousness in sleep, comes into a less disturbed contact with its origin, the heart of the creation; whence gifted with calmness and strength for itself, it grows able to impart comfort and restoration to the weary frame. The cessation of labor affords but the necessary occasion; makes it possible, as it were, for the occupant of an outlying station in the wilderness to return to his Father's house for fresh supplies. . . . The child-soul goes home at night, and returns in the morning to the labors of the school.

WC. chap. 48

Sonship

Whosoever . . . will do the will of God—not understand it, not care about it, not theorize it, but do it—is a son of God.

GW. 126–27

Son of our Father, help us to do what you say, and so with you die unto sin, that we may rise to the sonship for which we were created. Help us to repent even to the sending away of our sins.

HG. 22

To be a child is not necessarily to be a son or daughter. The childship is the lower condition of the upward process toward the sonship, the soil out of which the true sonship shall grow, the former without which the latter were impossible. God can no more than an earthly parent be content to have only children: he must have sons and daughters—children of his soul, of his spirit, of his love—not merely in the sense that he loves them, or even that they love him, but in the sense that they love like him, love as he loves. For this he does not adopt them; he dies to give them himself, thereby to raise his own to his heart; he gives them a birth from above; they are born again out of himself and into himself—for he is the one and the all.

SII. 123

None but a child could become a son; the idea is—a spiritual coming of age; *only when the child is a man is he really and fully a son.*

SII. 123

His children are not his real, true sons and daughters until they think like him, feel with him, judge as he judges, are at home with him, and without fear before him because he and they mean the same thing, love the same things, seek the same ends. For this are we created; it is the one end of our being, and includes all other ends whatever. It can come only of unbelief and not faith, to make men believe that God has cast them off, repudiated them, said they are not, yea never were, his children—and he all the time spending himself to make us the children he designed, fore-ordained—children who would take him for their Father! He is our Father all the time, for he is true; but until we respond with the truth of children, he cannot let all the father out to us; there is no place for the dove of his tenderness to alight. He is our Father, but we are not his children. Because we are his children, we must become his sons and daughters. Nothing will satisfy him, or do for us, but that we be one with our Father! What else could serve! How else should life ever be a good! Because we are the sons of God, we must become the sons of God.

SII. 124

While we but obey the law God has laid upon us, without knowing the heart of the Father whence comes the law, we are but slaves—not necessarily ignoble slaves, yet slaves; but when we come to think *with* him, when the mind of the son is as the mind of the Father, the action of the son the same as that of the Father, then is the son *of* the Father, then are we the sons of God.

SII. 127

Children we were; true sons we could never be, save through the Son. He brothers us. He takes us to the knees of the Father, beholding whose face we grow sons indeed. Never could we have known the heart of the Father, never felt it possible to love him as sons, but for him who cast himself into the gulf that yawned between us. In and through him we were foreordained to the sonship: sonship, even had we never sinned, never could we reach without him. We should have been little children loving the Father indeed, but children far from the sonhood that understands and adores. "For as many as are led by the spirit of God, these are sons of God."

SII. 129

We are the sons of God the moment we lift up our hearts, seeking to be sons—the moment we begin to cry *Father.* But as the world must be redeemed in a few men to begin with, so the soul is redeemed in a few of its thoughts and wants and ways, to begin with: it takes a long time to finish the new creation of this redemption.

SII. 131

So are we sons when we begin to cry Father, but we are far from perfected sons. So long as there is in us the least taint of distrust, the least lingering of hate or fear, we have not received the sonship; we have not such life in us as raised the body of Jesus; we have not attained to the resurrection of the dead.

SII. 132

When the sons of God show as they are, taking, with the character, the appearance and the place that belong to their sonship; when the sons of God sit with *the* Son of God on the throne of their Father; then shall they be in potency of fact the lords of the lower creation, the bestowers of liberty and peace upon it; then shall the creation, subjected to vanity for their sakes, find its freedom in their freedom, its gladness in their sonship.

SII. 134

The world exists for our education; it is the nursery of God's children, served by troubled slaves, troubled because the children are themselves slaves—children, but not good children. Beyond its own will or knowledge, the whole creation works for the development of the children of God into the sons of God.

SII. 136

When at last the children have arisen and gone to their Father; when they are clothed in the best robe, with a ring on their hands and shoes on their feet, shining out at length in their natural, their predestined sonship; then shall the mountains and the hills break forth before them into singing, and all the trees of the field shall clap their hands.

SII. 136

He was not the Son of God because he could not help it, but because he willed to be in himself the Son that he was in the divine idea. So with us: we must *be* the sons we are.

SIII. 13

Nothing I have seen or known of sonship, comes near the glory of the thing; but there are thousands of sons and daughters, though their number be yet only a remnant, who are siding with the father of their spirits against themselves, against all that divides them from him from whom they have come, but out of whom they have never come, seeing that in him they live and move and have their being.

SIII. 87

Sorrow

God loves not sorrow, yet rejoices to see a man sorrowful, for in his sorrow man leaves his heavenward door on the latch, and God can enter to help him. He loves, I say, to see him sorrowful, for then he can come near to part him from that which makes his sorrow a welcome sight.

HG. 100

So good a medicine is sorrow, so powerful to slay the moths that infest and devour the human heart, that the Lord is glad to see a man weep. He congratulates him on his sadness. Grief is an ill-favored thing, but she is Love's own child, and her mother loves her.

HG. 100

The Lord would have us know the sorrow is not a part of life; that it is but a wind blowing throughout it, to winnow and cleanse.

HG. 112

God says, . . . "Sorrow and pain are serving my ends; for by them I will slay sin, and save my children."

SP

Sorrow is catching.

SP

Every nature must have the subsoil plowing of sorrow, before it can recognize either its present poverty or its possible wealth.

V

Soul

"Father, you are in me, or I could not be in you, could have no house for my soul to dwell in, or any world in which to walk abroad."

These truths are, I believe, the very necessities of fact, but a man does not therefore, at a given moment, necessarily know them. It is absolutely necessary, nonetheless, to his real being, that he should know these spiritual relations in which he stands to his Origin; yea, that they should be always present and potent with him, and become the heart and sphere and all-pervading substance of his consciousness, of which they are the ground and foundation. Once to have seen them is not always to see them.

HG. 119

There are times, and those times many, when the cares of this world—with no right to any part in our thought, seeing either they are unreasonable or God imperfect—so blind the eyes of the soul to the radiance of the eternally true, that they see it only as if it ought to be true, not as if it must be true; as if it might be true in the region of thought, but could not be true in the region of fact.

HG. 119

The primal need of the human soul . . . is the man's need of God.

HG. 127

The instant a soul moves counter to the will of its prime cause, the universe is its prison; it dashes against the walls of it, and the sweetest of its uplifting and sustaining forces at once become its manacles and fetters.

HG. 227

No man can ever save his soul. God only can do that.

M

Your soul, however it became known to itself, is from the pure heart of God, whose thought of you is older than your being—is its first and eldest cause. Your essence cannot be defiled, for in him it is eternal.

M. 49

Fact is not the sole legitimate object of human inquiry. If it were, farewell to all that elevates and glorifies human nature—farewell to God, to religion, to hope! It is that which lies at the root of fact, yea, at the root of law, after which the human soul hungers and longs.

MOL. 78

Never soul was set free without being made to feel its slavery; nothing but itself can enslave a soul, nothing without itself free it.

SII. 38

To those who possess their souls in patience come the heavenly visions.

SII. 53

So needful is prayer to the soul that the mere attitude of it may encourage a good mood.

SII. 91

The Lord, the spirit, becomes the soul of our souls, becomes spiritually what he always was creatively; and as our spirit informs, gives shape to our bodies, in like manner his soul informs, gives shape to our souls. In this there is nothing unnatural, nothing at conflict with our being. It is but that the deeper soul that willed and wills our souls, rises up, the infinite Life, into the Self we call *I* and *me*, but which lives immediately from him, and is his very own property and nature—unspeakably more his than ours: this deeper creative soul, working on and with his creation upon higher levels, makes the *I* and *me* more and more his, and himself more and more ours; until at length the glory of our existence flashes upon us, we face full to the sun that enlightens what it sent forth, and know ourselves alive with an infinite life, even the life of the Father.

SIII. 53

Filled with the soul of their Father, men shall inherit the glory of their Father; filled with themselves, they cast him out, and rot. The company of the Lord, soul to soul, is that which saves with life, his life of God-devotion, the souls of his brethren. No other saving can save them. They must receive the Son, and through the Son the Father.

SIII. 54

Let no man who wants to do something for the soul of a man lose a chance of doing something for his body.

SP. 238

If the soul of a man be the temple of the Spirit, then is the place of that man's labor—his shop, his counting-house, his laboratory—the temple of Jesus Christ, where the spirit of the man is incarnate in work.

TW. 60

As the Son of Man came not to send peace on the earth but a sword, so the first visit of God to the human soul is generally in a cloud of fear and doubt, rising from the soul itself at his approach.

WM. 31

Strength/Weakness

The power of God is put side by side with the weakness of men, not that he, the perfect, may glory over his feeble children . . . but that he may say thus: "Look, my children, you will never be strong but with *my* strength. I have no other to give you."

AN. chap. 30

A moral, that is, a human, a spiritual being, must either be God, or one with God. This truth begins to reveal itself when the man begins to feel that he cannot cast out the thing he hates, cannot be the thing he loves. That he hates thus, that he loves thus, is because God is in him, but he finds he has not enough of God. His awakening strength manifests itself in his sense of weakness, for only strength can know itself weak. The negative cannot know itself at all. Weakness cannot know itself weak. It is a little strength that longs for more; it is infant righteousness that hungers after righteousness.

HG. 127

To trust in the strength of God in our weakness; to say, "I am weak: so let me be: God is strong"; to seek from him who is our life, as the natural, simple cure of all that is amiss with us, power to do, and be, and live, even when we are weary—this is the victory that overcomes the world.

SII. 148

To believe in God our strength in the face of all seeming denial, to believe in him out of the heart of weakness and unbelief, in spite of numbness and weariness and lethargy; to believe in the wide-awake real, through all the stupefying, enervating, distorting dream; to will to wake, when the very being seems athirst for a godless repose—these are the broken steps up to the high fields where repose is but a form of strength, strength but a form of joy, joy but a form of love. "I am weak," says the true soul, "but not so weak that I would not be strong; not so sleepy that I would not see the sun rise; not so lame but that I would walk! Thanks be to him who perfects strength in weakness, and gives to his beloved while they sleep!"

SII. 148

This is indeed a divine law! There shall be no success to the man who is not willing to begin small. Small is strong, for it only can grow strong. Big at the outset is but bloated and weak.

WW. 60

Suffering

For the love of Christ is an awful thing. There is nothing in that which goes halfway, or which makes exception. The Son of God loves so utterly that he will have his children clean, and if hurt and sorrow, pain and torture, will do to deliver any one of them from the horrible thing . . . the loving Christ, though it hurts him all the time, and though he feels every sting himself, will do it.

GW. 125

To free a man from suffering, he must be set right, put in health; and the health at the root of man's being, his rightness, is to be free from wrongness, that is, from sin.

HG. 5

This earnest of the promised deliverance may not, in all probability will not, be what the man desires; he will want only to be rid of his suffering; but that he cannot have, save in being delivered from its essential root, a thing infinitely worse than any suffering it can produce. If he will not have that deliverance, he must keep his suffering. Through chastisement he will take at last the only way that leads into the liberty of that which is and must be.

HG. 6

It is true that Jesus came, in delivering us from our sins, to deliver us also from the painful consequences of our sins. But these consequences exist by the one law of the universe, the true will of the Perfect. That broken, that disobeyed by the creature, disorganization renders suffering inevitable; it is the natural consequence of the unnatural—and, in the perfection of God's creation, the result is curative of the cause; the pain at least tends to the healing of the breach.

HG. 7

Suffering is *for* the sinner, that he may be delivered from his sin. Jesus is in himself aware of every human pain. He feels it also. In him, too, it is pain. With the energy of tenderest love he wills his brothers and sisters free, that he may fill them to overflowing with that essential thing, joy. For that they were indeed created.

HG. 15

He might, indeed, it may be, take from them the human, send them down to some lower stage of being, and so free them from suffering—but that must be either a descent toward annihilation, or a fresh beginning to grow up again toward the region of suffering they have left, for that which is not growing must at length die out of creation. The disobedient and selfish would fain in the hell of their hearts possess the liberty and gladness that belong to purity and love, but they cannot have them; they are weary and heavy-laden, both with what they are, and because of what they were made for but are not.

HG. 16

It is but common sense that a man, longing to be freed from suffering, or made able to bear it, should betake himself to the Power by whom he is.

HG. 20

Suffering is ground for rejoicing, for exceeding gladness. The ignominy cast upon them leaves the name of the Lord's Father written upon their foreheads, the mark of the true among the false, of the children among the slaves.

HG. 147

With all who suffer for the world, persecution is the seal of their patent, a sign that they were sent: they fill up that which is behind of the afflictions of Christ for his body's sake.

HG. 148

Praised be the grandeur of the God who can endure to make and see his children suffer. Thanks be to him for his north winds and his poverty, and his bitterness that falls upon the spirit that errs; let those who know him, thus praise the Lord for his goodness.

ML. 158

God made man for lordly skies, great sunshine, gay colors, free winds, and delicate odors; and however the fogs may be needful for the soul, right gladly does he send them away, and cause the dayspring from on high to revisit his children. While they suffer he is brooding over them an eternal day, suffering with them, but rejoicing in their future. He is the God of the individual man, or he could be no God of the race.

MOL. 28

God would have us reasonable and strong. Every effort of his children to rise above the invasion of evil in body or in mind is a pleasure to him. Few, I suppose, attain to this; but there is a better thing which to many, I trust, is easier—to say, your will be done.

MOL. 29

It is a law of nature that where there is sin there should be suffering; but even its cure helps to restore that righteousness which is highest nature; for the cure of suffering must not be confounded with the absence of suffering.

MOL. 224

Whoever would have a perfect Father, must believe that he bestows his very being for the daily food of his creatures. He who loves the glory of God will be very jealous of any word that would enhance his greatness by representing him incapable of suffering. Verily God has taken and will ever take and endure his share, his largest share of that suffering in and through which the whole creation groans for the sonship.

MOL. 238

We are so full of ourselves, and feel so grand, that we should never come to know what poor creatures we are, never begin to do better, but for the knock-down blows that the loving God gives us. We do not like them, but he does not spare us for that.

RS. 151

It is with the holiest fear that we should approach the terrible fact of the sufferings of our Lord. Let no one think that those were less because he was more. The more delicate the nature, the more alive to all that is lovely and true, lawful and right, the more does it feel the antagonism of pain, the inroad of death upon life; the more dreadful is that breach of the harmony of things whose soul is torture. He felt more than man could feel, because he had a larger feeling. He was even therefore worn out sooner than another man would have been. These sufferings were awful indeed when they began to invade the region about the will; when the struggle to keep consciously trusting in God began to sink in darkness; when the Will of The Man put forth its last determined effort in that cry after the vanishing vision of the Father; *My God, my God, why have you forsaken me?* Never had it been so with him before. Never before had he been unable to see God beside him. Yet never was God nearer him than now. For never was Jesus more divine. He could not see, could not feel him near; and yet it is "*My* God" that he cries.

SI. 165

The divine obedience was perfected by suffering.

SI. 181

He had been among his brethren what he would have his brethren be. He had done for them what he would have them do for God and for each other. God was henceforth inside and beneath them, as well as around and above them, suffering with them and for them, giving them all he had, his very life-being, his essence of existence, what best he loved, what best he was. He had been among them, their God-brother. And the mighty story ends with a cry.

SI. 181

Father, into your hands I commend my spirit. For it is your business, not mine. You will know every shade of my suffering; you will care for me with your perfect fatherhood; for that makes my sonship, and enwraps and enfolds it.

SI. 185

He knew what it would cost!—not energy of will alone, or merely that utterance and separation from himself which is but the first of creation, though that may well itself be pain—but sore suffering such as we cannot imagine, and could only be God's, in the bringing out, call it birth or development, of the God-life in the individual soul—a suffering still renewed, a labor thwarted ever by that soul itself, compelling him to take, still at the cost of suffering, the not absolutely best, only the best possible means left him by the resistance of his creature.

SII. 142

What Jesus did, was what the Father is always doing; the suffering he endured was that of the Father from the foundation of the world, reaching its climax in the person of his Son. God provides the sacrifice; the sacrifice is himself. He is always, and has ever been, sacrificing himself to and for his creatures. It lies in the very essence of his creation of them.

SII. 142

Jesus did nothing but what the Father did and does. If Jesus suffered for men, it was because his Father suffers for men; only he came close to men through his body and their senses, that he might bring their spirits close to his Father and their Father, so giving them life, and losing what could be lost of his own.

SII. 143

What better is the world, what better is the sinner, what better is God, what better is the truth, that the sinner should suffer—continue suffering to all eternity?

SIII. 123

Grant that the sinner has deserved to suffer, no amount of suffering is any atonement for his sin. To suffer to all eternity could not make up for one unjust word. Does that mean, then, that for an unjust word I deserve to suffer to all eternity?

SIII. 123

Justice is not, never can be, satisfied by suffering—nay, cannot have any satisfaction in or from suffering.

SIII. 125

The more we believe in God, the surer we shall be that he will spare nothing that suffering can do to deliver his child from death. If suffering cannot serve this end, we need look for no more hell, but for the destruction of sin by the destruction of the sinner. That, however, would, it appears to me, be for God to suffer defeat, blameless indeed, but defeat.

SIII. 129

It is no pleasure to God, as it so often is to us, to see the wicked suffer. To regard any suffering with satisfaction, save it be sympathetically with its curative quality, comes of evil, is inhuman because undivine, is a thing God is incapable of. His nature is always to forgive, and just because he forgives, he punishes. Because God is so altogether alien to wrong, because it is to him a heart-pain and trouble that one of his little ones should do the evil thing, there is, I believe, no extreme of suffering to which, for the sake of destroying the evil thing in them, he would not subject them. A man might flatter, or bribe, or coax a tyrant; but there is no refuge from the love of God; that love will, for very love, insist upon the uttermost farthing.

SIII. 131

They who do not know suffering, may well doubt if they have yet started on the way to be.

WM

Millions of human beings but for suffering would never develop an atom of affection.

WM

The man who would spare *due* suffering is not wise. Because a thing is unpleasant, it is folly to conclude it ought not to be.

WM. 10

There are tender-hearted people who virtually object to the whole scheme of creation; they would neither have force used nor pain suffered; they talk as if kindness could do everything, even where it is not felt. Millions of human beings but for suffering would never develop an atom of affection. The man who would spare *due* suffering is not wise. It is folly to conclude a thing ought not to be done because it hurts. There are powers to be born, creations to be perfected, sinners to be redeemed, through the ministry of pain, that could be born, perfected, redeemed, in no other way.

WM. 71

See what it cost him to redeem the world! He did not find that easy, or to be done in a moment without pain or toil. Yea, awfully omnipotent is God. For he wills, effects, and perfects the thing which, because of the bad in us, he has to carry out in suffering and sorrow, his own and his Son's.

WW. 23

Teacher/Teaching

He finds it very hard to teach us, but he is never tired of trying. Anyone who is willing to be taught of God will be taught, and thoroughly taught by him. People tell such terrible lies about God, judging him by their own foolish selves.

DG. 15

Nothing but Christ himself for your very own teacher and friend and brother, not all the doctrines about him, even if every one of them were true, can save you.

DG. 15

If they set themselves to find out what Christ thought and knew and meant, and to do it, they would soon forget their false teachers, and find it a good riddance.

DG. 15

Our Lord himself taught a divine morality, which is as it were the body of love, and is as different from *mere* morality as the living body is from the dead.

EA. 60

I believe that no teacher should strive to make men think as he thinks, but to lead them to the living Truth, the Master himself, of whom alone they can learn anything, who will make them in themselves know what is true by the very seeing of it.

SIII. 155

I will teach that which *is* good, even if there should be no God to make a fact of it, and I will spend my life on it in the growing hope, which *may* become assurance, that there is indeed a perfect God, worthy of being, the Father of Jesus Christ.

TW

Temptation

Like him, his Son also chose good, and in that choice resisted all temptation to help his fellows otherwise than as their and his Father would.

HG. 33

Throughout his life on earth, he resisted every impulse to work more rapidly for a lower good—strong, perhaps, when he saw old age and innocence and righteousness trodden under foot. What but this gives any worth of reality to the temptation in the wilderness, to the devil's departing from him for a season, to his coming again to experience a like failure? Ever and ever, in the whole attitude of his being, in his heart always lifted up, in his unfailing readiness to pull with the Father's yoke, he was repelling, driving away sin—away from himself, and, as Lord of men, and their Savior, away from others also, bringing them to abjure it like himself.

HG. 34

That men may rise above temptation, it is needful that they should have temptation.

MOL. 16

God chooses that men should be tried, but let a man beware of tempting his neighbor.

MOL. 17

I do not believe that the Son of God could be tempted with evil, but I do believe that he could be tempted with good—to yield to which temptation would have been evil in him—ruin to the universe.

SI. 134

The Lord could not have felt tempted to take vengeance upon his enemies, but he might have felt tempted to destroy the wicked from the face of the earth—to destroy them from the face of the earth, I say, not to destroy them for ever. To that I do not think he could have felt tempted.

SI. 134

Without this last trial of all, the temptations of our Master had not been so full as the human cup could hold; there would have been one region through which we had to pass wherein we might call aloud upon our Captain-Brother, and there would be no voice or hearing: he had avoided the fatal spot! The temptations of the desert came to the young, strong man with his road before him and the presence of his God around him; nay, gathered their very force from the exuberance of his conscious faith.

SI. 167

Testimony of George MacDonald

If I mistake, he will forgive me. I do not fear him: I fear only lest, able to see and write these things, I should fail of witnessing and myself be, after all, a castaway—no king but a talker; no disciple of Jesus, ready to go with him to the death, but an arguer about the truth.

SIII. 104

We are not bound to say all we think but we are bound not even to look what we do not think.

SIII. 107

I believe that he is my Savior from myself, and from all that has come of loving myself, from all that God does not love, and would not have me love—all that is not worth loving; that he died that the justice, the mercy of God, might have its way with me, making me just as God is just, merciful as he is merciful, perfect as my Father in heaven is perfect.

I believe and pray that he will give me what punishment I need to set me right, or keep me from going wrong.

SIII. 153

I believe that he died to deliver me from all meanness, all pretense, all falseness, all unfairness, all poverty of spirit, all cowardice, all fear, all anxiety, all forms of self-love, all trust or hope in possession; to make me merry as a child, the child of our Father in heaven, loving nothing but what is lovely, desiring nothing I should be ashamed to let the universe of God see me desire.

I believe that God is just like Jesus, only greater yet, for Jesus said so.

I believe that God is absolutely, grandly beautiful, even as the highest soul of man counts beauty, but infinitely beyond that soul's highest idea—with the beauty that creates beauty, not merely shows it, or itself exists beautiful.

SIII. 153–54

I believe in Jesus Christ, the eternal Son of God, my Elder Brother, my Lord and Master; I believe that he has a right to my absolute obedience whereinsoever I know or shall come to know his will; that to obey him is to ascend the pinnacle of my being; that not to obey him would be to deny him.

I believe that he died that I might die like him—die to any ruling power in me but the will of God—live ready to be nailed to the cross as he was, if God will it.

SIII. 153–56

I believe that God has always done, is always doing his best for every man; that no man is miserable because God is forgetting him; that he is not a God to crouch before, but our Father, to whom the child-heart cries exultant, "Do with me as you will."

I believe that there is nothing good for me or for any man but God, and more and more of God, and that alone through knowing Christ can we come near to him.

I believe that no man is ever condemned for any sin except one—that he will not leave his sins and come out of them, and be the child of him who is his Father.

SIII. 154

I believe that to him who obeys, and thus opens the doors of his heart to receive the eternal gift, God gives the spirit of his Son, the spirit of himself, to be in him, and lead him to the understanding of all truth; that the true disciple shall thus always know what he ought to do, though not necessarily what another ought to do; that the spirit of the Father and the Son enlightens by teaching righteousness.

SIII. 155

I believe that justice and mercy are simply one and the same thing; without justice to the full there can be no mercy, and without mercy to the full there can be no justice; that such is the mercy of God that he will hold his children in the consuming fire of his distance until they pay the uttermost farthing, until they drop the purse of selfishness with all the dross that is in it, and rush home to the Father and the Son, and the many brethren—rush inside the center of the life-giving fire whose outer circles burn.

I believe that no hell will be lacking which would help the just mercy of God to redeem his children.

SIII. 155–56

I believe that no teacher should strive to make men think as he thinks, but to lead them to the living Truth, to the Master himself, of whom alone they can learn anything, who will make them in themselves know what is true by the very seeing of it.

I believe that the inspiration of the Almighty alone gives understanding.

I believe that to be the disciple of Christ is the end of being; that to persuade men to be his disciples is the end of teaching.

SIII. 155–56

I believe in Jesus Christ. Nowhere am I requested to believe *in* any thing, or *in* any statement, but everywhere to believe in God and in Jesus Christ. In what you call *the atonement*, in what you mean by the word, what I have already written must make it plain enough I do not believe. God forbid I should, for it would be to believe a lie, and a lie which is to blame for much nonacceptance of the gospel in this and other lands. But, as the word was used by the best English writers at the time when the translation of the Bible was made—with all my heart, and soul, and strength, and mind, *I believe* in the atonement, call it the *a-tone-ment*, or the *at-one-ment*, as you please.

SIII. 156

I believe that Jesus Christ *is* our atonement; that through him we are reconciled to, made one with God. There is not one word in the New Testament about reconciling God to us; it is we that have to be reconciled to God. I am not writing, neither desire to write, a treatise on the atonement, my business being to persuade men to be atoned to God; but I will go so far to meet my questioner as to say—without the slightest expectation of satisfying him, or the least care whether I do so or not, for his *opinion* is of no value to me, though his truth is of endless value to me and to the universe—that, even in the sense of the atonement being a making-up for the evil done by men toward God, I believe in the atonement.

SIII. 156

Thinking

If there were no God to take thought for us, we should have no right to blame anyone for taking thought.

AN

But how is the work of the world to be done if we take no thought?—We are nowhere told not to take thought. We *must* take thought. The question is—What are we to take or not to take thought about? By some who do not know God, little work would be done if they were not driven by anxiety of some kind.

AN. 198

What then are we to take thought about? Why, about our work. What are we not to take thought about? Why, about our life. The one is our business: the other is God's. But you turn it the other way. You take no thought of earnestness about the doing of your duty; but you take thought of care lest

God should not fulfill his part in the goings on of the world.

AN. 198

And this gives me occasion to remark that the same truth holds with regard to any portion of the future as well as the morrow. It is a principle, not a command, or an encouragement, or a promise merely. In respect of it there is no difference between next day and next year, next hour and next century. You will see at once the absurdity of taking no thought for the morrow, and taking thought for next year.

AN. 206

Do you feel inclined to say in your hearts: "It was easy for him to take no thought, for he had the matter in his own hands?" But observe, there is nothing very noble in a man's taking no thought except it be from faith. If there were no God to take thought for us, we should have no right to blame any one for taking thought. You may fancy the Lord had his own power to fall back upon. But that would have been to him just the one dreadful thing. That his Father should forget him!—no power in himself could make up for that. He feared nothing for himself; and never once employed his divine power to save him from his human fate. Let God do that for him if he saw fit. He did not come into the world to take care of himself. That would not be in any way divine. To fall back on himself, God failing him—how could that make it easy for him to avoid care? The very idea would be torture. That would be to declare heaven void, and the world without a God. He would not even pray to his Father for what he knew he should have if he did ask it. He would just wait his will.

AN. 207

God's thoughts are power; they are like our thoughts, with this difference, that they are self-made, and ours are received from him. You cannot tell a moment before it comes what thought you are going to think. You cannot think at all in a certain sense; your thoughts are only the shadows of God's thoughts; but God is the living, original thought, and this is the atmosphere in which we poor little human creatures live.

The Christian World Pulpit

Our best thoughts come to us just simply up in our souls like our bad ones, only they come from a much deeper source. Bad ones are not half so deep as good ones, and it seems, "Can this be? am I not thinking this myself?" Yes; you are thinking it yourself, because God has thought it before you. And then you do think it yourself, for there is no possibility of dividing you from God. God thinks you out of himself, and you live because he lives; you have no independent existence at all.

The Christian World Pulpit

To have been thought about—born in God's thoughts—and then made by God, is the dearest, grandest, most precious thing in all thinking.

DE. 19

God's thoughts are not as our thoughts, or his ways as our ways—that the design of God is other and better than the expectation of men.

HG. 82

The God to whom we pray is nearer to us than the very prayer ere it leaves the heart; hence his answers may well come to us through the channel of our own thoughts.

PF

The man walking in that whereto he has attained will be able to think aright; the man who does not think right is unable because he has not been walking right; only when he begins to do the thing he knows, does he begin to be able to think aright; then God comes to him in a new and higher way, and works along with the spirit he has created.

SII. 262

A man who has not the mind of Christ—and no man has the mind of Christ except him who makes it his business to obey him—cannot have correct opinions concerning him; neither, if he could, would they be of any value to him: he would be nothing the better, he would be the worse for having them. Our business is not to think correctly, but to live truly; then first will there be a possibility of our thinking correctly.

SIII. 135

Our prayers must rise that our thoughts may follow them.

WM

Time/Eternity

For no sooner have I spoken the word *now*, than that *now* is dead and another is dying; nay, in such a regard, there is no *now*—only a past of which we know a little, and a future of which we know far less and far more.

AN. 3

If it were not for the clocks of the universe, one man would live a year—a century—where another lives but a day.

DG. 4

Eternity itself will be but an intense present to the child with whom is the Father.

DG. 4

The Son of man is content with my future, and I am content.

ML. 47

It takes a long time to finish the new creation of this redemption.

SII. 131

Trust

I heartily trust that man. He is what he seems to be.

DG

In him we live and move and have our being, which surely means that we are pretty close to him. Ah, yes, we must learn to trust him about our faults as well as about everything else.

DG. 20

If we do not trust him, and will not work with him, but are always thwarting him in his endeavors to make us alive, then we must be miserable; there is no help for it.

DG. 33

The only and greatest thing man is capable of is Trust in God.

RF

He who trusts can understand; he whose mind is set at ease can discover a reason.

SII. 43

Distrust is atheism, and the barrier to all growth.

SII. 49

The sigh, the exclamation, never meant that God might be doing something more than he was doing, but that the Father would have a dreary time to wait ere his children would know, that is, trust in him. The utterance recognizes the part of man, his slowly yielded part in faith, and his blame in troubling God by not trusting in him. If men would but make haste, and stir themselves up to take hold on God!

SII. 61

The true man trusts in a strength which is not his, and which he does not feel, does not even always desire.

SII. 148

To know that our faith is weak is the first step toward its strengthening; to be capable of distrusting is death; to know that we are, and cry out, is to begin to live—to begin to be made such that we cannot distrust—such that God may do anything with us and we shall never doubt him. Until doubt is impossible, we are lacking in the true, the childlike knowledge of God; for either God is such that one *may* distrust him, or he is such that to distrust him is the greatest injustice of which a man can be guilty. If then we are able to distrust him, either we know God imperfect, or we do not know him.

SII. 202

Unable to trust him for this world, neither can you trust him for the world to come. Refusing to obey him in your life, how can you trust him for your life?

SII. 257

The faith that a man may, nay, must put in God, reaches above earth and sky, stretches beyond the farthest outlying star of the creatable universe.

SIII. 21

In God we live every commonplace as well as most exalted moment of our lives. To trust in *him* when no need is pressing, when things seem going right of themselves, may be harder than when things seem going wrong. At no time is there any danger except in ourselves, and the only danger is of brushing in something else than the living God, and so getting, as it were, outside of God.

WM. chap. 22

The most degrading wrong to ourselves, and the worst eventual wrong to others, is to trust in any thing or person but the living God.

WM. 32

He who does not believe in God must be a truster in that which is lower than himself.

WW. 50

Truth

Do you not profess to have, and hold, and therefore teach the truth?

I profess only to have caught glimpses of her white garments—those, I mean, of the abstract truth of which you speak. But I have seen that which is eternally beyond her: the ideal in the real, the living truth, not the truth that I can *think*, but the truth that thinks itself, that thinks me, that God has thought, yea, that God is, the truth *being* true to itself and to God and to man—Christ Jesus, my Lord, who knows, and feels, and does the truth. I have seen him, and I am both content and unsatisfied. For in him are hid all the treasures of wisdom and knowledge.

AN. 159

To love the truth is a far greater thing than to know it, for it is itself truth in the inward parts—act-truth, as distinguished from fact-truth: in the highest truth the knowledge and love of it are one, or, if not identical then coincident. The very sight of the truth is the loving of it.

DG. 5

To think anything too good to be true is to deny God—to say the untrue is better than the true. . . . It will be something better and better, lovelier and lovelier that Christ will teach you.

DG. 445

A man must be good to see truth.

EA. 242

We need not trouble ourselves about our hearts, and all their varying hues and shades of feeling. Truth is at the root of all existence, therefore everything must come right if only we are obedient to the truth; and right is the deepest satisfaction of every creature as well as of God.

FS. 32

If he repents, it is of equally little consequence; for, setting himself to do the truth, he is on the way to know all things. Real knowledge has begun to grow possible for him.

HG. 39

For a moment he seemed to them a true messenger, but truth in him was not truth to them: had he been what they took him for, he would have been no savior.

HG. 71

All good news from heaven is of *truth*—essential truth, involving duty, and giving and promising help to the performance of it. There can be no good news for us men, except of uplifting love, and no one can be lifted up who will not rise.

HG. 82

You may wound the heart of God, but you cannot rend it asunder to find the Truth that sits there enthroned.

HG. 239

To him who has once seen even a shadow only of the truth, and, even but hoping he has seen it when it is present no longer, tries to obey it—to him the real vision, the Truth himself, will come, and depart no more, but abide with him for ever.

L. 235

You must follow the truth, and, in that pursuit, the less one thinks about himself, the pursuer, the better.

MM. 45

It was the truth in him that made him strong against the powers of untruth.

MOL. 162

We all need . . . healing. No man who does not yet love the truth with his whole being, who does not love God with all his heart and soul and strength and mind, and his neighbor as himself, is in his sound mind, or can act as a rational being, save more or less approximately.

MOL. 182

All spirit must rise victorious over form; and the form must die lest it harden to stone around the growing life. No form is or can be great enough to contain the truth which is its soul; for all truth is infinite, being a thought of God.

MOL. 258

Truth in the inward parts is a power, not an opinion.

PF. 264

To see a truth, to know what it is, to understand it, and to love it, are all one.

SI. 28

Is he not the Truth?—the Truth to men? Is he not the High Priest of his brethren, to answer all the troubled questionings that arise in their dim humanity?

SI. 53

If it be the truth, we shall one day see it another thing than it appears now, and love it because we see it lovely; for *all* truth is lovely. "Not to the unregenerate mind." But at least, I answer, to the mind which can love that Man, Christ Jesus; and that part of us which loves him let us follow, and in its judgments let us trust; hoping, beyond all things else, for its growth and enlightenment by the Lord, who is that Spirit.

SI. 70

Truth is truth, whether from the lips of Jesus or Balaam.

SI. 103

In its deepest sense, *the truth* is a condition of heart, soul, mind, and strength toward God and toward our fellow—not an utterance, not even a *right* form of words; and therefore such truth coming forth in words is, in a sense, the person that speaks.

SI. 103

The Son came forth to *be*, before our eyes and in our hearts, that which he had made us for, that we might behold *the truth* in him, and cry out for the living God, who, in the highest sense of all is The Truth, not as understood, but as understanding, living, and being, doing and creating the truth.

SI. 119

"I am the truth," said our Lord; and by those who are in some measure like him in being the truth, the Word can be understood. Let us try to understand him.

SI. 119

Think what an abyss of truth was our Lord, out of whose divine darkness, through that revealing countenance, that uplifting voice, those hands whose tenderness has made us great, broke all holy radiations of human significance. Think of his understanding, imagination, heart, in which lay the treasures of wisdom and knowledge. Must he not have known, felt, imagined, rejoiced in things that would not be told in human words, could not be understood by human hearts? Was he not always bringing forth out of the light inaccessible?

SI. 127

The Lord cared neither for isolated truth nor for orphaned deed. It was truth in the inward parts, it was the good heart, the mother of good deeds, he cherished. It was the live, active, knowing, breathing good he came to further. He cared for no speculation in morals or religion.

SII. 6

Truth is one, and he who does the truth in the small thing is of the truth; he who will do it only in a great thing, who postpones the small thing near him to the great thing farther from him, is not of the truth.

SII. 53

I forget that it is live things God cares about—live truths, not things set down in a book, or in a memory, or embalmed in the joy of knowledge, but things lifting up the heart, things active in an active will.

SII. 54

To the untrue, the truth itself must seem unsound, for the light that is in them is darkness.

SIII. 3

All truth is of him; no man can see a true thing to be true but by the Lord, the spirit.

SIII. 29

"How am I to know that a thing is true?"

By *doing* what you know to be true, and calling nothing true until you see it to be true; by shutting your mouth until the truth opens it. Are you meant to be silent? Then woe to you if you speak.

SIII. 29

According to the word of *the* man, however, truth means more than fact, more than relation of facts or persons, more than loftiest abstraction of metaphysical entity—means being and life, will and action; for he says, *"I am the truth."*

SIII. 56

A thing being so, the word that says it is so, is the truth. But the fact may be of no value in itself, and our knowledge of it of no value either. Of most facts it may be said that the truth concerning them is of no consequence.

SIII. 57

It cannot be to us a truth until we descry the reason of its existence, its relation to mind and intent, yea to self-existence. Tell us why it *must* be so, and you state a truth. When we come to see that a law is such, because it is the embodiment of a certain eternal thought, beheld by us in it, a fact of the being of God, the facts of which alone are truths, then indeed it will be to us, not a law merely, but an embodied truth.

SIII. 60

The truth *of a thing*, then, is the blossom of it, the thing it is made for, the topmost stone set on with rejoicing; truth in a man's imagination is the power to recognize this truth of a thing; and wherever, in anything that God has made, in the glory of it, be it sky or flower or human face, we see the glory of God, there a true imagination is beholding a truth of God.

SIII. 69

When the truth, the heart, the summit, the crown of a thing, is perceived by a man, he approaches the fountain of truth whence the thing came, and perceiving God by understanding what is, becomes more of a man, more of the being he was meant to be.

SIII. 70

A man may delight in the vision and glory of a truth, and not himself be true. The man whose vision is weak, but who, as far as he sees, and desirous to see farther, does the thing he sees, is a true man.

SIII. 70

The man who recognizes the truth of any human relation, and neglects the duty involved, is not a true man.

SIII. 71

The man who knows the laws of nature, and does not heed them, the more he teaches them to others, the less is he a true man.

SIII. 71

Man is man only in the doing of the truth, perfect man only in the doing of the highest truth, which is the fulfilling of his relations to his origin.

SIII. 71

When a man is, with his whole nature, loving and willing the truth, he is then a live truth. But this he has not originated in himself. He has seen it and striven for it, but not originated it. The one originating, living, visible truth, embracing all truths in all relations, is Jesus Christ. He is true; he is the live Truth.

SIII. 79

The obedient Jesus is Jesus the Truth. He is true and the root of all truth and development of truth in men.

SIII. 79

I was born to bear witness to the truth—in my own person to be the truth visible—the very likeness and manifestation of the God who is true. My very being is his witness. Every fact of me witnesses him. He is the truth, and I am the truth.

SIII. 103

The truth is *God*; the witness to the truth is Jesus. The kingdom of the truth is the hearts of men. The bliss of men is the true God. The thought of God is the truth of everything. All well-being lies in true relation to God. The man who responds to this with his whole being, is of the truth.

SIII. 105

To say on the authority of the Bible that God does a thing no honorable man would do, is to lie against God; to say that it is therefore right, is to lie against the very spirit of God. To uphold a lie for God's sake is to be against God, not for him. God cannot be lied for. He is the truth. The truth alone is on his side.

SIII. 116

Truth is indeed too good for men to believe; they must dilute it before they can take it; they must dilute it before they dare give it. They must make it less true before they can believe it enough to get any good of it. Unable to believe in the love of the Lord Jesus Christ, they invented a mediator in his mother, and so were able to approach a little where else they had stood away; unable to believe in the forgivingness of their Father in heaven, they invented a way to be forgiven that should not demand of him so much; which might make it right for him to forgive; which should save them from having to believe downright in the tenderness of his fatherheart, for that they found impossible. They thought him bound to punish for the sake of punishing, as an offset to their sin; they could not believe in clear forgiveness; that did not seem divine; it needed itself to be justified; so they invented for its justification a horrible injustice, involving all that was bad in sacrifice, even human sacrifice. They invented a satisfaction for sin which was an insult to God. He sought no satisfaction, but an obedient return to the Father. What satisfaction was needed he made himself in what he did to cause them to turn from evil and go back to him. The thing was too simple for complicated unbelief and the arguing spirit.

SIII. 140

You know what Christ requires of you is right—much of it at least you believe to be right, and your duty to do, whether he said it or not: *do it.* If you do not do what you know of the truth, I do not wonder that you seek it intellectually, for that kind of search may well be, as Milton represents it, a solace even to the fallen angels. But do not call anything that may be so gained, *the Truth.*

SIII. 152

Obey the truth, I say, and let theory wait. Theory may spring from life, but never life from theory.

SIII. 152

Do you so love the truth and the right that you welcome, or at least submit willingly to, the idea of an exposure of what in you is yet unknown to yourself—an exposure that may redound to the glory of the truth by making you ashamed and humble?

SIII. 235

For to be ashamed is a holy and blessed thing. Shame is a thing to shame only those who want to appear, not those who want to be. . . . For to be humbly ashamed is to be plunged in the cleansing bath of the truth.

SIII. 238

To those who care only for things, and not for the souls of them, for the truth, the reality of them, the prospect of inheriting light can have nothing attractive, and for their comfort—how false a comfort!—they may rest assured there is no danger of their being required to take up their inheritance at present. Perhaps they will be left to go on sucking *things* dry, constantly missing the loveliness of them, until they come at last to loathe the lovely husks, turned to ugliness in their false imaginations. Loving but the body of Truth, even here they come to call it a lie, and break out in maudlin moaning over the illusions of life. The soul of Truth they have lost, because they never loved her. What may they not have to pass through, what purifying fires, before they can even behold her!

SIII. 258

There must be things so entirely beyond our capacity that we cannot now see enough of them to be able even to say that they are incomprehensible. There must be millions of truths that have not yet risen above the horizon of what we call the finite.

TB. 316

What is the love of truth and the joy therein, if not a breathing into the soul of the breath of life from the God of truth?

TW. 31

A mere truism, is it? Yes, it is, and more is the pity; for what is a truism, as most men count truisms? What is it but a truth that ought to have been buried long ago in the lives of men—to send up forever the corn of true deeds and the wine of lovingkindness—but, instead of being buried in friendly soil, is allowed to lie about, kicked hither and thither in the dry and empty garret of their brains, until they are sick of the sight and sound of it and, to be rid of the thought of it, declare it to be no living truth but only a lifeless truism? Yet in their brain that truism must rattle until they shift it to its rightful quarters in their heart, where it will rattle no longer but take root and be a strength and loveliness.

TW. chap. 39

No one knows what a poor creature he is but the man who makes it his business to be true.

WM

To a pure soul, which alone can believe, nothing is so loathsome as a pretense of truth. A lie is a pretended truth. If there were no truth there could be no lies.

WM. 19

Understanding

With an obedient mind one learns the rights of things fast enough; for it is the law of the universe, and to obey is to understand.

AB. 175

One of the highest benefits we can reap from understanding the way of God with ourselves is, that we become able thus to trust him for others with whom we do not understand his ways.

AN

Men would understand: they do not care to *obey*—understand where it is impossible they should understand save by obeying. They would search into the work of the Lord instead of doing their part in it—thus making it impossible both for the Lord to go on with his work, and for themselves to become capable of seeing and understanding what he does.

HG. 17

God forbid I should seem to despise understanding. The New Testament is full of urgings to understand. Our whole life, to be life at all, must be a growth in understanding. What I cry out upon is the misunderstanding that comes of man's endeavor to understand while not obeying. Upon obedience our energy must be spent; understanding will follow.

HG. 19

Not anxious to know our duty, or knowing it and not doing it, how shall we understand that which only a true heart and a clean soul can ever understand? The power in us that would understand were it free, lies in the bonds of imperfection and impurity, and is therefore incapable of judging the divine. It cannot see the truth. If it could see it, it would not know it, and would not have it. Until a man begins to obey, the light that is in him is darkness.

HG. 19

To understand is not more wonderful than to love.

L. 57

The whole secret is to do the thing the Master tells you: then you will understand what he tells you.

MM

Had he done as the Master told him, he would soon have come to understand. Obedience is the opener of eyes.

SII. 19

He who does that which he sees, shall understand; he who is set upon understanding rather than doing, shall go on stumbling and mistaking and speaking foolishness.

SII. 98

Those who by insincerity and falsehood close their deeper eyes, shall not be capable of using in the matter the more superficial eyes of their understanding. . . . This will help to remove the difficulty that the parables are plainly for the teaching of the truth, and yet the Lord speaks of them as for the concealing of it. They are for the understanding of that man only who is practical—who does the thing he knows, who seeks to understand vitally. They reveal to the live conscience, otherwise not to the keenest intellect.

SII. 99

It was not for our understandings, but our will, that Christ came.

SII. 99

Everything, in truth, which we cannot understand, is a closed book of larger knowledge and blessedness, whose clasps the blessed perplexity urges us to open. There is, there can be, nothing which is not in itself a righteous intelligibility—whether an intelligibility for us, matters nothing. The awful thing would be, that anything should be in its nature unintelligible: that would be the same as *no God.*

SII. 200

To reason from a thing not understood, is to walk straight into the mire.

SIII. 30

I believe that the inspiration of the Almighty alone gives understanding.

SIII. 156

Universe

We are not at home in this great universe, our Father's house. We ought to be, and one day we shall be, but we are not yet. This reveals Jesus more than man, by revealing him more man than we. We are not complete men, we are not anything near it, and are therefore out of harmony, more or less, with everything in the house of our birth and habitation.

HG. 49

When we are true children, if not the world, then the universe will be our home, felt and known as such, the house we are satisfied with, and would not change. Hence, until then, the hard struggle, the constant strife we hold with *nature*—as we call the things of our Father; a strife invaluable for our development, at the same time manifesting us not yet men enough to be lords of the house built for us to live in.

HG. 50

It is not the fact that God is all in all, that unites the universe; it is the love of the Son to the Father.

SIII. 18

The bond of the universe . . . is the devotion of the Son to the Father. It is the life of the universe. It is not the fact that God created all things, that makes the universe a whole; but that he through whom he created them loves him perfectly, is eternally content in his Father, is satisfied to be because his Father is with him.

SIII. 18

Without Christ . . . there could be no universe.

SIII. 18

To be right with God is to be right with the universe; one with the power, the love, the will of the mighty Father, the cherisher of joy, the lord of laughter, whose are all glories, all hopes, who loves everything, and hates nothing but selfishness, which he will not have in his kingdom.

SIII. 81

"I and the Father are one" is the center-truth of the universe; and the circumfering truth is "that they also may be one in us."

SIII. 97

Vanity

The bondage of corruption God encounters and counteracts by subjection to vanity. Corruption is the breaking up of the essential idea; the falling away from the original indwelling and life-causing thought. It is met by the suffering which itself causes. That suffering is for redemption, for deliverance. It is the life in the corrupting thing that makes the suffering possible; it is the live part, not the corrupted part, that suffers; it is the redeemable, not the doomed thing, that is subjected to vanity.

HG. 220

The race in which evil—that is, corruption—is at work, needs, as the one means for its rescue, subjection to vanity; it is the one hope against the supremacy of corruption; and the whole encircling, harboring, and helping creation must, for the sake of man, its head, and for its own further sake too, share in this subjection to vanity with its hope of deliverance.

HG. 221

Corruption brings in vanity, causes empty aching gaps in vitality. This aching is what most people regard as evil: it is the unpleasant cure of evil. It takes all shapes of suffering—of the body, of the mind, of the heart, of the spirit. It is altogether beneficent.

HG. 221

The more things men seek, the more varied the things they imagine they need, the more are they subject to vanity—all the forms of which may be summed in the word *disappointment*. He who would not house with disappointment must seek the incorruptible, the true. He must break the bondage of havings and shows; of rumors, and praises, and pretenses, and selfish pleasures. He must come out of the false into the real; out of the darkness into the light; out of the bondage of corruption into the glorious liberty of the children of God. To bring men to break with corruption, the gulf of the inane yawns before them. Aghast in soul, they cry, "Vanity of vanities! all is vanity!" and beyond the abyss begin to espy the eternal world of truth.

HG. 222

Vengeance

Vengeance belongs to the Lord, who alone knows what use to make of it.

DG. 35

Will

All self-will is madness.

AN. 277

He says: "I tell you I am: act you upon that; for I know your conscience moves you to it; act you upon that, and you will find whether I am or not, and what I am." Do you see? Faith in its true sense does not belong to the intellect alone, nor to the intellect first, but to the conscience, to the will; and that man is a faithful man who says, "I cannot prove that there is a God, but, O God, if you hear me anywhere, help me to do your will."

The Christian World Pulpit

In our present imperfect condition, it seems to me that the absolute will has no opportunity of *pure* action, of operating entirely as itself, except when working in opposition to inclination.

DE

We did not come into this world because we willed it. We did not say what we should be. It is God in every man that enables that man even to stretch out his hand. The moment may come when he can lift it no more. Let him will, and will to do it with an agony of willing; yet he cannot raise his hand any more. He cannot do it. It is God; none else.

The English Pulpit of Today

For God's sake, do not cling to your own poor will. It is not worth having. It is a poor, miserable, degrading thing to fall down and worship the inclination of your own heart, which may have come from any devil, or from any accident of your birth, or from the weather, or from anything. Take the will of God, eternal, pure, strong, living, and true, the only good thing; take that, and Christ will be your brother.

GW. 128

The highest creation of God in man is his will, and until the highest in man meets the highest in God, their true relation is not yet a spiritual fact.

HG. 13

The highest in man is neither his intellect nor his imagination nor his reason; all are inferior to his will, and indeed, in a grand way, dependent upon it: his will must meet God's—a will *distinct* from God's, else were no *harmony* possible between them. Not the less, therefore, but the more, is all God's. For God creates in the man the power to will his will. It may cost God a suffering man can never know, to bring the man to the point at which he will will his will; but when he is brought to that point, and declares for the truth, that is, for the will of God, he becomes one with God, and the end of God in the man's creation, the end for which Jesus was born and died, is gained.

HG. 14

No man, least of all any lord of men, can be good without willing to be good, without setting himself against evil, without sending away sin.

HG. 34

If God himself sought to raise his little ones without their consenting effort, they would drop from his foiled endeavor. He will carry us in his arms until we are able to walk; he will carry us in his arms when we are weary with walking; he will not carry us if we will not walk.

HG. 83

God has . . . put us just so far away from him that we can exercise the divine thing in us, our own will, in returning toward our source. Then we shall learn the fact that we are infinitely more great and blessed in being the outcome of a perfect self-constituting will, than we could be by the conversion of any imagined independence of origin into fact for us—a truth no man *can* understand, feel, or truly acknowledge, save in proportion as he has become one with his perfect origin, the will of God.

MOL. 54

If there be a God at all, it is absurd to suppose that his ways of working should be such as to destroy his side of the highest relation that can exist between him and those whom he has cared to make—to destroy, I mean, the relation of the will of the Creator to the individual will of his creature.

MOL. 105

When the will of the man sides perfectly with the holy impulses in him, then all is well; for then his mind is one with the mind of his Maker; God and man are one.

PF

So long as we have nothing to say to God, nothing to do with him, save in the sunshine of the mind when we feel him near us, we are poor creatures, willed upon, not willing.

SI. 172

Do not, therefore, imagine me to mean that we can do anything of ourselves without God. If we choose the right at last, it is all God's doing, and only the more his that it is ours, only in a far more marvelous way his than if he had kept us filled with all holy impulses precluding the need of choice. For up to this very point, for this very point, he has been educating us, leading us, pushing us, driving us, enticing us, that we may choose him and his will, and so be tenfold more his children, of his own best making, in the freedom of the will found our own first in its loving sacrifice to him, for which in his grand fatherhood he has been thus working from the foundations of the earth, than we could be in the most ecstatic worship flowing from the divinest impulse, without this *willing* sacrifice.

SI. 174

God made our individuality as well as, and a greater marvel than, our dependence; made our *apartness* from himself, that freedom should bind us divinely dearer to himself, with a new and inscrutable marvel of love; for the Godhead is still at the root, is the making root of our individuality, and the freer the man, the stronger the bond that binds him to him who made his freedom. He made our wills, and is striving to make them free; for only in the perfection of our individuality and the freedom of our wills can we be altogether his children. This is full of mystery, but can we not see enough in it to make us very glad and very peaceful?

SI. 175

The highest condition of the Human Will, as distinct, not as separated from God, is when, not seeing God, not seeming to itself to grasp him at all, it yet holds him fast. It cannot continue in this condition, for, not finding, not seeing God, the man would die; but the will thus asserting itself, the man has passed from death into life, and the vision is nigh at hand. Then first, thus free, in thus asserting its freedom, is the individual will one with the Will of God; the child is finally restored to the father; the childhood and the fatherhood meet in one; the brotherhood of the race arises from the dust; and the prayer of our Lord is answered, "I in them and you in me, that they may be made perfect in one."

SI. 176

As God lives by his own will, and we live in him, so has he given to us power to will in ourselves. How much better should we not fare if, finding that we are standing with our heads bowed away from the good, finding that we have no feeble inclination to seek the source of our life, we should yet *will* upwards toward God, rousing that essence of life in us, which he has given us from his own heart, to call again upon him who is our Life, who can fill the emptiest heart, rouse the deadest conscience, quicken the dullest feeling, and strengthen the feeblest will!

SI. 178

If you are not willing that God should have his way with you, then, in the name of God, be miserable—until your misery drives you to the arms of the Father.

"I do trust him in spiritual matters."

"Everything is an affair of the spirit. If God has a way, then that is the only way. Every little thing in which you would have your own way, has a mission for your redemption; and he will treat you as a naughty child until you take your Father's way for yours."

SII. 51

It was not for our understandings, but our will, that Christ came.

SII. 99

The *will* is the deepest, the strongest, the divinest thing in man; so, I presume, is it in God, for such we find it in Jesus Christ.

SII. 153

When a man can and does entirely say, "Not my will, but yours be done"—when he so wills the will of God as to do it, then is he one with God—one, as a true son with a true father. When a man wills that his being be conformed to the being of his origin, which is the life in his life, causing and bearing his life, therefore absolutely and only of its kind, one with it more and deeper than words or figures can say—to the life which is itself, only more of itself, and more than itself, causing itself—when the man thus accepts his own causing life, *and sets himself to live the will of that causing life*, humbly eager after the privileges of his origin—thus receiving God, he becomes, in the act, a partaker of the divine nature, a true son of the living God, and an heir of all he possesses: by the obedience of a son, he receives into himself the very life of the Father.

SII. 153

Will is God's will, obedience is man's will; the two make one.

SII. 154

To will, not from self, but with the Eternal, is to live.

SIII. 11

The will, the power of willing, may be created but the willing is begotten. Because God wills first, man wills also.

SIII. 81

The Wise and Prudent

The Lord makes no complaint against the wise and prudent; he but recognizes that they are not those to whom his Father reveals his best things, for which fact, and the reasons of it, he thanks or praises his Father.

HG. 154

Why not reveal true things first to the wise? Are they not the fittest to receive them? Yes, if these things and their wisdom lie in the same region—not otherwise. No amount of knowledge or skill in physical science will make a man the fitter to argue a metaphysical question; and the wisdom of this world, meaning by the term, the philosophy of prudence, self-protection, precaution, specially unfits a man for receiving what the Father has to reveal: in proportion to our care about our own well-being is our incapability of understanding and welcoming the care of the Father.

HG. 154

The wise and the prudent, with all their energy of thought, could never see the things of the Father sufficiently to recognize them as true. Their sagacity labors in earthly things, and so fills their minds with their own questions and conclusions that they cannot see the eternal foundations God has laid in man, or the consequent necessities of their own nature. They are proud of finding out things, but the things they find out are all less than themselves. Because, however they have discovered them, they imagine such things the goal of the human intellect. If they grant there may be things beyond those, they either count them beyond their reach, or declare themselves uninterested in them: for the wise and prudent they do not exist. They work only to gather by the senses, and deduce from what they have so gathered the prudential, the probable, the expedient, the protective. They never think of the essential, of what in itself must be. They are cautious, wary, discreet, judicious, circumspect, provident, temporizing. They have no enthusiasm, and are shy of all forms of it—clever, hard, thin people, who take *things* for the universe, and love of facts for love of truth. They know nothing deeper in man than mere surface mental facts and their relations. They do not perceive, or they turn away from any truth which the intellect cannot formulate. Zeal for God will never eat them up: why should it? he is not interesting to them: theology may be; to such men religion means theology.

HG. 155

All those evil doctrines about God that work misery and madness have their origin in the brains of the wise and prudent, not in the hearts of the children. These wise and prudent, careful to make the words of his messengers rime with their conclusions, interpret the great heart of God, not by their own hearts, but by their miserable intellects; and, postponing the obedience which alone can give power to the understanding, press upon men's minds their wretched interpretations of the will of the Father, instead of the doing of that will upon their hearts. They call their philosophy the truth of God, and say men must hold it, or stand outside. They are the slaves of the letter in all its weakness and imperfection—and will be until the spirit of the Word, the spirit of obedience, shall set them free.

HG. 156

The babes must beware lest the wise and prudent come between them and the Father. They must yield no claim to authority over their belief, made by man or community, by church any more than by synagogue. That alone is for them to believe which the Lord reveals to their souls as true; that alone is it possible for them to believe with what he counts belief. The divine object for which teacher or church exists is the persuasion of the individual heart to come to Jesus, the Spirit, to be taught what he alone can teach.

HG. 157

Terribly has his gospel suffered in the mouths of the wise and prudent: how would it be faring now, had its first messages been committed to persons of repute, instead of those simple fishermen? It would be nowhere, or, if anywhere, unrecognizable. From the first we should have had a system founded on a human interpretation of the divine gospel, instead of the gospel itself, which would have disappeared. As it is, we have had one dull, miserable human system after another usurping its place; but, thank God, the gospel remains!

HG. 157

Had the wise and prudent been the confidants of God . . . the letter would at once have usurped the place of the spirit; the ministering slave would have been set over the household; a system of religion, with its rickety, malodorous plan of salvation, would not only have at once been put in the place of a living Christ, but would yet have held that place. The great Brother, the human God, the eternal Son, the living One, would have been as utterly hidden from the tearful eyes and aching hearts of the weary and heavy-laden as if he had never come from the deeps of love to call the children home out of the shadows of a self-haunted universe.

HG. 158

The Father revealed the Father's things to his babes; the babes loved, and began to do them, therewith began to understand them, and went on growing in the knowledge of them and in the power of communicating them; while to the wise and prudent the deepest words of the most babe-like of them all, John Boanerges, even now appear but a finger-worn rosary of platitudes. The babe understands the wise and prudent, but is understood only by the babe.

HG. 159

No wisdom of the wise can find out God; no words of the God-loving can reveal him. The simplicity of the whole natural relation is too deep for the philosopher.

HG. 163

The business of the universe is to make such a fool of you that you will know yourself for one, and so begin to be wise!

L. 26

The wise and prudent interprets God by himself, and does not understand him; the child interprets God by himself, and does understand him.

SIII. 224

The wise and prudent must make a system and arrange things to his mind before he can say, *I believe.* The child sees, believes, obeys—and knows he must be perfect as his Father in heaven is perfect. If an angel, seeming to come from heaven, told him that God had let him off, that he did not require so much of him, but would be content with less.

SIII. 224

Not one of the family had ever cared for it on the ground of its old-fashionedness; its preservation was owing merely to the fact that their gardener was blessed with a wholesome stupidity rendering him incapable of unlearning what his father, who had been gardener there before him, had had marvelous difficulty in teaching him. We do not half appreciate the benefits to the race that spring from honest dullness. The *clever* people are the ruin of everything.

TW. chap. 7

Witnessing

The testimony of their lives would go far beyond the testimony of their tongues. Their tongues could but witness to a fact; their lives could witness to a truth.

MOL. 66

The king crowned by his witnessing, witnessed then to the height of his uttermost argument, when he hung upon the cross—like a sin, as Paul in his boldness expresses it. When his witness is treated as a lie, then most he witnesses, for he gives it still. High and lifted up on the throne of his witness, on the cross of his torture, he holds to it: "I and the Father are one." Every mockery borne in witnessing, is a witnessing afresh.

SIII. 106

Infinitely more than had he sat on the throne of the whole earth, did Jesus witness to the truth when Pilate brought him out for the last time, and perhaps made him sit on the judgment-seat in his mockery of kingly garments and royal insignia, saying, "Behold your king!" Just because of those robes and that crown, that sceptre and that throne of ridicule, he was the only real king that ever sat on any throne.

SIII. 106

Is every Christian expected to bear witness? A man content to bear no witness to the truth is not in the kingdom of heaven. One who believes must bear witness. One who sees the truth, must live witnessing to it.

SIII. 107

When contempt is cast on the truth, do we smile? Wronged in our presence, do we make no sign that we hold by it? I do not say we are called upon to dispute, and defend with logic and argument, but we are called upon to show that we are on the other side. But when I say *truth*, I do not mean *opinion*: to treat opinion as if that were truth, is grievously to wrong the truth.

SIII. 107

The soul that loves the truth and tries to be true, will know when to speak and when to be silent; but the true man will never look as if he did not care. We are not bound to say all we think, but we are bound not even to look what we do not think.

SIII. 107

The Word

He has come, The Word of God, that we may know God: every word of his then, as needful to the knowing of himself, is needful to the knowing of God, and we must understand, as far as we may, every one of his words and every one of his actions, which, with him, were only another form of word. I believe this the immediate end of our creation.

MOL. 1

We must take his own words as true. Not only does he not claim perfect knowledge, but he disclaims it. He speaks once, at least, to his Father with an *if it be possible.* Those who believe omniscience essential to divinity, will therefore be driven to say that Christ was not divine. This will be their punishment for placing knowledge on a level with love. No one who does so can worship in spirit and in truth, can lift up his heart in pure adoration.

MOL. 79

The Word is that by which we live, namely, Jesus himself; and his words represent, in part, in shadow, in suggestion, himself. Any utterance worthy of being called a *truth*, is human food: how much more *The Word*, presenting no abstract laws of our being, but the vital relation of soul and body, heart and will, strength and rejoicing, beauty and light, to him who first gave birth to them all! The Son came forth to *be*, before our eyes and in our hearts, that which he had made us for, that we might behold *the truth* in him, and cry out for the living God, who, in the highest sense of all is The Truth, not as understood, but as understanding, living, and being, doing and creating the truth. "I am the truth," said the Lord; and by those who are in some measure like him in being the truth, the Word can be understood. Let us try to understand him.

SI. 118–19

By *the Word of God,* I do not understand *The Bible.* The Bible is a Word of God, the chief of his written words, because it tells us of The Word, the Christ; but everything God has done and given man to know is a word of his, a will of his; and inasmuch as it is a will of his, it is a necessity to man, without which he cannot live: the reception of it is man's life. For inasmuch as God's utterances are a whole, every smallest is essential: he speaks no foolishness—there are with him no vain repetitions.

SI. 142

The *Word* was made *flesh.* And so, in the wondrous meeting of extremes, the words he spoke were no more words, but spirit and life.

SI. 189

The Word is the Lord; the Lord is the gospel.

SIII. 166

No theology, except the *Word of God*, is worth the learning, no other being true. To know *him* is to know God.

SG

Words

The words of the Lord are the seed sown by the sower. Into our hearts they must fall that they may grow. Meditation and prayer must water them, and obedience keep them in the sunlight. Thus will they bear fruit for the Lord's gathering.

HG. 80

Words cannot convey the thought of a thinker to a no-thinker; of a largely aspiring and self-discontented soul, to a creature satisfied with his poverty, and counting his meager faculty the human standard. Neither will they readily reveal the mind of one old in thought, to one who has but lately begun to think.

HG. 205

If a man err in his interpretation, it will hardly be by attributing to his words an intent too high.

HG. 205

The Lord's own devotion was that which burns up the letter with the consuming fire of love, fulfilling and setting it aside. High love needs no letter to guide it. Doubtless the letter is all that weak faith is capable of, and it is well for those who keep it! But it is ill for those who do not outgrow and forget it! Forget it, I say, *by outgrowing it.* The Lord cared little for the letter of his own commands; he cared all for the spirit, for that was life.

MOL. 94

With vivid flashes of life and truth his words invade our darkness, rousing us with sharp stings of light to will our awaking, to arise from the dead and cry for the light which he can give, not in the lightning of words only, but in indwelling presence and power.

SI. 67

To men who are not simple, simple words are the most inexplicable of riddles.

SI. 68

Words for their full meaning depend upon their source, the person who speaks them. An utterance may even seem commonplace, until you are told that thus spoke one whom you know to be always thinking, always feeling, always acting. Recognizing the mind whence the words proceed, you know the scale by which they are to be understood. So the words of God cannot mean just the same as the words of man.

SI. 71

Whatever a good word means, as used by a good man, it means just infinitely more as used by God. And the feeling or thought expressed by that word takes higher and higher forms in us as we become capable of understanding him—that is, as we become like him.

SI. 71

To understand the words of our Lord is the business of life. For it is the main road to the understanding of The Word himself. And to receive him is to receive the Father, and so to have Life in ourselves. And Life, the higher, the deeper, the simpler, the original, is the business of life.

SI. 118

By *the word* of the God and not Maker only, who is God just because he *speaks* to men, I must understand, in the deepest sense, every revelation of himself in the heart and consciousness of man, so that the man knows that God is there, nay, rather, that he is here. Even Christ himself is not The Word of God in the deepest sense *to a man*, until he is this Revelation of God to the man—until the Spirit that is the meaning in the Word has come to him—until the speech is not a sound as of thunder, but the voice of words; for a word is more than an utterance—it is a sound to be understood.

SI. 142

No word . . . is fully a Word *of* God until it is a Word *to* man, until the man therein recognizes God. This is that for which the word is spoken. The words of God are as the sands and the stars—they cannot be numbered; but the end of all and each is this—to reveal God. Nor, moreover, can the man know that any one of them is the word of God, save as it comes thus to him, is a revelation of God in him. It is *to* him that it may be *in* him; but until it is *in* him he cannot *know* that it was *to* him. God must be God *in* man before man can know that he is God, or that he has received aright, and for that for which it was spoken, any one of his words.

SI. 143

If, by any will of God—that is, any truth in him—we live, we live by it tenfold when that will has become a word to us. When we receive it, his will becomes our will, and so we live by God. But the word of God once understood, a man must live by the faith of what God is, and not by his own feelings even in regard to God. It is the Truth itself, that which God is, known by what goes out of his mouth, that man lives by. And when he can no longer *feel* the truth, he shall not therefore die. He lives because God is true; and he is able to know that he lives because he knows, having once understood the word, that God is truth.

SI. 144

Our Lord was not in the habit of explaining away his hard words. He let them stand in all the glory of the burning fire wherewith they would purge us. Where their simplicity finds corresponding simplicity, they are understood.

SII. 31

When we speak of a man and his soul, we imply a self and a self, reacting on each other: we cannot divide ourselves so; the figure suits but imperfectly. It was never the design of the Lord to explain things to our understanding—nor would that in the least have helped our necessity; what we require is a means, a word, whereby to think with ourselves of high things: that is what a true figure, for a figure may be true while far from perfect, will always be to us. But the imperfection of his figures cannot lie in excess. Be sure that, in dealing with any truth, its symbol, however high, must come short of the glorious meaning itself holds. It is the low stupidity of an unspiritual nature that would interpret the Lord's meaning as less than his symbols. The true soul sees, or will come to see, that his words, his figures always represent more than they are able to present; for, as the heavens are higher than the earth, so are the heavenly things higher than the earthly signs of them, let the signs be good as ever sign may be.

SII. 224

One word of the Lord humbly heard and received will suffice to send all the demons of false theology into the abyss.

SII. 246

So long as a man will not set himself to obey the word spoken, the word written, the word printed, the word read, of the Lord Christ, I would not take the trouble to convince him concerning the most obnoxious doctrines that they were false as hell. It is those who would fain believe, but who by such doctrines are hindered, whom I would help. Disputation about things but hides the living Christ who alone can teach the truth, who is the truth, and the knowledge of whom is life.

SII. 252

God had not cared that we should anywhere have assurance of his very words; and that not merely, perhaps, because of the tendency in his children to word-worship, false logic, and corruption of the truth, but because he would not have them oppressed by words, seeing that words, being human, therefore but partially capable, could not absolutely contain or express what the Lord meant, and that even he must depend for being understood upon the spirit of his disciple. Seeing it could not give life, the letter should not be throned with power to kill; it should be but the handmaid to open the door of the truth to the mind that was *of* the truth.

SIII. 26

If any words that are his do not show their truth to you, you have not received his message in them; they are not yet to you the word of God, for they are not in you spirit and life. They may be the nearest to the truth that words can come; they may have served to bring many into contact with the heart of God; but for you they remain as yet sealed. If yours be a true heart, it will revere them because of the probability that they are words with the meaning of the Master behind them.

SIII. 29

The mind of man can receive any word only in proportion as it is the word of Christ, and in proportion as he is one with Christ. To him who does verily receive his word, it is a power, not of argument, but of life.

SIII. 31

The words of the Lord are not for the logic that deals with words as if they were things; but for the spiritual logic that reasons from divine thought to divine thought, dealing with spiritual facts.

SIII. 31

"You have not heard his voice at any time," might mean, *"You have never listened to his voice,"* or *"You have never obeyed his voice"*; but the following phrase, "nor seen his shape," keeps us rather to the primary sense of the word *hear*. *"The sound of his voice is unknown to you"*; *"You have never heard his voice so as to know it for his."* "You have not seen his shape";—*"You do not know what he is like."* Plainly he implies, *"You ought to know his voice; you ought to know what he is like."* "You have not his word abiding in you";—

"The word that is in you from the beginning, the word of God in your conscience, you have not kept with you, it is not dwelling in you; by yourselves accepted as the witness of Moses, the Scripture in which you think you have eternal life does not abide with you, is not at home in you. It comes to you and goes from you. You hear, heed not, and forget. You do not dwell with it, and brood upon it, and obey it. It finds no acquaintance in you. You are not of its kind. You are not of those to whom the word of God comes. Their ears are ready to hear; they hunger after the word of the Father."

SIII. 35

His argument was this: "If you had ever heard the Father's voice; if you had ever known his call; if you had ever imagined him, or a God anything like him; if you had cared for his will so that his word was at home in your hearts, you would have known me when you saw me—known that I must come from him, that I must be his messenger, and would have listened to me. The least acquaintance with God, such as any true heart must have, would have made you recognize that I came from the God of whom you knew that something. You would have been capable of knowing me by the light of his word abiding in you; by the shape you had beheld however vaguely; by the likeness of my face and my voice to those of my Father. You would have seen my Father in me; you would have known me by the little you knew of him."

SIII. 36

Every man must read the Word for himself. One may read it in one shape, another in another: all will be right if it be indeed the Word they read, and they read it by the lamp of obedience.

SIII. 167

Let your words be few, lest you say with your tongue what you will afterward repent with your heart.

SIII. 174

He spoke the words to the men to whom he looked first to spread the news of the kingdom of heaven; but they apply to all who obey him.

SIII. 233

She never imagined that words were necessary; she believed that God knew her every thought, and that the moment she lifted up her heart, it entered into communion with him; but the very sound of the words she spoke seemed to make her feel nearer to the Man who being the eternal Son of the Father, yet had ears to hear and lips to speak, like herself. To talk to him aloud, also kept her thoughts together, helped her to feel the fact of the things she contemplated as well as the reality of his presence.

SG. 178

Rudeness is a great and profound wrong, and that to the noblest part of the human being, while a mere show of indifference is sometimes almost as bad as the rudest words.

WW

Work/Works/Worker

God never buys anything, and is forever at work.

DG. 22

Strange helpers must we be for God, if, thinking to do his work, we act as if he were himself neglecting it! To wait for God, believing it his one design to redeem his creatures, ready to put to the hand the moment his hour strikes, is faith fit for a fellow worker with him.

DG. 22

We discover what we seem to discover, by working inward from without, while he works outward from within; and we shall never understand the world, until we see it in the direction in which he works making it—namely from within outward.

HG. 50

All that Jesus does is of his Father. What we see in the Son is of the Father. What his works mean concerning him, they mean concerning the Father.

MOL. 6

The joy of health is labor. He who is restored must be fellow worker with God.

MOL. 31

Some invalids are not cured because they will not be healed. They will not stretch out the hand; they will not rise; they will not walk; above all things, they will not work. Yet for their illness it may be that the work so detested is the only cure, or if no cure yet the best amelioration.

MOL. 59

Labor is not in itself an evil like the sickness, but often a divine, a blissful remedy.

MOL. 59

No amount of wealth sets one free from the obligation to work—in a world the God of which is ever working. He who works not has not yet discovered what God made him for, and is a false note in the orchestra of the universe. The possession of wealth is as it were prepayment, and involves an obligation of honor to the doing of correspondent work. He who does not know what to do has never seriously asked himself what he ought to do.

MOL. 59

Some sicknesses are to be cured with rest, others with labor. The right way is all—to meet the sickness as God would have it met, to submit or to resist according to the conditions of cure. Whatsoever is not of faith is sin.

MOL. 60

As at the first God said, "Let there be light," so the work of God is still to give light to the world, and Jesus must work his work, and *be* the light of the world—light in all its degrees and kinds, reaching into every corner where work may be done, arousing sleepy hearts, and opening blind eyes.

MOL. 62

Jesus did the works of the Father.

MOL. 68

The power to work is a diviner gift than a great legacy.

MOL. 112

Many a man's work must be burned, that by that very burning he may be saved—"so as by fire."

SI. 45

Do those who say, "Lo here or lo there are the signs of his coming," think to be too keen for him, and spy his approach? When he tells them to watch lest he find them neglecting their work, they stare this way and that, and watch lest he should succeed in coming like a thief! . . . Obedience is the one key of life.

SII. 62

"To you, O Lord, belongs mercy, for you render to every man according to his work." A man's work is his character; and God in his mercy is not indifferent, but treats him according to his work.

SIII. 132

He did not want any reception of himself that was not a reception of his Father. It was his Father, not he, that did the works!

SIII. 202

If ever the Lord claims to be received as a true man, it is for the sake of his father and his brethren, that in the receiving of him, he may be received who sent him. Had he now desired the justification of his own claim, the thing he was about to do would have been powerful to that end; but he must have them understand clearly that the Father was one with him in it—that they were doing it together—that it was the will of the Father—that he had sent him.

SIII. 202

No work noble or lastingly good can come of emulation any more than of greed: I think the motives are spiritually the same.

SG. chap. 44

Do you think the work God gives us to do is never easy? Jesus says his yoke is easy, his burden is light. People sometimes refuse to do God's work just because it is easy. This is sometimes because they cannot believe that easy work is his work; but there may be a very bad pride in it. . . . Some, again, accept it with half a heart and do it with half a hand. But however easy any work may be, it cannot be well done without taking thought about it. And such people, instead of taking thought about their work, generally take thought about the morrow, in which no work can be done any more than in yesterday. The Holy Present!

SP. chap. 3

Work is not always required of a man. There is such a thing as a sacred idleness, the cultivation of which is now fearfully neglected.

WC. chap. 55

He who, by fulfilling his own duties, teaches his neighbor to give every man the fair play he owes him, is a fellow worker with God.

WM. 46

God seems to take pleasure in working by degrees; the progress of the truth is as the permeation of leaven, or the growth of a seed: a multitude of successive small sacrifices may work more good in the world than many a large one.

WW

The right and privilege of ministering belongs to every one who has the grace to claim it and be a fellow worker with God.

WW. 13

It is the majesty of God's great-heartedness, and the majesty of man's destiny, that every man must be a fellow worker with God, nor can ever in less attain his end, and the conscious satisfaction of being.

WW. 48

God is the one only person, and it is our personality alone, so far as we have any, that can work with God's perfect personality. God can use us as tools, but to be a tool of, is not to be a fellow worker with.

WW. 48

No man ever did the best work who copied another. Let every man work out the thing that is in him! Who, according to the means he has, great or small, does the work given him to do, stands by the side of the Savior, is a fellow worker with him.

WW. 40

World

The world is not worse than it was. What we have to do is to let our light shine. Do you get any light? Let it shine. I do not mean, be an example to other people. You have no business to set yourselves up for an example. You have to be and to do, and that is letting the light shine. It now ought not to be possible to mistake a Christian for a man of the world.

The Christian World Pulpit

The world is his nursery for his upper rooms—for a higher and nobler state of being—a state which can be developed only by the doing of the will of God.

DG

There is more to be had out of the ordained oppositions in things than from the smoothest going of the world's wheels.

DG. 4

If the world had been so made that . . . people could without any trouble believe in the maker of it, it would not have been a world worth any man's living in, not even heirs, however well satisfied they might find themselves in it for a while; they would soon be sick of their own existence; neither would the God that made such a world, and so revealed himself to such people, be worth believing in.

DG. 33

We are not at home in this great universe, our Father's house. We ought to be, and one day we shall be, but we are not yet. This reveals Jesus more than man, by revealing him more man than we. We are not complete men, we are not anything near it, and are therefore out of harmony, more or less, with everything in the house of our birth and habitation. Always struggling to make our home in the world, we have not yet succeeded. We are not at home in it, because we are not at home with the lord of the house, the father of the family, not one with our elder brother who is his right hand. It is only the son, the daughter, that abides ever in the house.

HG. 49

When we are true children, if not the world, then the universe will be our home, felt and known as such, the house we are satisfied with, and would not change. Hence, until then, the hard struggle, the constant strife we hold with *nature*—as we call the things of our Father; a strife invaluable for our development, at the same time manifesting us not yet men enough to be lords of the house built for us to live in.

HG. 50

We cannot govern or command in it as did the Lord, because we are not at one with his Father, therefore neither in harmony with his things, nor rulers over them. Our best power in regard to them is but to find out wonderful facts concerning them and their relations, and turn these facts to our uses on systems of our own. For we discover what we seem to discover, by working inward from without, while he works outward from within; and we shall never understand the world, until we see it in the direction in which he works making it—namely, from within outward. This, of course, we cannot do until we are one with him. In the meantime, so much are both we and his things his, that we can err concerning them only as he has made it possible for us to err; we can wander only in the direction of the truth—if but to find that we can find nothing.

HG. 50

Think for a moment how Jesus was at home among the things of his Father. It seems to me, I repeat, a spiritless explanation of his words—that the temple was the place where naturally he was at home. Does he make the least lamentation over the temple? It is Jerusalem he weeps over—the men of Jerusalem, the killers, the stoners. What was his place of prayer? Not the temple, but the mountain-top. Where does he find symbols whereby to speak of what goes on in the mind and before the face of his Father in heaven? Not in the temple; not in its rites; not on its altars; not in its holy of holies; he finds them in the world and its lovely-low facts; on the roadside, in the field, in the vineyard, in the garden, in the house; in the family, and the commonest of its affairs—the lighting of the lamp, the leavening of the meal, the neighbor's borrowing, the losing of the coin, the straying of the sheep. Even in the unlovely facts also of the world which he turns to holy use, such as the unjust judge, the false steward, the faithless laborers, he ignores the temple. See how he drives the devils from the souls and bodies of men, as we the wolves from our sheepfolds! how before him the diseases, scaly and spotted, hurry and flee!

The world has for him no chamber of terror. He walks to the door of the sepulcher, the sealed cellar of his father's house, and calls forth its four-days dead. He rebukes the mourners, he stays the funeral, and gives back the departed children to their parents' arms. The roughest of its servants do not make him wince; none of them are so arrogant as to disobey his word; he falls asleep in the midst of the storm that threatens to swallow his boat. Hear how, on that same occasion, he rebukes his disciples! The children to tremble at a gust of wind in the house! God's little ones afraid of the storm! Hear him tell the watery floor to be still, and no longer toss his brothers! see the watery floor obey him and grow still! See how the wandering creatures under it come at his call! See him leave his mountain-closet, and go walking over its heaving surface to the help of his men of little faith! See how the world's water turns to wine! how its bread grows more bread at his word! See how he goes from the house for a while, and returning with fresh power, takes what shape he pleases, walks through its closed doors, and goes up and down its invisible stairs!

HG. 52–53

All his life he was among his Father's things, either in heaven or in the world—not then only when they found him in the temple at Jerusalem. He is still among his Father's things, everywhere about in the world, everywhere throughout the wide universe. Whatever he laid aside to come to us, to whatever limitations, for our sake, he stooped his regal head, he dealt with the things about him in such lordly, childlike manner as made it clear they were not strange to him, but the things of his Father. He claimed none of them as his own, would not have had one of them his except through his Father. Only as his Father's could he enjoy them—only as coming forth from the Father, and full of the Father's thought and nature, had they to him any existence. That the things were his Father's made them precious things to him. He had no care for having, as men count having.

HG. 53

The world was a blessed place to Jesus, because everything in it was his Father's. What pain must it not have been to him, to see his brothers so vilely misuse the Father's house by grasping, each for himself, at the family things! If the knowledge that a spot in the landscape retains in it some pollution suffices to disturb our pleasure in the whole, how must it not have been with him, how must it not be with him now, in regard to the disfigurements and defilements caused by the greed of men, by their haste to be rich, in his Father's lovely house!

HG. 54

The Lord loved the world and the things of the world, not as the men of the world love them, but finding his Father in everything that came from his Father's heart.

HG. 77

Multitudes of men, in no degree notable as ambitious or proud, hold the ambitious, the proud man in honor, and, for all deliverance, hope after some shadow of his prosperity. How many even of those who look for the world to come seek to the powers of this world for deliverance from its evils, as if God were the God of the world to come only!

HG. 85

When God can do what he will with a man, the man may do what he will with the world.

SII. 126

When I say *the world*, I do not mean the world God makes and means, yet less the human hearts that live therein; but the world man makes by choosing the perversion of his own nature—a world apart from and opposed to God's world. By *the world* I mean all ways of judging, regarding, and thinking, whether political, economical, ecclesiastical, social, or individual, which are not divine, which are not God's ways of thinking, regarding, or judging; which do not take God into account, do not set his will supreme, as the one only law of life; which do not care for the truth of things, but the customs of society, or the practice of the trade; which heed not what is right, but the usage of the time. From everything that is against the teaching and thinking of Jesus, from the world in the heart of the best man in it, specially from the world in his own heart, the disciple must turn to follow him. The first thing in all progress is to leave something behind; to follow him is to leave one's self behind. "If any man would come after me, let him deny himself."

SII. 211

The Lord's world will go on, and that without you; the devil's world will go on, and that with you.

SII. 256

How many hear and accept the words, "Be not conformed to this world," without once perceiving that what they call Society and bow to as supreme, is the World and nothing else, or that those who mind what people think, and what people will say, are conformed to—that is, take the shape of—the world.

SIII. 234

The true man feels he has nothing to do with Society as judge or lawgiver: he is under the law of Jesus Christ, and it sets him free from the law of the World.

SIII. 235

The glory of the true world is, that there is nothing in it that needs to be covered, while ever and ever there will be things uncovered. Every man's light will shine for the good and glory of his neighbor.

SIII. 237

That the loveliness of the world has its origin in the making will of God, would not content me; I say, the very loveliness of it is the loveliness of God, for its loveliness is his own lovely thought, and must be a revelation of that which dwells and moves in himself. Nor is this all: my interest in its loveliness would vanish, I should feel that the soul was out of it, if you could persuade me that God had ceased to care for the daisy, and now cared for something else instead. The faces of some flowers lead me back to the heart of God; and, as his child, I hope I feel, in my lowly degree, what he felt when, brooding over them, he said, "They are good"; that is, "They are what I mean."

SIII. 251

Never, in the midst of the good things of this lovely world, have I felt quite at home in it. Never has it shown me things lovely or grand enough to satisfy me. It is not all I should like for a place to live in. It may be that my unsatisfaction comes from not having eyes open enough, or keen enough, to see and understand what he has given; but it matters little whether the cause lie in the world or in myself, both being incomplete: God is, and all is well.

SIII. 261

The world is, as it were, the human, unseen world turned inside out that we may see it.

SP

This world looks to us the natural and simple one, and so it is—absolutely fitted to our need and education. But there is that in us which is not at home in this world, which I believe holds secret relations with every star, or perhaps rather with that in the heart of God whence issued every star, diverse in kind and character as in color and place and motion and light. To that in us this world is so far strange and unnatural and unfitting, and we need a yet homelier home. Yea, no home at last will do but the home of God's heart.

TW. 83

The world is a fine thing to save, but a wretch to worship.

WW

Worship

There is one kind of religion in which the more devoted a man is, the fewer proselytes he makes: the worship of himself.

AF. 151

Neither power nor wisdom, though infinite both, could constitute a God worthy of the worship of a human soul; and the worship of such a God must sink to the level of that fancied divinity.

EA. 277

There is no schism, none whatever, in using diverse forms of thought or worship: true honesty is never schismatic. The real schismatic is the man who turns away love and justice from the neighbor who holds theories in religious philosophy, or as to church-constitution, different from his own; who denies or avoids his brother because he follows not with him; who calls him a schismatic because he prefers this or that mode of public worship not his. The other *may* be schismatic; he himself certainly *is*. He walks in the darkness of opinion, not in the light of life, not in the faith which works by love. Worst of all is division in the name of Christ, who came to make one.

HG. 185

God will not compel the adoration of men: it would be but a pagan worship that would bring to his altars. He will rouse in men a sense of need, which shall grow at length into a longing; he will make them feel after him, until by their search becoming able to behold him, he may at length reveal to them the glory of their Father. He works silently—keeps quiet behind his works, as it were, that he may truly reveal himself in the right time.

MOL. 22

We . . . must worship him with a fear pure as the kingdom is unshakeable. He will shake heaven and earth, that only the unshakeable may remain . . . : he is a consuming fire, that only that which cannot be consumed may stand forth eternal.

SI. 31

It is the nature of God, so terribly pure that it destroys all that is not pure as fire, which demands like purity in our worship. He will have purity. It is not that the fire will burn us if we do not worship thus; but that the fire will burn us until we worship thus; yea, will go on burning within us after all that is foreign to it has yielded to its force, no longer with pain and consuming, but as the highest consciousness of life, the presence of God.

SI. 31

To love our brother is to worship the Consuming Fire.

SI. 32

The worship of fear is true, although very low; and though not acceptable to God in itself, for only the worship of spirit and of truth is acceptable to him, yet even in his sight it is precious.

SI. 36

The name is one "which no man knows except he that receives it." Not only then has each man his individual relation to God, but each man has his peculiar relation to God. He is to God a peculiar being, made after his own fashion, and that of no one else. Hence he can worship God as no man else can worship him.

SI. 110

Away with the thought that God could have been a perfect, an adorable Creator, doing anything less than he has done for his children! that any other kind of being than Jesus Christ could have been worthy of all-glorifying worship! that his nature demanded less of him than he has done! that his nature is not absolute love, absolute self-devotion—could have been without these highest splendors!

SII. 185

I worship the Son as the human God, the divine, the only, Man, deriving his being and power from the Father, equal with him as a son is the equal at once and the subject of his Father.

SIII. 4

Let us understand very plainly, that a being whose essence was only power would be such a negation of the divine that no righteous worship could be offered him.

SIII. 8

No woman, no man surely ever saw him as he was and did not worship!

TW. 83

The world is a fine thing to save, but a wretch to worship.

WW

Yoke

"I have rest because I know the Father. Be meek and lowly of heart toward him as I am; let him lay his yoke upon you as he lays it on me. I do his will, not my own. Take on you the yoke that I wear; be his child like me; become a babe to whom he can reveal his wonders. Then shall you too find rest to your souls; you shall have the same peace I have; you will be weary and heavy laden no more. I find my yoke easy, my burden light."

HG. 165

We must not imagine that, when the Lord says, "Take my yoke upon you," he means a yoke which he lays on those that come to him; "my yoke" is the yoke he wears himself, the yoke his Father lays upon him, the yoke out of which, that same moment, he speaks, bearing it with glad patience. "You must take on you the yoke I have taken: the Father lays it upon us."

HG. 166

A friend pointed out to me that the Master does not mean we must take on us a yoke like his; we must take on us the very yoke he is carrying.

HG. 166

"Take the other end of my yoke, doing as I do, being as I am." Think of it a moment: to walk in the same yoke with the Son of Man, doing the same labor with him, and having the same feeling common to him and us! This, and nothing else, is offered the man who would have rest to his soul; is required of the man who would know the Father; is by the Lord pressed upon him to whom he would give the same peace which pervades and sustains his own eternal heart.

HG. 167

But a yoke is for drawing withal: what load is it the Lord is drawing? Wherewith is the cart laden which he would have us help him draw? With what but the will of the eternal, the perfect Father? How should the Father honor the Son, but by giving him his will to embody in deed, by making him hand to his Father's heart!—and hardest of all, in bringing home his children! Specially in drawing this load must his yoke fellow share. How to draw it, he must learn of him who draws by his side.

HG. 167

Whoever, in the commonest duties that fall to him, does as the Father would have him do, bears his yoke along with Jesus; and the Father takes his help for the redemption of the world—for the deliverance of men from the slavery of their own rubbish-laden wagons, into the liberty of God's husbandmen.

HG. 168

Bearing the same yoke with Jesus, the man learns to walk step for step with him drawing, drawing the cart laden with the will of the Father of both, and rejoicing with the joy of Jesus. The glory of existence is to take up its burden, and exist for Existence eternal and supreme—for the Father who does his divine and perfect best to impart his glad life to us, making us sharers of that nature which is bliss, and that labor which is peace. He lives for us; we must live for him. The little ones must take their full share in the great Father's work: his work is the business of the family.

HG. 168

Starts your soul, trembles your brain at the thought of such a burden as the will of the eternally creating, eternally saving God? "How shall mortal man walk in such a yoke," say you, "even with the Son of God bearing it also?"

Why, brother, sister, it is the only burden bearable—the only burden that can be borne of mortal! Under any other, the lightest, he must at last sink outworn, his very soul gray with sickness!

HG. 168

He on whom lay the other half of the burden of God, the weight of his creation to redeem, says, "The yoke I bear is easy; the burden I draw is light"; and this he said, knowing the death he was to die. The yoke did not gall his neck, the burden did not overstrain his sinews, neither did the goal on Calvary fright him from the straight way thither. He had the will of the Father to work out, and that will was his strength as well as his joy. He had the same will as his Father. To him the one thing worth living for was the share the love of his Father gave him in his work. He loved his Father even to the death of the cross, and eternally beyond it.

HG. 169

When we give ourselves up to the Father as the Son gave himself, we shall not only find our yoke easy and our burden light, but that they communicate ease and lightness; not only will they not make us weary, but they will give us rest from all other weariness. Let us not waste a moment in asking how this can be; the only way to know that is to take the yoke on us. That rest is a secret for every heart to know, for never a tongue to tell. Only by having it can we know it.

HG. 169

If it seem impossible to take the yoke on us, let us attempt the impossible; let us lay hold of the yoke, and bow our heads, and try to get our necks under it. Giving our Father the opportunity, he will help and not fail us. He is helping us every moment, when least we think we need his help; when most we think we do, then may we most boldly, as most earnestly we must, cry for it. What or how much his creatures can do or bear, God only understands; but when most it seems impossible to do or bear, we must be most confident that he will neither demand too much, nor fail with the vital creator-help.

HG. 170

It is vain to think that any weariness, however caused, any burden, however slight, may be got rid of otherwise than by bowing the neck to the yoke of the Father's will. There can be no other rest for heart and soul that he has created. From every burden, from every anxiety, from all dread of shame or loss, even loss of love itself, that yoke will set us free.

HG. 170

Those who come at the call of the Lord, and take the rest he offers them, learning of him, and bearing the yoke of the Father, are the salt of the earth, the light of the world.

HG. 172

When he says, "Take my yoke upon you," he does not mean a yoke which he would lay upon our shoulders; it is his own yoke he tells us to take, and to learn of him—it is the yoke he is himself carrying, the yoke his perfect Father had given him to carry. The will of the Father is the yoke he would have us take, and bear also with him. It is of this yoke that he says, *It is easy*, of this burden, *It is light*. He is not saying, "The yoke I lay upon you is easy, the burden light"; what he says is, "The yoke I carry is easy, the burden on my shoulders is light." With the Garden of Gethsemane before him, with the hour and the power of darkness waiting for him, he declares his yoke easy, his burden light.

SIII. 219

Index

www.ingramcontent.com/pod-product-compliance
Lightning Source LLC
Chambersburg PA
CBHW060325100426
42812CB00003B/888
9781532688607